Revelation Revolution
Volume 1

By Dr. Kay Fairchild
and Lisa Perdue, R. N.

Copyright © 2003 by Dr. Kay Fairchild and Lisa Perdue, R.N.

Revelation Revolution Volume 1
by Dr. Kay Fairchild and Lisa Perdue, R.N.

Printed in the United States of America

ISBN 1-591606-99-3

All rights reserved. No part of this publication may be reproduced or transmitted in any form or by any means without written permission of the publisher.

Unless otherwise indicated, Bible quotations are taken from the Authorized King James Version of the Bible. Copyright © 1996 by Sage Software. The Companion Bible Authorized King James Version of 1611. Copyright © 1964, 1970, 1974 by Zondervan Bible Publishers.

Xulon Press
www.XulonPress.com

Xulon Press books are available in bookstores everywhere, and on the Web at www.XulonPress.com.

Contents

Introduction xi

Chapter One (Revelation Chapter 1)..1
    Revelation (Singular) 2
    The Little Book Is Open 2
    The Bitter Herbs 3
    Remove The Veil 5
    View The Finished Work..8
    The Testimony Of Jesus—The Spirit Of Prophecy 10
    Written To Bondservants...11
    Jesus—The New Beginning 12
    John—"God Is Good" 13
    Full Throttle..13
    Written By Sign And Symbol 14
    Let The Teacher Do The Teaching 16
    The Day Of The Lord..19
    In The Spirit On The Lord's Day 20
    The Isle Of My Death..21
    Time For Some "R and R"—Rest And Revolution.................21
    A People Determined To Know Nothing Except Christ
        And Him Crucified 22
    Hidden Treasure 23
    Changed From Glory To Glory 24
    The Father's Business—It Is Finished 25
    The Key Is Over The Door 26
    Jesus Has Blessed Us 27
    Jesus—The Firstfruit 28
    Jesus—King Of Kings..30
    A Great Multitude 31
    Seeing The Invisible 32
    Righteousness, Peace, And Joy—In The Holy Spirit................32
    Jesus—The First And The Last 35
    Jesus—The Lord's Day 37

Jesus—The Day Of Jubilee 40
Jesus—The Sabbath Day 41
Jesus Will Appear The Second Time 41
Jesus—The Promised Land 42
The Book Within 45
The Feasts Of The Lord 45
The Revelation Of Jesus Christ 47
Jesus, The Firstfruit 52
The Great Mathematician 53
I Am *That* I Am 54
Testimony—Can I Get A Witness? 56
Blessed To Be A Blessing 56
Holy Halitosis 57
Jesus Is Coming With Clouds—
   A Great Cloud Of Witnesses 60
Jesus Is Still Being Pierced Today 61
The Alpha And The Omega 63
The Key Of David 66
Seven Golden Candlesticks 68
Jesus Is Our Garment 77
The Testimony (Martyrdom) Of Jesus 78
Jesus Became Sin 81
The Spirit Of The Word 85
Adam Is Dead 86
The Sun Clothed Woman 87
Revelation 1:4 and Revelation 1:19 90
Passover—A Second Look 92
Unleavened Bread 93
Firstfruits 94
Pentecost 95
Tabernacles 95

Chapter Two (Revelation Chapter 2) 99
Complete In Jesus 99
Sacrifice The Ox 103
Divine Outline 105
"Caught Up" In Experience 106
The Blood Of Jesus 107

Like The Morning Spread Upon The Mountains 108
The Blood Is Speaking 110
Judgment Ended At The Cross 111
The Spirit Of Wisdom And Revelation 113
Three Major Feasts Of The Lord................................113
Passover..114
Unleavened Bread 116
Firstfruits 117
Pentecost...117
Tabernacles...117
The Seven Churches And Old Testament History.................118
The Seven Churches And The Seven Days Of Creation.......129
I Will Not Alter The Thing That Is Gone Out
    Of My Lips..134
Moses' Tabernacle..135
Revelation 1:19 and Revelation 1:4 136
The Seven Vials..142
Revelation—The Complement Of Genesis..............143
Old Testament History and the Seven Churches 149
Historical View Of Churches 150
Promise To Overcomers Is Most Holy Place Blessings.........158
The Holy City...160
We, The People, In Order To Form A More Perfect Union—
    Set Our Minds On Things Above! 163
Suffering With Jesus..164
The Seven Churches Speak of Re-Creation 166
Ephesus—Inventor of Works 167
Smyrna—Embitter; Mingle with Myrrh 169
Get The Message 174
Pergamos—Fortified; A Tower; A Castle; 176
OperationDragonSlayer..177
Thyatira—Female Woman 180

Chapter Three (Revelation Chapters 3 - 5)......................183
Sardis—A Gem 183
Philadelphia—Brotherly Love 185
Laodicea—A People 187
Paradigm Lift...189

The Three Feasts Of The Lord And Where They Take Place	190
Passover—The Outer Court	190
Pentecost—The Holy Place	191
Revelation—A Book Of Transition	194
Cold (Outer Court), Lukewarm (Holy Place), or Hot (Most Holy Place)	195
Trial Of The Ages	197
Tabernacles—The Most Holy Place	198
Leave Old Ministry	199
A Certain Man	200
I Bought A Piece Of Ground	202
I Bought Five Yoke Of Oxen	203
I Have Married A Wife	203
After This	204
Not A Fat Baby With Wings	206
Trumpeting A Clarion Word	207
The Last Trump	207
Chambers—Courts, Courts, Courts	210
The Song Of Songs, Which Is Solomon's— Let's Take It Up An Octave!	211
Off With The Veil—Let's Raise The Roof!	212
Jasper—Reuben—Behold, a Son	213
Emerald Rainbow	213
Mt. Ararat—The Curse Reversed	215
Rainbow—Different Levels Of Light Through Three-Sided Vessel	217
No Wedding, No Intimacy	221
Feast Of Firstfruits	222
The Four Living Creatures	224
When Maturity Comes The "In Part" Shall Be Done Away	228
Revelation—A Carbon Copy of Ezekiel	231
From "Woe" To "Holy"	234
The Book Within	237
The First Reason We Are The Book Within	239
The Second Reason We Are The Book Within	243
The Third Reason We Are The Book Within	255

The Fourth Reason We Are The Book Within 258
The Fifth Reason We Are The Book Within 259
The Sixth Reason We Are The Book Within 260
It Is Not A Future Event—
    But It Will Change The Events Of The Future! 268
Jesus Was A Fountain Sealed 270
The Seven Horns And The Seven Eyes Of
    The Slain Lamb 276
You Shall Hear A Word Behind You 279
Only The Lamb Slain Opens The Book 282

Chapter Four (Revelation Chapter 6) 285
Come And See..285
Ashes To Ashes—Dust To Dust
    Beauty For Ashes—Shake Off The Dust 287
Megiddo 288
As The Morning Spread Upon The Mountains 290
Metamorphosis 293
Divine Equine...294
"Name" Means "Nature"...298
A Finished Work Of Love 300
You May Kiss The Bride 302
Get The Message!..302
Before We Had The Written Word,
    The Word Was Written In The Stars 304
Behold The Lamb 306
Most Holy Place Mentality 308
The Church—The Book Within 310
Our Old Man Was Crucified With Christ 311
An Invitation To All Creation—Come And See! 312
Spiritual Indicators 313
It Is Our Destiny To Manifest 316
Heavenly Horsemen 321
The Last Enemy 323
In The Throne Zone..324
The Career Of Christ 327
The Rider..329
The White Horse 330

The Red Horse 333
It's All About Jesus 348
The Books Are Being Opened 352
The Spirit Of Truth Will Guide You Into All Truth 354
The Black Horse..356
The Pale Horse 380
The Fifth Seal—The Souls Under The Altar 385
The Sixth Seal 389
The River Of God...391
The Firmament Stretched Forth 392
The Terrible Crystal 395
The Star Of David 396
The Pivot Of God 396
The Father's Vision, The Father's Dream 397
God's Great Adventure..398
The Revelation Of Jesus Christ.....................................399

Chapter Five (Daniel 9:24-27)..403
The Origin Of The Religious World Order's Dispensational
    Theology..403
Daniel Chapter 9:24-27 407

Appendices
Appendix A—Christ's Spiritual Death 437
Appendix B—Jesus In Hell Scriptures...........................445
Appendix C—Three Feasts of the Lord 451
Appendix D—The 7 Churches of Revelation
    and Present Truth...453
Appendix E—The 7 Days of Creation and the
    7 Churches...455
Appendix F—The Feasts of the Lord............................457
Appendix G—The Literary Structure of Revelation.............459
Appendix H—Revelation 1:19 and Revelation 1:4................461
Appendix I—Five Schools of Thought on the
    Death of Christ 463

Endnotes..467

Introduction

This is a study of the book of Revelation from the perspective of the death, the burial and the resurrection of Christ—the finished work of Calvary. We will see in this book that the book of Revelation is not the revelation of *Newsweek Magazine*, it is not the revelation of *U. S. News and World Report*, but it is the revelation of Jesus Christ.

We're going to find out throughout this book, that Passover, Pentecost, and Tabernacles is depicted. When we study the seals, we're dealing with Passover. When we study the white horse, the red horse, the black horse, the pale horse, we're studying Passover. We're going to find out that the trumpets speak of Pentecost, and we're going to find out that the vials of blood that are poured out upon our heads speak of Tabernacles.

There are people that are beginning to catch a vision of the fact that the Melchisedec priesthood is ministering bread and wine. This study of the book of Revelation is to lift up the voice of Christ that is speaking in this hour, because he's speaking in no uncertain terms, a more sure word of prophecy, and he's speaking a more clear word than we have ever heard before, because it is time for it.

This is not a book of information, but it is an impartation of life. I am frustrated and excited both at the same time. I am frustrated in one sense because I know that if we do not approach the study of the book of Revelation with the same mindset and in the same spirit that John was in, then we're not going to get this. I'm frustrated in another sense because the teacher in me wants to teach very specifically and in detail, and doesn't want to miss one jot or tittle, doesn't want to assume anything, but I understand that I can't make you daily search the scriptures to see if these things be true. I hope you do.

I encourage you to meditate, to contemplate the book of Revelation, to put your spiritual antenna up as we study. You're going to see that as this begins to grip you, your ear will be nailed to the door[1] more and more. You're going to see a great tapestry woven with a scarlet thread.[2] You're going to see a great apothecary mixed, a great compounding.[3] You're going to see the grace of God. You're going to see the Lord Jesus Christ himself, and as 1 John 3:2 says, "When you see him as he is, you're going to be like him!"

All we're going to look at in the book of Revelation is him. Jesus is all I want to see anyway. When your ear is nailed to the door, he is all you want to hear about, he is all you want to see, and he is all you want to look for when you go to the Bible. From Genesis to Revelation we see a picture of Him!

When you're gripped by the ministry of bread and wine (the broken body and the shed blood), it will spontaneously bring forth a resurrection. There has to be a death before there is a resurrection. This is where we in the kingdom of God have missed it. We've taught all these great messages, but we've missed it because we should have been focusing on Christ Himself.

I used to be of the mindset that some of the hardest people to teach are Spirit-filled people in that "young-man" realm, who seem to think they already know it all, especially when teaching the cross of Calvary. But now I'm finding out that those who have entered into the kingdom of God[4] are hard to teach in the sense that they've heard too much. It is hard to break through that "much" that they've heard and give them something that is of real truth.

The hardest thing to do in the natural is to look away from the appearance realm when things look like they're going wrong. Looking away from the appearance realm has to be done by the Spirit. It is hard in the natural to look at your brother and sister and "know no man after the flesh" when you see their faults. The only way you can do that is to focus upon the fact that over 2,000 years ago, their old man, their Adam, as well as yours, was done away with. When we focus on the Christ, that will release the faith of

God to cause their life to get in line if it's out of order.

I'm believing that great grace is going to come—a greater manifestation of the grace of God than we have ever experienced before. When the apostles taught the death, burial and resurrection, there was *great grace* among them all, not only individually, but corporately. In Acts 4:33 we read:

> And with great power gave the apostles witness of
> the resurrection of the Lord Jesus; and great grace
> was upon them all.

People have said "Let the Bible interpret the Bible." If we understand the Bible correctly—if we understand the spiritual meanings as Paul said, "Spiritual things are spiritually discerned," then we can let the Bible interpret the Bible. We cannot understand the book of Revelation until we understand the tabernacle of Moses. Why? Because in the tabernacle, we see the pieces of furniture that are seen in the book of Revelation; the Ark, the candlestick, the golden altar of incense, and so forth. If we do not understand the tabernacle of Moses and how all the pieces of furniture relate to the cross, then we're not going to understand the book of Revelation.

There have been a lot of wild things taught about the book of Revelation. We can turn the television on and find "teaching" on the book of Revelation—or current events—with charts that reach from one end of the screen to the other, that speaks nothing but gloom and doom. No wonder people want to take the fire escape! As important as the book of Revelation is to the Church, one would think that the Church would want to understand the spiritual interpretation of the text—not just the literal. The literal letter kills, but the spirit brings life[5].

I can remember in my younger Christian days, going to a couple of the "Revelation Seminars" and some of the things they taught scared me terribly. I'd go home at night and maybe there would be a thunderstorm and I would think, "This is the big one!" Or the moon would be a little red and I would think "Oh, the moon is red! It's all over! This is the end of the world! The end is coming!" I would pray and repent over and over for the things I had already repented of, and it was because they taught this seven year tribulation. Some taught "pre-trib" and "mid-trib" and "post-trib," and some said, "Well, we don't know, it's all going to pan out in the end."

The book of Revelation is not about a seven year tribulation. When we get through this study, we will not have found any seven year tribulation whatsoever. We will not see half of the things we thought we saw there previously.

I can remember in my younger days, as a born-again, spirit-filled believer, going to the pastor of my Church and saying, "I'm interested in the book of Revelation" and I went to one particular passage of scripture. Just like it was yesterday, I remember him patting me on the shoulder saying, "Well, we'll understand it all by and by." And I thought, "I want to know now. Why can't we know now?" The truth of the matter was that he did not know the answer to the question I was asking. Paul spoke of this in 1 Corinthians 2:13-16 (Amplified Bible):

> And we are setting these truths forth in words not taught by human wisdom but taught by the Holy Spirit, combining and interpreting spiritual truths with spiritual language [to those who possess the Holy Spirit]. But the natural, nonspiritual man does not accept or welcome or admit into his heart the gifts and teachings and revelations of the Spirit of God, for they are folly (meaningless nonsense) to him; and he is incapable of knowing them (or progressively recognizing, understanding, and becoming better acquainted with them) because they are spiritually discerned and estimated and appreciated. But the spiritual man tries all things [he examines, investigates, inquires into, questions, and discerns all things], yet is himself to be put on trial and judged by no one [he can read the meaning of everything, but no one can properly discern or appraise or get an insight into him]. For who has known or understood the mind (the counsels and purposes) of the Lord so as to guide and instruct Him and give Him knowledge? But we have the

mind of Christ (the Messiah) and do hold the thoughts (feelings and purposes) of His heart.

This book is the product of the quest that began in those early years of my Christian life. It is compiled from a series of messages taught at New Life Ministries in both Ft. Wayne, Indiana and Portland, Indiana. Because of this, you will find repeated truths throughout the book as the Holy Spirit imprints the word in your heart and mind.

The book of Revelation has intrigued me for many years, but not until the Lord brought the message of the bread and wine, did this really begin to open up as never before. Some things that I once thought I understood were not according to the spiritual interpretation of the word of God. The study of the book of Revelation will take us on the adventure of our lifetime! Let's get started.

Chapter One

The book of Revelation is not just a historical book, but it is a spiritual book. It has been interpreted in the past as just an historical book. For example, in Revelation 1:4, John talks about him who is, and who was, and who is to come. Most people either talk about the "him who was" or "who is to come." What we want to do is take "him who was" and "who is to come" and bring it into "him who is." We want to bring the past and the future into the now. The way we are going to do that is in realizing that this is not just a historical book, but it is a spiritual book.

Some have taken the books of Revelation, Ezekiel, and Daniel and correlated them to current events that are happening in the world. Some of those things can be made to fit. I'm not saying that there is no validity to any of that. I am not saying that is all wrong. But some have made the Bible say anything they want it to say. Paul preached to some people who "were entirely ready and accepted and welcomed the message [concerning the attainment through Christ of eternal salvation in the kingdom of God] with inclination of mind and eagerness, searching and examining the Scriptures daily to see if these things were so" (Acts 17:11 Amplified Bible). This is the nobility of the Bereans:

Eight-fold Proof of Doctrine

1. Does it appear in seed form in Genesis?
2. Does it appear in type form in the Law?
3. Does it appear in song form in Psalms?
4. Was it prophesied by the prophets?
5. Did Jesus teach it?
6. Did the early Church proclaim it?
7. Do the epistles help us understand it?
8. Does it come to its consummation and manifestation in the book of Revelation?

Revelation (Singular)

In teaching the book of Revelation I am taking the posture of giving things to you rather than taking things away from you. But I do know that some things are going to be taken away from you because you are going to receive the Spirit of wisdom and revelation concerning the death, burial, and resurrection of Jesus Christ.

In Revelation 1:1 we read, "The Revelation" and I want to stop right there with the word "Revelation." That is the key to this whole chapter; in fact, it is the key to the whole book of Revelation. It tells us up front what this book is about. Notice "The Revelation" singular. It does not say "Revelation*s*." Nine times out of ten we hear teachers say "Turn to Revelations chapter 5." It is written "Revelation" (singular). Why? Because there is only one revelation.

Paul the apostle, who also had the revelation of the death, burial, and resurrection, used that word "revelation" (singular) many times in his epistles because he understood that there is only one revelation in the entire Bible and it is the revelation of the Lord Jesus Christ—the death, the burial, and the resurrection.

The Little Book Is Open

In Revelation 10:8 we read:

> And the voice which I heard from heaven spoke unto me again, and said, Go and take the *little book* which

is open in the hand of the angel who standeth upon
the sea and upon the earth (emphasis added).

Why is it a little book? It is a little book because it contains only one message. Man has made it many messages. But there is just one message. The gospel is Christ's life, death, burial, and resurrection.

He said go and take the little book which is *open*. We are living in a time where the little book, the one message is open. The revelation of Jesus Christ is now open. The bread and wine message is open to us. We are seeing it with clarity. We are seeing as never before that the Feast of Tabernacles is simply a second look at Passover.

The Bitter Herbs

The Israelites were to eat the lamb roasted with fire along with unleavened bread and bitter herbs. Proverbs 27:7 tells us that "to the hungry soul every bitter thing is sweet." Jesus had a soul that hungered for the Father's will—even if it meant drinking the bitter cup.

Look for a moment at Revelation 10:9:

And I went unto the angel, and said unto him, Give
me the little book. And he said unto me, Take it, and
eat it up; and it shall make thy belly *bitter*, but it shall
be in thy mouth sweet as honey (emphasis added).

When it's digested, you see the bitterness of the bitter cup that Jesus drank. We can't see how high he went until we see how low he went. Jesus drank that bitter cup—more bitter than anything that anyone could ever drink. When we see it, digest it, and we get it on the inside of us, we will see that Jesus, who knew no sin, became sin. It was more than just a physical death. He drank the bitter cup. When we drink something it is inside of us. So, Jesus became bitterness on the inside, because he became sin. When we really digest the person and the work of Christ, we see that it was a bitter cup and when he drank it, it was inside of him and he became sin. He did not just die physically. He also died spiritually and became sin and went into hell.

This is a big issue in the Kingdom of God because some still do not see this yet. Some do, and thank God, they're coming into this understanding more and more, but some say that Jesus just became a sin offering. If we want to say he became a sin offering, that's well and good, but let's make sure that we understand that in becoming the sin offering, he became sin. He became who we were; otherwise we could not have been there[6]. Some are challenged with the fact that Jesus became sin (2 Corinthians 5:21). We must eat the bitter herbs with the lamb.

It was bitter in his belly, but in his mouth, it was sweet as honey. Honey is a Promise Land provision. Remember the riddle that Samson gave forth to the Philistines? In the dead carcass of the lion was Promise Land provision, or honey. Honey also speaks of wisdom. What is the wisdom of God? 1Corinthians 1:18-25 tells us that the wisdom of God is the preaching of the Cross.

So in Revelation 1:1, we read "The Revelation," (singular) because there is only one revelation. There is only one message and the sooner we get this, the better off we're going to be. The sooner we understand this, the more we're going to hasten the coming of the Day of the Lord in our life individually and corporately. Continuing in verse 1, we read:

> The Revelation of Jesus Christ, which God gave unto him, to show unto his servants things which must shortly come to pass; and he sent and signified it by his angel unto his servant, John.

This book is about Jesus. When we come to the conclusion of this book, we will know that the book of Revelation is not about bugs as big as Volkswagens. When one is born of the spirit he hears by the spirit. When we finish the study of the book of Revelation we will know by the spirit that this book is not about Godzilla monsters that come up out of the sea to destroy people. It is not about locusts that come up out of the earth to sting people. It is not about Scud missiles. It's not about Russia. It is not about Iraq. It is not about the Middle East and the battle of Armageddon. It is not about a temple in the Middle East. It is not about a literal word that ministers death

(2 Corinthians 3:6). It is about the Lord Jesus Christ, the life-giving Spirit. This is the revelation of Jesus Christ. It is the unveiling of Jesus Christ, and that alone. And the understanding of that will change a *literal* world!

Remove The Veil

This book is about the removing of a veil that is over our minds—a veil that has been there for a long time and has hidden the glory of God. 2 Corinthians 3:14 gives us the key to having the veil lifted and that is the understanding of the death, burial, and resurrection:

> But their minds were blinded; for until this day remaineth the same veil untaken away in the reading of the old testament; which veil is done away in Christ.

In 1 Corinthians 11:26, Paul says we are to eat of the bread and drink of the cup to show the Lord's death until he comes. This scripture is not talking about the Lord coming from without. The Lord in us is much more personal than an external coming. This scripture refers to his *apokalupsis*, his *epiphaneia*, his uncovering, his outshining, his *parousia* that comes from spirit to soul and flows out of our body so others can see and can sense something of the nature of Christ and see the glory of God.

The Greek word for revelation is *apokalupsis*, meaning to uncover, to unveil something that is hidden. What has been hidden? Christ. Colossians speaks of Christ in you, the hope of glory. Christ in you is a *hope* of the manifestation of glory. Christ in you is not the manifestation of the glory, but when we get the veil removed, then the Christ, the glory, the nature of God is going to be unveiled, uncovered, and he is going to make his way out from spirit to soul and he is going to manifest out of our lives. If Christ in you is not unveiled, then the glory is yet a hope. A seed is planted in the ground not to stay covered, but to bring forth a stem, a branch, and to bring forth much fruit. That is what God is doing in this hour.

In the tabernacle of Moses, there was a veil between the Holy

Place and the Holy of Holies. At the death of Jesus, the veil in the temple was rent from top to bottom. In David's tent, which represents a people in maturity, there was no veil. That tells me that the veil was done away with in Christ, but it still has to be taken out of our minds. The thing that is going to bring about the revelation of Jesus Christ in our midst individually and corporately is receiving understanding of the death of Jesus. We have to understand that the old man was crucified and there is only one man left. After one sees that he was crucified, there is only one man left and that is Christ the Lord. That is why we are to "know no man after the flesh," including ourselves (John 7:24, 2 Corinthians 5:16, 1 Thessalonians 5:22).

The veil is not going to be taken away by giving people a list of do's and don'ts. Christ will be revealed when people awake to righteousness, wake up to who they are, wake up to the fact that there is only one man left and that is Christ. The world has a cliché, "accentuate the positive and you eliminate the negative." The death of Christ, and our identification with it, though it seems negative, is a positive thing.

In 2 Corinthians 3:14, we read that their minds were blinded. Remember, we are talking about *apokalupsis*, the revelation, which means to uncover something that is hidden. The key to uncovering that which is hidden, the key to removing the veil that is still upon our minds to a degree, is the understanding of the death of Christ—that is the marriage supper of the Lamb—the marriage of spirit and soul becoming one. The truth that is in our spirit comes to our mind, renews our mind, and is then expressed in our life.

In the natural, a woman receives seed in her womb and nine months later she births something. The womb of the woman speaks of the womb of the mind. Our spirit is an initiator and our soul is a projector—it projects out. What is in spirit that comes to soul is then projected out by the soul. The womb of our soul goes into labor. What is the labor? The labor is to fill our minds with the truths of the finished work. That is hard and that is a labor because your old heavens must pass away with a fervent heat and a loud noise. Why? Because it is easier to think we are something that we *are not* than to think that we are something that the *word* declares we *are*.

Continuing in 2 Corinthians 3:14-16:

> But their minds were blinded: for until this day remaineth the same vail untaken away in the reading of the old testament; which vail is done away in Christ. But even unto this day, when Moses is read, the vail is upon their heart. Nevertheless when it shall turn to the Lord, the vail shall be taken away.

Of course that does not mean that we are not to read the Old Testament. Paul said the veil is done away in Christ, who is the New Covenant. Paul understood that he was writing this *to them,* but *for us* (1 Corinthians 10:11, Hebrews 11:39-40). He was simply saying that we have read the New Testament with an Old Testament mentality. We see the God of the New Testament the same way we see the God of the Old Testament. You may be thinking, "Isn't he the same God?" Yes he is, but he deals differently. He dealt with them in a different way under the Old Covenant because they were not born again. Now, in the New Covenant, God deals with us from the mercy seat. Also, there is a difference between the Old Testament and the Old Covenant. Today we are to read the Old Testament with the mentality of the New Covenant.

So, the veil is untaken away in our minds, in the reading of the Old Testament; which veil is done away in Christ. Through the death of Jesus Christ, the veil has been *done away,* but now it has to be *taken away* and that is the key to having the revelation of the Lord Jesus Christ that the book of Revelation talks about. That is the key for the unveiling of the Christ in us.

Let me say that there are people that have been prayed for and have been healed that were not even born again. There are born again and spirit filled people who have been prayed for and have been healed. But I am not talking about that. I'm talking about something greater than an in-part manifestation. I'm talking about something greater than being healed from cancer and ten years later you have it again. I'm talking about receiving all of God, being made whole, God himself filling us in spirit, soul and body. I'm talking about the fullness, something that will never fade away, will never pass away, and will never be corrupted. I'm talking about Christ.

There is no veil in the New Testament except the veil that is over our mind. The primary work of the Holy Spirit is to remove the veil that is over our mind, to remove the veil that has been done away but is untaken away. How? John 16 says the Holy Spirit will not speak of himself, but he is going to glorify the Son. If he glorifies the Son, he's going to be speaking of and showing us the person and the work of Christ. If the Bible is an autobiography about Jesus, and it is, it is going to show us his person and his work. The work of the Holy Spirit is to remove the veil that is still there in our minds by teaching us about the person and the work of Christ and our identification with him. It will be removed when we walk up to the veil or the curtain that is called "the hanging." When we see that the veil was rent through his death, we see that his hanging was our hanging. We won't be like Judas and kiss the master, and then go out and hang *ourselves*. If Judas had waited just three more hours, he could have let Jesus' hanging be his hanging. But he went out and hung himself and threw down thirty (the number of maturity) pieces if silver (redemption) in the temple (which we are).

View The Finished Work

This is so prevalent in the Church today. We worship the Lord and walk out the door saying "What can I do to become more righteous?" There's nothing you can do. There is nothing you can do to become more righteous. You cannot add one cubit to your stature. What we have to do is walk up to the hanging and see that his hanging was our hanging as we see in Exodus chapter 40:33-34:

> And he reared up the court round about the tabernacle and the altar, and set up the *hanging* of the court gate. *So Moses finished the work.* Then a cloud covered the tent of the congregation, and the glory of the Lord filled the tabernacle (emphasis added).

What does this tell us in type? It tells us that when we walk up to the hanging and really see the spiritual meaning of the curtain of the tabernacle, that the veil was rent, that his hanging was our hanging, and that Jesus finished the work—then the glory of the Lord will fill the tabernacle. The veil will be *taken away* by the Holy Spirit revealing to us the treasures hidden in the death of Christ. In this particular passage we read that when they set up the hanging, Moses finished the work. Then a cloud covered the tent of the congregation and the glory of the Lord filled the tabernacle. The veil is going to be taken away as the Holy Spirit reveals that Jesus' hanging on the cross—his death over 2,000 years ago at Calvary—was our death.

When the tabernacle of Moses was completed, it was filled with God's glory. When David's tent was completed, it was filled with God's glory. Of course there are some other things that went along with that. But if you read about Solomon's temple, you will see that nothing happened until they put a bullock on the brazen altar and from the Ark of the Covenant in the Most Holy Place came a laser beam of light and supernaturally exploded that bullock on the brazen altar. At that moment, people fell down and worshipped the Lord for the first time. Then the glory of God filled the Most Holy Place. Jesus finished the work! When a people come to realize the work is completed, we will experience the fullness of God's glory filling his temple—and it will not be as a temporary visitation, but an eternal habitation.

The book of Revelation tells us what happens in the lives of people whenever they come to understand that his hanging was their hanging. In the Old Testament, we can see prophetic pictures of the death, burial, and resurrection. In the gospels, we find the historical surroundings of the death, burial, and resurrection. In Acts we see it proclaimed and declared, but Paul the apostle, in the epistles, is the only man that really *explained* it. All of the other writers took what Paul said to explain the death, burial, and the resurrection. Then the book of Revelation shows us the product that is coming forth out of a people that understand the death, burial, and resurrection.

So, the book of Revelation is a book that reveals what Jesus accomplished at the cross of Calvary. The book of Revelation is one of the most glorious books in that it gives us the conclusion of every Old Testament picture. One can teach every book of the Old Testament by teaching Revelation.

The Testimony Of Jesus—The Spirit Of Prophecy

Scholars argue that the only problem with spiritualizing the book of Revelation is that it takes away from the true prophetic nature of the book, because they say that all of these things are going to happen in the future. Some believe that there are things that are prophesied, like a future seven year tribulation, a literal temple in the Middle East, devastation, famine, pestilence, tumult, torture, and woe—and all of that has scared people to death. Some believe that if you spiritualize the book, you are taking away from the prophetic nature.

How can revealing Jesus take away from the prophetic nature when the spirit of prophecy is the testimony of Jesus? Let's look at Revelation 19:10:

> And I fell at his feet to worship him. And he said unto me, See thou do it not! I am thy fellow servant, and of thy brethren that have the testimony of Jesus. Worship God; for the testimony of Jesus is the spirit of prophecy.

There is no way that spiritualizing the book of Revelation can take away from the prophetic nature of this book, because the testimony of Jesus is the spirit of prophecy. If you're going to be involved in a true prophetic spirit of prophecy, it's going to talk about Jesus. The spirit of prophecy will bear witness to the person and the work of Christ. It will always lift up Jesus as he said, "In the volume of the book, it is written of me." Everything from cover to cover is about him. Yes, it is about us too, but primarily it is about the head. Look at 2 Peter 1:19:

> We have also a more sure word of prophecy, unto which ye do well that ye take heed, as unto a light that shineth in a dark place, until the day dawn, and the day star arise in your hearts;

What is a more sure word of prophecy? You will have a more sure word of prophecy, a more solid understanding of the word of

God, when you understand that the spirit of prophecy is the testimony of Jesus. When you understand that from cover to cover, the Bible is simply about Jesus and the work of Christ and that no matter what book you're studying, whether it is Exodus, Ruth, Nehemiah, or Esther (where the name of the Lord is written in acrostic five times throughout the book)—every book points to something that relates to the person and the work of Christ, then you have a more sure word of prophecy. You're going to have a more sure word of prophecy when you understand that the book of Revelation is not about Scud missiles. You're going to have a more sure word of prophecy when you understand that the book of Revelation is not about a battle of Armageddon, or locusts, or bugs as big as Volkswagens. You're going to have a more sure word of prophecy when you understand that the book of Revelation is simply about the revelation of Jesus Christ and it is God removing a veil in our minds to cause him to be unveiled and uncovered so the world can see.

Written To Bondservants

Continuing with Revelation 1:1:

> The Revelation of Jesus Christ, which God gave unto him, to show unto his servants things which must shortly come to pass; and he sent and signified it by his angel unto his servant, John,

Look at the words servants and servant. The word servants or servant in this passage means "bondservant." It would be an interesting study to see how many times the word bondservant is used in the book of Revelation. A bondservant is not a nominal, status-quo Christian. Not everyone in the body is a bride. Many in the body want to see how close they can live to the edge, how much sin they can be involved in and still be saved or still get by, but a bride is one that wants intimacy. A bondservant is one that loves his master. He is one that, even though he has fulfilled his time with his master, he doesn't want to live "footloose and fancy-free," but he wants to become a love slave, a bondservant, because he loves his master and he loves his family so much that he wants to keep on serving even though he is free to go. It will affect your family when you become a bondslave and have your ear nailed to the door with an awl. Look at Exodus 21:5-6

> And if the servant shall plainly say, I love my master, my wife, and my children, I will not go out free; then his master shall bring him unto the judges. He shall also bring him to the door, or unto the door post; and his master shall bore his ear through with an awl, and he shall serve him forever.

When we have our ear nailed to the door, we do not want to hear anything except the person and the work of Christ. When our ear is nailed to the door we do not want to hear any message unless it glorifies the Lord. We do not want to hear anything that would not lift Jesus up, and when he is lifted up, he is lifted up *within us.* That is all we want to see, that is all we want to hear, because when we see him as he is, we're going to be like him!

The book of Revelation is written for bondservants. Some may say, "I thought it was written for the whole body." Yes, it is written for the whole body, but specifically it is written for bondservants. If you are one in the body of Christ who is just satisfied with being born again and Spirit-filled, waiting for the rapture to take place so you can be snatched out of here, you're going to interpret this according to Scud missiles and locusts and a seven year tribulation and a battle of Armageddon. But if you have your ear nailed to the door, you are going to hear this spiritually.

Jesus—The New Beginning

Eight times (the number of new beginnings) we see in the book of Revelation "He that hath an ear, let him hear what the Spirit saith unto the churches." Everyone has an ear, so this must be talking about a specific group of people. Let me paraphrase it: "He that hath an ear nailed to the door is going to hear what the Spirit saith, (not "said" or "going to say," but *"saith,"* present tense, present truth) to the Church. Unless your ear is nailed to the door, you're not going to have a new beginning. If you want your ear nailed to the door, you're going to have a new beginning. Do you want a new beginning? Continue to eat lamb, continue to eat the bread and drink the wine, the broken body and shed blood, and your ear is going to be nailed to the door. All the way through this study, your ear will be continually nailed to the door.

John 10:9 tells us who the door is. Jesus is the door. If we will keep our ear nailed to the door, tuned in to him, then we are going to hear these things and there is going to be an unveiling. This book is about him. It is about him and it is about nothing else.

John—"God Is Good"

What a great choice the Holy Spirit made when he chose John to write this book. "John" means "Jehovah favored" or "God is good." John was the one that laid his head on the bosom of Jesus. He had his ear nailed to the door. He heard his heartbeat. He heard his heartthrob. He could feel his feelings because his ear was nailed to the door, and he had *the* revelation of Jesus Christ. On the isle of Patmos, John received the revelation of just how good God really is.

The only difference in the book of Revelation and the revelation that Paul received is that the book of Revelation is written in spiritual symbology and Paul's was written in a language that was easier to understand. The book of Revelation was written in a code and you can only understand the code by the Spirit. It is exactly the same revelation that Paul the apostle received when he received his gospel. Paul called it "my gospel" which is the death, burial, and the resurrection of Jesus Christ.

In Revelation 1:1, notice the phrase "… things which must shortly come to pass…." If it was to shortly come to pass *then*, it is at hand *now*. This is not just a futuristic book, but it is something that is present right now, as it says in Revelation 1:4, "Him who is and who was, and who is to come." We can take our past and our future and bring it into the now.

Full Throttle

The last phrase we read in Revelation 1:3 is, "For the time is at hand." The Greek actually says, "For the time is *in* your hand." If you study the word "hand," you will find that it means "throttle" or "to squeeze." So it is saying that the time is in your hand and the throttle is in your hand—which means we can hasten the coming of the Day of the Lord, the unveiling, the appearing of the Day of the Lord in our lives just as fast as we can labor to enter into rest.

Written By Sign And Symbol

Let's finish part b of Revelation 1:1: "And he sent and signified it by his angel unto his servant, John." The word "signified" is very interesting. It is #4591 in the Strong's Concordance and it means "to give a sign or to indicate by sign and symbol." For example, if you were driving down the road with kids in the back seat and they saw a McDonald's sign, you would not stop at the sign to get them a fun meal. You would go where the sign points to and get them a fun meal. A sign points to something else.

The book of Revelation is written by sign and symbol. For example, the pale horse in Revelation 6 according to the Greek, is a green horse. We've never seen a living, breathing, naturally occurring green horse, so it points to something else. A sign is not something that we center up around, but we center up around that to which it points. It is symbolic. We could break that word down to sign-if-ied—a sign that points to something else. We have to understand the code; we have to understand the symbology to understand the book of Revelation.

There are three things that are important to understand. First, we need to understand that this book is about Jesus. It is the revelation of Jesus Christ. Secondly, it is for a people that have their ear nailed to the door—bondservants. Thirdly, he tells us that he sent and signified it, meaning that it is written in sign and symbol. When we get into this book and see all kinds of pictures and icons, we must understand what they represent. They do not represent anything in the natural, or the literal. They represent something spiritual.

Let me give you the law of hermeneutics: If you interpret a set of scriptures, you must remain consistent with your law of interpretation. For example, when we see the word "Lamb" in the book of

Revelation, we do not think of a barnyard creature that bleats, we think of the Lord Jesus Christ. Why then, when we read Revelation, do we spiritualize the Lamb, but when we come to the temple, we are pouring concrete over in the Middle East? Why do we believe that the trumpet is a literal horn that an angel is going to blow and Christians all over the world are going to hear it? For that to literally happen, the trumpet would have to be the size of Mars. A trumpet blast of that magnitude would not rapture you; it would shatter you and everything around you into oblivion. The law of hermeneutics does not allow us to spiritualize one thing and then literalize something else. Jesus had something to say about man's doctrine called a literal, physical rapture, a literal, physical catching away, and we can find it in our Lord's prayer in John 17:15 (Amplified Bible):

> I do not ask that You will take them out of the world, but that You will keep and protect them from the evil one.

This is the prayer Jesus prayed. If we are praying any other prayer, we are not praying *with* Jesus, we are praying *against* Jesus. The issue is not whether there is a catching away, a rapture. Certainly there is a rapture. Paul experienced it, Philip experienced it, and John experienced it on the isle of Patmos. And all three men remained here on planet earth to minister from the realm they had been raptured into. There is definitely a rapture—but not in the way that many in the Church believe.

What amazes me is that people get into the book of Revelation and spiritualize what they understand, but they literalize what they do not understand. I do not say this to disparage anyone. I realize that people do the best they can with what they have and that is the way that most people have been taught to interpret the book of Revelation. They spiritualize the Lamb but they literalize the candlestick, or the temple, or the seals, when these things really have a spiritual meaning. Most people were never given the option to consider that a spiritual book might just have a spiritual meaning! They have never been given the freedom to find out what that spiritual meaning might be! Thank God this is changing. We're here to proclaim liberty to the captives and the opening of the prison *and of the eyes* of those who are bound! This is what Paul has to say about it in the Amplified version of Colossians 2:8 and 2:20:

> See to it that no one carries you off as spoil or makes you yourselves captive by his so-called philosophy and intellectualism and vain deceit (idle fancies and plain nonsense), following human tradition (men's ideas of the *material* rather than the *spiritual* world), just crude notions following the *rudimentary and elemental* teachings of the universe and disregarding [the teachings of] Christ (the Messiah).
>
> If then you have died with Christ to *material* ways of looking at things and have escaped from the world's crude and elemental notions and teachings of *externalism,* why do you live as if you still belong to the world? (Emphasis added).

Let The Teacher Do The Teaching

Once we understand the spiritual meaning, it is not hard for us to interpret the word of God correctly. There are some important things I want to show you so that you know why I am interpreting this book the way I am interpreting it, and so that you can interpret it for yourself. Yes, the Bible will interpret itself, but we must have a correct understanding of the Bible to begin with. Anyone can say "We use the Bible to interpret the Bible" but what is their understanding of the Bible? Do you see the Old Testament as prophetic pictures of the death, the burial, and the resurrection? Do you see that there were natural things, like Jesus' physical coming, that point to spiritual things, like Jesus' Spiritual coming in and through a people? The natural, literal temple in Jerusalem pointed to the temple which we are. All of that was natural at one time, but it points to something spiritual. I am going to show you how Jesus interpreted the scriptures and was consistent in his law of interpretation, like the law of hermeneutics states. Let's look at John 2:13-21.

And the Jews' passover was at hand, and Jesus went up to Jerusalem, and found in the temple those that sold oxen and sheep and doves, and the changers of money sitting; And when he had made a scourge of small cords, he drove them all out of the temple, and the sheep, and the oxen; and poured out the changers' money, and overthrew the tables; and said unto them that sold doves, "Take these things hence; make not my Father's house an house of merchandise." And his disciples remembered that it was written, "The zeal of Thine house hath eaten me up." Then answered the Jews, and said unto him, What sign showest thou unto us, seeing that thou doest these things? Jesus answered, and said unto them, "Destroy this temple, and in three days I will raise it up." Then said the Jews, "Forty and six years was this temple in building, and wilt thou rear it up in three days?" But he spoke of the temple of his body.

Jesus was making a transition. He was trying to show them that there is a transition from the Old Covenant into the New Covenant, but the Jews were showing Jesus the beauty of Herod's temple. Jesus was trying to show them that a New Covenant was standing before them and when it is enacted, God will not dwell in temples made by man's hands. Jesus said to them, "Destroy this temple, and in three days I will raise it up." To which the Jews said, "It took us 46 years to build *this* temple and you are going to raise it up in three days?" (Isn't it interesting that the number 46 just happens to be the number of Adam?[7]) Their carnal mind went right out of the safety zone! They wanted to kill him! They were greatly confused because they thought he was saying something other than what he was saying. They had no idea what he was talking about, because they were thinking in the natural of Herod's temple and Jesus was thinking spiritually.

He that hath an ear, let him hear what the Spirit saith. Jesus goes to Church and he sees men promoting their own ministry (selling oxen) instead of God's ministry of bread and wine. These ministers are exploiting their followers (selling sheep), and saying they have a corner on the market of "spiritual" things (selling doves). It was Passover! The only sacrifice needed is the one Jesus provided with his sinless life. But the Church is still offering their sacrifices of dead works and promoting religion.

Jesus made a scourge of small cords. If you take the word "cords" back to Moses' tabernacle, you will find that it means "remnant." With just a hand full of people that speak the truth of the finished work, Jesus is cleansing today's religious system—utterly destroying it! If Jesus cleansed the temple of Herod's day with zeal, with how much more zeal is he cleansing the religious system today?

He was showing them a transition from the literal interpretation to the spiritual interpretation. He said, "I'm going to go to the cross and I'm taking the first Adam with me and you are going to utterly destroy him when you crucify me!" He that knew no sin, became sin. The temple of the first Adam is the habitation of devils, and the hold of every foul spirit, and a cage of every unclean and hateful bird. *That* temple is going to be utterly destroyed! "But in three days, I'm going to arise as the last Adam, the life giving spirit, the true temple of God! And you too can become the temple of God if you'll just receive my sacrifice!" He said "I'm going to the cross as the first Adam. But I am going to arise as the last Adam, and redeem the whole fallen race!"

All he was trying to do was show them that in the Old Testament, *they thought* it was about Moses' tabernacle, *they thought* it was about David's tent, *they thought* it was about Solomon's temple, *they thought* it was about Ezekiel's temple, but these were all just signs pointing to Jesus. In the New Testament, there is a shift. *Jesus was establishing his principle of interpretation.* He was simply taking a picture in the Old Testament and bringing it out of the realm of enigma and types and shadows and showing the spiritual reality of it all. Jesus is the one who set up this principle of interpretation and we are going to teach it the way Jesus taught it. We are going to take Old Testament pictures and show you spiritual reality.

For instance, just a few years ago some in the Church were so hung up on, "This is the year of Jubilee." Yes 1998 was the one - hundred - twentieth Jubilee since Adam in Israel. It was the fiftieth year that natural Israel had been a nation. People were all excited about it in the Church, but they were not even teaching it according to the spirit of the word. They were saying, "If you'll send your money to this ministry, you will have a Jubilee because this is the year of Jubilee." They had no clue that Jubilee is the sounding of a long, loud blast of a ram's horn. It is speaking about a death that is going to bring more than a financial blessing or a physical healing; it is going to bring the wholeness of God, the manifestation of God himself. Many are so excited about the taking of a red heifer in Jerusalem and the sacrificing on the Feast of Tabernacles, and the cleansing of the temple sight. They're so excited about the blood of bulls and goats while the Holy Spirit is saying "What? Know ye not that ye are the temple of the Holy Ghost?"

I thank God for the revelation that the blood of Jesus Christ changes us on the *inside*. The Old Testament sacrifices could not do that. For example, in the book of Numbers, chapter 19, the red heifer ashes only cleansed the *outside* of the people who touched death. All of those sacrifices point to the Lamb of God who would become sin to cause us to become a new creature. Therefore, *we* are the temple of God. It's not about a temple over in the Middle East. As we get the veil over our minds taken away through understanding what the book of Revelation is all about, great grace is going to appear. We are going to experience an unveiling like we have never experienced before and it is going to bring a greater manifestation of joy and love and patience and faith.

You can tell people "love your neighbor" and people can *act* like they love their neighbor. And they can come in and hug you on the neck while they are thinking "I hope you break your leg when you walk out that door." You cannot teach people to love their neighbor. They have to be in union with the Christ. They have to have something take place in their minds in order to uncover Christ so that love can flow out and manifest. We must experience the revelation of Jesus Christ. The revelation of the death, the burial, and the resurrection must be realized. The Feast of Tabernacles is a second look at Passover and you're going to see it all the way through the word of God.

The Day Of The Lord

We are living in an hour that is the greatest hour that mankind has ever lived in because God is unveiling himself. He is uncovering himself through a people who have their ear nailed to the door. They are Christ-centered; their focus is nothing but him. "In the volume of the book it is written of *me.*" In the book of Psalm it also says that *our* members are written in the book. That is *our* identification. He primarily was the one that went to the cross. He primarily is the one that is written in the volume of the book, but we were there too. Our members are written in the book too. As we get that understanding and the spirit of revelation in the knowledge of him dawns on our consciousness, the day star is going to arise in our hearts, and we are going to see the Lord of glory manifest out of his temple. This is happening right now! As it continues to happen, the temple won't even be seen, the book of Revelation says—all that will be seen is the glory of God!

In The Spirit On The Lord's Day

In Revelation 1:10 John said, "I was in the Spirit on the Lord's day." He did not say that he was studying the literal letter of the word in Church one Sunday morning. The literal letter of the law can only minister death. The Spirit ministers life (2 Corinthians 3:6). And there is nothing wrong with Church on Sunday mornings, but the Lord's Day is not a day of the week. John was in the Spirit on the Lord's Day. If our head is full of dogmas and traditions of men and legalism, then we're going to interpret the book of Revelation and every other book according to that. We are going to interpret the word of God according to what has been placed in our minds. When we get the true understanding of the book of Revelation, there is going to be an unveiling not just in our understanding, but there is going to be an unveiling of the Christ in our lives individually and corporately. As we understand the word of God for the reason it has been given, to interpret it by the Spirit, we are going to see not just an unveiling in our minds, but that revelation will walk itself out. Then we will begin to manifest the nature of the Father and the glory of God will fill the temple. All nations will flow to Mt. Zion. We will manifest that for which we were created and we were created for God's pleasure, not for our pleasure. Then it can truly be said that God has a people that are a praise and a worship unto him.

We have heard many things taught from the book of Revelation that has ministered a lot of fear to the body of Christ. The book of Revelation as well as every book in the Bible is the revelation of Jesus Christ. As we begin to hear what the Spirit is saying to the Church, we will hear that the Holy Spirit is not speaking of himself, but he is glorifying the Son. If he is glorifying the Son, he is speaking of the person and the work of Christ. If I were reading an autobiography about a person, it would be about that person's life. The Bible, including the book of Revelation is an autobiography of Jesus. When we read the Bible, we don't just read it to get information or even revelation. Thank God for knowledge and revelation, but we read the Bible to see Jesus. This is where we have missed it in the past. We've read the Bible just to receive some information, or a golden nugget of truth, or a revelation, but if we go to the scriptures to see him, then he will be exalted and the Holy Spirit will show us the twelve redemptive aspects of the finished work of Calvary.

The Isle Of My Death

When John received this revelation, he was on the isle of Patmos. *Patmos* means "my death" or "my killing." While John was on this isle of his killing and his death, the Spirit began to reveal to him something concerning the death of Christ and how he, John, was identified with that death. We are living in a time when God is unveiling himself as he has never unveiled himself before.

Time For Some "R and R"—Rest And Revolution

We are living in the end of the sixth day. Peter said a day with the Lord is as a thousand years and a thousand years is as a day. It has been 6,000 years since Adam, which would be six days. We have come to the end of the sixth day and we are entering into the beginning of seventh day. "Seven" speaks of maturity, perfection, and rest. It has been over 2,000 years since Jesus walked upon the face of the earth, and was crucified at Calvary. So the time from the cross of Jesus Christ until now, has been two days. We have come to the end of the second day and we are entering into the dawning of the third day. The number "three" speaks of perfection and resurrection.

There is a resurrection taking place in the midst of a people who understand the three days and three nights that Jesus was in the heart of the earth. That does not mean that he was buried six feet under in the ground, because he was placed in the tomb of Joseph of Arimathaea. Joseph spent his whole lifetime carving out that tomb that he thought he was going to go into, but instead, he let Jesus' death be his death. So, when the Bible tells us that Jesus went into the heart of the earth, it means that he went into hell. Jesus, who knew no sin, became sin and he died spiritually and he went into hell. His hell was our hell. His death was our death. His suffering was our suffering. His judgment was our judgment.

This is the hour. We are living in the beginning of the seventh day, a time of rest and revolution. This is a time where a people are entering into rest as never before, as they see that it is a finished work, a "done deal." We are entering into the dawning of a new day—the third day—and there is an experiential resurrection that is beginning to take place as Revelation 20:5-6 declares. It is a superior resurrection, a *protos* (Strong's # 4413), a greater resurrection than those that will experience a resurrection after physical death.

The little book is now open. That tells us that the Holy Spirit is bringing us a word that has been condensed into one message—the message of the bread and wine. The Melchisedec priesthood is bringing forth the bread and the wine, ministering it unto the Church, and then unto the nations.

A People Determined To Know Nothing Except Christ And Him Crucified

Paul said he was determined to know nothing except Christ and him crucified. The Church today is groping and desiring the power of God, and I know they experience it in spurts here and there, but experiencing the unlimited ability and power of God is going to come through a people who understand the death, burial, and resurrection *and their identification with it.* It is going to come through a people who understand that Jesus did not just die physically, but he died spiritually when he became sin and he went into hell—and we went there with him. We were identified with him. He died according to the law of identification which we see for the first time in Genesis 15:9-10. Abraham did not divide the two birds because they were the same offering. This law is seen again in Leviticus 16 with the two goats and can be followed throughout the Bible. Paul wrote to Philemon and in verse 6 of the Amplified Bible he said, "[And I pray] that the participation in and sharing of your faith may produce and promote full recognition and appreciation and understanding and precise knowledge of every good [thing] that is ours *in [our identification with]* Christ Jesus [and unto His glory]" (emphasis added). The Webster's Dictionary definition of "identify" is: "to make identical; consider or treat as the same, to show to be a certain person or thing; fix the identity of; show to be the same as something or someone assumed, described, or claimed, to join or associate closely, to cause to be or become identical; to conceive as united (as in spirit, outlook, or principle); to be or become the same."

We will see Passover in Revelation chapters 2 through 4. We will see Pentecost in Revelation 6 and 7. We will see Tabernacles all the rest of the way through the book of Revelation. What the Holy Spirit wants us to understand is that Tabernacles is a second look at Passover.

Hidden Treasure

What has been hidden in the midst of the body of Christ? *He* has been hidden. I know that from time to time, we have manifested his nature and we've experienced the glory of God, but I believe that God has a people in the earth that are going to manifest the nature of the Father twenty-four hours a day, seven days a week, three-hundred and sixty-five days a year, and it is going to be dependent upon what is in our minds. That is not mind over matter or positive thinking, but it is the salvation of God—the truth of the person and the work of Christ that is in our spirit coming to our soul, renewing our mind (Romans 12). When our mind is renewed there is going to be a transformation—a total transformation in our whole life.

The veil was done away at the cross of Calvary, now it is being taken away from over our minds. The proverbial "stinkin' thinkin'" has to be taken away from our minds. Notice what it says in 2 Corinthians 3:14:

> But their minds were blinded: for until this day remaineth the same veil untaken away in the reading of the old testament;

The veil, the man of sin, has been completely done away with, but there is yet a veil over our minds. It is going to be taken away as we eat Lamb and experience the marriage supper. The marriage is not off yonder on some planet called heaven where there is a big long table that we just "pig out" as much as we want to. We are to eat of the Lamb, the bread and wine *now*. The marriage is spirit and soul becoming one—the mind renewed with the thoughts of the salvation that is in our spirit. Then we can manifest the nature of God and the glory of God can fill the house.

2 Corinthians 3:16 tells us:

> Nevertheless when it shall turn to the Lord, the vail shall be taken away.

How do we turn our heart to the Lord? One way is in going to the scripture to see him. "In the volume of the book it is written of me," Jesus said. In 1 John 3:2 we find that when we see him as he is, we are going to be like him, we're going to manifest him. So, we turn to the Lord when we go to the word of God not just to teach a bunch of messages, but we use scriptures taken from the word of God to teach *the* message. As we go there and get revelation of the little book—the one message—that has been condensed into the person and the work of Christ, we turn our mind to the Lord.

Changed From Glory To Glory

"When it shall turn to the Lord, the veil shall be taken away." You may be thinking, "What veil? I thought it was done away in Christ 2,000 years ago." Yes it was, but it has to be taken away from over our minds. 2 Corinthians 3:17-18 shows us what happens when we turn to the Lord—when the veil is taken away from our minds. We behold with open face the glory of the Lord and are changed into the same image, not another image, but the same image from glory to glory even as by the Spirit of the Lord. One translation says "from one degree of splendor to another degree of splendor." We are changed when we realize the veil was done away and is now being taken away as we renew our mind to the person and the work of Christ. As we turn to the Lord, as we behold the little book, then the veil that was done away is being taken away from the place where it yet remains—our mind. Colossians 1:27 declares that Christ in us is the hope of glory. If Christ is in us only, and there is not an expression and a manifestation, then it is just a hope of glory. Hope deferred makes the heart sick. How are we going to see that hope become an expression? We will see it as the veil is taken away.

The Father's Business—It Is Finished

Every time a temple or a tabernacle was finished, God filled it with his glory. Moses is a type of Christ in that he set up the hanging and finished the work. Look at the picture in Exodus 40:33:

> And he reared up the court round about the tabernacle and the altar, and set up the hanging of the court gate. So Moses finished the work.

What work did he finish? Bullinger writes:

> The Lord Jesus must have spoken from the time that all children spoke; but not one syllable that He uttered has the Holy Spirit been pleased to record in the Scriptures, until he was twelve years of age. And then only this one utterance from His birth till He entered on His ministry at His baptism. Only one sentence out of all those twenty-nine years. Surely words thus singled out by the Holy Spirit must be full of significance. What were they? They are written down for us in Luke 2:49: "Wist ye not that I must be about my Father's business?" Solemn words! Significant words! Especially in the light these first

words throw upon his last words, "It is finished." What was finished? The father's business.[8]

Jesus was the hanging in Exodus 40:33—he hung on the cross where he was crucified. His hanging was our hanging and we realize this as we realize our identification with Christ (Romans 6:6, Galations 2:20). We must walk up to the hanging and see that his hanging was our hanging.

The throttle is in our hand. We can "put the pedal to the metal." As fast as we can renew our minds with the truth about the person and the work of Christ and our identification with him, to that degree can we hasten the coming of the day of the Lord individually in our lives and corporately in the midst of the body of Christ.

So many times ministers go to the Lord at the beginning of the year and ask "What can I tell your people you are going to do in this New Year?" If our ear is nailed to the door, if we can really hear what the Spirit is saying, he will be saying to us, "It is not what I'm going to do; the question is 'What are *you* going to do?'" So many times we ask the Lord what we can tell the people to look forward to, but the Lord is saying "It is not what you're to look forward to, it is what you are to look back to." Our past determines our present and our future.

The Key Is Over The Door

The key to the interpretation of every book of the Bible is over the entrance. The meaning of the name of the book gives understanding as to what that particular book is about. Also, as we study the first few verses of a book we find the key. So, right up front we see that Revelation is a book of sign and symbol.

Continuing with Revelation 1:2:

> Who bare record of the word of God, and of the testimony of Jesus Christ, and of all things that he saw.

The word "record" in the Strong's is #3140, "to be a witness" or "give testimony," and it comes from #3144, which means "martyr."

The word "testimony" in this verse is #3141, which again, comes from # 3144 and it also means "martyr." John was a witness of the death of Jesus Christ when he saw himself crucified with Christ.

Revelation 1:3 declares:

> Blessed is he that readeth and they that hear the words of this prophecy, and keep those things which are written in it; for the time is at hand.

The same scripture in the Amplified Bible reads:

> Blessed (happy, to be envied) is the man who reads aloud [in the assemblies] the word of this prophecy; and blessed (happy, to be envied) are those who hear [it read] and who keep themselves true to the things which are written in it [heeding them and laying them to heart], for the time [for them to be fulfilled] is near.

Jesus Has Blessed Us

Happy? How happy could John be if he were *going to be* a martyr for the testimony of Jesus? When he saw that he *was* crucified with Christ at Calvary's cross and it was no longer John that lived, but Christ who lived in him, John was blessed, happy, and to be envied (Galations 2:19-21)! Happy? If this is a book about a seven year tribulation, how can we be happy? If this is a book about all those literal things we've been taught, then I don't think it would make us too happy. In fact, the majority of the Church world is unhappy and fearful because of the literal letter that only ministers death (Romans 7:6, 2 Corinthians 3:6). The thing that is going to make us happy and full of the joy of the Lord is the thing that satisfied little Ruth. When she ate bread and wine (the broken body and the shed blood) she was happy. That is the thing that is going to make us happy, fully satisfy us, cause the joy of the Lord to well up within us, birth praise, worship, and ministry out of us—eating bread and wine.

Blessed. That is an interesting word. In Acts chapter 3, we will see how we are blessed in reading verse 26:

> Unto you first God, having raised up his Son, Jesus, sent him to bless you, in turning away every one of you from his iniquities.

We are a blessed people. We are blessed to live in the time we are living in. We are blessed because the little book is opened and we are partaking of bread and wine. We are blessed because the Spirit of wisdom and revelation in the knowledge of him has been imparted to us. The word *blessed* here is where we get the English word *eulogy*. There has been a eulogy spoken over us. When was that eulogy spoken over us? At our death 2,000 years ago at the cross of Calvary. All the way through chapter 1 we see it. He is on the isle of Patmos, the place of *my* killing and *my* death, and he is feasting on bread and wine.

Revelation 1:4:

> John, to the seven churches which are in Asia: Grace be unto you, and peace, from him which is, and which was, and which is to come, and from the seven spirits which are before his throne;

Notice "grace and peace from him which is, and which was, and which is to come." When you understand what took place at the cross of Calvary, or the "which was" part, it is going to change your "which is" and your "which is to come." It will change because you're bringing the past into the "now" and that will bring the expression, the revelation of Jesus Christ in our "is" realm, our now, and it will intensify as time goes on. We have not seen anything yet, compared to what we're going to see and what we're going to experience in that which God reveals unto us. We've barely scratched the surface.

Jesus—The Firstfruit

What is "firstfruit?" Every fruit-bearing tree has some fruit that matures and ripens first, before the majority of the remaining fruit.

There is a firstfruit company in the earth today hearing from God, partaking of bread and wine, and going forth to rebuild the tabernacle of David. According to Acts chapter 15, this firstfruit company ministers to the Church world that is still entangled in religion, so that the residue—all of humanity—can come into the Kingdom of God.

We see the person and the work of Christ, bread and wine, from the beginning to the end of the Bible! In the very first verse of the Bible we see him. Look at Genesis 1:1. "In the beginning God created the heaven and the earth." The word "beginning" is the Hebrew word "firstfruit." Who is the firstfruit but Jesus Christ?

Genesis 1:2-3 declares, "And the earth was without form, and void; and darkness was upon the face of the deep. And the Spirit of God moved upon the face of the waters. And God said, Let there be light: and there was light." That literally happened. God created the heavens and the earth. But it is also a prophetic picture of the Lord Jesus Christ, the finished work, and our condition from the fall of Adam. Our earth was without form, and void. Darkness was upon the face of the deep and the Spirit of God fluttered and hovered and moved upon the face of the waters. God said, "Let there be light," and there was light. That happened at the cross of Calvary over 2,000 years ago. As we believe and receive that, and as the Holy Spirit draws us unto him, we are born again! God said through Jesus Christ at the cross of Calvary, "Let there be light!" We became a brand new creation in Christ Jesus.

In Genesis 1:11 we see bread and wine. "And God said, Let the earth bring forth grass, the herb yielding seed (there is the bread), and the fruit tree yielding fruit after its kind" (there is the wine).

In Genesis 4 we see some more pictures. Abel brought of the firstling of his flock in verse 4. That is a picture of the person and the work of Christ. But in verse 3, Cain brought of the fruit of the ground. People are still bringing of the fruit of their energy. It is not in works. By grace are you saved through faith, not by works lest any man should boast. You can't add one cubit to your stature by doing one good work. You are the righteousness of God because of what happened at the cross of Calvary 2,000 years ago. The works that we do, we do because we *are* righteous, not because we are trying to *get* righteous. That will lift a load off of your shoulder! That will bring you out of legalism! That will take the veil away from between your ears, which was done away at the cross of Calvary! That will cause us to be an expression of him! That will cause the unveiling, and will cause the Christ within us that has up until now been just a *hope* of glory, to become the reality of God in manifestation—to become an expression of God, an expression of his nature—and God will fill the house with his glory!

Jesus—King Of Kings

Again, in Revelation 1:5 we read:

> And from Jesus Christ, who is the faithful witness, and the first begotten of the dead, and the prince of the kings of the earth. Unto him that loved us, and washed us from our sins in his own blood,

Notice the three phrases here; "the faithful witness," "the first begotten of the dead," and "the prince of the kings of the earth." The faithful witness exposes the false prophet. The first begotten of the dead exposes the false prophet that tries to heal the deadly wound by saying you have two natures (Revelation 13).[9] We do not have two natures. We are not trying to rehabilitate Adam. God is not saving Adam. The carnal mind is not subject to God, neither will it ever be subject to God. We only have one nature. Our old man was crucified. He was that goat on the Day of Atonement that was sent out into the wilderness never to return again. Our old man is not going to return again. It may sometimes look like he has returned because of the residue of Adam that is yet in and over our minds, but we do not have two natures. Any man who is in Christ Jesus is a new creation, old things have passed away and all things have become new.

And the last phrase, "the prince of the kings of the earth" exposes Babylon's lie that says she is the ruler of the kings of the earth. The word "prince" is the Greek *archon,* from the word *archo* and it means "to be first in political rank or power, to reign, to rule over." Jesus is the Prince of the kings of the earth or the King of kings.

In verse 6 of Revelation chapter 1, he says:

> And hath made us kings and priests unto God and

his Father, to him be glory and dominion forever and ever. Amen.

How did he make us kings and priests? In the preceding verse, 5b, we see that it happened when he washed us from our sins in his own blood.

A Great Multitude

Now look at Revelation 1:7:

> Behold, he cometh with clouds, and every eye shall see him, and they also which pierced him; and all the kindreds of the earth shall wail because of him. Even so, Amen.

This particular verse is a big issue in a lot of Churches. Some believe that the clouds mentioned here are literal, atmospheric clouds that Jesus is going to return on. The word tells us he is coming *in* clouds, as seen in 1 Thessalonians 4:17, and as this verse tells us, he comes *with* clouds. Webster's dictionary lists one of the meanings of "cloud" as "a great crowd or multitude." "Clouds" are symbolic of a people that are filled with life-giving substance, bread and wine, to give to the earth, to water the earth. We can read in Jude about ministers who are clouds *without* water, without life-giving substance to give to the earth. Peter wrote about false teachers who are clouds that are carried with a tempest. We can read in Hebrews about a great cloud of witnesses who are heroes of faith. The word "cloud" here refers to people.[10]

Lucas and Washburn write in their book <u>Theomatics,</u> that the word "Cloud," singular, has the number value of 100 x 6. ("Theomatics" is known by the ancients as "gematria," or number in scripture.) The number 6 is the number of man. Any time you have a number followed by zeros, the zeros serve only to amplify and add clarity to that number. Therefore, the word "cloud" (600), refers to a many-membered body of Christ, a kingdom of priests unto God, a holy nation. The word "clouds," plural[11], has the gematria of 100 x 8. The number 8 is the number of new beginnings, the new day dawning, the new creation. So "clouds" refers to people who are in Christ and are new creations—an in-Christed people. In him, each day is a new beginning. His mercies are new every morning. He *is* the New Day. And this is the Day of the Lord!

Seeing The Invisible

Something helpful to keep in mind when we study the word and when we compare literal things (like clouds) to spiritual things, is Jesus' own words recorded in Luke 17:20-21 (Amplified Bible):

> Asked by the Pharisees when the kingdom of God would come, He replied to them saying, The kingdom of God does not come with signs to be observed or with visible display, nor will people say, Look! Here [it is]! or, See, [it is] there! For behold, the kingdom of God is within you [in your hearts] and among you [surrounding you].

Righteousness, Peace, And Joy—In The Holy Spirit

You can't see the kingdom, but when you *do* see it, this is what you'll see: righteousness, peace, and joy *in the Holy Spirit*. In Revelation 1:7, notice the phrase "and every eye shall see him." That is not because he is going to be on satellite television. Every eye is going to see him because he is a many-membered Christ! "Every eye shall see him, and they also which pierced him." Some are still piercing him today. In Isaiah 52 we read that his visage was marred. That passage is primarily about the fact that he was crucified. The Spanish translation says that when he was beaten, his body looked like hamburger meat. He was unrecognizable. He was also pierced in Spirit when he became sin and died spiritually.

People are still piercing him today by saying he just became a sin offering. It is of utmost importance that we understand that it was not just a physical death, but it was a spiritual death, because then we can realize that our sins are not just atoned for, or covered, as they were in the Old Covenant, but they were removed as far as the east is from the west. We received a brand new nature. I am not the same person I was before I accepted Jesus Christ as my savior and was born again. I received a new nature.

Revelation 1:8:

> I am Alpha and Omega, the beginning and the end, saith the Lord, which is, and which was, and which is to come, the Almighty.

In considering the phrase, "I am the Alpha and Omega," let's look at Genesis 1:1:

> And in the beginning God created the heaven and the earth.

The word "beginning" is firstfruit. Jesus Christ is the firstfruit of God (1 Corinthians 15:23). That is the Alpha. He is the author of our faith. Then we have the Omega, the end, the finality, the finisher of our faith. Everything begins and ends in him. 1 Corinthians 15:45-50 speaks of the first Adam, the first man of the earth and those that are earthy. Then it speaks of the last Adam, the life-giving spirit, the second man, the Lord from heaven and they that are heavenly. At the cross of Calvary, Jesus died according to the law of identification in that he fully identified with who we were in Adam. He did not just die *for* us. He was not just our substitute. He also died *as* us. He became all that we were and all that we inherited through Adam, and more. He totally did away with the first man at Calvary's cross. That only leaves one man, the Lord from heaven. If you are in the first man, Adam, you are in death. If you are in the last Adam, the second man, the Lord from heaven, you now possess eternal life. The word of God begins with Jesus in Genesis 1:1 and ends with Jesus in Revelation chapter 22—The Alpha and Omega, the beginning and the end, which is, which was, and which is to come, the Almighty.

Lucas and Washburn write in their book Theomatics[12]:

> The definition of the name *Adam* in Hebrew is simply "man." If one were to go to the text of the

Old Testament, he would find that the Hebrew words are full of multiples of 276 throughout the text of the creation of man. For the sake of illustration, we will show one verse containing two features. Here is Genesis 5:2, which has a number value of 2,760 or 276 x 10: *He created them male and female, and He blessed them* (276 x 10) *and called their name man, in the day when they were created.* The words "their name man" form the most distinct portion of the above verse. Here again, the same design is present: *Their name man* (276 x 3). Now here is something remarkable, The name *Adam* (or man) in Hebrew (Genesis 5:2) has a theomatic value of 46, and in the Greek (Romans 5:14) it is also 46. ... in the Greek the word *man* is 276, and *Adam* is 46 in both Hebrew and Greek. At this point you may be asking yourself the question, What relation does the number 46 have to the number 276? Watch! 46 x 6 = 276. Now the number six has been universally accepted by Bible scholars as being the number of man. There are many instances in Scripture where this is brought out. It was on the sixth day of creation that God created man. So 46 (the number of Adam in both Hebrew and Greek) times 6 (the number of man) equals 276 (the number of flesh and sin). When Jesus died on the cross, He took with Him man's sin. Scripture declares that Christ became sin for us, and it was in His body that He bore our sins ...We are now going to discover something of unique significance, In 1 Corinthians 15:22 we find these words: "For as in Adam all die, even so in Christ shall all be made alive." The word for *in* in the Greek is ... also the word for the number one in Greek. Therefore, this verse could have easily been translated: "As one Adam all die" instead of "As in Adam all die." ... *As Adam all die* is 276 x 11.

In light of this, look at an often misquoted scripture, Hebrews

9:27-28: "And as it is appointed unto men once to die, but after this the judgment; (and this is how it has been misquoted—the sentence does not end there, it goes on to say ...) *so Christ* was once offered to bear the sins or many; and unto them that look for him shall he appear the second time without sin, unto salvation." So, what have we discovered from the whole counsel of the word of God? Jesus took the first Adam (man) to the cross where he is crucified, dead, and buried. Jesus arose as the last Adam, the Omega—and we are in him! We no longer have the nature of the old man, but we have the nature of the new man, Christ. We are new creations in Christ Jesus. And when we take the second look at the cross, *he will appear the second time* without sin, unto full salvation!

Jesus—The First And The Last

In Revelation 2:8, when Jesus talks to the Church at Smyrna, he first tells them something about himself before he tells them what is required of them. Why? Because you have to understand the person and the work of Christ before you can be empowered to overcome. Paul said it this way in 1 Corinthians 15:34: "Awake to righteousness, and sin not." He did not say "fight this sin and that sin." He did not say to get in the pulpit every Sunday morning and preach on the works of the flesh and focus on that. He said "Awake to righteousness, and sin not." I am convinced that if we will minister a God-conscious message, rather than a sin-conscious message, we are going to see people walk in victory in every area, in every aspect of their lives. What I mean by a God-conscious message is a message that focuses on the person and the work of Christ.

Now let's look at Revelation 2:8 in light of our previous discussion:

> And unto the angel of the church in Smyrna write:
> These things saith the first and the last, which was dead and is alive.

He was telling them something about himself. "I was dead and now I am alive forevermore." He talks in verse 9 about their tribulation, poverty, and abuse then in verse 10 he says, "Fear none of these things which thou shalt suffer: behold, the devil shall cast some of you into prison, that ye may be tried; and ye shall have tribulation ten days: be thou faithful unto death, and I will give thee a crown of life." Some believe that the Christian life is one struggle after another. They say "I've got to work and I've got to spend ten hours a day in my prayer closet and I've got to just trudge along on this hard road and one day I'm going to overcome, if it kills me!" That is not what he is saying. We have taught too much processing and "if we suffer with him we will reign with him." I already suffered with him!

God does not bring things upon us that he nailed to the cross. He works in all kinds of situations, conditions and circumstances, but people do not go through a "Job experience" by the ordination of God. God does not put us in a Job experience. We may experience extraordinarily difficult trials and circumstances, but God is here with us to take us through them and deliver us from them—not to put us in them. What we have been taught about the book of Job is not even what the book is about! Job is a perfect type of Christ. He is a perfect type of Christ in that he lost everything and in the end, received more back than he lost! That is exactly what we read in the New Testament about Jesus, who for the joy that was set before him, endured the cross, despising the shame. Why? In Jewish families, the firstborn are considered sacred, the key to the family line. They receive double inheritance and are given a seat of honor over their brothers as well as the special covenant with God. Being the firstborn of many brethren, Jesus knew that he was going to get a people that he would reproduce himself through.

So he tells the Churches in Revelation about himself first. That is what we have to do. We have to minister bread and wine. We must minister a God-conscious message, rather than a sin-conscious message. We have to show people what happened at the cross of Calvary and how they are identified with that. The more we feed the sheep the message of the cross, placing it in their consciousness, empowering them to renew their minds to the person and the work of Christ, the more victory they will walk in. In doing so, we will hasten the coming of the Day of the Lord experientially in our individual and corporate lives.

Back to Revelation 1:9, 10:

> I, John, who am also your brother, and companion in tribulation, and in the kingdom and patience of Jesus Christ, was in the isle that is called Patmos, for the word of God, and for the testimony of Jesus Christ. I was in the Spirit on the Lord's day, and heard behind me a great voice, as of a trumpet,

We know the isle called Patmos means "my killing" or "my death" and he was there for the word of God, and for the testimony of Jesus Christ. That word "testimony" in the Greek means martyrdom. John was on the isle called "my killing," or "my death," for the word of God and for the testimony—or to come to understand the martyrdom or the death of Jesus Christ.

In verse 10 we read that he heard a great voice *behind* him. We see in verse 12 that he turned to see that voice and where did he turn? He turned *behind* him. That is what we need to return to. We need to return to what happened at the cross of Calvary and how we were identified with that. That is what we need to be focusing on. That is the little book. That is what we need to repent—or change our thinking about—and turn to.

Jesus—The Lord's Day

He said "I was in the Spirit on the Lord's day." The Lord's Day is not a Sunday, or a Saturday. The Lord's Day is the Most Holy Place where all of us are seated. Throughout scripture Jesus is referred to as "The Day." Jesus is the Lord's Day. *This* is the Day that the Lord has made; we will rejoice and be glad in it. It is a dimension in God. In the Lord's Day, if we hear what the Lord is saying, we are going to hear him saying that Tabernacles is a second look at Passover.

In Revelation 1:10-11 we continue:

> I was in the Spirit on the Lord's day, and heard behind me a great voice, as of a trumpet, Saying, I am Alpha and Omega, the first and the last; and What thou seest, write in a book, and send it unto the seven churches which are in Asia: unto Ephesus, and

unto Smyrna, and unto Pergamum, and unto Thyatira, and unto Sardis, and unto Philadelphia, and unto Laodicea.

The revelation that the apostle John received here is the same revelation that the apostle Paul received. John wrote it more in symbolic terms and Paul wrote it in common day language. Paul wrote to seven Churches also. We can see the parallel here.

So many people say that Laodicea, the last Church, represents the Church in the "last days." Laodicea does *not* represent today's Church in this hour, because there is nothing good said about Laodicea. There are a lot of *good things* said about today's Church! There are a lot of good things being said about a people today that fill their minds with bread and wine, eat nothing but Lamb, have their ear nailed to the door, and do not want to hear anything but Christ.

> Revelation 1:12-20: And I turned to see the voice that spake with me. And being turned, I saw seven golden candlesticks, And in the midst of the seven candlesticks one like unto the Son of man, clothed with a garment down to the foot, and girded about the paps with a golden girdle. His head and his hairs were white like wool, as white as snow; and his eyes were as a flame of fire; And his feet like unto fine brass. as if they burned in a furnace; and his voice as the sound of many waters. And he had in his right hand seven stars; and out of his mouth went a sharp twoedged sword; and his countenance was as the sun shineth in his strength. And when I saw him, I fell at his feet as dead. And he laid his right hand upon me, saying unto me, Fear not; I am the first and the last; I am he that liveth and was dead; and behold, I am alive for evermore, Amen, and have the keys of hell and death. Write the things which thou hast seen, and the things which are, and the things which shall be hereafter: The mystery of the seven stars which thou sawest in my right hand, and the seven golden candlesticks. The seven stars are the angels of the

seven churches; and the seven candlesticks which thou sawest are the seven churches.

John turned behind him and saw seven golden candlesticks, which are the seven Churches, and in the midst of them he saw Jesus. His eyes were as a flame of fire. Fire speaks of judgment. His judgment was our judgment. His feet were like unto fine brass, which speaks of judgment also. When Ruth came and uncovered Boaz's feet, she got a revelation that his judgment was her judgment. The twoedged sword speaks of the word of God. All of this is a revelation of the death, burial, and resurrection that John received on the isle of Patmos. The seven stars are the angels, or the pastors, and the seven candlesticks, are the seven Churches. Everything that is said about Jesus is said about the Church. Why? Because his death was our death. His suffering was our suffering. His judgment was our judgment. The Church has taught judgment in such an imbalanced way, as if God's wrath and judgment is going to come upon a wicked world. The world is reaping what they are sowing—but that is not God bringing judgment on them, it is their own doing. The religious Church is also reaping what she is sowing. Romans 4:15, James 2:10 and Galatians 5:4 tell us that judging one another and keeping people under the law will bring wrath, guilt, insecurity, and alienation. Religion is reaping what it has sown.

The judgment of God that is going to come upon this world is not going to be God kicking them down any further. They are down far enough. The judgment is going to be a Melchisedec priesthood that is going to bring a word of bread and wine to them and show them that they are not condoning their sin, but they are not condemning them. This will be a priesthood showing the mercy of God and that his judgment was their judgment 2,000 years ago at the cross of Calvary. That is a totally different mindset than what we've heard in religion, in the Church as a whole. Judgment is not unto condemnation. Judgment is unto victory (Matthew 12:20)! This is the revelation of Jesus Christ!

We have to enter into rest. In this day, we are entering into rest. How do we enter into rest? The word says we *labor* to enter into rest. That does not mean "labor" as in doing our good works. I'm not against good works. We show our faith by our works. But we don't do good works to make ourselves more righteous. We do good works because we *are* righteous. The laboring to enter into rest is laboring over the word, filling our mind with the truth of the word of God.

Jesus—The Day Of Jubilee

We read in Revelation chapter 1 about the Lord's Day. The Lord's Day is a dimension of rest or Jubilee that we come into. Jesus is our Jubilee. A few years ago the whole Church was declaring, "It's our Jubilee!" They were saying, "If you will send us your money, you are going to experience Jubilee, financial blessing, and healing." That is not Jubilee at all! I want more than healing. I want to be made whole! Wholeness means to be full of God himself, and then the healing will take care of itself! I am not against people laying hands on us for healing, but God wants to do something greater in this Day of Jubilee. "Jubilee" does not mean release; it does not mean what you "get." All of that comes along with it like tongues come with the shoes. "Jubilee" means "a long, loud blast of a ram's horn." Where in the world do you get a ram's horn? We get a ram's horn from the death of a male sheep.

There is a ram's horn that is being sounded in the midst of the Church and we are going to get more than just healed, we are going to get more than just financial blessing. Thank God for that, but we are going to be made every whit whole[13]. There is not going to be a need. The wealth of the sinner is laid up for the just that his covenant might be established. The Lord himself is the provision that declares this word through television, through the printed word, through audio and video tapes and other sources, all of which are flowing into and through the Melchisedec priesthood to the people. If we are preaching just a Jubilee as, "Send me your money and you'll get healed and you'll get your needs met, then our focus is very low on the totem pole! We need to have our spirit stretched! It is a long, loud blast of a ram's horn. Look what it says about the Sabbath day and Jubilee in Deuteronomy 5:14-15:

> But the seventh day is the sabbath of the Lord thy God: in it thou shalt not do any work, thou, nor thy

son, nor thy daughter, nor thy manservant, nor thy maidservant, nor thine ox, nor thine ass, nor any of thy cattle, nor thy stranger that is within thy gates; that thy manservant and thy maidservant may rest as well as thou. (And remember that thou wast a servant in the land of Egypt, and that the Lord thy God brought thee out thence through a mighty hand and by a stretched out arm; therefore the Lord thy God commanded thee to keep the sabbath day).

Jesus—The Sabbath Day

Jubilee correlates with Sabbath. We are laboring to fill our minds with the truth of the finished work that we may enter into rest. The Sabbath day is not a certain day of the week. It is not a Sunday or a Saturday. It has nothing to do with that. Sabbath speaks of rest. Notice, when they came into this rest, they were to *remember* how God brought them out of Egypt with a mighty hand and an outstretched arm. When they came out of Egypt, they took the blood and put it on the doorposts. That did not mean that the death angel was going to pass them by and there would be no death. It meant that the lamb's death *was* their death. So Sabbath and Jubilee is about the Feast of Tabernacles. Look what the Feast of Tabernacles is in verse 15—to remember the Lord! They are to remember Passover. Tabernacles is simply a second look at Passover.

Jesus Will Appear The Second Time

That is what we are doing. We are going back for a second look. Thank God for the first look when we were born again! We saw that Jesus died for us. The Church teaches that one man was crucified, died, buried, quickened, raised and seated. That is good as far as they go—that gets them born again. But we are going back to take a second look to see that we were there. That is why Paul could say, "I am crucified with Christ: nevertheless I live; yet not I, but Christ liveth in me: and the life which I now live in the flesh I live by the faith of the Son of God, who loved me, and gave himself for me." In

the King James it almost sounds like it is a daily crucifying. But it's not. It is daily waking up to the fact that it happened 2,000 years ago.
Look at 1 Corinthians 15:31-34:

> I protest by your rejoicing which I have in Christ Jesus our Lord, I die daily. If after the manner of men I have fought with beasts at Ephesus, what advantageth it me, if the dead rise not? let us eat and drink; for to morrow we die. Be not deceived: evil communications corrupt good manners. Awake to righteousness and sin not; for some have not the knowledge of God: I speak this to your shame.

Paul was persecuted by *beasts* at Ephesus, who were *people*. Paul's dying daily was not him crucifying his flesh, but daily renewing his mind to the fact that he was already crucified as to his old man and alive as to his new creation. You will be persecuted by religious beasts when you bear the message of the finished work of the cross.

We have been teaching too much "processing." To fill our minds with the finished work is a process. But we've looked at processing as suffering and as what we must go through saying, "If we suffer with him, we will reign with him," rather than looking at it as; "I already suffered with him. I am seated with him in heavenly places in a place of ruling and reigning." What we need to understand is that it is not so much a processing, but it is a provision. We need to understand that Tabernacles is a second look at Passover. With the second look we see it wasn't one man that was crucified, but that all men in Adam were crucified. With the second look we see that in Christ all men were reconciled—not saved—but all men were reconciled over 2,000 years ago at the cross of Calvary. Reconciliation is a provision for salvation. Reconcile means "to cancel, to satisfy, to atone for, to cover, and to change mutually." Salvation is the believing and receiving of that which has been provided.

Jesus—The Promised Land

We are coming into the Promised Land. Actually, we are already in the Promised Land, we're just waking up to the fact that we're already there. What is the Promised Land? Jesus is our Promised Land man. The Promised Land is expressing and manifesting *him*. I know we are not fully expressing and manifesting the full measure of the stature of Christ yet, but we are already in that place. We are not trying to *get into* the Holy of Holies. We were seated there over 2000 years ago. We are not trying to *get into* the Promised Land. We are already there. What we are to do is wake up to how we got there so we can have the expression of that.

When a person is born again, they are placed at the finish line. Now we need to look behind, look back to the cross, as we saw John do in the book of Revelation, and see how we got to the finish line. Looking at the sacrifice and our identification with it, is going to gradually remove, as it were, the layers of an onion that have hidden, that have veiled the Christ, and he will be uncovered.

In 1998, so many people were very excited because in natural Israel it was the historical Feast of Tabernacles. It was the one-hundred-twentieth Jubilee since Adam. They celebrated the fiftieth anniversary of natural Israel's birth as a nation. "Jubilee!" The Church was excited because they were taught that when the orthodox Jews began to re-institute those sacrifices, it meant that a literal rapture was going to happen before their sacrifices started and before the temple was built. They still believe that. Some even believe that Christianity will go back to offering the blood of bulls and goats. How absurd! Some Christians are excited because to them it is "a sign of the last days" and that before these things happen, a literal rapture will take place. If one's theology is based on a literal rapture when they re-institute these sacrifices, they are sadly mistaken.

If your theology is based upon the blood of bulls and goats, you crucify to yourself the son of God afresh, and put him to an open shame. Jesus was the sacrifice once and for all. If you believe that there is a temple over there in the Middle East that is going to be built, the Holy Spirit is saying, "What? Know ye not that *you are the temple* of the Holy Ghost?" It is a spiritual thing. It is a spiritual happening. The book of Revelation is a symbolic book. It is the unveiling of the Lord Jesus Christ. And yes, this is the time of Jubilee. Israel is not our time clock, but we can see things happening in natural Israel that are pictures pointing to the fact that those same things should be happening in us spiritually. And it *is* happening in us spiritually. We are living in the most exciting day mankind has ever lived in—the most strategic time—and the hardest thing we'll ever learn to do is nothing! The only labor we must do is renew our minds to the finished work, which brings us into rest.

> Isaiah 61:1-2: The Spirit of the Lord God is upon me; because the Lord hath anointed me to preach good tidings unto the meek; He hath sent me to bind up the brokenhearted, to proclaim liberty to the captives, and the opening of the prison to them that are bound; To proclaim the acceptable year of the Lord,"

That is the first message that Jesus preached. The acceptable year of the Lord is Jubilee and it is right now. We see the Old Testament pictures which were literal pictures, literal structures. There was a real Noah and a real Ark. There was a real Adam, but all of those pictures typify something spiritual. They typify the person and the work of Christ and what was accomplished at Calvary over 2,000 years ago. So the book of Revelation is the revelation of Jesus Christ, written to bondservants—those who have their ear nailed to the door. They are the ones who are going to "hear the words of this prophecy." If your ear is not nailed to the door, you will interpret it literally. If you are a bondservant, you really want to get intense with the Lord, to have intimacy with him. Then your ear will be nailed to the door and you will understand this book. It was written in sign and symbol. He signified it. It is a symbolic book, and I promise you, as we come to understand this, it will bring us into an experiential unveiling of the nature of Jesus Christ. The Christ in you won't just be hoping to someday manifest and expressing his glory, but he will be constantly manifested and expressed (Colossians 1:27). The revelation, the Spirit of wisdom and revelation in the knowledge of him will walk itself out.

Jesus Christ is not unveiled by works. I do not preach about tithing in my Church, but the people tithe. I do not minister a sin-conscious message, but I believe for the most part, they live above sin. We minister Christ crucified—and to us who are being saved, it is the power of God and the wisdom of God (1 Corinthians 1:18-25). The person and the work of Christ is the only thing that is going to satisfy. It is the only thing that is going to cause maturity. Like the little lily, we just draw out of that soil. We do not toil or spin in the energy of the flesh, we draw out of the soil that we were planted in, and we were planted in his death.

The eagles are gathered around the carcass. There was honey in the dead carcass of the Lion. The honey represents Promised Land provision, the wisdom of God, the power of God—the preaching of the cross. If you can answer the riddle within seven days of the feast, you're going to get thirty (maturity) changes of garments. It will bring you into maturity. Sons of Issachar, do you know what time it is?

The Book Within

As we unveil the truths of the book of Revelation and unseal the book, there is another book that is simultaneously being unsealed and that is the book of life within. When we read in Revelation 5:1 about the book that is sealed, it is not only talking about the book of Revelation, although, to a certain measure it *has* been sealed and we have not had the correct understanding of it. But the book that needs to be unsealed is the book within. That is the book that has been sealed on the backside with seven seals. It is the book that is unsealed by coming to understand the white horse, the righteous earth walk of Jesus, the red horse, his becoming sin, the black horse, his spiritual death, the pale horse, his going into hell.

The Feasts Of The Lord

There is a literary structure in the word of God[14]. In Revelation chapters 2 through 5 we find Passover. In the beginning of chapter 6, there are the first four seals with four horses, all depicting Passover. Then comes the fifth seal, which are the souls under the altar. Then with the sixth seal there was an earthquake and that speaks of Jesus' resurrection. So, we can see Passover depicted in Revelation chapter 2 through the first part of chapter 6 and that is all we will deal with in this volume.

Then we see Pentecost in Revelation chapters 6 and 7 and we will look at seals six and seven in upcoming volumes. We know that the baptism of the Holy Spirit is our seal until the day of redemption. We see in these two chapters the sealing of the saints.

In Revelation chapter 8, we see Tabernacles. We see a people come to maturity and fullness. We begin to experience Tabernacles in chapter 8 where there are seven trumpets. Included in the Feast of Tabernacles are the feasts of Trumpets and Atonement. In Revelation chapter 16, we see the Feast of Atonement as the seven vials of wrath (blood) poured out. Do you think those seven vials or bowls of blood that are poured out are literal? What good would that do? It is symbolic. The word "vial" in Revelation 16 is rendered "bowls" in the Old Testament and we find it in Exodus chapter 25:29 concerning the table of shewbread. These were "bowls to cover withal" or "bowls to pour out." And what did Jesus do but pour out his life's blood at the cross of Calvary? God's wrath was *fully* poured out at the cross and Jesus Christ our Lord *fully bore* that wrath for us and as us when he poured out his precious blood, removing all sin.

These bowls or vials on the table of shewbread were filled with wine, which is symbolic of blood. Remember, the number "seven" represents fullness. So we see that the seven vials of wrath are seven vials of blood which fully redeemed us. The seven vials of blood are being poured out upon our minds as we come to understand atonement, the fullness of the blood, and what took place physically in the shedding of his blood. There was outward bleeding that Jesus experienced. When he was bruised, he experienced inward bleeding. He was bruised for our iniquities, the inward bleeding. And we want to see the *fullness* of the Day of Atonement. So, we have the Feast of Atonement in Revelation chapter 16.

In Revelation chapters 21 and 22, God says he's going to tabernacle with people. That's where we see maturity. That is where we see Christ fully manifested within his body. That is what the book of Revelation is about. It is not about bugs as big as Volkswagens. It is not about a seven year tribulation. It is not about a literal dragon. It is not about a literal temple. It is not about any of those things that have been interpreted literally. As I wrote earlier, the law of hermeneutics says we must stay consistent with interpretation, meaning if we spiritualize one thing in the book of Revelation, we must spiritualize it all. I could go to any Church in America and teach that the Lamb represents the Lamb that went to the cross. But then they want to literalize everything else. That is inconsistent with the law of interpretation. It is not taking away from the prophetic nature of the book when we teach that "In the volume of the book, it is written of me" in Revelation. When it is written about the Revelation of Jesus Christ, the prophetic nature of the book is not taken away as some scholars say, because the spirit of prophecy is the testimony of *Jesus*. The word "testimony" means *martyrdom* of Jesus. So, the spirit of prophecy is going to testify to the death of Christ.

The Revelation Of Jesus Christ

Look at Revelation 1:1-4 again:

> The Revelation of Jesus Christ, which God gave unto him, to shew his servants things which must shortly come to pass; and he sent and signified it by his angel unto his servant John, who bare record of the word of God, and of the testimony of Jesus Christ, and of all things that he saw. Blessed is he that readeth, and they that hear the words of this prophecy, and keep those things which are written therein: for the time is at hand. John to the seven churches which are in Asia: Grace be unto you, and peace, from him which is, and which was, and which is to come; and from the seven Spirits which are before his throne;

In Revelation 1:1, we have the key which is the revelation of what? Not Newsweek Magazine, not CNN, not anything that we see as current events. Our intent is to establish truth, not to belittle anyone. I know the current events teachers have their reasons for teaching it the way they do. But this book is written to servants—*bondservants,* that have their ear nailed to the door. If your ear is nailed to the door, you're going to see the symbolism. If your ear is not nailed to the door, you're going to interpret it like many in the

Church do today and you're going to see it as literal vials and literal trumpets and literal horses and everything is going to be literal to you. But I'm not concerned with what the present day multitudes are interpreting, because it is the *multitudes* that are in the valley of decision. I'm concerned with what the remnant is hearing from the throne in this, the Lords Day. God has always had a remnant—a firstfruit company—and he says I will not do anything unless I first reveal it to my servants, the prophets. He that hath an ear, let him hear what the Spirit is saying to the Church!

But we see the key in verse 1. It says it is the revelation of Jesus Christ. It is an unveiling of him. Notice, as I stated earlier, it says "the revelation," not "revelation*s*," but "the revelation," singular, as in Revelation 10 where it talks about the *little* book. It is a *little* book because it is just one revelation—the revelation of Jesus Christ. Something opened up to me when I thought about the cup. Jesus drank the bitter cup. If I take a drink of water, it does not affect the outside of me primarily. It does eventually, because it hydrates me. But it goes on the inside. So, Jesus drank the bitter cup. He took sin and bitterness *into* him. That's what it means to roast the lamb rather than soddening it down with water[15]. He took that cup. He became sin.

We found out that the word "revelation" is *apokalupsis* and it means to unveil or to uncover something that has been hidden. And Christ has been hidden. He has been *in* us, but he has been hidden for the most part—Christ in you, the *hope* of glory. But we do not want to just stay there in that realm of Christ in you, the hope of glory. That is the Holy Place realm. It is even in a measure the Outer Court realm because people have Jesus when they are born again. But when you receive the baptism of the Spirit, you come into the Christ realm, so it is Christ *in* you. But we want to see Christ *on* us. We want to see Christ in us *and* on us. How does he come on us? Well, he is in us and he comes *on* us as he comes from our spirit to our soul. Then, as the glory fills the temple, he is going to be seen to the extent that the mortal will put on immortality. Mortality is swallowed up by life (2 Corinthians 5:4).

So the key to unveiling the book of Revelation is to take away the veil, and that is what the book of Revelation is going to do. As we gain the understanding, it will do that. It will take away more of the veil that has been over our minds that was *done* away with at the cross of Calvary. We are waking up to the truth that the veil was rent from the top to the bottom and we are seeing that his hanging was our hanging. If Judas would have waited just three more hours, he could have allowed Jesus' hanging to be his hanging. Your self-crucifixion will not produce the righteousness of God. Only one man's crucifixion produced that—and you are in him.

When they set up the hanging in Exodus 40, and Moses finished the work, it says the glory came and filled the temple. Then in the New Testament, the veil was rent from the top to the bottom. As the veil is rent from the top—from our minds—it will eventually be removed from our members (Romans 6 and 7) and will become a walk as the veil continues to be rent to the very bottom. As we renew our minds to our new creation identity, we become a walking revelation of that new creation—from the top to the bottom the veil is rent. And this will happen both individually and corporately. Can you see the power of the body of Christ all over the world who knows their identity? His Kingdom will know no end, and its glory will know no bounds! We are not "mankind," we are the body of Christ in earth as it is in heaven!

The book of Revelation is not a historical book about some historical man that walked the shores of Galilee per se, but it is about an historical man that accomplished something at the cross. It is not just about his miracles and how he was a good teacher and that sort of a thing. It isn't what he did in that sense so much as it is about what he accomplished when he went to the cross, when he was crucified, died, buried, quickened, raised, and seated.

There is an argument among the body of Christ saying we are taking away from the prophetic nature of the book of Revelation. If we get Revelation 19:10 established in our mind, we won't have any doubt about how this is taught. When we have it established in our mind that it is a symbolic book and that the spirit of prophecy is the testimony of Jesus, we will not have any problem in understanding this book. Let's look at Revelation 19:9-10 again:

> And he saith unto me, Write, Blessed are they who
> are called unto the marriage supper of the Lamb.
> And he saith unto me, These are the true sayings of

God. And I fell at his feet to worship him. And he said unto me, See thou do it not! I am thy fellow servant, and of thy brethren that have the testimony of Jesus. Worship God; for the testimony of Jesus is the spirit of prophecy.

We see in verse 9 that we are eating from a table with Lamb. It is causing an experiential marriage. We are already in union, we are already one, but the marriage is being consummated as spirit and soul become one by eating Lamb. What does it mean to eat Lamb? We are taking Jesus into our mind, saturating our belief and understanding with him, which produces the action, the being of him in our lives. We are giving *him* a body to live and move and have *his* being in. Another way of saying it is, we have walked up to the hanging and we see that his hanging was our hanging. Another way of saying it is, we are filling our mind with the truth until the veil over our minds is *taken* away that was already *done* away at the cross.

In verse 10 we read about brethren that have the testimony of Jesus. In other words, they understand the death of Christ. "Testimony" is the Greek word "martyrdom." Then we read, "Worship God; for the testimony of Jesus is the spirit of prophecy." So the spirit of prophecy is always going to testify concerning the martyrdom of Jesus. If we are teaching this book of prophecy and if we want to say that it is a book of prophecy, then we need to understand that the book of prophecy testifies to the martyrdom of Jesus.

It was written to bondservants, people who have their ear nailed to the door. In the book of Revelation, you can see eight times that he says, "He that hath an ear." Now we all have ears, but not all in the body of Christ have their ears nailed to the door. Why? Because the cloud moved on but the Church has not moved with it. Solomon told the Shulamite to find a Shepherd who dwells in a tent and feed there. A tent speaks of being on the move. But the Church decided to build a permanent structure called Pentecost and they've said "This is it! We've got it made! We'll just hang out here with the gifts and the blessings and wait for a literal rapture because it can't get any better than this!" But the Lord has moved on to the Feast of

Tabernacles and those who are feasting with him today are those who live in tents—and God is not ashamed to be called their God (Hebrews 11:9, 16)! So, he that hath an ear that is nailed to the door *will hear* what the Spirit is *presently* saying unto the Church. I shared with you how John, who wrote this book, was the one who laid his head on the bosom of Jesus. His ear was nailed to the door. Jesus said in John 10:9, "I am the door."

We also talked about the phrase in Revelation 1:1 that says, "Which must shortly come to pass." If it was shortly to come to pass then, it is at hand right now. When you look at the end of Revelation 1:3 it says, "For the time is at hand." The Greek says, "The time is *in* your hand." The word "hand" there is the word "throttle," "to squeeze," "a time and a place." It means the throttle is in our hand. We've heard the cliché, "put the pedal to the metal." The throttle is in our hand and as fast as we can fill our mind with the pictures of the finished work of Calvary and what they represent, to that degree are we going to hasten the coming of the day of the Lord *experientially* in the corporate Son (the body of Christ). And that will only happen as it happens in the lives of each individual in his many-membered body.

Then it says in Revelation 1:1, "He sent and signified it." We established that the word "signified" is "sign-if-ied" which simply means that this book is written in sign and symbol. I took you also to John 2 when we talked about hermeneutics and I shared with you the way Jesus taught. I'm teaching this the way Jesus would teach it. In fact, I'm believing it *is* him teaching it! We are at the end of the sixth day and the beginning of the seventh day, a time for people to enter into rest! "Seven" means rest, Sabbath day, Jubilee—and this is the time! This is The Day that the Lord has made! Let us rejoice and be glad in it! We are at the end of the second day from Jesus, and the beginning of the third day—it is time for a resurrection! As Hosea wrote, "We were smitten, we were torn, we were bound up, we were healed. After two days he will revive us; *in the third day he will raise us up, and we shall live in his sight!*" The second day is over. It is not a time to revive something that died and then have it die again and revive it again. But it says we will live in the third day in his sight. It literally says "we will live *as his presence!*"

Jesus, The Firstfruit

We saw in saw in Genesis 1:1 a picture of the person and the work of Christ where it says, "In the beginning God created the heavens and the earth." The word "beginning" is the Hebrew word "firstfruit." We read that our earth was without form and darkness covered the face of the earth and the Spirit hovered or fluttered, one translation says, over the face of the waters and God said, "Let there be light" and there was light. We know Jesus, the firstfruit, was slain from the foundation, but to really have it experienced in our life, we have to understand that it was made apparent and happened physically and spiritually at the cross of Calvary over 2000 years ago. We were generated, because we were in God from before the foundation. We were de-generated, and then we were re-generated. We were created, we were de-created, and we were re-created. Regeneration and recreation came about as a result of the finished work of Calvary.

In Genesis 1:12, we read that on the third day God brought forth the herb bearing seed which speaks of bread, and the fruit bearing tree which speaks of wine—the bread and the wine. In Genesis 4:4, Abel brought the firstling of his flock, which is the firstfruit. That typifies Jesus, the firstfruit. Cain brought of the work of the ground, the energy of the flesh—that speaks of religion. At least ninety percent of born-again, spirit-filled Christians today believe that to mature, you have to *do* certain things. That is going to change, thank God, but most think that it is in *doing* rather than in *viewing*.

We looked at a number of scriptures and saw that Cain just brought forth something of his own works. You can make Adam learn the Bible from cover to cover and God still won't receive his sacrifice. Many are thinking that God is going to save Adam, modify Adam, and reform Adam. God is not the least bit interested in that. Just like when he told Abraham to offer his *only* son, Isaac. Abraham had another son, Ishmael. God did not recognize that son, but because he is the God of all flesh, he blessed Ishmael and he had twelve sons! But the covenant is not with a "good idea," that we conceived in the flesh, it is with a God-initiated, God-breathed, God-inspired promised seed!

The Great Mathematician

We found out so far that the book of Revelation is about a Jubilee and we know that in Isaiah 61, Jesus declared that *he* was the acceptable year of the Lord. He was the Jubilee. We talked about the nation of Israel experiencing a chronological Jubilee, the one-hundred-twentieth Jubilee since Adam. We will discuss this further in a moment, but first, a word about number in scripture. Lucas and Washburn write:

> Now in order to confirm the Greek number code as we have given it, a person needs to look no further than Webster's dictionary. The complete number code is found in the section entitled "Special Signs and Symbols," which lists all of the Greek letters with their appropriate values. The Hebrew number code, following a similar concept, has been in use since the time before Christ. In fact, if you were to look in a present-day Hebrew Bible, you would find the chapter and verse numbers given with the letters of the Hebrew alphabet.
> ... Following each letter of the alphabets there is a number. This number is the equivalent *number,* or *theomatic,* value of that particular letter. ... Now this is not only true of the individual letters, but it is also applicable to each and every single word in the Bible. ... Not only do words have number values, but also complete thoughts and sentences as well.[16]

If you look in the Strong's concordance for the words "hundred" and "twenty," there are a lot of 120's there that are very symbolic with what God is doing right now in feeding bread and wine. It has been over fifty years since Israel became a nation (the fiftieth year represents Jubilee). Natural Israel, the place in the Middle East, is not the time clock of God. We will explore this subject in depth later, but for now understand that when the Jews of Jesus' day rejected him, they gave up their position of being God's own peculiar people. Now whosoever will can be God's own peculiar people through

Jesus Christ our Lord. If God has a time clock in that sense, the time is in *our* hand.

At the beginning of every year Christians say, "What can we tell the people to look forward to? What can we tell people that God is going to do in 2002?" If we're hearing what God is saying he will tell them "It's not what you have to look forward to, it is what you have to look behind to." It is not what he is going to do; he has already done the work! It's what *we're* going to do. We've got to see that it is a "done deal." It is a finished work.

It's not about red heifers to be sacrificed in the Middle East during the time of Tabernacles. If our theology takes us back to the blood of bulls and goats and to a literal temple, I *with* the Holy Spirit say, "What? Know you not that *you* are the temple of the Holy Ghost?" We read in Hebrews 10:1-7 that God does not take pleasure in the offering of the blood of bulls and goats but he says in verse 7, "In the volume of the book it is written of *me*," meaning: this is an autobiography of Jesus and we go to the word to see him. And if we go there to see him, he is going to show us the bread and the wine—especially because of the time we're living in—God is raising up a Melchisedec priesthood. Then in Psalm 139:16 we read, "In thy book are all my members written." That simply tells us how we are connected with the finished work of Calvary. We are all members of Christ's' one body.

I Am *That* I Am

In Revelation 1:4 we saw him who is, and who was, and who is to come. It is a book about "he is." He is in the midst of his people. When we see him as he is, not in some physical heaven, but *in us,* we will be like him. It is a book about what happened in the past and the finished work—"he was." It is also a book about the future—"is to come." And we can bring the past and the future into the "is" realm by understanding the finished work of Calvary. "Is" speaks of the present Christ who lives within us, the resurrected Christ—the I Am. "Was" speaks of the finished work. "Is to come" speaks of the fact that as we change what is in our minds (and remember, the throttle is in our hand), as we renew our minds to the pictures and what they represent, *then* we come to the "is to come."

Most people teach he is and he was and he is to come as him splitting a sky and coming back on a cloud. But we know that the clouds represent people. So the "is" is the resurrected Christ that lives within us, the "was" is the finished work, the "is to come" is the resurrected Christ within us intensifying—the salvation of God coming from spirit to soul and manifesting in a walk of uncompromising righteousness.

Jesus was crucified between two thieves. There are two things that can rob us from the "I am-ness" of Jesus Christ—having a mindset that is penned in the past, and having a mindset that is fixed on the future. We must realize that the past is crucified, dead, and buried, as far as who we were in Adam, and we are not going to dig it back up again. And then we must repent of our future fixations. The thief who repented was promised that he would be in paradise with Jesus—and three days later it was so[17]. We must fix our focus on the Lord Jesus Christ and embrace our "Now God," drawing our thoughts out of the Most Holy Place, which releases the "Now faith" that Hebrews 11 speaks of. "Now faith" places us in heaven *today* with Jesus Christ our Lord. The Spirit is saying, "I am *that* I am—the now God, the Christ in you today." Jesus brought the past together with the future and he said, "I Am." Yes Jesus was—the word declares that he was slain before the foundations of the world. And yes Jesus is to come, but only as we realize that Christ is in us today, will we see him as he is, and only when we see him as he is, will we be like him. God is not confined to past or future time as we once were when we were in Adam—he is eternal—he is outside of the box of time that we have tried to put him in, and yet he fills time *and* eternity—he fills all in all. We will never understand God or his ways with a carnal mind. We must have the mind of Christ to understand spiritual things.

Our coming into the fulfillment of the manifestation of the resurrected Christ expressing himself, is exactly what Jesus was talking about when the Jews came to him and showed him Herod's temple and the beauty of it. Jesus said, "Destroy this temple and in three days I will raise it up ... but he spake of the temple of his body." Jesus was referring to his body that was crucified, dead, and buried—and he was also referring to us. In this third day, we are beginning to understand Hosea 6:1-3—We were torn, we were healed, we were smitten, we were bound up. In the second day he revived us, but in this third day he is raising us up and we shall live in his sight—we are living in his presence. Then shall we know, if we follow on to know the Lord: his going forth is prepared as the morning; and he shall come unto us as the rain, as the latter and former rain unto the earth. Now—right now—in this third day, we are seeing that when he said, "Destroy this temple and in three days I will raise it up ... but he spake of the temple of his body," he was also talking about us!

Testimony—Can I Get A Witness?

In Revelation 1:2 we read:

> Who bare record of the word of God, and of the testimony of Jesus Christ, and of all things that he saw.

John got this message of the "testimony," which is #3144 in the Strong's Concordance, and it means "martyrdom" or a "martyr." Jesus was martyred. So were we. So, John came to bear record of the word of God, and of the martyrdom of Jesus Christ. Where was he when he bore record of the martyrdom of Jesus Christ? He was on the isle of Patmos which means "my killing" or "my death."

In Revelation 11:19, John finds that the testimony of Jesus is *in the temple* of God. In other words, this testimony or martyrdom is *him* coming to testify about the death of Jesus. What John is realizing is that this testimony is going to bring him into an understanding of "Patmos," which means "the place of *my* killing." There, he will come to understand that his killing is not in the future, but in the past; and he is going to have to look behind him to see that.

Blessed To Be A Blessing

In Revelation 1:3 we saw, "Blessed is he that readeth." One version states, "Happy is he that reads and understands and keeps the words of this book." How can you be happy if you think you're going to go through a seven year tribulation and fire and brimstone is going to come on you and a beast is going to come forth. How is that going to make you happy? I guess some would have their way of explaining it by saying, "It makes us happy because we know that when that comes, the Lord is going to come and we're going to be raptured literally." But the word "blessed" will take you back to Acts 3:26 where it is written that the Lord Jesus blessed us in turning us away from our iniquities. When did he turn us away from Adam— our iniquities, our own desire in the natural? When we were crucified over 2000 years ago. The word blessed comes from the Greek word *eulogeo,* where we get the English word "eulogy." So there were some good and healthy words that were spoken over us at our death over 2000 years ago at the cross of Calvary. Hallelujah! What an exciting day we live in! Yes, I'm enraptured in his presence, but my feet remain on holy ground! I'm discovering the depths of *inner* space and that speaks peace to the storm of outer space.

If we read, if we understand, and if we keep the words of this book as it says in verse 3 ... maybe you're thinking, "I wish it didn't say "keep" the words of this book. How can I *keep* the words of this book?" The words of this book are kept simply by realizing there's been a death and it's done and it's over with. We've taught so much "processing" in the midst of the Church. The processing is the process of filling my mind with the truth. But we've taught it as a processing of "all this suffering" and "all this stuff that I've got to go through and then I'll be tried as gold." I know God uses those things, and we are tried as gold in the fire, but we need to come to understand that it is not a processing as we've thought in the past. It is rather a provision. If it's a finished work, it is a provision—even more than a provision—it is our possession! It is just a matter of us waking up to that, rather than thinking, "I've got to go through all of this and all of that," and the like. The incorrect teaching we have received is what has held back the day of the Lord within our lives experientially.

Holy Halitosis

What is it that has held us back from expressing the Lord? The man of sin, the first Adam. The religious system has taught from 2 Thessalonians, that the thing that has held back the coming of the

Lord (and they teach it as a physical coming only), has been the Holy Spirit. They say the reason for this holding back is to give more people a chance to accept their salvation before the literal, physical rapture. But what is 2 Thessalonians really talking about? The man of sin is the first Adam—who we were before we received our salvation in Christ the Lord. The antichrist is not just someone who is against Christ, but it is all the false images we've had *about* Christ. 1 John chapter 4 speaks of *the spirit* of the antichrist and he says there are *many* false prophets. The antichrist has a religious system that teaches with "all power and signs and lying wonders, and with all deceivableness of unrighteousness" (2 Thessalonians 2:9-10). *That* has kept Jesus from being manifested out of our lives.

When we understand that the man of sin was dealt with at the cross and that only the *residue* of the man of sin remains in our mind, then we realize that there was a death which was *our* death. We no longer believe that we are a "rehabilitated" Adam. We now understand that the first Adam was done away with at the cross and the Last Adam, the life giving spirit, arose—and we are in him! We're not a converted Adam, we are new creations! When we fill our mind with the gospel of truth, we *take away* the veil that was done away with at the cross, and he that shall come, will come. And in this day of the Lord, he is slaying that wicked one with the breath of his lips (Isaiah 11:4)! That's what I call "holy halitosis!" Of course we all know that this is actually very good breath, very God breath, because the Lord is slaying the residue of Adam with the *spirit* of the word—not with the literal letter of the word.

Malachi 3:2 says, "But who may abide the day of his coming? And who shall stand when he appeareth? For he is like a refiner's fire and like fuller's soap." There are two questions there. Who may abide the day of his coming? And who shall stand when he appeareth? He will. The answer to both questions is "He will." He is the only one that is going to stand. When we understand that the old man was done away with and his residue is taken away from our minds, the only one that's left to stand is Jesus. He is the only one that's left—and we are in him.

Revelation 1:4-6:

> John to the seven churches which are in Asia: Grace

be unto you, and peace, from him which is, and which was, and which is to come; and from the seven spirits which are before his throne; And from Jesus Christ, who is the faithful witness and the first begotten of the dead, and the prince of the kings of the earth. Unto him that loved us, and washed us from our sins in His own blood, and hath made us kings and priests unto God and his Father; to him be glory and dominion for ever and ever. Amen.

John is writing to what he sees as a Church soon to be full and complete in Christ, so he sees it and writes it as *seven* Churches. And notice; they are in Asia. Where does the sun rise? It rises in the east. John is getting a grasp in chapter 1 of what he later describes fully in chapters 21 and 22, the mature Church, the resurrected body of the Lord Jesus Christ in earth as it is in heaven. Then John shows us his standard. Crookedness (deceitfulness, Babylon) is really revealed for what it is when it is held in view of, and in comparison with a straight standard of measure. Jesus is the standard—the faithful witness. That exposes the false prophet (Revelation 16:13, 19:20, and 20:10).

Then we read that Jesus is the first begotten of the dead. Jesus, being the first begotten of the dead, exposes the beast that says the deadly wound was healed (Revelation 13). We're not healing a deadly wound. How would we heal a deadly wound? By saying that we have two natures. No! Let's leave alone the deadly wound that was inflicted to Adam. Let him stay buried in our thinking! All we have is a residue of Adam in our thinking and not even much of that anymore. I'm encouraging you! Some say, "We've come a long way baby, but we've still got a long way to go." No, we've come a long way and we do not have that much further to go because he's doing a quick work, cutting it short in righteousness. We are hearing a message from the throne. There is a priesthood being raised up in the midst of the Church. Our hands are being filled with bread and wine.

Then he says in Revelation 1:5, "And from Jesus Christ, who is the faithful witness and the first begotten of the dead, and *the prince of the kings of the earth.* Unto him that loved us, and washed us from our sins in His own blood." The prince of the kings of the earth exposes Babylon's lie that she is the prince, the ruler of the kings of the earth. How did Jesus do that? Well, John tells us right there in verses 5 and 6, "Unto him that loved us, and washed us from our sins in His own blood, and hath made *us* kings and priests unto God and his Father; to him be glory and dominion for ever and ever. Amen." He did all that at the cross.

Jesus Is Coming With Clouds— A Great Cloud Of Witnesses

Let's look at Revelation 1:7 again:

> Behold, he cometh with clouds; and every eye shall see him, and they also which pierced him: and all kindreds of the earth shall wail because of him. Even so, Amen.

We dealt with the phrase "Behold, he cometh with clouds." The clouds are not talking about atmospheric clouds as nearly 90 percent of the Church says, but clouds represent people. The cloud of witnesses in the book of Hebrews is a people—and they are not just people that have died. We are surrounded right now with a cloud of witnesses. A witness is one who doesn't have a second-hand report of something, but a first-hand report. We're getting a first-hand report! I am surrounded by a great cloud of witnesses when I minister the word. We are compassed about with a cloud of witnesses as we live unto God.

What is a cloud of witnesses? A cloud of witnesses is a people that are full with bread and wine—full with life-giving substance to give the earth. And if you remember the Greek meaning for the word "witness," then you know that a cloud of witnesses is a people who realize they have been crucified with Christ. A cloud of witnesses is a people who realize their old man is dead in Christ. And when you say "Amen," you are not saying "Amen" to the preacher so much as you're saying "Amen" to the voice of your own spirit. When we can learn to say "Amen" we're simply saying, "Yes, I agree, God let it happen!"

The next phrase in Revelation 1:7 is, "Behold, he cometh with clouds; *and every eye shall see him."* This does not refer to him appearing on satellite television when he comes at some future time. Every eye is going to see him because he is a many-membered person (1 Corinthians 12:12-14). Also, spiritually speaking, every eye is going to see him. Can your spirit see him right now? We are to know no man after the flesh. We are to know one another as new creations (2 Corinthians 5:16). So if every eye is going to see him, we're already seeing him. How? Through the eye of spirit. If your eye be single, your whole body shall be full of light. Every eye *should* be seeing him right now. And when we see him as he is, we are going to be like him. When we see him as he is, in ourselves and in one another, we are going to begin to manifest him as never before.

Jesus Is Still Being Pierced Today

Revelation 1:7 continues, "Behold, he cometh with clouds; and every eye shall see him, *and they also which pierced him."* We see in Isaiah 52 that his visage was marred. People are still piercing him because they sodden down the lamb rather than roast it with fire. Many people today are still piercing him by teaching on radio, television, and in their pulpits that there was just one man that died. They are piercing him. He died as us. We crucify him afresh and put him to an open shame when we do not look at all the aspects of what he accomplished at Calvary. They won't teach that he *drank in* the bitter cup. They won't teach the two goats on the Day of Atonement, one being his physical death and one being his spiritual death. They won't tell that he had an outward bleeding and also was bruised and had an inward bleeding. It was not only a physical death. Having just partial knowledge of Christ's death would have not done a whole lot for any of us if we were standing there at the foot of the cross when he was crucified, other than touch our emotions. But when we see that he died spiritually, it changes the inside of us. I'm not saying that people who do not understand that have not had their spirit changed. But if we want to mature to the fullness, the way God desires us to mature, we've got to understand that he died spiritually, he became sin, and went into hell. He was bruised for our iniquities. There was an inward bleeding. He died spiritually.

His visage was so marred more than any man, and his form more than the sons of men. In Psalm 22, one of the Messianic Psalms, David writes as if he himself were hanging there on the cross. He sees Jesus hanging on the cross, looking down upon his body and he says, "My bones are out of joint." Conversely, in the Song Of Solomon 5:16 we find that he is *altogether* lovely. When Jesus is *altogether* he is *lovely!* But in the religious system, his bones are out of joint. We're talking about the body of Christ! At sundry times and in diverse manners, God spoke in time past unto us by the prophets, but today, he speaks to us by his son Jesus. He that hath an ear, let him hear what the Spirit of Jesus is saying to the Church: "My bones are out of joint! If just a remnant with an ear to hear will be one with me, we will unite my body. I am prophesying unto the dry bones of the Methodists and the Baptists and the Pentecostals and the Presbyterians and the Catholics and the denominations and the non-denominations and the nations and saying unto them, Hear the word of the Lord! I am prophesying to the wind! I am prophesying to the whole house of Israel and saying unto them, O my people, I am opening the graves of your minds, and causing my Spirit that is buried deep within your earth to come up out of your graves, bringing you into myself, the Promised Land. My Spirit is in you awakening your understanding and showing you that you are already living in me—the Promised Land! Awake thou that sleepest, and arise from the dead, and I shall give thee light. Thy dead men shall live, together with my dead body shall they arise. Awake and sing, ye that dwell in the dust; for thy dew is like the dew of herbs, and the earth shall cast out the dead. Come into the Most Holy Place and cover yourself with me. *I am coming out of my place* to show you that your punishment was fully meted at the cross, three days ago. You shall disclose your blood and shall no more cover your slain. Stand upon your feet, an exceedingly great army (Ezekiel 37, Ephesians 5:14, Isaiah 26)!"

Jesus is the Promised Land Man. So shall he sprinkle many nations; the kings shall shut their mouths at him: for that which had not been told them shall they see; and that which they had not heard shall they consider (Isaiah 52:14-15). The half that has never yet been told is *being told* today, in this great day of the feast! Kings are shutting their mouths. They are seeing and they are considering. Selah.

The Alpha And The Omega

In Revelation 1:8 we read that Jesus is the Alpha and the Omega. Then we saw the Alpha, the beginning, the firstfruit in Genesis 1:1. If you understand 1 Corinthians 15:35-50 by the spirit of the word, you see that Jesus became the first man, Adam on Calvary's cross. He became one with the first man, Adam, that fell. And Jesus became the last Adam, the Omega, the life-giving spirit, when he was quickened. In the Kingdom of God, many teach that Jesus went to the cross as the *last* Adam. But the truth is, Jesus went to the cross as the *first* Adam that fell. Be careful how you read that. Jesus did not fall—he took the fall. He, who knew no sin, became sin. When he said, "Into thy hands I commend my spirit," at that point he became sin, he died spiritually, and he went into hell and that's why he had to be born again. He had to be born from death to life—not because he sinned—but because God wasn't going to raise who he had become—he became sin. We hear the statement, "He arose." Yes he did arise, but most people think that the same man, the first Adam that went to the cross and was crucified, is he that arose. Jesus did arise, but he had to be made over again, becoming the firstborn from the dead (Colossians 1:18). It wasn't the nature of the first Adam, the man that became one with all humanity that arose, because he had to be born again, as one translation says. Jesus arose as the last Adam, a life giving spirit.

Now you can begin to understand 1 Corinthians 15:22, "For as in Adam all die, even so in Christ shall all be made alive." Jesus completely did away with the man of sin, the first Adam. You are free to make the choice of either remaining in Adam—who is dead—or being born into the One man who is alive for evermore, the Lord Jesus Christ. In Genesis 1:1 Jesus is "the beginning" ("the firstfruits" in the Hebrew), or the "Alpha." In Revelation chapter 22 Jesus is the end, "the Omega." There is only one man left and that is Christ the Lord—the Alpha and Omega, the beginning and the end.

We have discussed some of Revelation chapter 2. Before the Lord told each of the Churches what was required of them, he first said something about himself. Why? Because we overcome by the blood of the Lamb, which is the shedding of Jesus' blood, and by the word of *our* martyrdom, as we read in Revelation 12:11:

> And they overcame him by the blood of the Lamb, and by the word of their testimony; and they loved not their lives unto the death.

We overcome him by the blood of the Lamb—his death—and the word of *our* martyrdom. At the end of that verse it says they loved not their lives unto *the* death. What death? The death that happened at the cross of Calvary. We were crucified with Christ. Our sin nature is dead and our new life is hidden in Christ (Colossians 3).

In Revelation chapters 2 and 3 Jesus speaks to all seven Churches. In the light of the previous discussion, notice that before Jesus tells them what is required of them, he first tells them something about himself. In Revelation 2:8, he is talking to the Church at Smyrna, and look what he says before he tells them what is required:

> And unto the angel of the church in Smyrna write; 'These things saith the First and the Last, which was dead, and is alive;

That is something about the finished work. He was crucified and now he arose as that new man. He was the firstbegotten of the dead, meaning what? Other men were raised from the dead before him. So, if he were the firstbegotten of the dead, that would mean he would have to be born from death to life—born again, if you will—come forth from death to life. Continuing with Revelation 2:9-10:

> I know thy works, and tribulation, and poverty (but thou art rich), and I know the blasphemy of them which say they are Jews, and are not, but are the synagogue of Satan. Fear none of those things which thou shalt suffer; behold, the devil shall cast some of you into prison, that ye may be tried; and ye shall have tribulation ten days: be thou faithful unto death, and I will give thee a crown of life.

Verse 10b states, "Be thou faithful unto death, and I will give thee a crown of life." Be faithful unto what death? Does that mean I am just supposed to trudge along and just be faithful no matter what comes along in my life? Am I supposed to take it with a grain of salt and say things like "Well, this must be God giving me cancer because he is trying to perfect me." No. What death are we supposed to be faithful to? *The* death. We overcome by the blood of the Lamb and the word of our martyrdom, our testimony.

In Revelation 2:12, Jesus talks to the church at Pergamos:

> And to the angel of the church in Pergamos write;
> 'These things saith he which hath the sharp sword
> with two edges;

This is not talking about a literal sword. Revelation chapter 1 tells us that Jesus has a twoedged sword coming out of his mouth. That is simply talking about the word of God coming from Jesus. If the word of God is coming from Jesus, and it is—he is the word—what is the word going to be? It is going to be bread and wine. We overcome first by understanding the person and work of Christ. So everything Jesus says to the Churches—*before* he tells them what they're to do and what is required of them—is about himself and his finished work, because that is how they overcome.

In Revelation 2:18, before he talks to the Church in Thyatira he says:

> And unto the angel of the church in Thyatira write;
> 'These things saith the Son of God, who hath his
> eyes like unto a flame of fire, and his feet are like
> fine brass;

What is this talking about? The fire and the brass speak of judgment. His judgment was our judgment. When we understand that, we overcome by the blood of the Lamb and by the word of our martyrdom, the word of our testimony. Let's look at what he says in Revelation 3:1:

> And unto the angel of the church in Sardis write;

> 'These things saith he that hath the seven Spirits of
> God, and the seven stars;

"Seven" means "fullness." How do we come to the fullness of Christ in experience? The "seven Spirits" represent more than an in-part realm. This represents operating in the fullness of the Holy Spirit. You may be wondering, "What does all of this mean?" If you remember, in Revelation 1:20 the Lord explained the seven stars as the angels or messengers of the seven Churches. He said that those seven stars are in his right hand. The right hand speaks of the valiancy and power of God. The power of God is the preaching of the cross. "Hand" speaks of the five-fold ministry. So the seven stars are the messengers who fully understand everything that happened from the cross to the throne. These messengers who minister the bread and the wine are the apostles, prophets, evangelists, pastors and teachers. Ministering the fullness of the message of the cross will bring the Church to fullness (seven Churches). We must break the word down—grind it at the millstone and explain it. Jesus is showing the Church in Sardis some of the aspects of the finished work of Calvary.

The Key Of David

In verse 7 of Revelation chapter 3 he says:

> And to the angel of the church in Philadelphia write;
> 'These things saith he that is holy, he that is true, he
> that hath the key of David, he that openeth, and no
> man shutteth, and shutteth, and no man openeth;

What is the key of David? He is telling them first of all about himself, his person and work, before he tells them what is required. Isaiah 22:20-25 is another golden apple in a silver frame:

> And it shall come to pass in that day, that I will call
> my servant Eliakim the son of Hilkiah: and I will
> clothe him with thy robe, and strengthen him with
> thy girdle, and I will commit thy government into his

> hand; and he shall be a father to the inhabitants of Jerusalem, and to the house of Judah, And the key of the house of David will I lay upon his shoulder; so he shall open, and none shall shut; and he shall shut, and none shall open. And I will fasten him as a nail in a sure place; and he shall be for a glorious throne to his father's house. And they shall hang upon him all the glory of his father's house, the offspring and the issue, all vessels of small quantity, from the vessels of cups, even to all the vessels of flagons. And in that day, saith the Lord of hosts, shall the nail that is fastened in the sure place be removed, and be cut down, and fall; and the burden that was upon it shall be cut off: for the Lord hath spoken it.

This is another picture of the finished work of the cross. "Eliakim" means "resurrection of God." "Hilkiah" means "God is my portion." Isaiah is describing Jesus, the servant son of God. After emptying himself, Jesus is clothed again in royal, priestly garments and received the authority of the Kingdom as the King of kings because of his finished work of the cross. And look, he has the key of the house of David. Why doesn't it say the key to the tabernacle of Moses, or the key to Solomon's temple? Well, Jesus is from the lineage of David, of course, and that is the first thing that comes to mind. We also know that the tabernacle of David had no veil—and that is the only house God is interested in restoring (Acts 15:16). This speaks of a people of maturity.

Notice in verse 24, *we were hung there with him at the cross:* "And they shall hang upon him all the glory of his father's house, the offspring, and the issue, all vessels of small quantity, from the vessels of cups, even to all the vessels of flagons. Then in verse 25, the nail that fastened Jesus in a sure place was removed when Jesus was cut off—when he died for us and as us.

But what did Jesus open and shut? He opened the way into the Holy of Holies for us. He opened the age of grace and closed the age of judgment. He opened a new Day for all who are in him. He opened the New Covenant and closed the Old Covenant. He opened up the day of the great grace of God and no man can shut it, no religion can shut it, no works can shut it—not even a bunch of preaching and teaching of judgment and gloom and doom can shut it! Jesus closed the Day of Judgment and legalism and bitterness and condemnation when the wrath of God was fully vented on him at the cross. And no man can open it again, no matter how much they preach it and teach it—the door is closed!

Again in Revelation 3:14, he first shows them an aspect of himself:

> And unto the angel of the church of the Laodiceans write; 'These things saith the Amen, the faithful and true witness, the beginning of the creation of God;

The last phrase, "the beginning of the creation of God," is the firstfruit. What does the firstfruit typify? It typifies the person and the work of Christ, the beginning of the creation of God.

Seven Golden Candlesticks

We have taken a glance at the seven candlesticks being the seven Churches in Revelation chapter 1. Let's look at the details of the seven candles. First these candles represent Jesus. Secondly, they represent you and I. Some may ask how that can be. Jesus was the word made flesh. We are becoming the word made flesh—living epistles read of all men.

Those that interpret the book of Revelation literally say that the candlestick is a nice, gorgeous piece of furniture just inside the eastern gate. But we need to understand what the candlestick is. John saw the candlestick and it was *behind* him. Notice what it says in Revelation 1:10:

> I was in the Spirit on the Lord's day, and heard behind me a great voice, as of a trumpet.

In verse 12, he turned to see the voice and what did he see? Where did he turn? He turned behind him. So the candlestick is something connected to the person and the work of Christ because he turned behind him and he saw a candlestick:

> And I turned to see the voice that spake with me.
> And being turned, I saw seven golden candlesticks;

Now, here's something very interesting. We know that the candlestick was situated in the Holy Place of Moses' Tabernacle. It was there to light the table of shewbread so the priests could partake of the bread and the wine. On that table of shewbread were two stacks with six loaves on each stack, which represent the twelve redemptive aspects of the finished work: crucified, died, buried, quickened, raised, seated—crucified with, died with, buried with, quickened with, raised with, seated with. At the end of what day did the priest come and eat the bread and drink the wine? At the end of the sixth day and the beginning of the seventh day. Seven speaks of rest. The first stack of six loaves represents Jesus' substitutionary work when he died *for* us. The second stack of six loaves represents his dying according to the law of identification. That is what he did *with* us. The second stack of bread represents the *second look*—and to those who look for him shall he appear the *second time* without sin unto full and complete salvation (Hebrews 9:28).

Detailing the candlestick according to Exodus 25, we know first of all that it was made of pure gold. It had no wood on it. Primarily it represents Jesus. This candlestick was beaten. The branches were not made and then attached. The branches represent the body. We were not an afterthought of God. His beating was our beating. The branches were beaten out of the same piece of gold as the vine or the central shaft. It was all beaten out of one piece of gold. What was it that produced the Church? That beating—the finished work where he was beaten produced the branches from Christ, the vine.

There were a total of seven branches including the central shaft. Revelation 5:6 speaks of the seven eyes of the Lord. Seven here is speaking of perfection of perception. With that golden candelabrum, that light which is synonymous with the word and with understanding, we can see all things. The Holy Spirit has been given to lead and guide us into all truth. He will not speak of himself, but he reveals the son, the person and the work of Christ.

Secondly, the candlestick had one central shaft and that represents Jesus. It also represents that he walks in the midst of the Church as we see in Revelation 1:13:

> And in the midst of the seven candlesticks one like unto the Son of Man, clothed with a garment down to the foot, and girt about the paps with a golden girdle.

There is a central shaft and the branches come from it, they were not attached later. They were beaten out of the same piece of gold—they are *one* with the central shaft. This simply tells us that Jesus walks in the midst of the Church. He is in the midst of the branches. He is the vine. We are the branches. It is significant to note that the central shaft is taller than the branches. Jesus Christ the Lord is eminent. He is the head, we are his body.

The Hebrew word for the central shaft is" yarek" and it means "thigh, loins, body, and side." The branches come out of the side, not the front. Again, the Lord has the preeminence. The woman came out of Adam's side. We are bone of his bone and flesh of his flesh. "Yarek," the main shaft also speaks of reproduction. We are a reproduction of him. The branches were beaten out of the same piece of gold as the central shaft meaning that we are not an afterthought of God. We are not before or in front because he has the pre-eminence. We come out of his side. We are joined in close connection, as closely as a vine and a branch. If you look closely at a vine and a branch you cannot tell where one ends and the other begins. They are one.

If we are abiding in the vine, we are going to have the same result as the root whenever our mind is renewed to the person and the work of Christ. I could come and beat you up every Sunday demanding, "Love your neighbor!" Then you may *act* like you love your neighbor while secretly wishing they'd break their leg. But when we really abide in the vine *experientially*, when we get the truth, the salvation of God, out of our spirit and into our minds and the veil is *taken* away that was *done* away at the cross of Calvary, we are going to experience the same result as the vine. The scripture says in John 15:3-4, "Now ye are clean through the word which I have spoken unto you. Abide in Me and I in you. As the branch cannot bear fruit of itself, except it abide in the vine; no more can ye, except ye abide in Me." What has happened in the Church by teaching legalism is that people have lowered the fruit of the spirit down into the works of the flesh. Love is automatic when you are hooked up with the vine.

Thirdly, there are three branches on each side of the candlestick for a total of six branches. Each branch has nine sets of ornaments for a total of fifty-four ornaments. They have knobs, thirtyfold (Passover, Outer Court). They have buds, sixtyfold (Pentecost, Holy Place). And with the central shaft, they have almonds, hundredfold (Tabernacles, Most Holy Place). The branches on each side of the shaft have nine sets of ornaments representing nine gifts of the Spirit and nine fruit of the Spirit. If the Church has only the nine gifts, they're going to be lop-sided. We must have the nine gifts and the nine fruit (one fruit, nine manifestations). The central shaft has four each of knobs, buds, and almonds for a total of 12 ornaments on the central shaft. When we add the total number of ornaments on the candlestick we have a total that equals the number of the books of the Bible—sixty-six. Thy word is a lamp unto my feet, and a light unto my path (Psalm 119:105).

And fourthly, the oil that flowed out to the branches flowed from the central shaft. All anointing comes from the anointed one—Jesus Christ the Lord. Some people think we have to have the writings of Nostradamas and Josehpus and all that sort of thing, but all we need is in the Bible. I'm not saying that you should not read other books. I read other books too. I'm simply saying that all we need is Jesus. He is all we need! We get full light and understanding from him.

If you remove the central shaft and take away it's four almonds that leaves only eighteen almonds (fruit). Eighteen is the number of the beast. Six plus six plus six equals eighteen. If Jesus isn't walking amongst the candlesticks, the beast is. Galations 5:19-21 lists eighteen works of the flesh, which includes the phrase "and such like.' If Jesus, the firstfruit, is not in the midst of the Church, the fruit produced is that of false teachers. Jesus said we will know them by their fruits.

What do the bowls, knops, and flowers represent? A bowl was like a cup-shaped leaf, like an envelope of a flower called a "calyx." Then there was a knop which was a bud, and there was a flower which represents a blossom or fruit. What we see when we look at those three things—the bowl, the knop, and the flower, is growth and maturity. The path of the just goes from step to step until it climaxes into full fruit as Proverbs 4:18 and Isaiah 35:1-2 tell us. From the bowl or the calyx comes the knop or the bud and then from the bud comes the flower. These three represent growth. They do not represent just one aspect of the finished work of Calvary, but they represent every detail of the finished work of Calvary. We are roasting it with fire, not soddening it down with water. We are not stopping with the fact that it was a physical death, but with Paul's system of truth we are systematically teaching every detail about the finished work of Calvary.

The bud, leaf and flower pattern also speak of reproduction. Life is a growth from bud to leaf to blossom. The bowl encloses or protects the bud and holds the seed of next year's life which will bring forth the flower or the fruit. That speaks of the fact that we should not keep the light for ourselves only, but we should minister it to others. The candelabrum lit everything in the Holy place realm. We must bear fruit after our own kind. That speaks to us to share the word that God gives us.

The lamps were set in order as we read in Exodus 39:37. The branches were set in order and in 1 Corinthians 15:23 we see, "Every man in his own order." The branches represent the body. Again, we can bring in Paul's system of truth. Every lamp required oil individually. Every one of those branches had to receive oil from the central shaft that came up into it individually, meaning: we must have a revelation for ourselves. We can't just get it from a teaching that we might hear. We need to be as the Bereans and daily search the scriptures to see if these things be true. We must bear record of the word of God *ourselves*. We must testify to the martyrdom of Jesus ourselves so we can receive the spirit of wisdom and revelation in the knowledge of him.

Remember, the candlestick was made of pure gold—there was no wood in it. That means that *we* are not the light. We bear witness of the light. It is pure gold. It is Jesus, and we bear witness to that light. We are not God and we will never be God. We bear witness to the light of God, the scripture says. We manifest and we express the light. We are one. My husband and I are one but we are not the same people. We are not the light, but we bear witness to the light. Yet Jesus told his disciples, "Ye are the light of the world." What did he mean? Well, the gold that is used to make the furniture in the tabernacle speaks of the divine nature. It is not our old nature that is the light of the world because there is no wood (humanity) in this candlestick. Only when we see that our old nature was nailed to the cross and we now have his nature, the divine nature, will we be the light of the world.

The Holy Spirit did not record any dimensional measurements of this golden candelabrum because there is no limit to the light. But he does give us the quality (pure) and the weight (which speaks of glory). It weighed 125 pounds. On today's market it would be worth about $770,000 so they did not spare any money when they made this piece of furniture. It was not made in sections. It was all hand beaten. The branches were not added. We do not have another life, we have the same life. "When Christ who *is* thy life shall appear, then shall ye appear with him in glory." When we received Jesus as savior we did not get another life, we got the very same life he has. The candlestick was not made in sections. It was all hand beaten. The branches were not added later after the central shaft was made. We do not have another life. We have the same life.

The oil that was used for the fuel was beaten also. In Gethsemane, where Jesus prayed and sweat great drops of blood, he was in a place called "The olive oil press." That is where the oil was pressed from the olives and was put in the golden candelabrum. The oil was beaten out of those olives. Even the utensils, the tongs and the snuff dishes were beaten which speaks of one beating. His beating was our beating.

For the care and maintenance of the candlestick they made tongs and snuff dishes. The tongs were like scissors in which the hand fit. Often when we see the word "hand" in scripture, it speaks of ministry. The snuff dishes were used when the ministry trimmed the wicks, the charring of yesterday's word, so that the light can burn with the *present* truth. When they trimmed the wicks, the ashes fell down into the snuff dishes and what did the Lord say in the book of Isaiah? "I'm going to give you beauty for ashes."

So the hand represents ministry. The apostle is the first of the ministry gifts. We could compare the ministry of the apostle to the thumb, which balances the hand. The prophet is the index finger or the pointing finger of ministry. He points the way and says, "This is the way, walk ye in it." The evangelist is the longest finger, the longest outreach of ministry. The pastor is the ring finger, the one we need to be in covenant with. The teacher is the smallest finger. It can get in the ear where there is an itch. There are many today seeking teachers, having itching ears, so be careful little ears, what you hear. It is important for the health and vitality of the body of Christ to have a normal, functioning hand of ministry. In the religious system the hand is withered or has some fingers missing or is taken with palsy.

Then John comes to the conclusion in Revelation 1:18-20, where Jesus said:

> I am he that liveth, and was dead; and behold, I am alive for evermore. Amen; and have the keys of hell and of death. Write the things which thou hast seen, and the things which are, and the things which shall be hereafter; the mystery of the seven stars which thou sawest in my right hand, and the seven golden candlesticks. The seven stars are the angels of the seven churches: and the seven candlesticks which thou sawest are the seven churches.

He is to write about the mystery of the seven stars and notice; there is no period after verse 19. Then he says the seven stars are angels, or the messengers of the seven Churches. Messengers are those of us who proclaim God's message—not our message—but the message of the cross. The seven candlesticks represent the seven Churches. John sees the revelation of none other than Jesus Christ when he turns behind him. He's on the isle of "my killing." He sees nothing but the person and the work of Christ and how it affects the Church. In Revelation 1:12 John turned to "see" the voice. Who was speaking? Jesus was speaking to him. Then in verses 12 through 15, John described "the voice" that he saw:

> And I turned to see the voice that spake with me,
> And being turned, I saw seven golden candlesticks.
> And in the midst of the seven candlesticks one like unto the Son of Man, clothed with a garment down to the foot, and girt about the paps with a golden girdle. His head and his hairs were white like wool,

as white as snow; and his eyes were as a flame of fire; and his feet like unto fine brass, as if they burned in a furnace; and his voice as the sound of many waters.

In the midst of the Church he saw Jesus. His head, (his authority,) and his hairs were white like wool because of the righteousness of God. His mind was filled with righteousness. His voice was as the sound of *many waters,* meaning there is one voice speaking, but it is coming out of a many-membered body. His eyes were as a flame of fire and his feet were like fine brass because his judgment was our judgment. John saw us, the Church, as one with Christ. He saw Christ in the *midst* of the Church because what is true of Jesus is true of us. Out of the mouth comes the word. We are to speak the bread and wine. He goes on to say in verse 16, "And he had in his right hand seven stars: and out of his mouth went a sharp twoedged sword: and his countenance was as the sun shineth in his strength." One translation says "his countenance was as the sun at high noon." That speaks of the presence of God that clothes us.

When John turned to look behind him, he saw the candlesticks, he saw the testimony, the martyrdom of Jesus and he saw one like the son of man *in the midst of the Church.* What John saw was the finished work of Calvary and how we were there—how we are identified with Christ in his death. The seven golden candlesticks represent the Church with the fullness of the light of Christ, the fullness of the understanding of everything that Christ accomplished in his death, burial, and resurrection.

In the tabernacle of Moses, the wicks of the candlestick had to be trimmed of yesterday's charring in order to accommodate the present-day flame. We can't just eat manna. Manna ceased. We've got to be ready for the old corn (Joshua 5:11-12). The snuff dishes enabled Aaron to keep the charred ashes that were snipped off by the ministry, from falling into the pure oil. This represents a present word that is clear as crystal—no debris. We want to get to the place that when the word comes from our spirit to our mind and flows out of our mouth, it does not pick up the debris of the dogmas and the traditions of man, but it comes out as pure as it was when it started its journey from spirit to mind. It must be pure.

This candlestick of pure gold weighed 125 pounds. We were weighed also. We were weighed in the balance and found wanting, more than 2000 years ago. The light of the candelabrum will show us that God did weigh us. You can read about it in Daniel chapter 5. The king of Babylon was weighed and found wanting. It is interesting that it was over by the candlestick that the writing came on the wall. God is weighing us by asking us what he asked little Ruth—"Who are you (Ruth 3:9)?" You are a widow. We were widowed over 2000 years ago. Who are you? Adam, your first husband is dead. Adam was weighed in the balance and found wanting. He could not produce life. His days were numbered; his kingdom was numbered and came to an end at the cross of Calvary over 2000 years ago. In Genesis God said, "Adam, where art thou?" God is saying the same thing today, "Adam, where art thou? When I think of that story, I think of a 2000-pound Tweety Bird going through the Garden of Eden saying "Here Sylvester! Here kitty, kitty, kitty!" God wants *us* to see where Adam is. He is at the cross—crucified—and all there is left of him is a residue, a veil, which we have to deal with in our minds.

In 1 John 1:7 we find the link between walking in the light of the one beaten work of the cross and being cleansed and having true fellowship. If we walk in the light (of the candlestick) as he is in the light, we have fellowship one with another, and the blood of Jesus Christ, his Son, cleanseth us from all sin. True fellowship will automatically flow as we walk in the light of the gospel—the death, burial, and resurrection, shown by the candlestick.

When they carried this candlestick, there was no place for rings like some of the other furniture so they put it upon a bar to carry it, according to Numbers 4:9-10. What does that bar represent? We are going to rule with a rod of iron—uncompromisingly righteous government. It represents the word. The candlestick *reveals* the word.

The bowls were made after the fashion of almonds. An almond rod speaks of authority and resurrection. This candlestick was in the form of an almond tree. An almond tree is called a "hastener" because after the dead of winter, the almond tree grows faster than any other tree. God said, "I'm going to hasten my word to perform it." In Jeremiah 1:11-12 we can see this paralleled:

> Moreover, the word of the Lord came unto me, saying, Jeremiah, what seest thou? And I said, I see a rod of an almond tree. Then said the Lord unto me, Thou hast well seen; for I will hasten my word to perform it.

The almond had three things connected with it: buds, blossoms and fruit. In Numbers, at the time of the rebellion, Korah and his company were coming against Moses. Later they came against Aaron. God said, "I want you to take twelve almond rods with the names of the fathers of the twelve houses of Israel written on them, and lay them before the Ark, lay them before my presence. In the morning, the almond rod that buds, blossoms and bears fruit—that man shall be the leader." It was Aaron's rod that budded, blossomed and yielded almonds.

Revelation chapter 1 speaks of the candlesticks which represent Christ and the Church. Revelation's seven golden candlesticks show us the voice of God. The voice comes out of the Church declaring the finished work of Jesus Christ.

Jesus Is Our Garment

Revelation 1:13-15 reveals the garment that goes down to the feet. Jesus is fully clothed spiritually. His head and his hair were as white as wool. His head of authority comes from knowing who he is and from understanding the death. His understanding was a flame of fire. Understanding has to do with that which is in our minds that cleanses us. His feet were like fine brass. His judgment was our judgment. His voice was as the sound of many waters. It is a corporate voice speaking about a finished work.

This is why we have to understand the Tabernacle of Moses in order to understand the book of Revelation. In the book of Revelation we see the furniture of Moses' tabernacle. If we understand the true meanings of the pieces of furniture, we'll understand the book of Revelation.

Another thing we must correctly understand is the seven feasts of the Lord. When we understand those, it is real easy to understand the book of Revelation as the word describes this symbolic book.

The Testimony (Martyrdom) Of Jesus

Each Easter we think about the lily because the lily is very important symbolically. Lilies represent resurrection. The lily doesn't toil nor spin but draws life out of the soil it is planted in. We draw resurrection life out of the death we have been planted in, as Paul wrote in Romans 6:5: "For if we have been planted together in the likeness of his death, we shall be also in the likeness of his resurrection." At the time of Pentecost, 120 trumpets blew and they gathered 120 lilies. 120 is the number that speaks of the Melchisedec priesthood. When the glory of God filled Solomon's temple and no one could stand to minister, the priests blew 120 trumpets or 120 ram's horns. Those ram's horns came from the death of a male sheep. So the trumpets are declaring the death of Christ and our identification with it.

Paul the apostle said in 1 Corinthians 11:26 "Eat the bread, drink the cup, and when you do that, you show the Lord's death until he comes." Not until he comes "out there," but until he comes *in us* and *through us.* In other words, the key that is going to take the veil away from our minds that has already been done away at the cross is the understanding of the death of Christ. The thing that is going to bring revelation—the unveiling of the Christ out of our lives, is our coming to understand the death of Christ. Many people in the Kingdom of God are saying, "Give us resurrection life!" The only way we are going to get the correct life flowing—not just *bios* life, but the *Zoe* life—life as God has it—is to minister the death of Christ. It is *not* going to come in trying to save Adam. When we minister the death of Christ, then subsequently and automatically life will come forth—and it won't be life that modifies an old man, but it will be resurrection life! You must have a death before you can have a resurrection. When we identify with the death of Christ, we are going to see him appear!

Remember, the eagles are not gathered around resurrection life, they're gathered around a carcass. They're gathered around the death of Christ (Matthew 24:28, Luke 17:37). The riddle of the ages is about that carcass. You probably remember the story of Samson who slew a lion with his own hands. Later, when he was traveling down the same path where that heroic scene took place, he turned aside to see the lion carcass, and in that lion carcass he found honey. An interesting side note to ponder, though not the topic of this discussion—Samson had to break the law to get to the honey. After all of this took place, Samson put forth a riddle to his companions. Look at the story in Judges 14:8, 12-14:

> And after a time he returned to take her, and he turned aside to see the carcass of the lion: and, behold, there was a swarm of bees and honey in the carcass of the lion. And Samson said unto them, 'I will now put forth a riddle unto you: if ye can certainly declare it me within the seven days of the feast, and find it out, then I will give you thirty sheets and thirty change of garments: But if ye cannot declare it me, then shall ye give me thirty sheets and thirty change of garments.' And they said unto him, 'Put forth thy riddle, that we may hear it.' And he said unto them, 'Out of the eater came forth meat, and out of the strong came forth sweetness.' And they could not in three days expound the riddle.

There were three days remaining of the seven day feast. If the young men could answer the riddle by the seventh day of the feast, and tell Samson what the dead lion carcass and the honey represented, they would receive thirty sheets and thirty changes of garments. Jesus is the Lion of the tribe of Judah. Honey is a Promised Land provision. The word "sheets" in Hebrew means "to envelop," "a wrapper," and "fine linen." This speaks of our being clothed, being absolutely enveloped in righteousness. "Thirty" speaks of maturity. In the book of Hebrews and in the book of James we read about "the peaceable fruit of righteousness," and "the fruit of righteousness which is sown in peace." Fruit also speaks of maturity. Righteousness and peace are the first two levels in the Kingdom of God, which is righteousness, peace, and joy in the Holy Spirit (Romans 14:17).

In 2 Peter 3:8 we find, "But, beloved, be not ignorant of this one thing, that one day is with the Lord as a thousand years, and a thousand years as one day." Let me paraphrase: You need to know that we are living in the end of the sixth day from Adam, and the beginning of the seventh day—the day of rest. We are living in the end of the second day from the cross of Jesus Christ and the beginning of the third day—the resurrection of the body of Christ. As far as "feast days" are concerned, we are living in the end of the seventh day of the Feast of Tabernacles and the beginning of the eighth day (Nehemiah 8:18). If you can answer the riddle of the ages by the seventh day of the feast, you're going to be fully clothed in righteousness; you're going to come into maturity, resulting in rest as well as the resurrection power of Jesus Christ. How? In being made conformable unto his death (Philippians 3:10). And there, my friend, is the answer to the riddle of the ages—the death of Jesus Christ—the Promised Land Man.

Enoch walked with God 300 years. 300 is the number that speaks of complete deliverance. He walked, left foot, right foot—death, resurrection. The word says that he was taken and not found because he had *this testimony* that he pleased God. He understood that he was dead to the old man and alive to God. The only way you can know that you please God is to know that you were crucified with Christ and that now you are in the One who pleased God for all men. Enoch was translated (Hebrews 11:5). As we understand death and resurrection, we not only are translated out of the kingdom of darkness into the Kingdom of his dear son, but we experience translation power.

What is the power of God? The Church is groping for the power of God. The power of God is the preaching of the death, the preaching of the cross. What is the wisdom of God but the preaching of the cross? No wonder Paul said that he determined to know nothing save Christ and him crucified! Why didn't he say that he was determined to know nothing except the resurrection of Christ? Because he knew that resurrection automatically comes out of the death. The people of God have the cart before the horse when it comes to this. It is not something that is *going* to happen; it is something that has already happened. We *have been* translated out of the kingdom of darkness into the Kingdom of his dear son—at the cross of Jesus Christ our Lord. We've been taken and not found. We are not another man outside of Christ. We are hidden in Christ who is God's One Man in dominion over the earth.

Some years ago, we bought a building for the Church, and we began to move into it. Everyone was excited and jubilant because we finally got out of a store front and got our own building. I was excited but yet on the inside I was miserable, I was frustrated and I said, "Lord, what's wrong, what's going on?" The Lord said to me, "You're frustrated in your spirit with a righteous indignation because you've heard the people of God preach the height of Zion, but they haven't told you how to get there. I'm going to show you how to get there." Since then, God has been adding people to me that are teaching the same thing. This message is exploding everywhere! The message of the death of Christ.

Jesus Became Sin

This is not milk. It is not something we've already known, it is not the simplicity of the gospel. The simplicity of the gospel is enough to get us saved; we saw Jesus died *for* us. But you really challenge people's thinking when you tell them that Tabernacles is a second look at Passover. In the second look we see more than the truth that Jesus died for us. We saw that when we came to Christ. But with the second look we see that Jesus died *as* us. He became sin. He died spiritually. He went into hell and was the firstborn from the dead. One translation says that he had to be born again—not because he sinned, but because God was not going to raise up from the dead the sin that he had become—the first Adam that he had become. He had to be made all over again. He was God but he emptied himself. He then became our sin. We must not sodden the lamb down with water. We must roast it with fire. We are going to tell the whole story! When we take the second look, we can tell the half that has never yet been told! The other half is that we were there.

What does Revelation 1:5 mean when it says that Jesus is the *first* begotten of the dead? Certainly others were raised from the dead. So, what does the first begotten of the dead mean? He died spiritually. He was the first one that was born from spiritual death to spiritual life. Some people want to know why I make such a deal of that. You will never see how high he went until you first see how low he went. It is important because you will not see how high you are until you see how low he went—and you went with him. The scripture says no man ascends, and let me paraphrase here; no man will *experience* resurrection life unless he first descends into the lower parts of the earth. That is not talking about Jesus being buried six feet under when he died. We know that he was buried in a tomb. Joseph of Arimathaea had spent all of his life carving out this tomb for himself. At Jesus' death, instead of *Joseph* going in that tomb, he let Jesus' death be his death. So, when it says Jesus descended into the lower parts of the earth, it does not mean that he was buried six feet under. It means he went into hell. Hebrews 1:6 in the Amplified Bible says this concerning "firstborn:" "Moreover, when He brings the firstborn Son *again* into the habitable world, He says, Let all the angels of God worship Him" (emphasis added).

It is vitally important that we do not sodden down the lamb with water, but we roast it with fire because the book of Revelation talks about the marriage supper of the Lamb. If we eat enough Lamb, we are going to see spirit and soul become one. We're going to get the salvation that is in our spirit to flow into our minds, and then our desires and our emotions and everything about our soul is going to be in line with the spirit and we are going to experience what "revelation" means: an *apokalupsis*, an unveiling, an uncovering of something that has been hidden.

In Revelation chapter 1, we found out that Revelation is not the revelation of Newsweek Magazine. It is not the revelation of locusts. It is not the revelation of a seven year tribulation. It is not the revelation of a literal temple being built in the Middle East. It is not the revelation of the offering of the blood of bulls and goats and getting a red heifer and sacrificing it to cleanse the temple site in order to build a temple. It is not about that. It is simply the revelation of Jesus Christ.

We are going to look into the literary structure of the book of Revelation. Then we are going to look at all seven Churches in the book of Revelation. We will discuss how those seven Churches cannot be talking about the different dispensations of Church history, because according to that theory, Laodicea would be the last of the Church age—which they say would be us—and there is nothing good said about Laodicea. But there are wonderful, glorious, magnificent things foretold about us, the third day Church, as John Newton so deftly penned in his eighteenth century hymn,

Glorious Things Of Thee Are Spoken:

Glorious things of thee are spoken, Zion, city of our God
He whose word cannot be broken, formed thee for His own abode:
On the Rock of Ages founded, what can shake thy sure repose?
With salvation's walls surrounded, thou mayst smile at all thy foes.

See, the streams of living waters, springing from eternal love,
Well supply thy sons and daughters, and all fear of want remove:
Who can faint, while such a river ever flows their thirst to assuage?
Grace which, like the Lord, the Giver, never fails from age to age.

Round each habitation hovering, see the cloud and fire appear
For a glory and a covering, showing that the Lord is here!
Glorious things of thee are spoken, Zion, city of our God;
He, whose word cannot be broken, formed thee for His own abode.

The seven Churches in Revelation are not dispensations of Church history. We will see how each of those Churches can be lined up with day one of creation through day seven. We will also see how the seven Churches line up with what happened in the Old Testament. We'll look at the release from Babylonian captivity, and the wilderness wandering. Then we see that everything promised to the overcomers comes out of the Most Holy Place.

Revelation chapter 16 speaks of seven vials of blood (wrath) being poured out on our head. What good would it do for me to pour out a vial of blood upon someone's head? It would do nothing but make them wet, stain their clothes, and make them smell like blood. The Church has taught that the seven vials of blood are going to be poured out on a wicked world, and even some in the Church, who didn't live the way they should live. They believe the wrath of God is going to be poured out during some seven year tribulation or at the end of some seven year tribulation, depending on what they believe—whether it is "pre-trib," "mid-trib," or "post-trib." But I'm telling you, I *want* seven vials of blood poured out upon my head because that means that my mind is being renewed to the death of Christ so the manifestation of life can come forth! This is the revelation of Jesus Christ! If you've been terrorized with this kind of religious teaching all of your life, it is quite difficult for you to even read this book right now. But if you are willing to have your ear nailed to the door, you and your whole house will be brought into the glorious liberty of the children of God.

Remember the "little book" in Revelation chapter 10? Why a *little* book? The people of God have had so many messages. I've said it before and I'll say it again and I'm not trying to criticize anyone: Sometimes deeper life people are the hardest to teach because they've heard so many messages and so much "stuff" that it is difficult for them to understand that the death of Christ is not just the simplicity or the milk. It is not milk! In fact, there is no way you can avoid judging according to the appearance realm and "know no man after the flesh"(John 7:24, 2 Corinthians 5:16, 1 Thessalonians 5:22). That is not possible with the carnal mind. Only as your mind is renewed to the finished work of Calvary and the spirit begins to flow through you, can you look at your brother or sister, or situation in your life and not judge it according to the natural.

So when we teach that we are taking a second look, that Jesus was not just our substitute, he didn't just die for us, but he died *as* us, something is released through that understanding. He died according to the law of identification. In other words, his death was our death, and his resurrection was our resurrection. You may not realize it, but we are challenging many kingdom minds. They want to teach that Jesus just became a sin *offering*. That's okay if they want to say that. But if he just became a sin offering like the animals, and sin was just *laid* on him, then you're just a forgiven sinner. You're just a sinner saved by grace. Your sin was just covered. My sin was not just covered! I was forgiven, but I am also a new creation in Christ Jesus! Something *more* happened than just being forgiven. My old nature, Adam, was destroyed and I received the new-creation nature of Jesus Christ my Lord! We who are in Christ do not have two natures. Now, it may *look* like we do because of the residue of Adam that is yet in our minds, but that veil has to be taken away. It was done away at the cross, now it has to be taken away. The understanding of the book of Revelation is going to help take away more of that veil. That is the key. Then the revelation will walk itself out.

We've heard this phrase time and time again and I have even

taught it in the past—"It is a processing." But it is not merely a processing—it is a provision. The processing is to fill our minds with the finished work of the cross. That takes some time and some processing. We are to labor to enter into rest—and that has nothing to do with works. It has nothing to do with paying tithes. It has nothing to do with perfect Church attendance. Laboring to enter into rest is simply laboring over the word to fill our mind with the truth. That is not saying I do not believe in good works. I do. But we don't do good works to become more righteous. We are righteous because of what happened at the cross. We do good works because we *are* righteous. We *want* to do good works. We *want* to gather together. Something is wrong with the body of Christ when they want to sit out of Church week after week.

We have already seen that it is *one* revelation—the death, burial, and resurrection of Jesus Christ. It is a little book because there is only one revelation. All the messages are about Jesus. It is condensed. It is a little book, and remember, Revelation chapter 10 says that the little book is now open. Why? Because we are living at the end of the sixth day and the beginning of the seventh day—the day of the Lord.

Melchisedec feeds the people what? Remember the principle of first mention? In Genesis 14 Melchisedec gave Abram bread and wine—the broken body and the shed blood of the Lamb of God. We will see that carried true all the way through the word of God. Melchisedec is going to feed the people Lamb, and he is going to roast it with fire—not sodden it down with water. He is going to give nothing but bread and wine. He is going to minister the bread and the cup, showing forth his death until the Lord comes, until a people mature, until a people express fully and completely, individually and corporately, the Lord Jesus Christ.

The Spirit Of The Word

In Revelation chapter 1, the words "servant" and "servants" in the Amplified Bible is "bondservants." A bondservant is one who has his ear nailed to the door. If your ear is not yet nailed to the door, it will be by the time we get to the end of this study. The servant that wanted to stay on and serve his master when his time was up, because he loved his master and loved his family, had his ear nailed to the door. Like I said earlier, isn't it interesting that John, who was given the revelation, is the one who laid his head on the bosom of Jesus. John laid his ear on the door. Jesus is the door. There are many people that are interpreting the book of Revelation literally, and they are scaring people to death! Their ear is not nailed to the door. If their ear was nailed to the door, they would realize that he *signified* it by his angel unto his servant, John. "Signified" means it is written in sign and symbol. It is a symbolic book.

According to hermeneutics, if we spiritualize one aspect, we must spiritualize it all. I could go into any Church in America today and teach from the book of Revelation that the Lamb is a picture of the spotless Lamb that went to the cross, and they would agree. But they want to literalize everything else. They want to make the temple literal in the literal Middle East. They want to make the beast, the false prophet, and most everything else literal, but yet they will spiritualize the Lamb. That is inconsistent with the law of interpretation.

Adam Is Dead

We have discussed 1 Corinthians 15:45 which talks about the first man, Adam, and the last Adam. Adam, the man, fell in sin and turned the garden into a graveyard. Jesus became who Adam was when he became sin and died on the cross. Then Jesus became the last Adam, the life-giving spirit, in his quickening and in his raising and turned the graveyard into a garden. Many in the kingdom of God say that Jesus went to the cross as the last Adam. That is not what happened. He went to the cross as the first man, Adam. The blood that Jesus shed was precious, pure blood because he lived a sinless life. But when Jesus said, "Father, into your hands I commit my spirit," that was the moment that he became sin and died spiritually. At that point he was saying in so many words, "Whatever we have to do to get the job done Father, I yield to it." Then he went into hell.

Isaiah prophesied in chapter 53 verse 9, "And he made his grave with the wicked, and with the rich in his death." When we look at that Hebrew word "death," we find in the Cambridge Bible and in other translations, that it is an intensive plural—"deaths." Not only did Jesus die a physical death, but a spiritual death also. Or we could say his death was two-fold: physical *and* spiritual.

In Revelation 1:9, we find that John was on the isle of "Patmos" which means, "my death" or "my killing." He was not only seeing the death of Christ, but he was seeing his identification with it. Later on, John turned to look *behind* him. What is behind us? We are not just looking forward. Yes, things are going to intensify and happen in the future. But we are going to see it happen in the "is" realm *and* in the future when we look behind us and listen to the voice of Jesus that is speaking. If we look behind us we are going to see the cross of Calvary. That is what John wrote in Revelation 1:10—he heard *behind* him a great voice as of a trumpet. He looked *behind* him in verse 12. He is on the isle of his killing and looks behind him and sees the cross and his identification with it. He also sees seven candlesticks which is the Church, so he saw the Church's identification with the death, burial, and resurrection.

John turned behind him and he saw the cross and the seven candlesticks and in the midst of the seven candlesticks in verse 13, he saw one like the Son of man. He did not just see that Jesus died *for* him. He saw the candlesticks. He died *as* all of us. In the gospel of John, Jesus said, "And I, if I be lifted up from the earth, will draw all men unto me." The Greek says, "I will "drag" all men unto me.[18]" All were reconciled, whether they wanted to be or not—not saved—but they were all reconciled. The word "reconciled," # 2644 in the Strong's Concordance, is *katallasso*: meaning: "to change mutually." It even sounds like drag—"lasso." When we accept that, then salvation begins in our lives.

The Sun Clothed Woman

In the midst of the seven candlesticks is one like unto the Son of man, clothed with a garment down to the foot. We are clothed with the son. Revelation 12 talks about a woman who gives birth to a manchild. This is the *apokalupsis*, the unveiling of Christ, with his nature, his glory, flowing out. She is clothed with the sun and the moon (reflected light) is under her feet. We're not just a reflection of Jesus. We are clothed with the son! We are an expression of the son! Then we read that she has on her head a crown of twelve stars: crucified, died, buried, quickened, raised, seated—crucified with, died with, buried with, quickened with, raised with, seated with. Her mind is renewed to that and *because* her mind is renewed to that, she can birth the manchild.

Notice, we are clothed totally and completely with a garment down to the foot. This speaks of a total manifestation of Christ. We make such a big deal in the Church about how we dress when we go to Church. I enjoy being nice and clean and fresh. I like nice clothes just like anyone else. I am not against dressing nicely for Church at all—I dress for Church too. We represent the Lord and we are mindful of that every day—not just on Sundays. But again, the majority of the Church has lowered a spiritual treasure down to the works of the flesh—so much so that if someone dares to come to Church "dressed down," or not looking as good as the Pharisees look, watch out, because you're going to be "stoned" with the law of the doctrine of man! Look what Jesus said in Matthew 6:25 and 28-29:

> Therefore, I say unto you, Take no thought for your life, what ye shall eat, or what ye shall drink; nor yet for the body, what ye shall put on. Is not the life more than meat, and the body than raiment? And why take ye thought for raiment? Consider the lilies of the field, how they grow; they toil not, neither do they spin: And yet I say unto you, That even Solomon in all his glory was not arrayed like one of these.

Jesus always said more than what we read on the surface level. He spoke into many dimensions. He says here, "Is not *the* life more than meat, and *the body* than raiment?" What life? The *psuche* life of the soul, not the *bios* life of the body. The Greek word *soul* is written in the feminine gender. David said, "My soul shall make *her* boast in the Lord." Jesus compares our soul to the lily that draws its life out of the soil it is planted in. We likewise, draw our life out of the death of Christ that we have been planted in. He said that even Solomon was not clothed like one of these lilies. Why? Solomon could not be clothed with the righteousness of God because the cross of Jesus had not yet come. Our soul, our woman, is clothed with the righteousness of God. So, when we go to Church, we are not there to impress God or man with what we put on our natural body. We cannot win people to God with outward apparel, but with the hidden man of the heart, the ornament of a meek and quiet spirit, which is in the sight of God of great price. Jesus is saying, "Your three piece suit and your silk tie are nice, but step aside because I'm looking for a sun-clothed woman—the body of Christ! And if you're not fully clothed with me like she is, you are naked!"

Look again at Revelation 1:12-16:

> And I turned to see the voice that spake with me. And being turned, I saw seven golden candlesticks; And in the midst of the seven candlesticks one like unto the Son of Man, clothed with a garment down to the foot, and girt about the paps with a golden girdle. His head and his hairs were white like wool, as white as snow; and his eyes were as a flame of fire; and his feet like unto fine brass, as if they burned in a furnace; and his voice as the sound of many waters. And he had in his right hand seven stars: and out of his mouth went a sharp twoedged sword: and his countenance was as the sun shineth in his strength.

So, in Revelation 1:13, John sees Jesus clothed with a garment down to the foot. What *body* was Jesus talking about in the previous scripture, Matthew 6:25? We, *the body* of Christ, both individually and corporately, must be fully clothed in his righteousness so much so that we are not seen—only the Lord Jesus is seen. We could compare this with Enoch who *walked* with God 300 years—left foot, right foot—death, resurrection. Left foot—death. Right foot—resurrection. And what happened? He was taken and not found. I don't want to be found! Yes, Adam is dead and he is not found, but I don't even want any *residue* of Adam to be seen.

Jesus was girt about the paps with a golden girdle, gold symbolizing his divine nature. His head and his hairs were as white as snow. Isaiah said, "Though your sins be as scarlet, they shall be as white as snow." His eyes were as a flame of fire, speaking of cleansing. How are we cleansed? We are cleansed through the word, the gospel. What is the gospel? The gospel is not just any word out of the Bible, but the gospel is the death, burial, and resurrection of Jesus Christ. Paul said, "I am not ashamed of the gospel of Christ; for it is the power of God unto salvation." Then Paul said in his letter to the Corinthians that the power of God is the preaching of the cross. The gospel is the message of the death, burial, and resurrection of Jesus Christ. It is the power of God. It is the wisdom of God.

Paul said, "Awake to righteousness and sin not." How does one awake to righteousness? By understanding what happened at the cross. There was a death and your old man died. The more you see that, the more you awake to who you are in Christ and the more resurrection comes forth out of your life. The more you live above sin, the more you live above *anything* that is not normal for a Christian to live and walk in. Now when you are tempted to sin, you can say, "No, it is not in my nature to sin because I have *his nature, the righteousness of God.*"

In Revelation 1:15, we find that Jesus' feet were like unto fine brass, as if they burned in a furnace. This speaks of the judgment of God that Jesus suffered for us and as us. His judgment was my judgment. Then John describes the voice of Jesus in the last part of verse 15 as "the sound of many waters." Why *many* waters? Because it is one voice, but in a many-membered body.

In verse 16, Jesus had in his right hand seven stars and out of his mouth went a sharp twoedged sword. That is the word. And his countenance was as the sun shineth in his strength. His joy is complete!

Then Jesus said in verse 18, "I am he that liveth, and was dead." He was not saying he was just physically dead, but also spiritually dead—dead all the way through. He drank the bitter cup. It got on the *inside* of him. He *became* sin. He died spiritually. He was not just a sin *offering*. He was the goat that was sent out into the wilderness. The goat that was killed was his physical death on the Day of Atonement. The other goat that was sent out into the wilderness never to return again was his spiritual death.

Revelation 1:4 and Revelation 1:19

Let's compare Revelation 1:4 and Revelation 1:19:

Revelation 1:4. John to the seven churches which are in Asia: Grace be unto you, and peace, from him which is, and which was, and which is to come; and from the seven Spirits which are before his throne;

Revelation 1:19. Write the things which thou hast seen, and the things which are, and the things which shall be hereafter;

What did John see that the first part of verse 19 refers to[19]? When he turned, he saw a finished work. He saw something that "was," as verse 4 says. Notice the "things which are" in verse 19. It correlates with the phrase in verse 4, "which is." This refers to trumpeting one message loud and clear. When you see the *things which were* at the cross, you will begin to *trumpet* those things in the here and now. There are seven trumpets in the book of Revelation. Again, seven represents fullness. When you turn as John did, and take a second look at the cross, you will begin to trumpet the fullness of the finished work. You will not sodden it down with water, you will roast it with fire.

Then notice the last phrase in verse 19, "which shall be hereafter." The corresponding phrase in verse 4 is, "which is to come." These phrases both refer to the seven vials of blood (or wrath) poured out on our heads in chapter 16. That is the *product* of what is true because of what happened at Calvary.

The things that John "hast seen" in verse 19 are the things "which was" in verse 4. That is the past. That is what happened at the cross of Calvary. The things "which are" in verse 19, are the *trumpeting* of what he saw that happened over 2000 years ago. And the "things which shall be" is the vials poured out on our heads, the *manifestation* of what is true and has already happened.

Some say the book of Revelation is not written in correct order. If you are in the same spirit that John was, in this Lord's Day, you will see that the book of Revelation is a prophetic masterpiece. It is beautiful just the way it is. First of all, it is prophetic because it is the testimony of Jesus Christ, which is the spirit of prophecy. We see fore-telling and forth-telling throughout. John is a revolving prophet in this book—everywhere he turns, he prophesies. He stands in chapter 1 and turns back to take his second look at the cross, and it takes him nearly eight chapters to tell what he saw in that second look. The same thing happened to Moses when he saw the first five books of the Bible in just one look of where God *had been.* The book of Revelation is no more out of order than the Pentateuch. God is not the author of confusion. When we get in the Spirit with this book, as well as with every book of the Bible, we can see the flow.

Passover—A Second Look

Now let's look at the three feasts of the Lord. In chapters 2 and 3 of Revelation we see Passover, where seven times the Lord says, "to him that overcomes." How do we overcome? We find the answer in Revelation 12:11:

> And they overcame him by the blood of the Lamb,
> and by the word of their testimony; and they loved
> not their lives unto the death.

How we overcome has to do with Passover, the blood of the Lamb. But it does not stop there. It goes on to say, "and by the word of *their* martyrdom." We must understand what was—he was crucified. The preaching of the cross is the *power* of God. Because of the preaching of the cross we are going to release the unlimited power of God when we understand that we overcome by the blood of the Lamb, the death, and the word of *our* death, *our* testimony, *our* martyrdom. With the second look at Passover, we see that we were crucified with Christ.

So, in chapters 2 and 3, there are seven places where the Lord Jesus speaks of overcoming. The eighth time (the number of new beginnings) he uses the phrase, "he that overcomes," appears as a master brush stroke in chapter 21, where we see the New Jerusalem. The word of God is a divine masterpiece. It is an inexhaustible source of hidden treasures.

Notice it goes on to say in Revelation 12:11, "And they loved not their lives unto *the* death." In other words, we are not going to try to hold on to our lives and say we have two natures, or "we still have an

Adam." It may *look* like it, because we have some residue of his thinking yet, but we do not have two natures. We're not going to love the old man and try to reform him, save him, and modify him. We could even get him to memorize the Bible from cover to cover and God still will not receive him. We're not holding on to the carnal impulses of Adam. It is not about us any longer—it's all about Jesus.

We are going to overcome by the blood of the Lamb, the death, and by the word of *our* death because his death *was* our death. We are not going to love our lives—even unto *the* death. We are not going to try to dig up an old man because God is not saving him. We are going to realize that he was crucified at *the* death that took place more than 2000 years ago. That is Passover.

Unleavened Bread

The Feast of Passover includes Unleavened Bread and Firstfruits. We have looked at Passover. Now let's look at Unleavened Bread. In Revelation chapters 2 and 3, the Lord told the Churches some things that were required of them. Before he told them what was required of them, he first told them something about himself and his finished work. At the time of Passover and Unleavened Bread the Israelites were to kick out all the dust and the dirt from their dwelling place. Jesus told them what was required of them saying, "You've got to kick this dirt out. You've got to kick this sin out." But before he tells them that, he first tells them something about himself, the person and the work of Christ; because that is the only way they will have the power to kick out the dust and the dirt. You can't kick out the dust and the dirt by fighting sin, but by renewing the mind with the truth about the finished work. Romans chapter 12 declares that if we renew our mind, we will experience a transformation. So, here we have Unleavened Bread when he tells them what is required of them, what they are to kick out.

Look at 1 Corinthians 5:7-8:

> Purge out therefore the old leaven, that ye may be a new lump, as ye are unleavened. For even Christ our passover is sacrificed for us: Therefore let us keep the feast, not with old leaven, neither with the leaven

of malice and wickedness; but with the unleavened bread of sincerity and truth.

The original Greek text omitted the last two words in verse 7, "for us." Now we understand why. Christ our Passover was sacrificed for us *and* as us.

Firstfruits

Firstfruit speaks of the resurrection. In Revelation chapters 4 and 5, we read about being seated in a throne. We were crucified, we died, and we were buried. Then there was a quickening and a resurrection. We were seated in the heavenlies. We are already seated with him in the throne. We are not *trying* to get in the throne. We are not *trying* to get into the Holy of Holies by going through some veil. The veil was rent and we were seated in the throne. When we were born again we were placed at the finish line. The only veil that has to be taken away is the veil of our darkened understanding that remains in our un-renewed minds. We are in the Most Holy Place seated with Christ. From that place we are looking back out to see the Holy Place and beyond—all the way out to the brazen altar. We see *how* we got to the finish line by renewing our mind with what took place at that brazen altar—the sacrifice, the death of Christ. We are coming to realize it is not a processing; it is a provision and a possession. It is a "done deal." It is finished. It is over with. When we wake up to righteousness, sin will no longer be an issue and we will no longer practice sin.

When Israel went in to take the Promise Land, they did not take anything in with them. They kicked things out. How do we apply this to our lives? We are complete in Jesus—we do not need any *more* of Jesus in our spirit. When we accepted Jesus as our savior, our spirit became wall to wall Jesus. We need to allow the fullness of Christ that is in our spirit to fill our mind, our will, our intellect, and our emotions and manifest through our lives, which are *his* body, the Church. The Israelites kicked things out. We need to kick out the things that are between our ears. We need to kick out the principalities and powers that govern our minds. The veil that is still untaken away needs to be taken away—and kicked out! The only way this can happen is by renewing our minds. When our mind is renewed to the death, burial, and resurrection—how it all happened and everything that took place during those three days and three nights—the word will walk itself out in our lives! So Revelation chapters 4 and 5, reveal resurrection or the Firstfruits, a part of Passover.

Pentecost

Pentecost is the next feast. Now it is becoming clearer that we must understand the seven feasts of the Lord and the Tabernacle of Moses to understand the book of Revelation. In Revelation chapters 6 and 7 we see the sealing of the saints. When we are baptized with the Holy Spirit, we are sealed until the day of redemption.

Tabernacles

The last feast is Tabernacles. Included in Tabernacles is the Feast of Trumpets, the Day of Atonement, and the Feast of Tabernacles. In Revelation chapter 8 we see the Feast of Trumpets in the seven trumpets. We see Atonement in Revelation chapter 16 when the seven vials of blood are poured upon our heads. During the Day of Atonement the Israelites did a number of things. First, they were to afflict their soul. That represents renewing our minds to the finished work of Calvary. So, the pouring out of these seven vials is the afflicting of the soul—it is the renewing of our minds to the finished work. The understanding and the application of Christ and him crucified will bring you to the *experience* of the Day of Atonement in your life. Also, on the Day of Atonement they were to offer a bullock, a burnt offering, which represents Jesus Christ who finished the work at Calvary. They could do no work on that day. They were to rest. That is what we are learning to do in this, the Day of Atonement. And then we find the Feast of Tabernacles in Revelation chapters 21 and 22 where we find God tabernacling with the people. There you have the feasts of the Lord.

This is not a book to scare people to death. It is about the death of Christ. It is the revelation of Jesus Christ and everything in this book will give us a greater understanding that it is a finished work. It happened over 2000 years ago. As we come to more revelation and understanding by the spirit of this book, the veil over our minds that was done away at the cross is going to be taken away and there is going to be a greater uncovering and unveiling of the Lord Jesus Christ. He is going to be seen in the earth. We are going to manifest his nature.

The Church is teaching the book of Revelation saying, "Get ready world, you're going to be judged! The wrath of God is going to be poured out!" They are already reaping what they are sowing. The Amplified Bible says in Galatians 6:8, "For he who sows to his own flesh (lower nature, sensuality) will from the flesh reap decay and ruin and destruction ...." Some of the ways we sow to the flesh are our negative thoughts, wrong motives, and legalistic ways. "For when we were in the flesh, the motions of sins, which were by the law, did work in our members to bring forth fruit unto death" (Romans 7:5). Yes, the world, including the Church world is going to be judged. The judgment that they are going to receive is going to be ministered through a people, a Melchisedec priesthood, who realize that we have already been judged.

Judgment must first begin in the house of God. We must first understand that his judgment was our judgment. Then we are going to go forth and tell them, "God is not mad at you." We're not going to condone their sin, but we are going to tell them that his judgment was their judgment. This is the victory that is going to win the world. It is the goodness of God that leads men to repentance. If what they call "good preaching" was going to win the world—"good preaching" that judges this and judges that and judges everyone who is "not like me" and everyone who "does not believe or think the way I do,"—the world would have been won a long time ago! If miracles would have done it, the world has seen enough miracles to save everyone! The world is going to be won by a people who manifest and express the nature of God and are filled with God's glory—a people who go forth as a priesthood with nothing but bread and wine—the broken body and shed blood. This priesthood goes forth because they know that the cross is the power of God and the wisdom of God, and they understand that the cross is what is going bring an expression of the Lord in others.

The book of Revelation is written to those who have their ear nailed to the door, a people who want to experience the Feast of

Tabernacles in completeness and in fullness. This is a people who are not afraid of change.

There is a whole kingdom realm of people who are teaching messag*es*. There is only one message. They have been preaching for thirty years, "We're going to experience Tabernacles!" We will experience Tabernacles by realizing that Tabernacles is a second look at Passover. It is more than the first look. When you take a second look, you see it all. We are going to look and look and look and look. We are going to be like Israel in the wilderness and we are going to be made whole for a look. We will not be just *healed* for a look, as when they put the serpent on the pole. We are going to be as that little harlot, Rahab, who put a scarlet cord in the window and she and her whole family received *in one day* what it took Israel forty years to get—and some of them still did not get it. We've made it so hard that we haven't seen the forest for the trees. It is not by works, lest any man should boast. Yes, we do works, but not to become more righteous or more holy.

Chapter Two

Complete In Jesus

The understanding of the book of Revelation which, in the Greek is *apokalupsis*, is that something is going to be revealed that has been hidden. Something is going to be uncovered that has been hidden. It is not going to be revealed and uncovered by *adding* something. A veil cannot be removed by adding something to it. It is removed simply by taking the veil away. Christ is not going to be unveiled and uncovered by "getting more" of something. If we have received his sacrifice, we don't need one ounce more of Jesus. Our spirit contains the completeness, the totality of him. We are complete in him. Yet born-again, spirit-filled people are singing and saying, "We need more of Christ." We don't need any "more" of Jesus. What we need is for that fullness and that completeness of him that is in our spirit to come all the way through into our soul (our mind, our will, and our emotions) and be expressed out of our lives. He has already given us his all! We are perfect in him. We are complete in him. All of the nature, all of the anointing, all of the power of God abides within our spirit.

What we need to do is *wake up* to the fact that the veil that was done away at the cross, is now being taken away from our mind as our understanding, which was darkened by that veil, is "lightened." "Lighten" is one of the meanings of the word "revelation" or *apokalupsis*. Other meanings of the word "revelation" from the

Strong's Concordance are: "disclosure, appearing, coming, manifestation, be revealed, revelation." Notice "appearing" and "coming." If we teach a literal rapture as the appearing or the coming of the Lord, then we have all been "left behind" because the Lord *appeared* and *came* to John on the isle of Patmos in the revelation. Let's backtrack a little to see where Jesus prophesied this.

John's gospel records the interaction of the risen Lord and the seven apostles at the Sea of Galilee. This is a classic. We all know the story. Three times Jesus asked Peter if he loved him. This is the same guy that denied Jesus three times before the cock crowed prior to the crucifixion. O, the mercy of God! But there is more to that chapter. The remaining verses are not so well known. In the next verse Jesus told Peter how he (Peter) was going to die and thereby, glorify God. Peter immediately turned to look at John and then asked Jesus, "Lord, and what shall this man do?" Have you ever wondered what Jesus meant when he said, "If I will that he tarry *till I come,* what is that to thee?" There was quite a bit of discussion about that statement according to John chapter 21. This is the same John that wrote the Revelation of Jesus Christ. John *did* tarry until Jesus came. Jesus came to John on the isle of Patmos. The rapture is a spiritual event. The rapture is comparable to initial salvation in that we did not all receive Christ en masse. God is a personal God. The rapture is a personal experience. The rapture is an intimate working of the Holy Spirit just as initial salvation is. The Holy Spirit drew us, we responded. The rapture of the Church happens one person at a time.

If I were to ask someone in the religious system what the requirements were to "make the rapture," they would tell me something like, "Jesus is coming for a Church without spot, blemish or wrinkle." If that is true, none of them will "make it!" What a shock! Why would I say that? Because they see themselves with spots, blemishes, and wrinkles. They see themselves with two natures—one is a sin nature and one is a born-again nature. If you will read that passage in Ephesians 5:25-27 you will see that it does not even say "Jesus is coming for a Church without spot, blemish or wrinkle." What it says is, "Husbands, love your wives, even as Christ also *loved* the church, and *gave* himself for it; that he might sanctify and cleanse it with the washing of the water by the word, *that he might present it to himself* a glorious church, not having spot, or wrinkle, or any such thing; but that it should be holy and without blemish." He loved the Church and gave himself for it (past tense) *so that* he might present it to himself a glorious church, not having spot, or wrinkle, or any such thing; but that it should be holy and without blemish—and all of that happened at the cross of Calvary, as we will discover throughout the course of this study.

Whether there is or is not a rapture is not the controversy. Certainly there is a rapture. Paul experienced it, Philip experienced it, John experienced it and people all over the world are experiencing it today. But it is not a rapture as the religious system has taught. Blaise Pascal was a philosopher/mathematician who sought to provide prudential reasons for believing in God. His argument was that if one believes in God, but God does not exist, that person has lost nothing. But if one does not believe in God, and God does exist, that person has lost everything. This is known as Pascal's wager. We can apply his formula to the rapture of the Church. It would be safer and wiser to believe that the rapture is a spiritual rapture in which people grow up and mature, manifesting the nature of the Lamb which draws others to the Lord—not a literal rapture that is only a fire escape. 2 Peter 1:3 says that God has placed everything within us that pertains to life and godliness. We have been given every spiritual attribute necessary for growth and maturity in this life.

Many in the Church believe that when the Lord returns to literally rapture them away, they will all of a sudden be what they are supposed to be. The attitude is that the people "left behind" are simply getting what they deserve. Pascal's wager is a concept that shows us that it is much safer to believe that God wants us to "grow up" rather than "go up." Paul experienced a spiritual rapture when he was caught up into the third heaven. All the while he was on the earth. In John 3:13 Jesus, in talking with Nicodemus, said that he was in heaven while he was standing on the earth right there in front of Nicodemus.

The phrase "caught up" means "to love with a love embrace." The Most Holy Place is the loving room of God. It is a place of experiential oneness with the Lord where we are matured to the point of intimacy with him and we reproduce his nature through our lives. To understand that the rapture is a spiritual growing up and not a literal going up is wisdom and maturity. But to believe that the Lord is one day is going to get us out of this awful mess while some who have never even heard the true gospel are going to be left here to suffer is to believe according to the letter of the word and not according to the spirit of the word (2 Corinthians 3:6). Believing according to the letter of the word *is* the veil that remains untaken away. The veil that was done away must now be taken away and that is only accomplished when our mind turns to the Lord *who is Spirit;* and where the Spirit of the Lord is, there is liberty to behold the glory of the Lord that changes us from glory to glory (2 Corinthians 3:6-18). We are called as a firstfruit company of people to win the world to Christ—not to physically escape. The manifested sons of God are to redeem the groaning creation according to Romans 8:19. We are raptured dimensionally, not directionally—spiritually, not physically.

The veil is being taken away primarily by seeing the death of Christ and how the work got done. Some teach that we have to walk by the way of the cross. I agree. But their explanation of us walking by the way of the cross is: "You have to crucify the emotions, the appetites, crucify the flesh and die to self." You will not find that anywhere in the word of God. You may be thinking, "But Paul said I die daily. I keep under my body and bring it into subjection." Yes Paul said that. But we have interpreted the word so cruelly. We have interpreted it according to an old mindset, not according to the Spirit of Life. What Paul said was that every day he realized that he died with Christ. Paul had also come to understand that one man was given dominion over the earth—the last Adam, the Lord Jesus Christ—and Paul was in him. The Spirit of Jesus Christ was given dominion over Paul's flesh, the earthen vessel of Paul's body, so Paul's flesh was in subjection to the Spirit. The Spirit was not in subjection to Paul's flesh because only One Man has dominion over the earth. Paul's old nature no longer ruled Paul's flesh. The Lord Jesus lived and ruled and reigned in Paul's flesh. And this is going to happen in us as we, like Paul, wake up to the fact that it *already* happened. Then we will be empowered.

If we are purified and processed by the way some have taught it, then we are getting involved in works again. You might as well believe in reincarnation, because reincarnation is a doctrine of works. It tells you that your karma today determines what your life form will be tomorrow. It tells you that if you do good works, those works are going to determine who you are going to be in the next life. That is a doctrine of works. By grace are you saved through faith, not by works, lest any man should boast.

So, if we take what we've heard concerning processing and the wilderness experience (and many use scripture to proof-text this doctrine), then we will forever be in a state of processing. Works cannot mature us. We must understand suffering correctly and one of the things we've got to understand is: if we suffer with him we will reign with him and our suffering took place at Calvary. I'm not saying we don't suffer anything and I am not saying that God does not use those things. Certainly he does. But God's way of maturing us is causing us to be cleansed by the word.

Sacrifice The Ox

We must come to understand that in the Old Testament God dealt with the people in the physical and natural level because they did not have a new nature. But today, we are a new creation with a new nature, the nature of God, and he deals with us *through his word*. We are purged, we are cleansed through his word. As soon as we get that message and lay down our ox (the former beliefs we had about suffering), we are going to see the unveiling of Christ.

It is not a processing, it is a provision. The throttle is in our hand now. This is the time of Jubilee. The filling of our mind with what took place at Calvary takes some time, and in that sense it is a process. To renew our mind takes some time. But it is not a processing as we have thought. People say, "The cross of Calvary is heavy upon me," meaning they have to suffer, and the more they suffer the more they're going to be conformed into his image. That is works. The moment we think that, we are in works. We've got to wake up and see that it is a "done deal." His suffering was our suffering more than 2000 years ago. It is already done. It has already happened.

I hear so many deeper life preachers say, "Oh, but we're *life* preachers. We're kingdom life ministers!" Well, yes we are ministering life, but we must minister life correctly. If we just teach on resurrection life and nothing else, what we are doing is trying to reform an old man. But if we show them that they were widowed more than 2000 years ago and they get established in the fact that the old man was crucified, he died, and was buried, *then* resurrection life can begin to spring forth from spirit to soul and out of our body. Jesus said, "I am the resurrection." *The* Resurrection will quicken our body. We'll live above what the body realm tries to dictate to us.

John 3:13 and Ephesians 4:9 tell us that no man ascends (being seated in heavenly places), unless he first descends (that is the death of Christ and our identification with it). There are treasures in darkness, Isaiah prophesied. I did not understand that for so many years. There are treasures in the death! Enoch walked with God—left foot (death), right foot (resurrection)—for 300 years (the number of complete deliverance) and he was not found. Revelation *does* tell us that there is coming such an expression of the Lord that the temple will not even be seen. Only the glory will be seen! And that is what the whole book of Revelation is about.

We do need to go back and take a second look at a lot of things, but only those things that apply to the person and the work of Christ. That is the message. We were not just separated from God in our mind. We were separated in our spirit. We were dead in sins and in trespasses. Jesus laid the ax to the root. Otherwise, why would Jesus become sin if we were only separated in our thinking? Man's fall affected his spirit. It started in the mind but went all the way down to the core of our being and that is why Jesus had to become sin and die spiritually.

There are some that border-line on new age and metaphysical ideas that tell you the only place we were separated was in our mind. We were separated from God in our spirit, in our soul, and death was in our body—the whole man! That's why Paul said "I pray God your whole spirit *and soul and body* be preserved blameless unto the coming of our Lord Jesus Christ." If we were just separated in our mind, then Paul would not have prayed for our whole spirit *and* soul *and* body. "And" is a conjunction which shows three different parts of the whole: spirit and soul and body. It is important that we understand this. If we were only separated in our mind, then for what reason did Jesus become sin and die spiritually? He laid the ax to the root. We were bad to the core! We were "bad to the bone," as they say.

Divine Outline

In the book of Revelation we see God's own divine outline. Let's look at Revelation 1:19: "Write the things which thou hast seen, and the things which are, and the things which shall be hereafter." Let's break this down—let's grind the corn with the millstone. "The things which thou *hast* seen" are the seven seals John saw in chapters 5, 6 and 8. He saw the book within that was sealed on the backside with seven seals. He saw the white horse, the opening of one seal which represents the righteous earth walk of Jesus. The second seal was the red horse—Jesus became sin. The third seal was the black horse—Jesus died spiritually. The fourth seal was the pale horse—Jesus went into hell. The fifth seal was the souls under the brazen altar getting the revelation that his death was our death. The sixth seal displaces former rulers. The seventh seal was silence in heaven for about a half an hour. Understanding the first 6 seals will bring you to rest, or silence. We will discuss all of these things in detail throughout the course of this study.

So the phrase "write the things which thou hast seen," refers to the things John *had* seen, specifically the seals, which were the righteous earth walk of Jesus and what happened at the cross. John wrote about what was shown when he looked behind him—the cross of Calvary and our identification with it.

Then Jesus said to John, "Write the things which *are*." This speaks of trumpets. A trumpet is a clear sounding word. These are not the seven trumpets spoken of in Revelation chapter 8, which we will discuss later. The trumpeting here was: "You have seen what happened to Jesus in the opening of the seals and looking behind you. Now I want you to write the things which *are* as a *result* of what you saw happen to Jesus."

Then Jesus said, "Write the things that *shall* be." So, not only was John to write the things that happened, that which he *had seen*, but he was to write the things that *are true because of* what happened to Jesus, and then he was to write about the *product* of *what is going to come* because of what happened to Jesus—the vials of Revelation chapter 16.

We have the seals—John saw what happened to Jesus. We have trumpets—John gave voice to what he saw. Then we have the vials—that which "shall be" because of the blood that Jesus poured out. As I stated earlier, if I poured a vial of blood on someone, nothing would happen to them other than them smelling like blood, their clothes would be stained, and they would be a little wet. But that which "shall be" represents that "which is to come" when the seven vials are poured out. Seven means fullness. So that which shall be represents the fullness of the understanding of the blood of Jesus Christ poured upon our head, renewing our mind to the finished work of the cross. Then we are going to see the product of that which was and that which is, come forth into manifestation—the manifestation of the body of Christ!

So we have seals, trumpets, and vials—the things which thou hast seen, the things which are, and the things which shall be hereafter. This is similar to the phrase in Revelation 1:4; "him which is, and which was, and which is to come." "That which was" is what John saw happen to Jesus. "That which is" is the *result* of what happened to Jesus—we were there. "That which is to come" is the product—the resurrection of the many-membered body of Christ in the earth! All the way through the book of Revelation we see this truth conveyed.

"Caught Up" In Experience

As we consider the candlesticks in Revelation chapter 1 we need to understand that those Churches were in the Holy Place realm because the Holy Place dimension is where the candlestick was in the tabernacle of Moses. The thing that the book of Revelation will do in our lives individually and corporately is move us from the Holy Place mentality and bring us *experientially* into the Most Holy Place mentality. We know we are already seated there in spirit, but what we're doing now is opening our spiritual eyes and looking around in the room of the Most Holy Place to see our surroundings. When we see what is in the Most Holy Place and what it represents, *we are going to experience that dimension.* We are not just going to be there spiritually. We are going to be walking in it and experiencing it. We are going to manifest the product—living epistles—walking word—manifested many-membered body of Christ. Right now, right here on planet earth, there is a remnant who are experiencing this "caught up" life.

The Old Testament gives us prophetic pictures of the death, burial, and resurrection. The gospels give us historical surroundings. The gospels claim it. Acts proclaims it. Paul explains it. John exclaims it. Revelation gives us the *product* of it and that is what we want to see. As Gary Garner, a gifted teacher and Bible scholar explains, the product is: A people move in experience from the Holy Place to the Holy of Holies.

As we understand the book of Revelation, it will remove Babylon, which means "confusion." Because the death, burial, and resurrection are *explained,* it becomes a millstone, as Paul was. A millstone grinds the wheat or breaks down the word so that it can be understood. Paul was a millstone in the sense that he explained the finished work. That millstone destroys Babylon, as Revelation 18:21 says. Explaining destroys confusion. Then we begin to *experience* the realm that we are already seated in.

The Blood Of Jesus

When we study the seven vials of wrath (or blood) that are poured out, we will find that the word "vial" in Revelation chapter 16 is only used three times in the Septuagint. Each time it speaks of the bowl on the table of shewbread. If the Greek word for "vial," in reference to the seven vials of blood being poured out, is the same Hebrew word that is used for the bowl or the cup on the table of shewbread, what does that say to us? The vial or cup on the table of shewbread was full of wine. The wine symbolizes the blood of Jesus Christ. The other thing on the table was bread. The bread is symbolic of the body of Christ.

The Lord is simply showing us that the understanding of the fullness (seven) of the blood (vials) being poured out on our heads comes as we eat the bread and drink the wine. This understanding comes as we show ourselves his death until he comes personally to us and shows us that we too are dead and our new life is hidden in him (Colossians 3:3). Then we shew bread—we show forth his death until he comes—through his many-membered body. The vials of God's wrath were fully poured out upon our Lord Jesus and consequently, Jesus poured out his life's blood on Calvary's cross. He fully bore God's wrath for us and as us. We were crucified with Christ. The seven vials of blood that are poured out in Revelation chapter 16 represent the fullness of the understanding of the blood of Jesus. The seven vials of blood also speak of the seven bleeding spots on the body of Jesus when he was wounded, and crucified.

In Revelation 9:5, we read about a people that are tormented for five months. They want to die. They are begging to die. In the Old Testament, you can't live, and that is part of the curse. In the New Testament, you can't die! All you can do is wake up to the fact that you already died! People are trying to *kill themselves* in the Church. They are trying, like Judas, to hang themselves. They are trying to crucify their flesh and die to self. And this went on for five months, Revelation chapter 9 says. Five months! Isn't it interesting that there are five months from the end of Passover to the beginning of Tabernacles![20]

Like The Morning Spread Upon The Mountains

This is a spiritual book! It has nothing to do with literal bugs and locusts that come out of the earth and sting us. It has nothing to do Godzilla monsters and a seven year tribulation and a literal temple in natural Israel. Religion can make it sound somewhat convincing. They can teach all the current events and attempt to line them up with the books of Ezekiel, Daniel, and Revelation. The problem is; current events do not remain current. Current events shift with the currents. So the "prophecy" they made yesterday was washed away in the tide of today's headlines and the "prophecy" they make today will need revision tomorrow. All the while they are out of touch with spiritual reality because they do not understand that the spirit of prophecy is the testimony of Jesus. The spirit of prophecy is the preaching of the cross. The spirit of prophecy is The Solid Rock that no storm will ever wash away. The religious system has the audacity to preach to their members "Don't watch horror movies," yet they terrorize the people with a message of horror! I am not condoning horror movies, I am exposing Babylonian confusion. Wake up Church! Paul said that the veil is only over the minds of those who are *perishing!* Look at 2 Corinthians 4:2-4 in the Amplified Bible:

> We have renounced disgraceful ways (secret thoughts, feelings, desires and underhandedness, the methods and arts that men hide through shame); we refuse to deal craftily (to practice trickery and cunning) or to adulterate or handle dishonestly the Word of God, but we state the truth openly (clearly and candidly). And so we commend ourselves in the sight and presence of God to every man's conscience. But even if our Gospel (the glad tidings) also be hidden (obscured and covered up with a veil that hinders the knowledge of God), it is hidden [only] to those who are perishing and obscured [only] to those who are spiritually dying and veiled [only] to those who are lost. For the god of this world has blinded the unbelievers' minds [that they should not discern the truth], preventing them from seeing the illuminating light of the Gospel of the glory of Christ (the Messiah), Who is the Image and Likeness of God.

Reveille! Blow the trumpet in Zion! Sound the alarm! That means it's time to wake up Church! Morning is spread upon the mountains! In verse four of this passage, Paul talks about unbelievers. The Church world is full of "unbelieving believers." For the majority of the Church world, the Day of the Lord is a day of darkness and gloominess. But those who follow the cloud and not the crowd are not taken by surprise—they're already awake, living in the New Day. Look at Joel 2:1-2:

> Blow ye the trumpet in Zion, and sound an alarm in my holy mountain: let all the inhabitants of the land tremble: for the day of the Lord cometh, for it is nigh at hand; A day of darkness and of gloominess, a day of clouds and of thick darkness, *as the morning*

spread upon the mountains: a great people and a strong; there hath not been ever the like, neither shall be any more after it, even to the years of many generations (emphasis added).

The Blood Is Speaking

Do you know that the book of Ezekiel is the Old Testament book of Revelation? It is the same thing. We could just lay Ezekiel right over the top of Revelation because it is a carbon copy. At the end the book of Ezekiel, there is a people, and it says of them, "The Lord is there." They are called "The Lord is there!" In the end of the book of Revelation, there is a people who understand the death, burial, and resurrection—and exactly how they are identified with it—and the Lord is in the midst of them. The same message is in both the Old Testament book of Ezekiel and the New Testament book of Revelation—the *One Thing* that makes heaven what it is—the Presence of the Lord!

We are going to see nothing in the book of Revelation but the unfolding of the person and the work of Christ. The blood is speaking better things today. The little book is open now—the One Message. Thank God for that truth and thank God that he is balancing things and he is giving us a way to teach the message so that people will understand.

If we start teaching from the perspective of the death of Christ and bring the people on up from Passover and Pentecost, to Tabernacles, every truth will just fall into place as we teach it systematically. The problem has been that we have not used the wisdom of God. We ran with these things. We were excited about these things. They were controversial and they were different and they made us feel good. Thank God for them! But now God is opening the little book. There is a condensing into one message. Now we know what the gospel really is. The death of Christ is an all-inclusive message. With it, you can minister to people on every level. The wings of the Cherubim can be heard way out in the Outer Court! Some minds will be challenged when we teach that Jesus became sin, died spiritually and went into hell. Our minds have to be challenged if we're going to have them renewed.

The blood is speaking something in Hebrews 12:24:

> And to Jesus the mediator of the new covenant, and to the blood of sprinkling that speaketh better things than that of Abel.

The blood is saying something to us today. A lot of people do not want to go back and take a second look at the cross because "that is elementary." No, it is not elementary to see that Jesus became sin and died spiritually. To be able to look beyond the appearance realm and "know no man after the flesh" is not elementary. You cannot do that unless you have a revelation of the cross of Calvary and have taken a second look. Then you will be able to discern spiritually on a consistent basis.

The blood is speaking. It speaks of better things than that of Abel. Able brought a sacrifice of covenant, the slain lamb. Cain brought a sacrifice of religious works. Cain was angry with Abel because God had respect for Abel's sacrifice, but he rejected Cain's sacrifice, so Cain killed Abel. The religious killed Jesus. The blood of Jesus, the Lamb speaks better things—a covenant not based on works. Your works and your anger cannot produce the righteousness of God.

These vials of blood that are poured out are saying something to us and revealing something to us that is causing the veil to be taken away from our mind. This is bringing salvation to our *soul* to such a degree that we *become* that fifth seal that is opened in Revelation chapter 6. We are a soul under the altar that has been beheaded because we see that his death was our death. We see that he wore the crown of thorns so that we could have the mind of Christ. We see that his judgment was our judgment. The book of Revelation reveals the truth that his judgment was our judgment.

Judgment Ended At The Cross

John 12:31 says, "Now is the judgment of this world." Now—over 2000 years ago—is the judgment of this world! People are teaching that this world is *going* to be judged, including much of the Church world. They are already reaping what they have sown. Those that sow judgment are reaping bitterness, unforgiveness, a critical spirit, strife, jealousy, wrath, factions, seditions, heresies, and the like. As people sow to the flesh, they reap some undesirable consequences. But the true and righteous judgment that they receive will be to find out that they were judged over 2000 years ago. A priesthood to whom judgment has been given will minister this to them. This priesthood understands that Jesus Christ's judgment was their judgment.

It would behoove the Church to do a study on the word "judgment." The breastplate in the Old Testament was the breastplate of judgment. The breastplate in the New Testament is the breastplate of righteousness. Judgment in the Old Testament was unto death. Judgment in the New Testament is unto victory. The majority of the Church world is "ministering" judgment unto condemnation and they are reaping what they are sowing. The judgment that God desires is righteous judgment. God desires mercy, but the majority of the Church world still wants people to pay for their sins. Why did Jesus say "I will have mercy and not sacrifice?" Because out of the great mercy of God, *he was* the sacrifice! Judgment ended at the cross! Why did Jesus say "I will have mercy and not sacrifice?" Because the sacrifices were offered under the law (Hebrews 10:8) and they were made to *remember* sin, to give us a sin consciousness (Hebrews 10:3). But Jesus, the once for all sacrifice, came to make us a new creation with the mind of Christ. He came to give us a God-consciousness so we could enter into rest (Hebrews 10:12). God does not remember our sins and we are in him (Hebrews 10:17). Therefore, we who are in him do not have a sin consciousness, but the mind of Christ.

We are going to go forth and *give* judgment to the world, including the Church world, by telling them that Jesus' judgment was their judgment. We will *give* them judgment by telling them that God is no longer mad at them. Again, from John 12:31-32: "*Now* is the judgment of this world; *Now* is the prince of this world cast out. And I, if I be lifted up from the earth, will draw all men unto me." The judgment that was exacted upon this world, took place over 2000 years ago. God exacted the punishment that was due all of us at the cross of Calvary. The wages of sin is death. In Adam, we came into sin. We were dead in sins and trespasses in our whole being and over 2000 years ago, we got what we deserved—

death. In Adam, all died. In Christ shall all be made alive.

I have been judged. This truth is revealed to me. There is no way in this world that I will ever be convinced that I have not already been judged. I am being bored through with that message and gripped by the cross. My ear is being nailed to the door. This truth is being bored through us and when we really get gripped by the cross, nothing else will satisfy us. We must do more than just proclaim it. We must explain it. We will not understand spiritual truths by osmosis. We must hear it by the spirit. We must be bored through. We have to be gripped by the cross. We must come to understand that the true gospel is the death, the burial, and the resurrection and not a bunch of other messages. We must partake of the bread and the wine. We must eat Lamb. You've got to feed on it and feed on it and feed on it until the marriage is experienced between spirit and soul.

Paul said in 1 Corinthians 11:26, "For as often as ye eat this bread, and drink this cup, ye do show the Lord's death till he come." Most people misquote this saying, "We're to eat the bread and drink the cup until he comes." That is not what it says. We are to eat of the bread, drink of the cup and in doing that, we are showing forth the *Lord's death*—not life—*death*. As we do that, life will automatically come. When Jesus died, resurrection life followed. But we are to show forth the Lord's death till he come. So we are to talk about his death, study his death, become firmly planted in his death, until he appears from spirit to soul and out through our bodies on a consistent, regular basis.

The Spirit Of Wisdom And Revelation

The revelation John received was actually not a "new" revelation. Everything he received came from his knowledge of the Old Testament. But it was Jesus Christ, the light, which gave him the enlightenment of what he already knew, which changed his common, ordinary knowledge to wisdom and revelation *in the knowledge of* the Lord Jesus Christ. The revelation that John received in the New Testament was from a higher place than that of the Old Testament. We could go to Zechariah 1:8 and see horses, but they were spotted horses. John had head knowledge of the Old Testament, but when he "comes up hither," he sees it from a higher perspective—from the one who *is* the New Covenant. They are spotted horses in Zechariah, but John saw white and red and black and pale horses. The cherubim in Ezekiel have four wings, but John sees a higher order—seraphim with six wings. Why? It is a greater message. It is the highest revelation of our Lord, Jesus Christ—the Most Holy.

John and Paul had the same revelation. They both wrote to seven Churches. John's revelation is in visionary, symbolic, terms and Paul's revelation is in more common language. The same thing occurred with Zechariah and Haggai. Zechariah said something like, "I see horses flying through the clouds." Haggai said it more in common terms like, "Let's go out and cut down a tree and get the wood and build a house"—and they were both saying the same thing at the same time to the same people. What does this tell us? One is more practical and the other is visionary, symbolic, and spiritual. In the Old Testament as well as the New Testament the message comes both in practical terms and in visionary, symbolic, and spiritual terms.

Three Major Feasts Of The Lord

Let me give some structure of the book of Revelation that will correlate with the three feasts of the Lord. As was stated earlier, if we are going to understand the book of Revelation in any way, we have to understand Moses' Tabernacle, the pieces of furniture, and what they typify spiritually. We must also understand the feasts of the Lord. We will see some of the furniture in Moses' Tabernacle in the book of Revelation and if we do not understand what it signifies and how it is related to the finished work, we are not going to have a clue about what is disclosed in the book of Revelation.

Passover

So let's look at the three feasts of the Lord as the structure of the book of Revelation. First we have Passover. In Leviticus 23, Israel was commanded to keep three general feasts: Passover, Pentecost, and Tabernacles. Throughout the book of Revelation, we are going to see Passover, Unleavened Bread, Firstfruits, Pentecost, Trumpets,

Atonements, and Tabernacles. In Revelation chapters 2 through 5, we see Passover, Unleavened Bread, and Firstfruits. The Passover is when Jesus died and he shed his blood. In chapter 2, Jesus said seven times to the Churches, "To him that overcomes." How do we overcome? Passover. Revelation 12:11 tells us they overcame him by the blood of the Lamb, and by the word of their testimony; and they loved not their lives unto the death.

The Israelites came out of Egypt by the sacrifice of a Passover lamb. When they took the blood and put it on the doorposts and the side posts, the lamb's death *was* their death. Jesus' death was our death. So, Passover represents the shedding of the blood of Jesus. It goes on to say in Revelation 12:11b, "And they loved not their lives unto the death." One of the ways that you *could love* your live is by thinking that you've got to go out like Judas and hang yourself spiritually. We have been programmed by the religious system to think, "I've got an old man here, I have two natures and I must die to self every day." You are loving your *old* life (which is already dead), and trying to reform yourself thinking that you have to work harder to be good, to be righteous, to save Adam. But we're not to love our life. We're not trying to heal a deadly wound. We're realizing that the old man is crucified, dead, and buried and we do not love him *unto the death*. In other words, we're seeing that he was done away with more than 2000 years ago at *the death*. At Passover, all the firstborn of Egypt were slain. Egypt represents sin. The firstborn of sin was Adam. He was the first one born from life unto death. All the firstborn of Egypt were slain at the cross. Jesus, however, is the firstborn from the dead, the first one born from death to life. The death of the ages took place at the cross of Calvary over 2000 years ago. Now, all who are in Christ are alive with just one nature—the righteousness of God.

Another thing we will see in the book of Revelation is the same thing we saw in the Garden of Eden. When John turned to see the candlesticks, they were like almond trees. So, you can say he turned and saw a garden. We saw a garden in Genesis; we will see a garden in Revelation. Remember the voice that came after Adam had fallen and sinned? The voice said, "Adam, where art thou?" That is really the same question being asked in the book of Revelation, "Adam, where art thou?" And we have to find out where Adam is. He is crucified, he is dead, he is buried. We also have to find out where the residue of Adam is. That residue is in our mind. Throughout the entire Bible there are stories that show us that Adam, our old (spirit) man is dead and that Eve, our old woman, our soul (carnal mind, will, and emotions) is also dead—both exchanged with the spirit and the mind of Christ.

There are many examples of doing away with the old man and the old woman in the Old Testament. One such story is that of Elisha. Before he could follow Elijah, he had to go kiss his Father (his old man) and his Mother (his old woman, his soul, his carnal mind) good-bye. Then in the New Testament Paul continues explaining that the first man, Adam, is dead and the last Adam, the life-giving spirit lives eternally—and we are in him. Then we come to the book of Revelation where Jesus says right up front in Chapter 1, and in the verse of the number of new beginnings—verse 8—"I am Alpha and Omega, the beginning and the ending." Jesus did away with the old man and gave us a new beginning in him. All things begin and end in him. Doesn't that make you want to be found in him, where every day is a new beginning? Well hang on, because throughout the book of Revelation, as our understanding is enlightened, the residue, the veil that was done away at the cross of Calvary is going to be taken away from our mind and we will see that there is only One Man left.

Unleavened Bread

The next feast is Unleavened Bread. In Revelation chapter 2 and 3, the Lord told the seven Churches the things that he required of them. Before he told them what he required of them, he told them something about *himself*. Then he told them something about *themselves* that was identified with the cross of Calvary. Why? Because we overcome by the blood of the Lamb and by the word of *our* testimony, the word of *our* death. We overcome as we identify with Jesus' death. So, in chapters 2 and 3 we see the Feast of Unleavened Bread. Do you remember what else they did during Passover in Israel when they came out of Egypt? They had to get all the leaven out of the house. They had to sweep all of the dirt out. That is what was required of them. When Jesus told them what was required of them he was saying, "You have to sweep all the leaven out of your house." But that is only done through a realization of the death, and how the work was finished.

Firstfruits

The Feast of Firstfruits appears in Revelation chapters 4 and 5, in reference to the throne. This feast represents our being seated with him in heavenly places. So, Passover is Revelation chapters 2 and 3—to him that overcomes. And how do we overcome? We overcome by the blood of the Lamb and by the word of our testimony—that is Passover. Unleavened Bread is Jesus telling them what he requires of them, what they need to get out of the house. Then Firstfruits is our seating in the heavenly places in chapters 4 and 5. We will deal with all of this in detail when we reach those topics in this study.

Pentecost

Pentecost is the next feast. We will partake of this feast and savor the details in the following chapter. The Feast of Pentecost speaks of the Holy Place dimension where we are baptized with the Holy Spirit and sealed until the day of redemption.

Tabernacles

The last feast, the Feast of Tabernacles, encompasses three feasts: Trumpets, Atonements, and Tabernacles. In Revelation chapter 8 we see seven trumpets. When they celebrated the Feast of Tabernacles they blew the trumpets. When the trumpets were sounded the camp was to gather together. The ram's horns were blown at the Feast of Tabernacles to tell the people to get ready to do what they were supposed to do on the Day of Atonement. The trumpet has been sounding. The ram's horn has been sounding. The seven trumpets in Revelation chapter 8 represent the fullness of the long, loud blast of the ram's horn that came from the death of Christ. The trumpets are declaring the death of Christ, preparing you for the Day of Atonement.

On the Day of Atonement they sacrificed a bullock, which represents Jesus. They were to rest and do no servile work. They were to afflict their souls—or we could say it this way—typically, they had seven vials of blood poured upon their heads. To afflict the soul is to fill the mind in gaining understanding of the finished work of Calvary. The Day of Atonement is what is spoken of in Revelation chapter 16 where the seven vials are poured out. Those are not seven literal vials. Seven speaks of fullness. This signifies the fullness of the blood poured upon our heads—fully understanding the finished work of the cross. Our soul really gets afflicted as our old heavens (our old thoughts) pass away with a fervent heat and a loud noise and our mind is renewed to the New Creation Man.

Then Tabernacles is revealed in Revelation chapters 21 and 22 where John writes, "Behold, the tabernacle of God is with men, and he will dwell with them, and they shall be his people, and God himself shall be with them, and be their God." That is the Feast of Tabernacles. So, the structure of the book of Revelation is that of the feasts of the Lord.

The Seven Churches And Old Testament History

Now, in Revelation chapters 2 and 3 we will look at the seven Churches and Old Testament history. We discussed that Jesus did not tell them what he required of them until he first told them something about himself. You may wonder, "Why Ephesus and Smyrna and Pergamos and Thyatira? Why Sardis, and Philadelphia and Laodicea? Why not the Church in Jerusalem? Why not the Corinthian Church? Why not the Church in Rome?" Very little is written about these seven Churches. So why these particular Churches? We will see the reason is that they line up with Old Testament history until the time of Jesus' death, burial, and resurrection.

Some have said that if we line up the Laodicean Church with Church history as we have known it, then today's Church would be the Laodicean Church. That cannot be, because there is nothing good said about the Laodicean Church if you're going by what God is saying. If you were to judge today's religious system and see the lukewarmness, then you would say, "Yes, that is the Laodicean

Church." But do you know what God said about them? He said he was going to spew them out of his mouth. That is not what God spoke about today's Church. Whom did he spew out of his mouth but natural Israel, the Jews? The Laodicean Church is not this present Church age. However, it's true he wants us either hot or cold, but if we're lukewarm, caught somewhere in the Holy Place, he says he is going to spit us out of his mouth. God does not want us to stay in the Pentecostal experience! He wants us to go on to the Feast of Tabernacles.

We must see how vital it is that we overcome by the blood of the Lamb and by the word of our martyrdom, and that we love not our life (the old man) unto the death, but we see him crucified. The reason for this emphasis is because we cannot overcome anything in our lives on a consistent basis until we begin to realize who we are in Christ because of a death. Awake to righteousness and sin not. That will empower you.

In Revelation chapter 2, let's look at the things Jesus told each of these Churches about himself. These are the things Jesus said *before* he told them what was required of them in getting the dirt, the leaven, out of their house. Every one of these things he told the Churches about himself represent an aspect of the person and the work of Christ. Why? There is no overcoming, there is no doing what he said he required of us unless it is done through the blood of the Lamb and the word of our testimony. Revelation 2:1 begins:

> Unto the angel of the church of Ephesus write; These things saith he that holdeth the seven stars in his right hand, who walketh in the midst of the seven golden candlesticks;

What are the seven stars in this verse? At the end of chapter 1, in verse 20, the seven stars are the angels of these Churches, or the messengers. So he is walking in the midst of the Church of Ephesus and he is holding the messengers in his right hand—not in the left hand, but in the right hand. What does that tell us? It tells us something about the person and the work of Christ. The right hand speaks of valiancy and power. What is the power of God but the preaching of the cross? So right there in verse 1 of chapter 2, before

Jesus tells them what is required of them, he first tells them something of his person and his work. The right hand, the power, is the preaching of the cross and because of the cross, where is Jesus? He is in the midst of a people. The people of John's era understood these things. They understood that the right hand symbolized power. They understood that the preaching of the cross is the power of God.

We will find the Church of Smyrna in Revelation 2:8:

> And unto the angel of the church in Smyrna write;
> 'These things saith the first and the last, which was dead, and is alive;

Again we find something about the person and the work of Christ. He is Alpha and Omega, the first and the last. We previously discussed how Jesus identified with the first Adam in becoming sin. And then in his quickening and resurrection, he became the last Adam. He was dead and is alive, as he says in this verse. How was he dead? Was he just dead physically and put in a tomb? No, he was dead spiritually. He was the firstbegotten of the dead. As we have said, there were others who were raised from the dead, so how could Jesus be the firstbegotten of the dead? He was the first one born from spiritual death unto life. He was the first born again man. He was the first of a new creation man. So something about the person and the work of Christ is spoken to the Church in Smyrna.

To the Church of Pergamos in Revelation 2:12, we read:

> And to the angel of the church in Pergamos write;
> 'These things saith he which hath the sharp sword with two edges;

I hear preachers say that the flaming sword was in front of the garden to let people in, not to keep people out. But I see it both ways. The garden speaks of maturity. The flaming sword is there for *both* reasons. Yes, if you go in through the word and the flame, which is understanding that his judgment is your judgment, you will come into the garden of maturity. But, if you do not go in that way, the sword is there to keep you out the garden. It's going to keep you out of maturity. Yes, the flaming sword *was* there to let people in, if they came in the right way. But it was also there to keep people out if they tried to come in any other way than through the cross. You can only come into the garden, which represents full maturity, the experience of the Most Holy, when you come *by The Way*.

If we try to come through works, through legalism, if we try to come by smiting the rock twice, like Moses, we will not enter in. To smite the rock twice is to believe that Jesus' smiting at Calvary was not really enough. Those who believe this add their own works to "earn" their salvation because they lack the humility that simply accepts God's free gift. This is called religion and the Church is full of it. To smite the rock twice is to believe that Jesus' smiting was not our smiting, so they expect God to put them through the sickness, the judgment, the sorrow, the grief and the wrath that the sweet Lord Jesus was smitten to take *away* from us! I have heard preachers say, "Nothing evil can touch our lives unless it passes through God's hands." For Jesus to take that all away at Calvary to have God turn around and put it back on us is a house divided. A house divided against itself shall not stand. Just as God does not bring sin into our lives to mature us, neither does he bring sickness into our lives to make us suffer or to "process" us in order to mature us. If we believe that God puts disease and troubles on us to mature us, we are smiting the rock twice. We must let his smiting be ours. Moses smote the rock twice and could not enter into the Promised Land of fullness. If we think that we enter in by "all the hell I go through," then we will not enter in. If we think that is the way we are matured, then that flaming sword will keep us out of the garden of maturity. It is a sharp *two*edged sword. It cut off Adam and now the understanding of it is cutting off the residue of Adam in our mind. The veil that was done away is taken away from our mind. Twoedged.

So in looking at Pergamos, we are taken back to the flaming sword by the garden. We have the same thing in Revelation that we have in the garden, which simply represents a revelation that his judgment was our judgment. Understand *that* word, *that* sharp sword with two edges, and you will come into maturity. It cuts going in, and it cuts coming out. But listen, that is not talking about some hard dealing that we have to go through as if the word is just going to cut us up. No, the word is going to show us that our old man was cut off over 2000 years ago. Our roots are not in Adam. That was cut off from us. Our genetic upbringing and our environmental upbringing was cut off at the cross of Calvary by that sword. The flaming, two-edged sword cut the old man off with one edge, at the entrance wound. And now it is cutting off the residue that remains in our mind with the other edge, at the exit wound. And we are *not* going to heal the deadly wound!

Revelation 2:18:

> And unto the angel of the church in Thyatira write; 'These things saith the Son of God, who hath his eyes like unto a flame of fire, and his feet are like fine brass;

What is that telling us? The spirit is revealing in the fire and the fine brass that his judgment was our judgment. In chapter 1, John saw in the candlesticks one like unto the Son of Man. He saw Jesus there and he saw how we are identified with him. His feet were as fine brass. In the book of Ruth, Naomi represents the religious Church, and natural Israel. Ruth represents the true Church, Spiritual Israel—and by the way, Ruth was a Gentile widow from Moab. Do you remember how irate the Jews were when Jesus told them that Elijah was not sent to Israel, but to a Gentile woman who was a widow? I wonder what would have happened if Jesus had reminded them that Boaz married Ruth, a Moabitess who, according to the law, will *never* enter the house of the Lord!

Ruth represents a people who realize that their old man, Adam, is dead. Boaz represents Jesus. Before Ruth could become one with Boaz and birth a servant (Obed means "servant") she had to come and uncover his feet. She had to get a revelation in type, that his death was her death. Do you know where Boaz was when Ruth uncovered his feet? It was the time of the wheat and barley harvest. Corns of wheat are symbolic of death according to John 12:24. Barley represents resurrection. He was lying in the threshing floor at midnight by a heap of wheat. When she uncovered his feet, she got a revelation that his judgment, his death, was her judgment and her death. How many times we see that his judgment was our judgment! That is the only way we can overcome. When we see that his death was our death and we are the righteousness of God in Christ Jesus, we are awaking to righteousness and we'll sin not. We can get the leaven out of our house now.

According to Genesis 1:5, each new day begins with night. It was midnight. When Ruth uncovered Boaz's feet at midnight, a new day began for her. Then as some other things took place, she could become one with Boaz, which represents the Lord Jesus Christ, the New Day.

Next, we see Sardis in Revelation 3:1:

> And unto the angel of the church in Sardis write;
> 'These things saith he that hath the seven Spirits of God, and the seven stars;

The seven spirits of God refer to the fullness of the Spirit of God. Isaiah 11:2 lists the seven-fold Spirit of God by name: The spirit of the Lord, the spirit of wisdom and understanding, the spirit of counsel and might, the spirit of knowledge and the fear of the Lord. Seven is the number of fullness. We are moving into the fullness of the Spirit. We are not throwing the gifts of the spirit away, but we are "coming up hither," as we will study later in Revelation chapter 4. We are taking the gifts with us, but not with us in the way we operated in them in the Holy Place. We are going to move in the seven spirits of the Lord, the fullness of the spirit of God. What is the fullness of the power of God? The preaching of the cross.

We have the power of God in the Church. We have seen people healed. We have seen some die. We have seen some healed only to become ill with the same sickness. We have the seen the power of God, but we have only seen smidgens of it here and there. We have been taught the "in part" as the whole. We have to realize that if we are going to operate in the seven spirits of God, the full power of God, it is going to be as we understand that he is a great big God, the devil is defeated, and the old man is dead. It is going to come as we understand what happened at the cross of Calvary and how we were identified with it. It is going to come as we roast the lamb with fire and not sodden it down with water. We don't smite the rock twice. Instead we allow the Lord to grant us the spirit of wisdom and revelation in the knowledge of him. So that, the eyes of our understanding being enlightened, we may know what is the hope of his calling and what is the riches of the glory of his inheritance in the saints. That is where we are in such a time as this—the time for this word to come forth. Why? Because the little book is now open. As we digest it we see that Jesus' cup was bitter *and* it was sweet as honey (Revelation 10:9).

Look at Revelation 4:5:

> And out of the throne proceeded lightnings and thunderings and voices: and there were seven lamps of fire burning before the throne, which are the seven Spirits of God.

Out of the throne proceeded lightnings and thunderings and voices. Lightning comes before thundering. Lightning speaks of illumination or understanding, and *then* you trumpet, then you thunder it out. But you cannot trumpet until you understand. Revelation 4:5 continues, "And there were seven lamps of fire burning before the throne, which are the seven Spirits of God." Seven represents fullness. The fullness of the Spirit of God comes by understanding these seven lamps of fire burning before the throne.

When you come before God, what is the throne room? It is the Most Holy Place. What is in the throne room? The Ark of the Covenant is there. What was the Ark of the Covenant made of? It was made of wood overlaid with gold. The wood represents Jesus' humanity, the gold is his deity. Everything about the Ark speaks of the finished work. The Ark is in the Most Holy Place, which speaks of the throne, and the Ark itself represents the throne. The seven fold Spirit of God is connected with the throne. "Throne" speaks of authority and power. What is the power of God but the preaching of the cross?

The next Church is Philadelphia, in Revelation 3:7:

> And to the angel of the church in Philadelphia write; These things saith he that is holy, he that is true, he that hath the key of David, he that openeth, and no man shutteth, and shutteth, and no man openeth;

What is this key of David? Both "key" and "David" speak of ruling and reigning. Where does one rule from? The throne. And we are seated in the throne. How do we come to understand that we are in the heavenlies? How do we come to understand that we are complete in him? How do we come to understand that we are at the finish line? We understand these things by coming out to the brazen altar to see how we got there. Then we will rule with him in experience. If we suffer with him, we reign with him. When did we suffer? More than 2000 years ago at the cross of Calvary. Again, that is not "all the things I have to go through," even though God can use those things. It is not God's will for us to "go through hell" to be purified, when we have his word that cleanses us. In this hour, God is causing a people to realize that Jesus' suffering was our suffering, and that constitutes our beginning to walk in this ruling and reigning position. We've got to get this "suffering" junk out of our mind. We do not need anymore "spiritual junk food." It gives us hardening of the arteries and we'll have a hard heart! I do not want to have to spit out the bones to get to the meat. I want a pure word! It is time for a people to hear a pure word. I do not want a mixture any more. I want purity.

The seventh Church, Laodicea, we find in Revelation 3:14:

> And unto the angel of the church of the Laodiceans write; 'These things saith the Amen, the faithful and true witness, the beginning of the creation of God;

Notice the phrase, "the Amen" which means "trustworthy" and "verily." The Amen is trustworthy and is truth. He is adding emphasis to the faithful and true witness," or according to the Greek, the faithful and true *martyr.* In other words, he says "I am trustworthy, I am the truth, I am the faithful and true martyr. Then he uses the phrase "the beginning of the creation of God." The beginning of *what* creation of God? We know that it was Jesus that created the heavens and the earth, the visible and the invisible. But the "beginning of the creation of God" is not talking about the physical, visible world that was created in Genesis, even though we can see the death, burial, and resurrection in Genesis chapter 1. The beginning of the creation of God speaks of the fact that Jesus became sin, and then became the first one born from death unto life. Jesus so fully identified with Adam—who we were—that he became sin. God was not going to raise who he had become. Jesus was the firstborn among many brethren, in that he was the first one to be born again. God is not saving Adam, so Jesus is the firstborn from the dead. He was the first of a new creation, the beginning of the creation of God. One translation says he had to be born again. He was the first one born from death unto life.

The religious Church will not teach that Jesus became sin because they say that it somehow takes away from Jesus' deity and that it "demonizes" him. The truth is that it does neither. But it *does* show the depths of his love! The religious Church will not teach the finished work of Calvary for three apparent reasons. The first reason is that they only know what they've been taught by man and man's doctrine. All this time they have been heaping unto themselves teachers, having itching ears and the precious Holy Spirit's still small voice is drowned out by the loud, demonstrative outer voice of religion. Isaiah prophesied of the day when we would not let this happen any more. In Isaiah 30:20, he said "…yet shall not thy teachers be removed into a corner any more, but thine eyes shall see thy teachers." The Amplified version says it this way: "… yet your Teacher will not hide Himself any more, but your eyes will constantly behold your Teacher." Hallelujah! The Lord is revealing himself to us like never before! It is his will—he *wants* us to see him! He wants to be unveiled and uncovered in us and through us!

Then in the New Testament John writes to us and says that we do not need any man to teach us (the law) because *sons* already have God's word written on their hearts. He was not saying that we no longer need teaching. We do. We need teaching that ministers to the new creation that we are. But we do not need teaching that ministers law to a dead old man. Sons do not need any man to teach us the law! We know our Father's will because he lives in our temple. We have a daily disclosing of his will to us, his sons. The anointing abides in us.

The Church that remains in Babylonian captivity has never been free to think with the mind of Christ. They have been taught to believe whatever they're told. We have to be careful because it's easy to lump everyone together in the same category and call it a religious system. There are sincere people in every Church. It is also easy to blame "the system" and not take responsibility for our own individual lives. People do the best they can with what they have been given, so we're not blaming our spiritual or natural parents. But when the truth is revealed, we are responsible to change if we must and make any adjustments necessary to walk in the truth and to walk in the light that God gives us. The Church, for the most part, has *not* taught the people to be as the Bereans and daily search the scriptures to see if what they have been told is true. They sodden, sons roast. They must come out of Babylon to be able to hear the still small voice of the Holy Spirit.

The second reason the Church will not roast the Lamb with fire is because they are interpreting spiritual things with carnal minds. Spiritual things are spiritually discerned. That is why the Holy Spirit told John to write, "I was in the Spirit on the Lord's day." If you have been born again, your spirit does know the truth. That is why there is such a divine discontentment in the Church today. There is a war going on between confusion and the Spirit. Sincere Christians are desperately hungry for more because their Spirit tells them that there is so much more. As a matter of fact, they are experiencing a famine. But their souls, their minds, have been blinded by the veil of the god of this world. The Holy Spirit wants to show them how to remove the veil.

The third reason that the majority of the Church world will not teach the finished work of Calvary is a very dark and deceptive one hidden deep within their motives. In fact, it is hidden so well that most of them are not even consciously aware of it. But the Holy Spirit is shining his impeccable, glorious light in this day when everything that is hidden will be revealed. This reason is quite pathetic and very repulsive and it is this: CONTROL. Religion controls with FEAR. Pharisees control with fear. Pharisees hate anything they can't control and anything they can't own. And they are afraid themselves that if people understand the finished work, they won't be able to tell them what to do any longer. They won't be able to "glory in your flesh," as Paul said. I've heard them use the excuse that if people receive the message of grace, the message of the finished work, then they will no longer serve the Lord! Paul dealt with that one too. They say that, because that is the first thing that comes to their own minds—that is what they would do themselves. But to the pure in heart, all things are pure. That is the very reason God wrote the book of Revelation to bondservants. A bondservant is mature. A bondservant is one who will never leave his master, even though he is free to go! The book of Revelation is not written for the immature, but for those who are of age to receive the full inheritance.

The majority of the Church world serves God from a foundation of fear. The fear of punishment. The fear of a seven year tribulation. The fear of being "left behind." The fear of not earning God's love. How close could you be to an abusive husband or father that you are afraid of? Would you be courageous enough to confide in him? Would he be your best friend? How often would you steal away to be alone in his presence? Would you serve him because you love him or because you are just trying to live one more day—trying with all the energy you've got—to appease him so much that he won't hurt you—just for today?

If you find yourself in this condition, there is a wonderfully beautiful, liberating message Father God has for you. It is found in 1 John 4:18-19 and I'm quoting the Amplified Bible:

> There is no fear in love [dread does not exist], but full-grown (complete, perfect) love turns fear out of doors and expels every trace of terror! For fear brings with it the thought of punishment, and [so] he who is afraid has not reached the full maturity of love [is not yet grown into love's complete perfection]. We love *Him,* because He first loved us.

This is what God wants for each one of us—the full maturity of love's complete perfection. You may be in a place right now where this does not even seem possible to achieve in this lifetime. But all things are possible to him that believes! Never stop believing. Believe. Always believe.

So, in the book of Revelation, before Jesus tells the Churches what is required of them, he first tells them something about the person and the work of Christ. Why? Because we overcome by the blood of the Lamb and by the word of our martyrdom and we love not our lives unto *the* death. We love not our *old* lives unto *the* death. We're not trying to get an old man resurrected, modified, or saved. We are realizing that at the death of the ages, the wrath of God was vented. The wages of sin is death and we were dead in sins and trespasses. The judgment and the wrath of God were exacted upon us over 2000 years ago. That is what we've got to go out and tell a dying world, including a dying Church world—dying because of all the religious literal-letter interpretation that has captivated them in Babylonian confusion.

The sad thing is, that when one begins to minister the truth of the finished work to people in the Outer Court or in the Holy Place in their experience, their first response is, "I'm confused." It's true. They *are* confused. They *came* confused. They had help from the Babylonian religious system to *get* confused. That is the Hebrew definition of Babylon—confusion! The Pharisees and Sadducees were greatly confused with Jesus' parables! The letter kills. The spirit gives life.

The Seven Churches And The Seven Days Of Creation

So, we see that Jesus first tells every one of these seven Churches something about himself before he tells them what is required of them. Now, let us take a look at the days of creation in line with these seven Churches.[21] These Churches, taken in their order, complement the seven days of creation. Ephesus would represent day one. Look what Revelation 2:5 says about Ephesus:

> Remember therefore from whence thou art fallen, and repent, and do the first works; or else I will come unto thee quickly, and will remove thy candlestick out of his place, except thou repent.

The word "repent" here does not mean coming to an altar and accepting Jesus as Savior. These people were already in the Holy Place dimension in their experience. The word "repent" refers to changing your mind. This is the renewing of the mind. To repent is to draw your thoughts out of the realm of spirit instead of drawing your thoughts out of the residue of Adam's memory. To repent is to have the veil that is over your mind taken away so that Jesus can express and appear.

Notice the phrase "or else I will come unto thee quickly, and will remove thy candlestick out of his place, except thou repent." In other words, "I am going to take the light, (the candlestick represents the light) out of the midst of you, unless you repent. What did God say on day one of creation? "Let there be light." Jesus calls himself the one who is in the midst of the candlestick, and he is light. So, the Church at Ephesus correlates with day one of creation when God said "Let there be light." In other words, "If you do what I say, there is going to be light." If you repent, and do what God says here, there is going to be light. Day one is, "Let there be light."

On day two in Genesis 1:6, there was a separation. In Smyrna, there were some people that were really Jews and then there were some people that just said they were Jews. Look what Revelation 2:9 says:

> I know thy works, and tribulation, and poverty (but thou art rich), and I know the blasphemy of them which say they are Jews, and are not, but are the synagogue of Satan.

When Jesus uses the word "Jews" in this scripture, he is speaking of God's own peculiar race—the new creation. He is not referring to natural Israel (Romans 9:6-7). Jesus is making a separation between religious people and spiritual people—the true Church. He could have said, "I know the blasphemy of them which say they are Christians, and are not, but are the synagogue of Satan," and it would have meant the same thing. In Revelation 2:9 we find a heavenly people and a natural people. In Genesis 1:6, there was a separation between the heaven and the earth. Day two of creation lines up with the Church in Smyrna, a heavenly people and an earthly people.

Day three of creation represents Pergamos as we find in Revelation 2:17:

> He that hath an ear, let him hear what the Spirit saith unto the churches. To him that overcometh will I

> give to eat of the hidden manna, and will give him a white stone, and in the stone a new name written, which no man knoweth saving he that receiveth it.

In Genesis 1:9-11, we see that on the third day, the land and the plants appeared that brought forth seed or food—the bread and the wine. The promise to the overcomers in Revelation 2:17 is hidden manna and a white stone. The "white stone" is "a verdict of acquittal or ticket of admission." So here we have manna, we have food. Your ticket of admission to partake of this hidden manna, this food, is in realizing that all in Adam were judged and found guilty at the cross and received the punishment of death. Now, all who are in Christ, the last Adam, have been given the law the Spirit of Life in Christ Jesus that sets us free from the law of sin and death! All who are in Christ have a white stone—a verdict of acquittal!

The next Church, Thyatira, coincides with day four of creation as we read in Revelation 2:26-28:

> And he that overcometh, and keepeth my works unto the end, to him will I give power over the nations: And he shall rule them with a rod of iron; as the vessels of a potter shall they be broken to shivers: even as I received of My Father. And I will give him the morning star.

On day four of creation, the sun, moon, and stars were created as rulers. In this scripture Jesus says, "You're going to rule the nations and I am going to give you the morning star. I am going to cause you to rule and reign with me." So, on day four the sun and the moon and the stars came forth as heavenly rulers over all creation.

In Genesis 1:20-22, the birds of the heavens, the animals on the land, and the fish in the sea were created on the fifth day. There are three realms there, heavens, land, and sea. Sardis speaks of day five of creation and we find a heavenly people in Revelation 3:4:

> Thou hast a few names even in Sardis which have not defiled their garments; and they shall walk with me in white: for they are worthy.

In Revelation 3:3, we see a carnal people:

> Remember therefore how thou hast received and heard, and hold fast, and repent. If therefore thou shalt not watch, I will come on thee as a thief, and thou shalt not know what hour I will come upon thee.

The Lord is speaking to people who need to repent and change their carnal thinking. So we have the birds in the heavens, and the animals on the land. In Revelation 3:1 we see the fish in the sea—those who are dead:

> And unto the angel of the church in Sardis write; 'These things saith he that hath the seven spirits of God, and the seven stars; I know thy works, that thou hast a name that thou livest, and art dead.

We have spiritual people in verse 4, carnal people in verse 3, and dead people in verse 1. Those represent respectively, the birds in the heaven, the animals on the land, and the fish in the sea. Scripture references to "sea" speak of wickedness.

Church number six is Philadelphia in Revelation 3:12:

> Him that overcometh will I make a pillar in the temple of my God, and he shall go no more out: and I will write upon him the name of my God, and the name of the city of my God, which is new Jerusalem, which cometh down out of heaven from my God: and I will write upon him my new name.

On day number six God created man. The letter to the Church at Philadelphia reveals that if you overcome, you're going to be a pillar. *Men* become the tabernacle of God, as Adam was in the beginning before he fell asleep in sin. These pillars are those who have awakened to righteousness.

The last Church, Laodicea coincides with the seventh day of creation as we find in Revelation 3:21:

> To him that overcometh will I grant to sit with me in my throne, even as I also overcame, and am set down with my Father in his throne.

The word "sit" speaks of rest. On the seventh day, God rested. If the Laodicean Church overcomes, they are promised to sit with him, denoting rest. This complements the seventh day of Creation.

Those who overcame received the Most Holy Place. What does it mean to be an overcomer? We have thought that we have to just hustle and bustle and work and sweat. But that has never produced the righteousness of God. Awake to righteousness and then you will overcome. When we understand that we are in the Overcoming One because of what happened at the cross of Calvary we become empowered to live above sin. We are empowered to manifest the nature of Christ and that empowers us for everything. We are empowered for the revealing, for the unveiling of the Christ *within*, which for the most part, has just been a hope of glory. The full expression of glory has not been consistent. We have manifested his nature and his glory from time to time, but there is going to be a people who, at all times, consistently manifest his glory. Nothing will flow out of the river but purity. There will be a sea as clear as crystal—no debris, no dogma, no traditions or doctrines of man, no condemnation, and no guilt will flow out to anyone. It shall be a free river of life and as Ezekiel says, everything it comes in contact with, is going to live!

How is it going to happen? As we eat the bread and drink the cup, we show forth his death until he comes, and this is what the whole book of Revelation is about. All the way through this series, we are going to see a revelation, a revealing, an unveiling, an uncovering of the Lord Jesus Christ. It is the revelation of Jesus Christ. I want my mind completely filled with every aspect of the death of Christ. I *want* the seven vials of blood poured on my head. No man ascends unless he first descends. That is why Paul said in 1 Corinthians 1:23, "We preach Christ crucified." As we understand every aspect of the death of Christ, resurrection will take care of itself. It will just break forth. We already have eternal life. We already have resurrection life. It is just a matter of getting it out, and opening the flow out of us. As we roast the lamb with fire—not sodden it down with water—showing that Jesus became sin, manifestation will take place.

I Will Not Alter The Thing That Is Gone Out Of My Lips

I thank God for the understanding of the spirit of his word that allows us to interpret the book of Revelation according to scripture. Nearly every other interpretation of the book of Revelation has been eschatologically interpreted, meaning it has been interpreted according to what's happening in *world* events which are constantly changing. When we interpret the scripture according to current events which are always changing, then the interpretation is always changing too. But in Psalm 89:34, a Psalm of the Davidic covenant, we find that God said, "My covenant will I not break, nor will I alter the thing that is gone out of my lips." If we're *in* the world but not *of* the world, why would we interpret scripture according *to* the world? Eschatology is the study of last things, for example, death and resurrection. There is nothing wrong with eschatology as long as it is not based on things of the world. It must be based on the sure foundation of Jesus Christ and his finished work.

I can remember some years ago, hearing teaching on the book of Revelation, and they were teaching that the antichrist was Henry Kissinger. They changed their mind about that. Then they said the antichrist was Ronald Reagan because all of his names had six letters (666). Then world events changed and the antichrist was said to be someone else. They were always changing their ideas of who the antichrist was. They were always revising their books. They are still revising their books. They have failed the Deuteronomy test. Then they excuse their error by teaching that Satan must always have an antichrist ready because he does not know when the so called "literal rapture" of the Church is to take place.

They taught that the ten horns were the ten nations of the European Common Market. There are no longer ten nations in the European Common Market, so something is wrong, if we are going to interpret the book of Revelation according to the eschatology of gloom and doom. When we understand that it is the revelation of Jesus Christ, then we interpret the book of Revelation according to the word of God, allowing the Bible to interpret it.

Moses' Tabernacle

There were seven pieces of furniture in the Tabernacle of Moses. The Ark and the mercy seat were made separately and are counted as two pieces of furniture. If all the furniture in the tabernacle of Moses is placed in its proper place, it forms the shape of the cross. If Jesus were superimposed on that cross, he would have a head of gold (the Ark of the Covenant), and his feet (the brazen altar), would be brass, showing that his judgment is our judgment.

Every piece of furniture was a bleeding spot, where Jesus shed blood. There were seven pieces of furniture (seven vials, seven trumpets). Seven is the number that speaks of fullness. I want the fullness of the revelation of the death of Christ. Automatically, that will take care of the resurrection life of the Lord Jesus Christ in our lives as an ongoing experience.

Interpreting according to scripture is the only way to view the book of Revelation. It is the only view that says that the book of Revelation is the revelation of Jesus Christ. When our ear is nailed to the door, and when all we want to see is him, the word says we will be like him. When all we want to see *in one another* is him, and when all we want to see when we go to the word is him—because our ear is nailed to the door—there is going to come an uncovering and an unveiling of Jesus Christ. The Greek meaning of "revelation" is "to unveil or uncover something that has been hidden." Jesus Christ has been hidden.

I am not saying that he has not been manifested in the Church. We know that he has been manifested in the Church. I am saying that he has been hidden because he has not been manifested on a consistent basis. Evangelism is not so much trying to win a soul here and a soul there, though evangelism does win souls. But God has a higher meaning of evangelism and it is this: When a people manifest his nature at all times, the glory fills the temple to such a degree that the temple is not even seen—only the glory is seen. *Then* people will *flow* to Mt. Zion and say, "Men and brethren, what must we do to be saved?" *That* is the highest realm of evangelism, and that is where we are, in this time.

If the body of Christ is flowing correctly, pastors are able to send people from their Churches out to minister a *pure* word. If the body of Christ goes to the place that God wants it to go to, there will be people in the body who can go preach a word of fullness, a word that will bring an uncovering of the Christ, a word that will bring the joy of the Lord, a word that will bring maturity to the body of Christ.

Revelation 1:19 and Revelation 1:4

The chart in appendix H compares these two scriptures. What were the things that John saw that he was commanded to "write" in Revelation 1:19? He was on the isle of "my killing," "my death," and he looked behind him. He saw a finished work—and he saw how the Church was involved with that finished work.

Then in Revelation chapter 6, John had a vision of the horses. These are part of "the things which thou hast seen" in Revelation 1:19. When he saw the horses, he saw something that happened over 2000 years ago. In the horses and in the seals, John saw what Jesus accomplished at the cross. So the "hast seen" is what John saw. The first seal was the white horse, the perfect earth walk of Jesus. He was tempted in all points but never sinned, and that is what qualified him to be the spotless Lamb that went to the cross. John saw a white horse—the holy, righteous earth walk of Jesus. That is seal number one.

Then John saw seal number two, the red horse, which reveals that Jesus became sin. The third seal opened and John saw the black horse, which represents Jesus dying spiritually. The fourth seal was the pale horse, which was Jesus going into hell. The fifth seal was the souls slain under the brazen altar. That is what is happening right now. We are being beheaded of any residue in our minds. We are at the finish line, but we are coming out to find out how we *got* to the finish line. The reason we can experience this is because Jesus wore a crown of thorns. He identified with the cursed thinking of Adam when he wore that crown of thorns. Now we can come to understanding and receive the Spirit of wisdom and revelation in the knowledge of him, as Paul prayed in Ephesians 1:17. We can have the veil that was done away at the cross (2 Corinthians 3:14), taken away from our minds as we come to understand this. This constitutes our being beheaded under the brazen altar (Revelation 6:9 and 20:4).

The next seal was an earthquake, which represents the resurrection. There was an earthquake at the resurrection. The seventh seal was silence in heaven for about half an hour. When you find out that the work is completed, there will be some silence. You'll be like Abraham. A great horror of darkness will come upon you and you will realize that you have been involved in works of the flesh that cannot add one cubit to your stature. We have to understand that it is not works, although we do works. But the works must spring forth from the spirit, and they *will* when we understand the death, burial, and resurrection and our identification with it. The revelation will walk itself out when we get true understanding—not just information, not just head knowledge. My desire is not to just fill your head with a bunch of information, but with truth. Truth has life.

Remember, in Revelation 5:1, the book *within* was sealed on the backside with seven seals. We have a book within. As we gain understanding, the book within is opened. As the seals of understanding are loosed or broken, then out will flow the book of life on a consistent basis.

In Revelation chapter 1, they were experiencing the Holy Place dimension because it talks about the candlestick, and the candlestick is in the Holy Place dimension. When we get into Revelation chapter 4, Jesus tells John to "Come up hither." That is telling us that we are not throwing the gifts away, but we are not just about gifts. The baptism of the Holy Spirit is a down payment. It is the Greek word *arrhabon*, and it means "an engagement ring.[22]" You are just engaged in the Holy Place. That is where the Holy Spirit shows up on your doorstep with a box of chocolate covered prophesies and a bouquet of the word of knowledge, as Lynn Hiles says. That is wonderful, and that is what we need in that realm, but that is just the engagement period. Everything in the Holy Place realm is necessary—but not sufficient. We must go on to maturity.

In Revelation chapter 4, when Jesus says, "Come up hither," he is not talking about a literal rapture. He is talking about our coming into the experience of the Most Holy Place where we are already positionally seated. He is not asking us to throw the baby out with the bath water—we will continue to move in the gifts of the spirit. He is not taking the gifts away but he is bringing us up into a higher dimension where we don't think that we have to have a prophecy and we don't run after a prophecy. He is bringing us into a place where we can hear him clearly because we have the mind of Christ. And of course, when we hurt we want someone to lay hands on us. We are certainly believing the Lord to heal our bodies until total manifestation comes. I've heard people say, "God gives us a little heaven to go to heaven with." We also need a little healing to go to wholeness with. There is nothing wrong with the gifts. We are not throwing them out; we are just saying there is something higher. The gifts of the "in part" realm are necessary but not sufficient to mature us. We must "come up hither" and when we do, we'll find out what the gifts are really for. Everything takes on a higher perspective when viewed from the Most Holy Place. From here we see the whole picture. From here we see reality.

This is what the little Shulamite woman experienced. This is what little Ruth experienced when she came to Boaz, who represents Jesus Christ. When Ruth uncovered his feet, guess where he was. At midnight—which is the *end* of one day and the *beginning* of another day—he was laying, resting, by a heap of corn or grain. A corn of wheat speaks of death. Ruth uncovered his feet and saw that his judgment was her judgment. Then when Boaz redeemed her, they consummated the marriage and gave birth to a manchild. That is where we are spiritually. The book of Revelation is about this higher level of intimacy.

The next thing John saw in Revelation 1:19 was "the things which are." This is talking about trumpets, but not the seven trumpets in Revelation chapter 8. There are different trumpets in Revelation and we do not want to get them confused. Here, "the things which are" is talking about trumpeting or sounding something which is true *because of* what happened at the cross of Calvary. Then it goes on to say, "and the things which shall be hereafter." This is the *product* of what is true because of what happened at the cross of Calvary.

Then, Revelation 1:4 speaks to the same three tenses also, but John begins with the present, flashes back to the past, and then to the future, *which is now!* In Revelation 16, we see the Day of Atonement where our mind is renewed to the fullness of the death of Christ and our identification with it. The "which is to come" is Revelation chapters 21 and 22, where we see *as a result of* the seven vials of blood poured upon our heads in chapter 16, a city out of which flows a pure river of life! *And* everything the river comes in contact with is going to live and receive life! This is what we see in the book of Revelation—Passover, Unleavened Bread, Firstfruits, Pentecost, Trumpets, Atonements, and Tabernacles. It's all about Jesus Christ.

Previously we have seen Passover, Unleavened Bread, and Firstfruits. We find Pentecost in Revelation chapters 6 and 7, in the sealing of the saints. The book of Ephesians tells us that when we receive the baptism of the Holy Spirit we are sealed with the Holy Spirit of promise. That sealing is just the down payment. In the book of Revelation we see that we have also been sealed on the backside with *seven* seals—the fullness of what is yet to come. As we understand the horses, and as we understand that John received the symbolic book of Revelation, those seals, one by one, are broken, and out of our bellies flow the river of life. When we do not try to interpret the book of Revelation literally, but we see that it was written in sign and symbol, we can mount these four horses as they gallop over the mountain tops (Joel 2). We are blowing the trumpet in Zion, trumpeting the same message that John trumpeted in the book of Revelation.

The last feast is Tabernacles, which has three aspects: Trumpets, Atonements, and Tabernacles. We see seven trumpets in Revelation chapters 8, 9, and 11. These are not seven literal trumpets that toot. "Seven" means fullness. These are people that have their mind renewed to the death, burial, and resurrection and their identification with it, and they are trumpeting the word that will bring people into fullness. They are ministering a word from the throne. The Melchisedec priesthood is seated, and they minister *from* the throne. They minister a word that causes a people to realize that they are in the throne too. In *spirit*, we are already in the Most Holy Place. What we are doing now is looking around with our *mind* in the Most Holy Place to see what is there. When we see what is in the Most Holy Place and how we got there, something is going to happen within our lives. There *has* to be a change! We are living in the time of that change!

The "God in the sky" theory began with the Jews. But Elijah did not find the Lord in the wind, the earthquake, or the fire. He found the Lord in the still, small voice. The most exciting hour we have ever lived in, is this hour—right now. We are not going to go somewhere as in some physical heaven. Heaven is not a place, it is a Presence! Heaven is wherever God is and God dwells in us! He has planted eternity in our hearts and in our minds (Ecclesiastes 3:11, Amplified Bible)! The Kingdom of God goes wherever we take it because it is in us (Luke 17:20-21)! We are not going to go somewhere. We are going to GROW somewhere! We are going to experience what Paul experienced—being caught up into the highest heaven (2 Corinthians 12:2). We are being lifted out from among the dead even though we are in the body (Philippians 3:11, Amplified Bible). And yet Paul still lived on earth and ministered from the throne to the people on the earth.

As important an event as "the literal rapture" is to the Church, one would think God would have written about it in the Bible, especially in the book of Revelation! The Church is declaring, "We want to see the coming of the Lord!" How much do you want to see his coming? Do you want it enough to grow up? Our maturing hastens his coming. The word declares that Jesus is the King of kings. He is coming to rule and to reign as the King of kings, so we must be about the business of maturing into kingship. We must give him some kings to be the King *through*. The word declares that without holiness, no man shall see the Lord. We, in him, and he in us, *is* the event! Our coming up hither—our maturing to the point that we can have intimacy with the Lord and reproduce his nature out of out lives is *his event—his inheritance!* And it is beginning to happen as these seals are broken.

Trumpets then, an aspect of Tabernacles, is what we see in Revelation chapters 8, 9 and 11, as the seven trumpets. We will deal with these seven trumpets in depth in those chapters.

Atonements is seen in Revelation chapter 16 where we see the seven vials of blood poured out upon our heads, which again, is understanding the fullness of the death of Christ. In Revelation chapter 9, we read about men who are tormented for five months and they want to die, but they can't die. In the Old Testament, they could not live because of the curse, but in the New Testament, they can't die! Why? Because it is already done. It is the death of your old man, your old nature. In the New Testament, the worst thing that can happen to us is *not* getting the revelation that we were already crucified. Just over 2000 years ago I died and went to heaven. As we receive that revelation, we begin to walk in it. The revelation will walk itself out because the anointing is on the word.

So in Revelation chapter 9, they are tormented for five months and they can't die. The period of time from the end of Passover to the beginning of Tabernacles, is five months. They beg to die for five months! Begging won't kill your old man—*believing* shows you that he's already dead. It's not in *doing,* but in *viewing.* There are some glorious truths that we are going to see when we get to these chapters of Revelation. The book of Revelation is going to release the life of God out of us. And it is going to reveal the process by which that life is released out of us. We will come to the place where we *experience* Revelation chapter 22—no more curse! Out of the place where Jesus is resting flows a river of life! A pure river of life that comes from the throne and the Lamb—and it comes right out of us. Jesus said, "Out of your belly shall flow rivers of living waters." Strong's Concordance says that the "belly" is the "heart" or the "womb." What is in our belly if we are eating the Feast of Passover? Rest. A pure river of life. Jesus is birthed out of our bellies. Tabernacles is a second look at Passover. This is the objective of ministering the book of Revelation. The objective is not just to give out revelation, or another "really neat way" to look at the book of Revelation. It is to experience what is there to be experienced. It is to find that place of rest.

In Matthew chapter 27 Judas hung himself, which is a picture of trying to crucify the flesh. If he would have waited, he could have let Jesus' hanging be his hanging. Many in the Church are committing suicide in that sense, because they do not understand that the old man is dead. I read a news letter from deeper life ministers talking about "glorious things" like "trudging along until one day the climax will happen and BOOM! We'll be what we are supposed to be." They were saying that the way it is going to happen is as we go through hell, and suffering, and going through trials. But they have not taken a second look. All they were talking about has already happened! God's way of cleansing us is through the word. We need to get out of the wilderness experience, and the wilderness mentality of "Woe is me; I've got to go through this." Not until Isaiah saw *and understood* that the old man was dead was he able to see the

Lord high and lifted up with his train filling the temple. When Isaiah saw *and understood* that the old man was dead *and* when he saw *and understood* that the Lord was high and lifted up, he was able to speak, "Holy, holy, holy, is the Lord of hosts; the whole earth is full of his glory." We need to be like Isaiah and move from "Woe, woe, woe" to "Holy, Holy, Holy" as the coal is taken from the brazen altar and touches our lips, empowering us to speak with authority concerning the death of Christ! Old King Uzziah died! The old man is crucified, dead, and buried.

Maturity does not happen by "what the devil throws at us." The Church is preaching such a powerful devil! All I want to minister is a great big God, a defeated devil, and a dead old man! That is what is going to bring this unveiling of the Lord Jesus in our lives.

The last aspect of Tabernacles is the Feast of Tabernacles. This is what Revelation 1:4 states as "which is to come" and what Revelation 1:19 states as "the things which shall be." The Feast of Tabernacles is manifested in Revelation chapters 21 and 22, where God Tabernacles with the people. This aspect will intensify as time goes on, as we will see.

The Seven Vials

We have talked about some interesting things concerning the word "vial" in Revelation chapter 16 in reference to the "vials of wrath." The word that is used for "vial" or "vials" is used only three times in the Septuagint. It is the "bowl" or cup that was on the table of shewbread (Exodus 25:29, Exodus 37:16, and Numbers 4:7). The bowl on the table of shewbread was full of wine, which represents the blood of Jesus. That tells me that the vials being poured out upon the earth is not something literal that is going to happen in the earth to a Church world that just doesn't have it together, or to a world that is in sin. The "vials of wrath" are vials of blood that are being poured out upon the earth or being poured out upon our heads. This is symbolic of our coming to the table of shewbread, which gets us into the experience of the Most Holy—partaking of bread and wine and entering into rest—period. What a great revelation! That is as exciting as the word "testimony"—the martyrdom of Jesus Christ and *our* "testimony," or our martyrdom. We overcome by the blood of the Lamb (the death) and by the word of our martyrdom! We are dead and our new life is hidden in Christ (Colossians 3). If we are going to let the Bible interpret the Bible, we will find these things there.

Revelation—The Complement Of Genesis

These Churches can represent the seven days of creation (see Appendix E). Further in this study, we will see that these Churches represent a *new* creation. Revelation is about a book that brings a *de*generation of what Adam brought. We were generated—we were with God from before the foundation of the world. Then we were *de*generated through Adam's sin. Now we are *re*generated. We were created, *de*created, and *re*created. The book of Revelation is about a de-creation of all the things that Adam brought upon the face of the earth and it is about the recreation—what God brought through Christ Jesus.

Day 1

In Genesis 1:3, God said, "Let there be light." In Revelation 2:5, Jesus tells the Church at Ephesus that if they do not overcome, their light is going to be taken away. If they overcome, they will keep the light. In Revelation 2:5, Ephesus speaks of day one of creation:

> Remember therefore from whence thou art fallen, and repent, and do the first works; or else I will come unto thee quickly, and will remove thy candlestick out of his place, except thou repent.

Day 2

In Genesis 1:6, there was a separation on day two when God said, "Let there be a firmament in the midst of the waters, and let it divide the waters from the waters. In Revelation 2:9, we see a separation in the Church at Smyrna:

> I know thy works, and tribulation, and poverty (but

thou art rich), and I know the blasphemy of them which say they are Jews, and are not, but are the synagogue of Satan.

In Smyrna, the second Church, we find the separation of a heavenly people from an earthly people.

Day 3

In Genesis 1:9-11, God created plants on the third day that brought forth bread and wine. In Revelation 2:17, the third Church at Pergamos will have hidden manna and a white stone—their own personalized admission ticket to experience the Feast of Tabernacles, if they overcome—by seeing that they are *in* the Overcoming One:

> He that hath an ear, let him hear what the Spirit saith unto the churches. To him that overcometh will I give to eat of the hidden manna, and will give him a white stone, and in the stone a new name written, which no man knoweth saving he that receiveth it.

Day 4

In Genesis 1:14-18, God created the sun, the moon, and the stars as rulers on day four. Now look at the promise to the overcomers at the fourth Church, Thyatira, in Revelation 2:26-28:

> And he that overcometh, and keepeth my works unto the end, to him will I give power over the nations: And he shall rule them with a rod of iron; as the vessels of a potter shall they be broken to shivers: even as I received of My Father. And I will give him the morning star.

The phrase, "and keepeth *my* works" is not talking about giving tithes or the works that *we* do, although we do give tithes and do good works—but we do these things because we *are* the righteousness of God. The phrase "and keepeth my works" refers to our understanding that his works were *finished* from the foundations of the world. Remember, Jesus is speaking to his bondservants—those who are able to understand spiritual language because their ear is nailed to the door. Jesus knows that we understand that we can't work to add one cubit to our stature because by grace we are saved through faith, not by works lest any man should boast. In Revelation chapter 1 we found that we are blessed if we *keep* these things that are written. We keep these things in our understanding, not in our works. We overcome by the blood of the Lamb and by the word of our testimony. Romans 12:2 tells us that when we renew our minds we will be transformed. We will overcome by realizing we're in the overcoming one.

In Revelation 2:27 we see the phrase, "As the vessels of a potter shall they be broken to shivers: even as I received of My Father." Again, this is not some horror story. Jesus is using symbolic language to tell his bondservants that Adam, the flesh, does not rule us—we're governed by the Spirit. Adam was broken to shivers at the cross and all who are in Christ are governed by the Spirit of Jesus. He has given us power over the nations and we are ruling with a rod of iron. Iron does not bend, it does not compromise. We are a people who are uncompromisingly righteous.

On day four, God created the sun, the moon, and the stars as rulers. In Revelation 2:28, he gives us the morning star. So Jesus tells the overcomers at Thyatira that he will give them the morning star so that they can rule and reign.

Day 5

In Genesis 1:20-22 the birds in the heavens, the animals on the land, and the fish in the sea were created on day five. This represents spiritually alive people, carnal people, and spiritually dead people. In Revelation chapter 3, verses 4, 3, and 1, we see the spiritual, the carnal, and the dead people of the fifth Church at Sardis. Look at the spiritual people in Revelation 3:4:

> Thou hast a few names even in Sardis which have
> not defiled their garments; and they shall walk with

me in white: for they are worthy.

Those are the birds in the heavens, the heavenly people. Then we have the animals on the land, the carnal people, in Revelation 3:3:

> Remember therefore how thou has received and heard, and hold fast, and repent. If therefore thou shalt not watch, I will come on thee as a thief, and thou shalt not know what hour I will come upon thee.

Here he is talking to born-again, spirit-filled people. He says they need to repent; they need to change their minds. Obviously they had some carnality. They represent the animals on the land. We have a heavenly people, a carnal people, and the fish in the sea, (sea speaks of humanity), a dead people, as we see in Revelation 3:1:

> And unto the angel of the church in Sardis write; 'These things saith he that hath the seven Spirits of God, and the seven stars; I know thy works, that thou hast a name that thou livest, and art dead.

So, in the fifth Church, we have a spiritual people, a carnal people, and a dead people.

Day 6

Then on the sixth day, God made man. In Genesis 1:26-27, God created man in his image and after his likeness and gave him dominion. Man became the tabernacle or dwelling of God. Revelation 3:12 says:

> Him that overcometh will I make a pillar in the temple of my God, and he shall go no more out: and I will write upon him the name of my God, and the name of the city of my God, which is the new Jerusalem, which cometh down out of heaven from my God: and I will write upon him my new name.

Those who realize that they are in the overcoming one are pillars in the tabernacle of God. The letter to the sixth Church at Philadelphia reveals an overcoming people as pillars in his house. People are the house of God. We are the tabernacle of God!

When we get into Revelation chapter 4, we see that Jesus tells John, "Come up hither." Remember, in Revelation chapter 1 the candlesticks are in the Holy Place. Now he says that he wants the people that are in the Holy Place mentality to open the door, and if they open the door, he will sup with them as he promised in Revelation 3:20. He did not say, "We're going to have breakfast in the Outer Court and then we're going to have lunch in the Holy Place." He said, "We are going to sup." That is the "super supper!" That is the Feast of Tabernacles. What announces the beginning of the Feast of Tabernacles? The trumpet, or the voice with the clear sounding message that John heard in Revelation 4:1.

In Israel, the biggest meal of the day was at the *end* of the day. What happens after the big meal at the end of the day? Intimacy and rest. We are presently in the seventh day from Adam, the third day from Jesus—the Lord's Day—the day of Tabernacles—the day of rest. He says if you'll open the door, I'll come in and we'll experience a Feast of Tabernacles, we'll have a super supper. He is the door and he is continually being opened up to us in our understanding. There is more than one door in the book of Revelation—door #1 (Revelation 3:8), door #2 (Revelation 3:20), and door #3 (Revelation 4:1). A door is a greater entering into salvation. We are continually being saved. We are continually being changed from glory to glory. Remember, Revelation is symbolic.

Jesus begins to deal with the seventh Church in Revelation 3:14. He is saying that he does not want us to be cold, in the Outer Court, just coming in and having breakfast. He does not want us to be caught in the middle, just having lunch with him in the Holy Place. He wants us to sit down to a hot meal with him in the Most Holy Place! If we are not cold and not hot, but lukewarm, somewhere caught in the middle, he says he is just going to spew out. It's as if he is saying, "If you're caught somewhere in the middle, I just feel sick at my stomach."

Jesus is telling John in chapter 4, "Come up hither." Come up to the super supper. Obviously, a door must have been opened in chapter 4. There must be a people who open the door. There must be a people who do not want to mess around in the Outer Court and just have breakfast with the Lord. There must be a people who don't want to just "do lunch" with the Lord. There must be a people who realize they are vitamin deficient and need a full course meal with the spinach (the bitter herbs) and meat (the Lamb) and things that will make them mature and grow in health and wholeness. Surely there is a people who are saying, "We want to partake of the Feast of Tabernacles with you, Lord!"

We are already eating the super supper. We are already seated at the King's table. We already have five more messes than the rest of Joseph's brothers (five is the number of grace). The present day ministry of the Holy Spirit in a Melchisedec priesthood is taking a veil away in the minds of those who have religion—those who have been blinded by the god of this world. The veil is being removed as they come to understand the grace of God!

Day 7

In Genesis 2:2, God rested on the seventh day. In Revelation 3:21 we see the seventh Church at Laodicea, who were lukewarm, wretched, miserable, poor, blind and naked *in the Holy Place realm*—born-again and Spirit-filled—but still immature:

> To him that overcometh will I grant to sit with me in
> my throne, even as I also overcame, and am set
> down with my Father in his throne.

The word "sit" speaks of rest. When we are sitting, we are resting in the Most Holy Place dimension. To overcome is to sit and be at rest with him. We are laboring to enter into rest, to fill our minds with the truth about the finished work of Calvary. We've opened the door and we are partaking of the super supper. It is not some big meal far away on a planet called heaven where there are people at a big table eating chicken and throwing the bones down on the people on the earth, as we have been taught. What a carnal thought! We are partaking of the bread and the wine, which is referred to as the marriage supper of the Lamb. What is on the menu? Roasted Lamb.

Old Testament History and the Seven Churches

As we know, some teach the seven Churches of Revelation as the dispensations of the history of the Church, but when we come to Laodicea, there is nothing good said about that Church. But everything said about us, today's Church, is good—even better—it's God! Haggai 2:9 tells us that the present day Church will have more glory than the former house. The Old Testament is full of wonderful things to say about the third day Church, the Kingdom of God. I heard someone on television recently, talking about "the pathetic state of the Church today." We need to make a distinction between religious Babylon and the true Church, the Kingdom of God. These seven Churches speak of a new creation.

When Adam transgressed in the garden, we were not just separated from God in our thinking, or Jesus would not have had to become sin. We were "bad to the bone." We were dead in sin and trespasses. If we were just separated from God in our minds through the fall of man, then the only thing Jesus would have needed to do is wear a crown of thorns to deal with our cursed thinking. If we were separated from God in mind only, the crown of thorns alone would have brought us into union with God. If we were only separated from God in our mind, Jesus would not have had to die spiritually. The crown of thorns that Jesus wore dealt only with the *residue* of Adam's *thinking*. But Jesus did much more that just wear a crown of thorns. He laid the ax to the root because we were *dead* in sins and trespasses! He became sin that we might be made the righteousness of God in him (2 Corinthians 5:21).

Metaphysical, eastern philosophies have crept into the Church and they are teaching that sort of thing, but we were *totally* separated. If not, Paul wouldn't have said, "I pray God your whole spirit and soul and body be preserved blameless unto the coming of our Lord Jesus Christ." The conjunction "and" joins the three different parts of us. When Jesus went to the cross of Calvary, he took upon himself even *more* than the first Adam brought into the world by the fall—Hebrews says "much more"—because Jesus was doing nothing but ministering love to the people. That is all he was doing—ministering love to people who crucified him on an old rugged cross. He took upon himself all that Adam had become, and more!

Everything was included in the death of Christ.

Historical View Of Churches

Jesus taught the disciples to pray, "Thy kingdom come, thy will be done *in* earth as it is in heaven," because he *wants* to answer that prayer. He *is* answering that prayer. He is doing it as a people have their mind renewed to the fact that it is a finished work. It has already happened. It is not something that is *going* to happen, although we do have things to look forward to as this intensifies, as we realize these truths and they walk themselves out in our lives. But we need to realize that he did all he is going to do—we're not waiting on him to do something—he is waiting on us! The throttle is in our hand. The time is at hand, as we read in Revelation 1:3. The Greek says "the time is in your hand." The Kingdom of heaven is at hand! He is waiting on us to get this understanding! Natural Israel is not God's time clock. *We* are his time clock, if he has a time clock in that sense[23]. He is waiting on us and the renewal of our minds. As we partake of the Lamb, the experience of the marriage between spirit and soul can happen, so that the revelation, the *apokalupsis,* the unveiling of that which is hidden, can come forth and manifest *as* his Kingdom.

Ephesus

Let us look at the seven Churches and their correlation with Old Testament history. All seven of these Churches were in Asia Minor. In Revelation 2:7, the Church at Ephesus correlates with the Garden of Eden:

> He that hath an ear, let him hear what the Spirit saith unto the churches: To him that overcometh will I give to eat of the tree of life, which is in the midst of the paradise of God.

The tree of life was in the garden (Genesis 2:9). The piece of furniture in the Holy of Holies is the Ark of the Covenant. In the Ark of the Covenant are the unbroken tables of stone (a Book of record), Aaron's rod that budded, and the pot of manna. Aaron's rod represents the tree of life. Even in the dimension of the Most Holy Place, our minds must be filled with the death of Christ in order for us to experience oneness with the mercy seat and manifest the grace and the mercy of God. The tables of stone are *inside* the Ark. God said he would write his word on the tablets of our hearts. Aaron's rod, the tree of life is *inside* the Ark. The pot of manna is *inside* the Ark. Archeologists have been searching for the Ark of the Covenant, but they have been digging in the wrong earth! God has hidden it very well! It is *Christ in us!*—the hope of *realizing* the glory! It's time to unearth the Ark!

Smyrna

In Revelation 2:10, the Church at Smyrna represents the age of the Patriarchs:

> Fear none of those things which thou shalt suffer. Behold, the devil shall cast some of you into prison, that ye may be tried, and ye shall have tribulation ten days; be thou faithful unto death, and I will give thee a crown of life.

In the Old Testament, Joseph, a perfect type of Christ, was the one who was in prison and received a crown of life (Genesis 41:38-44). He was sold into slavery and was in prison in Potiphar's house. Then he became ruler over all the land of Egypt.

Pergamos

Pergamos, of Revelation 2:14 represents the wilderness wandering period of the Old Testament:

> But I have a few things against thee, because thou hast there them that hold the doctrine of Balaam who taught Balac to cast a stumbling block before the children of Israel, to eat things sacrificed unto idols, and to commit fornication.

We find this account of the wilderness wandering in Numbers beginning with chapter 22, to the final account in Numbers 31:16. They worshipped Baal, they were prostitutes, and later, Jezebel entertained the prophets of Baal and supported Baal worship.

Thyatira

The Church at Thyatira represents the time of the kings. Thyatira speaks of "a female woman." Jezebel's influence goes all the way to the book of Revelation where we see in chapter 17, a woman clothed in scarlet with a golden cup. This golden cup is not empty like the silver cup, the bitter cup that Jesus drank. The golden cup is full of abominations and the filthiness of her fornication. Jezebel thinks that she is the ruler of the kings of the earth. That is what we saw in the people's lives during the time that the kings ruled. Look at Revelation 2:18-27:

> And unto the angel of the church in Thyatira write; 'These things saith the Son of God, who hath his eyes like unto a flame of fire, and his feet are like fine brass; I know thy works, and charity, and service, and faith, and thy patience, and thy works; and the last to be more than the first. Notwithstanding I have a few things against thee, because thou sufferest that woman Jezebel, which calleth herself a prophetess, to teach and to seduce my servants to commit fornication, and to eat things sacrificed unto idols. And I gave her space to repent of her fornication; and she repented not. Behold, I will cast her into a bed, and them that commit adultery with her into great tribulation, except they repent of their deeds. And I will kill her children with death; and all the churches shall know that I am he which searcheth the reins and hearts: and I will give unto every one of you according to your works. But unto you I say, and unto the rest in Thyatira, as many as have not this doctrine, and which have not known the depths of Satan, as they speak; I will put

upon you none other burden. But that which ye have already hold fast till I come. And he that overcometh, and keepeth my works unto the end, to him will I give power over the nations: And he shall rule them with a rod of iron; as the vessels of a potter shall they be broken to shivers: even as I received of my Father.

The people of the Old Testament were highly influenced by the worship of Baal and by "that woman Jezebel." We find much in 1 and 2 Kings concerning that woman. Then, in Revelation 2:27, we see the rule of the King of kings.

How does Jezebel teach God's servants to commit fornication? We have to remember that Revelation is a spiritual book, written in sign and symbol. The name "Jezebel" means "an unchaste dwelling." Jezebel teaches God's servants to commit fornication by teaching that we can have intimacy with Jesus and not be married to him. We cannot be married to Jesus until we see that our first husband, Adam, is dead. He was nailed to the cross, crucified, died, and buried. We were widowed at the cross. But when the last Adam, Jesus, the life-giving spirit arose, we arose with him. Now we are free to be married to Jesus and give birth to his nature through our lives. We were married at the resurrection of Jesus. Because of our Babylonian captivity in the religious system, we have not fully understood what actually happened during those three days and three nights from the cross to the throne. We were widowed from the old man and we were married to the New Man. Both happened. Until we see that our old man is dead and was crucified with Christ and now we are brand new creations, we are in idolatry, which is spiritual fornication. Jesus has a bride without spot or wrinkle who is saying, "I was widowed at the cross but Jesus, my kinsman redeemer married me and wants me to "come up hither" so the marriage can be consummated." Compare this with the great whore in Revelation 18:7 who says, "I sit a queen, and am *no* widow, and shall see no sorrow."

And how does Jezebel teach God's servants to eat things sacrificed to idols? Notice in Revelation 2:19 that Jesus mentions "works" not once, but twice! Then he says that the last works are *more* than the first works! A suitable environment for Jezebel's idol worship! Remember the Church at Ephesus? Jesus told them to repent from where they had fallen and do the *first* works. Do you remember when you were born again? You heard that Jesus died on the cross to purchase your salvation and you humbly came and simply believed and received. That was your first work. That is all he wants. When we begin to add to Jesus' finished work of the cross, we get into religious works of the flesh, AKA—self righteousness. God does not want our filthy rags. He wants our first works—humility, believing, and receiving. But we will understand more with verse 18, where Jesus told Thyatira something about himself in order to help her make the changes she needed to make in order to overcome. What did he say? "My judgment was your judgment. You don't have to work for your salvation anymore. I've paid the price." Then in verses 26 and 27 Jesus said, "If you get the message, I will give you power over the nations and we will rule with a rod of iron." In verse 28, they receive what their soul has been longing for—the morning star, the Lord Jesus.

We can find out a little more about eating things sacrificed to idols from Psalm 50. I encourage you to read this Psalm in light of Revelation 3:18-29. But look at Psalm 50:13-14: "Will I eat the flesh of bulls or drink the blood of goats? Offer unto God *thanksgiving* and pay thy vows (could he mean marriage vows?) unto the Most High." He desires *mercy* instead of sacrifice. Why? Because out of God's great mercy, Jesus *was* the one and only perfect sacrifice! God's judgment and wrath was fully vented at the cross of Calvary once and for all—and Jesus bore it *all!* Will he eat the flesh of our dead works and drink the blood of our self-crucifixion? Only when we can identify with the finished work of the cross, realizing that we were crucified with Christ, our old man is dead and our new man is risen in Christ, will we be able to enter into rest and cleanse ourselves from dead works.

Psalm 50:21 says, "These things hast thou done, and I kept silence; thou thoughtest that I was altogether such an one as thyself ...." This is what God is saying to Jezebel and her first Adam husband—"You thought I was just like you!" We have created an *image* of God in the Church—a God that is judgmental and critical and fault-finding and condemning. Jezebel, the un-renewed mind of man, the doctrine of man in the Church, causes us to eat things sacrificed to this "god" that *we have created!* How do we "eat" those things? By making them part of our belief system. What Jezebel and her children are saying is, "We've got to work! We must pay for our sins because what Jesus did was really not enough. And no matter how much we work, it will never be good enough because God is just waiting for us to mess up one time so he can knock our lights out."

Are you beginning to see the Babylonian confusion that controls the religious system? Our works *will* never be good enough. That is why Jesus came. And he *finished* the work. And guess what else happened. Our lights *were* knocked out—at the cross where we were crucified with Christ. When we accepted our salvation, we accepted the reality that our lives in Adam were sacrificed with Jesus at the cross. We accepted the reality that only one man lives in this temple (our body) and that is Jesus Christ. We accepted the reality that Adam is dead and our new life is hidden in Christ. But because of the veil that blinds our minds, we have never known the terms of the Covenant agreement! And no one but the Holy Spirit can tell us what is written in the will. Today, the Holy Spirit is removing the veil so we can read the contract that he has *already written* on our minds, because we've come into the maturity required for the inheritance.

Unger's Bible dictionary says that idolatry is "the paying of divine honor to any created thing ... the worship of Jehovah under image or symbol! We have had an *image* of God presented to us in the Church! We have *created* an image of him in our low thinking carnal minds. The majority of the Church world has not been worshipping God. They've been worshipping the Pharisees—submitting to their "rule"—in bondage to a religious system. Every "woe" Jesus said of the Pharisees, he was saying of Jezebel (Matthew 23:13-39). We must renew our minds to the fact that the old man is dead and there is only one man left—Christ the Lord—and he loves us with an everlasting love. His mercy endures forever. His grace endures forever. His love endures forever and ever, and ever. Amen.

Sardis

Sardis, we find in Revelation 3:1:

> And unto the angel of the church in Sardis write; 'These things saith he that hath the seven Spirits of God, and the seven stars; I know thy works, that thou hast a name that thou livest, and art dead.

This represents the time of Israel's Babylonian captivity. The people were dead spiritually as recorded in Jeremiah 25:1-14. In this passage, Jeremiah tells them that their deadness is one of the reasons they entered into Babylonian captivity. The reason people are in Babylonian confusion today is because they have a residue of death yet in their minds. Paul wrote to Timothy about a woman, that even while she lives, she is dead. That does not necessarily mean that she was not a born-again and spirit-filled person. You can be twice dead and plucked up by the roots while you sit there on the Church pew—or worse yet, in the pulpit! We have a lot of people today in the Church who are born-again and spirit-filled, yet they are dead in dogmas and traditions of man. The word of God is powerful, yet, if we are unenlightened, there is something else that we can give power that causes the word of God to have no effect in our lives—traditions and doctrines of man make the word of God of none effect! You can have your head so full of traditions and doctrines that you are dead as far as progressing in God.

Philadelphia

Philadelphia represents the release of Babylonian captivity in Revelation 3:8:

> I know thy works: behold, I have set before thee an open door, and no man can shut it: for thou hast a little strength, and has kept my word, and hast not denied my name.

In 2 Chronicles 36:22-23, in Isaiah 45, and in the book of Ezra, we find that by the mouth of Cyrus, the Israelites were released from Babylonian captivity and they began to build the temple. This is the open door. They could leave Babylonian captivity and go back home.

Laodicea

In Revelation 3:16-20, Laodicea represents the Jews in Jesus' day:

> So then because thou art lukewarm, and neither cold or hot, I will spue thee out of my mouth. Because thou sayest, "I am rich, and increased with goods, and have need of nothing;" and knowest not that thou art wretched, and miserable, and poor, and blind, and naked: I counsel thee to buy of me gold tried in the fire, that thou mayest be clothed, and that the shame of thy nakedness do not appear; and anoint thine eyes with eyesalve, that thou mayest see, As many as I love, I rebuke and chasten: be zealous therefore, and repent. Behold, I stand at the door, and knock: if any man hear my voice, and open the door, I will come in to him, and will sup with him, and he with me.

This does not represent the present day Church, because only good things are said about the third day Church. God saves the best for last. No matter what kinds of problems we see in the Church today, lukewarmness and so forth, God still says something good about us. God still speaks blessing over us. The word "bless," in Acts 3:26, is *eulogeo,* from which we get the word "eulogy." A little more than 2000 years ago, he spoke a eulogy over us. We were blessed at the cross. Jesus blessed us in turning us away from our iniquities. Even when we were in iniquity, dead in sins and trespasses, he still spoke a good, healthy, word of blessing over us. That word was about our death and resurrection.

Revelation 3:16-20 represents the Jews in Jesus' day, which he spewed out of his mouth. He divorced natural Israel. Jesus said "I would have gathered you like a hen gathers her chicks, but you would not. You wouldn't open the door and let me come in and sup with you." In Jesus' time, the Jews wanted absolutely nothing to do with that. But even though God divorced natural Israel, he will have mercy on her that had not obtained mercy (Hosea 2:23). At Calvary, mercy was given to *all* men (John 12:32).

Promise To Overcomers Is Most Holy Place Blessings

Everything that was promised to the overcomers in Revelation, were Most Holy Place provisions. As we saw in Revelation chapter 1, these people were in the Holy Place in their experience. The purpose of the book of Revelation is to bring us from a Holy Place experience (by seeing the death of Christ and our identification with it), to a Most Holy Place experience where we are ruling and reigning from the throne.

Ephesus

In Ephesus, they are promised to eat of the tree of life which is in the midst of the paradise of God. Where do we see the tree of life in the Most Holy Place? In the Ark, in Aaron's rod that budded.

Smyrna

The Church at Smyrna was promised a crown of life. If we identify with the death of Christ, we have a crown of life. In the Most Holy Place, there was a crown that held the mercy seat on top of the Ark of the Covenant. This represents our mind being renewed to the death of Christ so that *we can become a mercy seat* and minister nothing but the grace and mercy of God.

Pergamos

To the Church at Pergamos, is the promise of hidden manna. Where is hidden manna? In the Most Holy Place, it was in the golden pot, which was in the Ark.

Thyatira

The Church at Thyatira was promised that they would rule and reign. We rule and reign from the Most Holy Place, the throne.

Sardis

The fifth Church, Sardis, was promised white linen. The bottom layer of the covering of the Most Holy Place was made of white linen, which speaks of the righteousness of God.

Philadelphia

The Church of Philadelphia was promised to be a pillar in the house of God. A pillar is a load-bearing part. The name "Philadelphia" means "love as brothers." Paul said in 1 Corinthians 13:7, "Love *bears up* under anything and everything that comes, is ever ready to believe the best of every person, its hopes are fadeless under all circumstances, and it endures everything [without weakening]" (Amplified Bible). That's the kind of pillar I want to be, how about you? The pillars in Moses' tabernacle represent strength and maturity. We do not come into our full strength until we are fully mature. Then, when we minister to someone, when we encourage someone, we become a strength to them. We become a pillar in their temple. God's will for us is to grow up in every way and in all things into Him who is the head, Christ. Listen to the harmony of that scripture in the light of Philadelphia, the Church of love:

> Rather, let our lives lovingly express truth [in all things, speaking truly, dealing truly, living truly]. Enfolded in love, *let us grow up* in every way and in all things into Him Who is the Head, [even] Christ (the Messiah, the Anointed One) (Ephesians 4:15, Amplified version, emphasis added).

When love is mature in our lives, we become a pillar in the house of God. In the ancient house of God, the height of the brazen altar was a cubit and a half. When we speak of height in this sense, we speak of growing up or maturing. The brazen altar represents the cross. A cubit and a half is about thirty inches. Thirty is the number of maturity. The height of the Ark of the Covenant, the mercy seat, and the table of shewbread? A cubit and a half. All of these pieces of furniture typify the death of Christ. Death. Maturity. What is the message? We follow the Lamb wherever he goes (Revelation 14:4). We follow him in humility—simply trusting our heavenly Father. We follow him in courage—taking our stand against religion even if they scourge us in the synagogues and crucify our character in the streets. In love—laying our lives down daily—realizing that persecution brings into manifestation the life of Jesus (2 Corinthians 4:9-11). Peter said, "If ye be reproached for the name of Christ, happy are ye; for the Spirit of glory and of God resteth upon you." This is the full maturity of love's complete perfection (1 John 4:18).

Laodicea

Laodiceans were promised to sit on the throne. That is the Ark of the Covenant—ruling and reigning from the Most Holy Place. Again, this comes as we follow him, looking away [from all that will distract] to Jesus, who is the Leader and the Source of our faith [giving first incentive for our belief] and is also its Finisher [bringing it to maturity and perfection]. He, for the joy [of obtaining the prize] that was set before him, endured the cross, despising and ignoring the shame, and is now seated at the right hand of the throne of God (Hebrews 12:2, Amplified Bible).

The Holy City

When we get to the end of the book of Revelation, we see the holy city as a cube. Every Most Holy Place in the temples and the Tabernacles was a cube, and they grew bigger as time went on. The Most Holy Place in Moses' tabernacle was 10 x 10 x 10. Solomon's was 20 x 20 x 20. In Revelation, the holy city, the new Jerusalem, the Most Holy Place is progressive—and it is foursquare—balanced. Four is the number of creation. When I think of "balance" and "creation," I see a creation that is no longer groaning in the pains of labor and longing for God's sons to be made manifest, but a creation that is set free from its bondage to decay and corruption. I see a creation that has gained an entrance into the glorious freedom of God's children!

The city in Revelation chapter 21 lies in a square. Its length and width and height are equal, measuring 12,000 furlongs or 1500 miles. Both of these numbers are spiritually significant. When we consider the New Jerusalem as 12,000 x 12,000 x 12,000 furlongs, we see the message of the Kingdom of God that knows no end. The number 12 signifies governmental perfection (the Kingdom of God). 12 is the product of 3 (the perfectly divine and heavenly number) and 4 (the number of all that is created). The message is this: the new Jerusalem's King is the creator of heaven and earth and his Kingdom is the canopy of every created thing in heaven and on earth and under the earth and on the sea and all that is in it, crying out together, "To him who is seated on the throne and to the Lamb be ascribed the blessing and the honor and the majesty, glory and splendor, and the power, might and dominion forever, through the eternities of the eternities! Amen!"

When we consider the New Jerusalem, the Most Holy city as 1500 x 1500 x 1500 miles, we see the message of the glory of God. The gematria for "glory of God" is 1500. His glory will fill the earth as the waters cover the sea! It is foursquare glory! It is joy unspeakable and *full of glory* and the half that has never yet been told is now being told! 1500 is also the gematria for "Lord of Glory." And—get this—1500 is the gematria of "light" and "power!" This city has no need of the sun nor of the moon to give light to it, for the splendor and radiance and glory of God illuminate it, and the Lamb is its lamp! The gematria for the phrase in Acts 4:31, "They were all filled with the Holy Spirit and spoke the word of God with boldness," is 1500 x 4![24] All creation brings glory to God in this Kingdom age!

The book of Revelation is about Passover, Pentecost, and Tabernacles. It is about the death of Christ and our identification with it. We are going to see the death, the burial, and the resurrection all the way through the book of Revelation. If this book is the revelation of Jesus Christ, and not the revelation of Newsweek Magazine or what is happening in the world, if it is a symbolic book, then we cannot spiritualize the Lamb and literalize everything else as many in the Church are doing. The *purpose* of this book is to unveil, and uncover, and reveal Christ in manifestation out of a people—to resurrect the body of Christ up out of the earth of our vessels! This is the third day! We are in the here and now with a little book that is opened—and it has only one message—Christ and him crucified and what that means to us, as Lynn Garner sings. The *product* of this book is seen in Revelation chapters 21 and 22. That is what we have to look forward to as the people of God.

We eat of the bread, we drink of the cup, and we are showing forth his death until the unveiling—until the veil that was done away is *taken away* and he is revealed. Now we will begin to see the nature of Christ manifested in our lives consistently. That is what we want. We do not want to just see an "in part" manifestation of Christ from time to time. True evangelism is a people who are experiencing what we are talking about. Then people will run to you and say "Men and brethren, what can we do to be saved? We see something not only *in* you, but flowing *out* of you."

So, it is time for the Church to grow up. Not go up. GROW UP. People say, "We're going to be taken out of this mess here on earth." That is not consistent with scripture. The sons of God are to redeem the groaning creation. We are needed here. Doors are going to open and we are not going to be able to run fast enough with this word (Joel 2:7, Amos 9:13). Why? Because it is time. It is time for this revelation to be revealed so that the seals which have sealed up the book within can be broken. We are not going to condemn or condone, but we are going to minister mercy. We are going to minister judgment to the world as we tell them, "God is not mad at you. You received his wrath at the cross of Calvary over 2000 years ago. His judgment was your judgment." This message is already being declared all over the world.

These words are not to be knowledge that would just puff us up. This is not just information that we can run with to tell people that we have something greater than they have. This is a manifestation and an expression of an impartation of life to each and every one, that we would become a praise and a worship unto God. And we will express that for which we were created. His appearing is taking place the second time, without sin, unto salvation as we partake of bread and the wine—not by anything that we could do, but as we just realize that it was done more than 2000 years ago. As we rest in that, the unveiling will take place. We will manifest the love and mercy of God to a lost and dying world, and to a Church world that is filled with Babylonian confusion.

We, The People, In Order To Form A More Perfect Union— Set Our Minds On Things Above!

As we come to understand the book of Revelation there are changes that take place in the soul part of us. And when we talk about the renewing of the mind, we are not talking about "positive thinking," or mind over matter. People in the *world* can teach you to think positive. *Adam* can do that. *Adam* can memorize scripture. We've got to get beyond just some positive thinking. We've had enough of that in the Church realm; in fact, there is a lot of that in the kingdom of God along with some metaphysical things that has crept in as a result of the idea of the philosophy, "just think positive."

What we need to do is meditate on *how* he brought about the good report. We need to meditate on what he did to bring us to the place that we *can* think the lovely thoughts. Otherwise, it is not any different than positive thinking. For too long we have tried, in the faith realm, to *make* ourselves think on the good report and think on the things that are just and holy and so forth, without ever really coming to an understanding of how and what took place so that we *can* think those thoughts. Colossians 3:1-4 encourages us in this process:

> If then you have been raised with Christ [to a new life, thus sharing His resurrection from the dead], aim at and seek the [rich, eternal treasures] that are above, where Christ is, seated at the right hand of God. And set your minds and keep them set on what is above (the higher things), not on the things that are on the earth. For [as far as this world is concerned] you have died, and your [new, real] life is hidden with Christ in God. When Christ, Who is

our life, appears, then you also will appear with him in [the splendor of His] glory. (Amplified Bible).

When we begin to think in those terms, it is an entirely different dimension.

When the children of Israel were at rest in Moses' tabernacle, there were three tribes on each side of the tabernacle, north, south, east, and west. Visually, that forms a cross. When the tabernacle and its furniture are assembled in their proper places, they too form a cross. So, we have a cross within a cross that has to do with rest. A cross within a cross foreshadows the fact that Jesus was not the only one on the cross, but we were there too (Romans 6:6). Again, we see the same picture when Israel came out of Egypt, slew the lamb, and put the blood on the door post and the side posts—a double cross. We are transformed by the renewing of the mind. We are matured by the renewing of the mind, by something that takes place in our minds. This does not happen by what we suffer and by what we go through, although we learn from our experiences. But the point is, God does not put things of the curse on us for the purpose of maturing us. God does not put back upon us anything that was nailed to the cross for any reason, and if you believe that he does, you are worshipping an idol—not the one true God.

God can use the trials we go through to work obedience and patience, and certainly we learn from those experiences. The book of Hebrews says that Jesus learned obedience by the things which he suffered. But some are of the mindset that their suffering *adds* to the work that Jesus did. They seem to brace themselves to expect every type of suffering. If that is true, then they have reason to boast, which is what works always gets us into. It is by grace through faith, not of works, lest any man should boast.

Suffering With Jesus

David Wilkerson wrote: "Throughout scripture, the greatest revelations of God's goodness came to people in their times of trouble, calamity, isolation and hardship. We find an example of this in the life of John. For three years, this disciple was "in Jesus' bosom." It was a time of utter rest, peace, and joy with no troubles or trials. Yet, in all that time, John received very little revelation. He knew Jesus only as the Son of man. So, when did John receive his revelation of Christ in all his glory? It happened only after John was dragged from Ephesus in chains. He was exiled to the Isle of Patmos, where he was sentenced to hard labor. He was isolated, with no fellowship, no family or friends to comfort him. It was a time of utter despair, the lowest point in his life. Yet that's when John received the revelation of his Lord that would become the final element of Scripture: the Book of Revelation. In the midst of that dark hour, the light of the Holy Ghost came to him. He literally saw Christ as the Son of God. John had never received this revelation while he was with the other apostles or even during Jesus' days on earth. Yet now, in his darkest hour, John saw Christ in all his glory, declaring, 'I am he that liveth, and was dead; and behold, I am alive for evermore, Amen; and have the keys of hell and of death.'" That is great grace—when we find grace in spite of suffering, not necessarily as a result of suffering.

How can we give grace to others who are suffering unless we can be touched with the feeling of their infirmities as Jesus was, through his being tempted in all points as we are? We suffer in order to become grace-givers, not to become more righteous and certainly not because God is punishing us. We're not going through suffering to make ourselves better. As Paul said, it is for *their* sakes. The suffering we experience should produce the result of being able to comfort others as we were comforted by the Holy Spirit in our suffering—not for ourselves to become more righteous. That's where we get it wrong—we think it is all about us! It's not about us! It is about his purpose! Paul said there was a purpose in his suffering and the purpose was so that the resurrection life of Christ could flow *from* Paul *to them!* Death worked in Paul that life could flow! There is a lot of death you feel when you're ministering to people. When we come into the Holy of Holies experientially, there is no more suffering, but most of the time, it seems that the pattern in scripture is that we get there through a lot of suffering. That's what 2 Peter 3:10 is talking about when it says the old heavens pass away with a fervent heat and a loud noise. He is speaking of our "old man" ideas about spiritual things. They will pass away with a fervent heat and a loud noise—that sounds like some suffering! But we'll see a new heaven and a new earth, in which righteousness dwells (2 Peter 3:13)! Later, we will study the passage in Revelation 9, about men being tormented for five months—sounds like some suffering.

So, what is the suffering that Jesus learned obedience from? There are five types of suffering mentioned in the New Testament.
1. Temptation (James 1:12).
2. Persecution (Matthew 5:10-12, 2 Timothy 3:12).
3. Affliction, which is defined as pressures of life (2 Corinthians 4:17, 8:2).
4. Suffering wrongfully (1 Peter 2:20).
5. Reproach for the gospel (Luke 6:22, Romans 15:3, 1 Timothy 4:10, 1 Peter 4:14).

The Seven Churches Speak of Re-Creation

Not only do each of the seven Churches of Revelation represent the days of creation and the stages of Old Testament history up until the time of Jesus' crucifixion, but the present day Church can also gain from what Jesus said to each of these Churches. Each of the seven Churches represents a *re*-creation. The names of each of these Churches reveal even more to us if we understand their meaning from the Greek context.

For example, the Church at Ephesus correlates with day one of creation and the Garden of Eden. Jesus told them if they did not repent, he would remove their light, but if they overcame they would eat from the tree of life in the midst of paradise. We are eating of the tree of life in the midst of paradise right now. We are partaking of the bread and wine in the Most Holy Place. Aaron's rod that budded speaks of the tree in paradise that we are eating of. Aaron's rod also speaks of priestly ruling and reigning. We also see Jesus' death in the Most Holy Place when we see the wood (humanity) overlaid with gold on the inside and the outside, making up the Ark of the Covenant. We also see the mercy seat representing God's mercy which was appropriated by the death of Christ.

Ephesus—Inventor of Works

The name Ephesus means "inventor of works." We have invented a lot of man-made works. Of course we show our faith by our works, but we are not one ounce more righteous or holy, nor do we grow and mature by our works. We are to cease from our own labors and trust in his labor, his works, which took place at the cross of Calvary. We are to labor to enter into rest by filling our minds with the truth. In light of this, let's look at Revelation 2:1-7:

> Unto the angel of the church of Ephesus write; 'These things saith he that holdeth the seven stars in his right hand, who walketh in the midst of the seven golden candlesticks; I know thy works, and thy labor and thy patience, and how thou canst not bear them which are evil, and thou has tried them which say they are apostles, and are not, and has found them liars: And hast borne, and hast patience, and for my name's sake hast labored, and hast not fainted. Nevertheless I have somewhat against thee, because thou hast left thy first love. Remember therefore from whence thou art fallen, and repent, and do the first works; or else I will come unto thee quickly, and will remove thy candlestick out of his place, except thou repent. But this thou hast, that thou hatest the deeds of the Nicolaitanes, which I also hate. He that hath an ear, let him hear what the Spirit saith unto the churches; To him that overcometh will I give to eat of the tree of life, which is in the midst of the paradise of God.

The seven stars speak of the pastors, and not just the pastors, but *all* ministers, and every one of us are ministers. This is not exclusive. I am not saying that he is holding in his right hand some elite group, because we are all called to be ministers. An angel is one with a message and we can all have the message. Since the cross, we are all held in his right hand. In the Old Testament God used his left hand because they were not born again and he dealt with them according to a natural, physical level many times. But because we are born again, his way of cleansing us is through the word and the renewing of the mind and specifically, to the person and the work of Christ. The right hand speaks of the power of God. The power of God is the preaching of the cross. So, he first tells them something about the person and the work of Christ before he tells them to sweep out the leaven.

In thinking about the meaning of the name Ephesus, an inventor of works, I also began thinking about humility. We need to become like a little child. I remember when our kids were little, I used to have them stand up on a countertop or table and tell them to jump in my arms. They just knew Mom wasn't going to drop them. They were just humble enough, trusting enough to know that I was not going to let them fall in the floor. When we realize that the work was finished at the cross of Calvary that works within us a child-likeness, a trust, and a true humility. A lot of people think humility means that you can't pay your bills, you have holes in your shoes and you can barely scrape by. True humility is casting your care on him because your mind is filled with what happened at the cross of Calvary and you *know* that he cares for you. He is our peace. Our peace is a person!

In Matthew 18, Jesus told the disciples that unless they were converted and became as a little child, they could not enter into the kingdom of God. He was simply talking about trust. How do we come to the place where we really trust him? We *say* we trust him. Our money says, "In God we trust." Do we *really* trust him? We cannot really trust in the full sense of the word, until our mind is filled with the truth of what happened at the cross of Calvary over 2000 years ago. James 4:10 says "Humble yourselves in the sight of the Lord, and he shall lift you up." 1 Peter 5:6-7 says "Humble yourselves therefore under the mighty hand of God, that he may exalt you in due time: Casting all your care upon Him; for He careth for you." Trust him. He is a God of integrity. He did what he said he would do. Now it must be believed.

"Ephesus" means "an inventor of works" and we do not want to invent any man-made works. We have had enough man-made works. We are to keep *his* works, just as in chapter 1, "Blessed is he that … keep those things which are written." That is not "keep" in the legalistic sense; it is keeping his works before our minds as far as our understanding, in awakening to righteousness and seeing what happened at the cross of Calvary. What did Jesus mean when he said that the Church at Ephesus had left her first love? He first loved us. In 1 John 4:10, that love is connected to Calvary. Our first works were simply when we first believed. In John 6:28, the people asked Jesus, "What shall we do, that we might *work* the *works* of God?" Jesus told them, "This is the works of God, that ye *believe* on him whom he hath sent." Believe. Simply believe!

The Church has had the cart before the horse. Paul did not say do this and do not do that, he said, "Walk in the Spirit and you will not fulfill the lusts of the flesh." He said, "Awake to righteousness and sin not." But what we've been doing in the Church is fighting sin. The little Shulamite said "I am black like the tents of Kedar." Kedar was a son of Ishmael. In other words, "I'm something of the flesh; the king is never going to love me." Then the king takes her to the mountain of Bether. In the Strong's, the word "Bether," #1336, refers the reader to the previous definitions, which mean "to cut in pieces, to thrust through, to chop up, a section, part, piece, a craggy place." This is what the priests did with the sacrifices in the Old Testament, all of which are types of the perfect sacrifice of our Lord, Jesus Christ. So, the king takes her to the mountain of Bether, which means "the mountain of suffering" or "the mountain of covenant," because God cut covenant with himself, and showed her that there was no spot in her. She came to the place where she could rightly divide who she was—that's only done by seeing that his suffering was our suffering. The spots were removed; the blackness of the tents of Kedar was removed at the cross of Calvary. As soon as she found out these were removed, she was able to enter into a love relationship with the king.

Smyrna—Embitter; Mingle with Myrrh

The next Church, Smyrna, in Revelation 2:8-11:

> And unto the angel of the church in Smyrna write; 'These things saith the first and the last, which was dead, and is alive; I know thy works, and tribulation,

and poverty (but thou art rich), and I know the blasphemy of them which say they are Jews, and are not, but are the synagogue of Satan. Fear none of those things which thou shalt suffer: behold, the devil shall cast some of you into prison, that ye may be tried; and ye shall have tribulation ten days: be thou faithful unto death, and I will give thee a crown of life. He that hath an ear, let him hear what the Spirit saith unto the churches; He that overcometh shall not be hurt of the second death.'

Again, he is showing them first, before he tells them what is required, some of the person and the work of Christ. We could say it this way in comparison with the little Shulamite; he is showing them that their blackness and their spots were taken away at the cross of Calvary over 2000 years ago. Then they will be empowered to get the leaven out of their house.

Look at the phrase "shall have tribulation ten days." The number ten signifies completeness of divine order. It implies that there is nothing wanting and that the whole cycle is complete. Abraham's faith was proved by a completed cycle of ten trials. When our faith is proved, being faithful unto *the* death, we have (already possess!) a crown of life.

The phrase "be thou faithful unto death" does not mean that you just have to trudge along until the day you die and whatever comes your way, just let it roll over you like a steam roller. That is not what the scripture teaches. The scripture teaches that we can renew our minds with the finished work of Calvary. This is talking about *"the* death" here. He is talking about overcoming by looking at *the* death. As we look at his death, we are empowered to be faithful unto this death by seeing that we are crucified with Christ.

Look at the end of verse 10: "be thou faithful unto death, and I will give thee a crown of life." When we understand *the* death, we see that we already have a crown of life. There was a crown on top of the Ark of the Covenant that held the mercy seat, speaking of the mind of Christ concerning the mercy of God. In Hosea 6:6, he said, "I desire mercy and not sacrifice." The Ark made of wood, represents Christ becoming one with us in his death, and the gold, his resurrection. When we are faithful unto death by filling our mind with *the* death, ceasing from our own works, we have the crown of life. *That is* the crown of life.

Verse 11b in this passage tells us "He that overcometh shall not be hurt of the second death." When we get further in this study we will talk more about the second death. But let me give you a sneak preview from Hebrews 9:27-28. This scripture is usually misquoted as "it is appointed unto *man* once to die, but after that the judgment." And they usually quit right there after that statement. That is not even the end of the sentence! It continues into verse 28. This is what it really says:

> And as it is appointed unto men once to die, but after this the judgment: so Christ was once offered to bear the sins of many; and unto them that look for him shall he appear the second time without sin, unto salvation.

In the first phrase, "men" is talking about men in Adam. It is not talking about man, the new man, Christ Jesus. It speaks of all men that were in Adam. We had an appointment with death, but that appointment was met over 2000 years ago at the cross of Calvary. Notice, "And as it is appointed unto men once to die, but after this the judgment: (the sentence continues) *so Christ was once offered* to bear the sins of many; and unto them that look for him shall he appear *the second time* (with our second look at the cross) without sin, unto salvation. Period. End of sentence.

As we awake to righteousness the veil is being taken away. As we walk in the Spirit, not fulfilling the lust of the flesh, the veil is being taken away. As we realize that our appointment with death was met over 2000 years ago at the cross of Calvary, the veil is being taken away and the Lord Jesus is going to *apokalupsis*—he is going to appear. It does not say anywhere in the Bible that there is going to be a second coming of the Lord. The scripture says that he shall *appear the second time* without sin, unto salvation. This takes place when a people understand that his judgment was our judgment and that our appointment with death was met over 2000 years ago. Then the veil that was done away, is *taken* away and he appears the second time *without sin,* unto salvation—unto full and complete salvation. The coming of the Lord is actually comings (plural) of the Lord.

Notice the phrase "without sin." Remember, Tabernacles is a second look at Passover. When we take our second look at the cross, we see the body of Christ individually and corporately without sin. We see ourselves and each other as the righteousness of God in Jesus Christ. We know no man after the flesh. We know all men in Christ as a finished work of love. We cannot see this with the carnal mind. The carnal mind can only see the natural world. As the Spirit of God becomes one with our soul, we are able to see spiritually in all dimensions. Yes, Jesus is appearing bodily—and we are the body he is appearing through. We are the body of Christ.

So, in studying the Church at Smyrna, we need to understand that "Smyrna" means "embittered" and "to mingle with myrrh." We could apply that many different ways. First of all, these people were greatly persecuted by the legalists of their day. They were persecuted by embittered people. We can also take it back to the bitter cup that Jesus drank at the cross of Calvary. The word of God tells us that the flesh always persecutes that which is of the spirit. We see this happening in the present day Church. We see spiritually mature Christians get the left foot of fellowship from the Church. People cross the street so they don't have to pass by us or talk to us. Some of us even experience persecution from our own families. If so, you can identify with the people in Smyrna who were persecuted by people who had heads full of works and legalism.

Circumcision was a big thing during this time. According to the Old Covenant, literal circumcision was the seal of the Covenant. That carried over into the New Covenant Church where Jews tried to proselytize the believers back into this literal circumcision and their legalistic order. Look at Galations 6:12-17:

> As many as desire to make a fair shew in the flesh, they constrain you to be circumcised; only lest they should suffer persecution for the cross of Christ. For neither they themselves who are circumcised keep the law; but desire to have you circumcised, that they may glory in your flesh. But God forbid that I

should glory, save in the cross of our Lord Jesus Christ, by whom the world is crucified unto me, and I unto the world. For in Christ Jesus neither circumcision availeth any thing, nor uncircumcision, but a new creature. And as many as walk according to this rule, peace be on them, and mercy, and upon the Israel of God. From henceforth let no man trouble me: for I bear in my body the marks of the Lord Jesus.

This was happening to the Church at Smyrna and continues to happen in the Church today. But even the circumcised could not keep the law—and still can't. If we try to keep the law, we must keep the *whole* law. There is no way we can keep the whole law and Jesus knew that, and that is why he came. But the circumcised want us to be circumcised so they can glory in our flesh—so they can glory in our works. But look what Paul said: "God forbid! I'm not going to glory in circumcision; I'm not going to glory in works of the flesh. I'm going to cease from my own labors and realize the work was accomplished at the cross of Calvary over 2000 years ago." He said, "I glory in one thing, and that is the cross of our Lord Jesus Christ!"

Legalists or Pharisees attempt to rule over us with law, legalism, and the doctrine of man, that they may glory in our flesh. This has produced an enslaved Church—captives of Babylon—captives of a religious system that says it is "blasphemy" to question what we have been taught, to question our faith in a system. Our faith must be the faith of Jesus Christ. We are at the place where it is no longer "my faith," but it is the faith of Jesus Christ, the Son of God. The life that we now live must be lived by the faith of the Son of God! Look at Galations 2:16 and 20:

> Knowing that a man is not justified by the works of the law, but by *the faith of Jesus Christ,* even we have believed in Jesus Christ, that we might be justified by *the faith of Christ,* and not by the works of the law: for by the works of the law shall no flesh be justified. I am crucified with Christ: nevertheless I

live; yet not I, but Christ liveth in me: and the life which I now live in the flesh I live by *the faith of the Son of God,* who loved me, and gave himself for me (emphasis added).

This is the day when everything that can be shaken is being shaken. Babylon has fallen! Has she fallen in your world?

Get The Message

So, in Galations 6:17, Paul said, "Let no man trouble me: for I bear in my body the marks of the Lord Jesus." What does that mean? It simply means that he realized that Jesus' death was his death. We've been taught that we must bear our cross. Listen, there is no way we can bear our cross the way we've been taught to "bear our cross." We were taught that it means to suffer, to go through all kinds of trials. But that is not what *God* meant when he wrote this to us. Bearing our cross means that we bear it in our understanding. It means that we renew our minds to what took place at the finished work of Calvary. His cross *was* our cross over 2000 years ago.

Yes Paul was physically beaten, shipwrecked, and suffered greatly for the cause of Christ. And we may go through these things, but those things do not make us more righteous and Paul knew that. We need to know that we are who we are by the grace of God. We need to know that we were crucified with Christ. If we get the message, we won't turn away if any of those things happen—we will continue to be bold. Our times are in *his* hands.

If I tell you that my physical sufferings are something that God has put on me to purify me, that falls under the category of "works of the flesh" or "dead works." He *can use* those things, but for the most part, the Church has been out of balance with this teaching to the point that it is no longer the cross of Calvary and the grace of God that has *already* made me pure and righteous, but it is "what I'm going through" that is making me righteous. That is the same as Moses smiting the rock twice. Moses never entered into the Promised Land because of that. We, as kingdom people, need to get out of the wilderness mentality. When our mind is renewed to the person and the work of Christ, there is going to be a quickening of

Spirit life in our spirit, soul, and body. We are going to be quickened, not just healed, but quickened unto life.

So, the overcomers in the Church at Smyrna will not be hurt of the second death. What does that mean? Some teach that it refers to immortality of the body—not dying physically. And they say, "I am not going to go by way of the grave." What we have failed to realize is that we already died—not that we're not going to die. The children of Israel did not escape death when the death angel went through. The lamb's death *was* their death. They already died. The Church at Smyrna is not going to partake of the second death because they realize that their old, Adamic nature died with Jesus at the cross (Romans 6:6, Galations 2:20). They will not be hurt by the second death—spiritual death—because as far as this world is concerned, they have died, and their new, real life is hidden with Christ in God (Colossians 3:3).

Look at this from 1 Corinthians 15:51-53:

> Behold, I shew you a mystery: We shall not all sleep, but we shall all be changed, in a moment, in the twinkling of an eye, at the last trump: for the trumpet shall sound, and the dead shall be raised incorruptible, and we shall be changed. For this corruptible must put on incorruption, and this mortal must put on immortality.

The text says "in the twinkling of an eye." Notice it does not say the blinking or the batting of an eye, nor does it say when you shift your eye from side to side. What is it that makes our eye twinkle? When light not only hits it, but penetrates it. So, when the light of God's word is in our hearts and in our mind—not just head knowledge, but the spirit of wisdom and revelation—our eye, our spirit, is going to twinkle because of the light. Then, do you know what is going to happen? Let's read on, continuing the sentence in verse 52: "at the last trump: for the trumpet shall sound, and the dead shall be raised incorruptible, and we shall be changed." What is the spiritual interpretation of this text? We are not just looking for the literal, natural interpretation of physical death. We want to be able to apply this to our lives today. Paul says it's a mystery. In this day, God is revealing his mysteries to his *huios* sons—his mature sons. That which is hidden is being revealed because he wants us to receive the revelation of Jesus Christ!

"The dead" refers to those who are still in Adam experientially. This *includes* born again, spirit-filled Christians who believe they still have two natures—a sin nature and a new-creation nature. This kind of death is that of being dead in the grave of the womb of our minds. In the Old Testament, when a woman had a miscarriage, they spoke of the womb as a grave. Jeremiah said that his mother's womb might have been his grave. In the New Testament, we see that our mind is a womb. As long as we live like we have two natures, the womb of our mind will be our grave. Unless we give birth to the nature of Christ in our lives, we, ourselves will be the miscarriage. So, the dead will be raised incorruptible—that is Christ! We will no longer think and act like we have two natures. We shall be changed! We will realize that we have followed Jesus in the regeneration (Matthew 19:27-30) and that we are brand new creations! Quickening life will then come forth that will bring more than just healing, but it will bring wholeness—a hundredfold!

He says, "This corruptible must *put on* incorruption (Christ)." Adam is crucified, dead, and buried. Our new life is hidden in Christ. We are clothed with Christ. This mortal *must* put on immortality. But *put ye on* the Lord Jesus Christ, and make not provision for the flesh, to fulfill its lusts—Romans 13:14. For as many of you as have been baptized into Christ have *put on* Christ—Galations 3:27. And that ye *put on* the new man, which after God is created in righteousness and true holiness—Ephesians 4:24. And have *put on* the new man, that is renewed in knowledge after the image of him that created him—Colossians 3:10. And above all these things *put on* love, which is the bond of perfectness—Colossians 3:14. *This mortal must put on immortality.* When? When something takes place from spirit to mind and the veil is taken away. The renewing of the mind brings transformation.

Pergamos—Fortified; A Tower; A Castle;

The name Pergamos means "fortified; a tower; a castle." Revelation 2:12-14:

And to the angel of the church in Pergamos write; 'These things saith he which hath the sharp sword with two edges; I know thy works, and where thou dwellest, even where Satan's seat is: and thou holdest fast my name, and hast not denied my faith, even in those days wherein Antipas was my faithful martyr, who was slain among you, where Satan dwelleth. But I have a few things against thee, because thou hast there them that hold the doctrine of Balaam, who taught Balac to cast a stumblingblock before the children of Israel, to eat things sacrificed unto idols, and to commit fornication.

Again, as we let the Bible interpret the Bible, the sharp sword with two edges takes us right back to the garden where the flaming sword was. We get into the garden, or into maturity as we go through the word, (the sword) with the flame (which represents his judgment was our judgment). If we do not come in God's prescribed way, we are not going to experience maturity. It has to be God's way, which is drawing out of the soil we are planted in—the death.

OperationDragonSlayer

In Revelation 2:13, again, Jesus says to the Church at Pergamos, "I know your works." Then he said, "I know your address too—and you live where Satan's seat is!" And he is talking to the Church?!! Ouch! What can he possibly mean? Remember, this is a symbolic book. In Revelation 12:9-10, Satan is called the accuser of our brethren. In Lucas and Washburn's book, "Theomatics," the theomatic value of "the accuser of the brethren' is 276 x 13. The phase found in 2 Corinthians 4:4, "the god of this age has blinded" is 276 x 19. The phrase in Hebrews 9:15, "the first covenant" (the law) is 276 x 6. The phrase in 2 Corinthians 3:3, "stone tablets" is 276 x 2. The phrase in Matthew 5:20, "the righteousness of the scribes and Pharisees" is 276 x 18. The phrase in Romans 3:20, "By works of the law shall no flesh be justified" is 276 x 14. The phrase in 2 Corinthians 3:6, "the letter killeth" is 276 x 4. And last, but certainly not least is this: both "Satan" and "religion" have the same theomatic values. In Matthew 16:23, the name "Satan" is 276 x 2. In Acts 26:5, the word "religion" is 276 x 2!

Church, we've got to cast down the great dragon, that old serpent, religion, *which deceives the whole world!* How is he cast down? We must cast him down and out of our thinking as Paul said, "Casting down imaginations and every high thing that exalteth itself against the knowledge of God, and bringing into captivity every thought to the obedience of Christ." Then we will hear a loud voice saying in heaven, "Now is come salvation, and strength, and the kingdom of our God, and the power of his Christ: for the accuser of our brethren is cast down!" Right now, your spirit and my spirit is hearing that loud voice in heaven speaking since the cross of Jesus Christ our Lord—and his sound goes forth to the ends of the world—the kingdoms of this world *are* become the kingdoms or our Lord and of his Christ; and he shall reign forever and ever!

We found out when we discussed Old Testament history with these seven Churches that this Church had to do with idols that the people were worshipping. Baal worship and all kinds of corrupt things were going on. This took place in the wilderness. Some in the Church today are in the wilderness. Some in the Church have worshipped a lot of idols and one of them is: "You are God." There are a lot of metaphysical things being ministered in the Church today. There has been an imbalance. Let's read 1 John 5:21 in light of Revelation 2:14: "Little children, keep yourselves from idols." The word "idol" here is *eidolon* and it means "false images and ideas about God." Another false image about God is the image the Church teaches, that God is a mean God and if you don't get every jot and tittle correct he is going to lower the boom and knock your lights out—or he is going to send you into a seven year tribulation where scorpions sting your flesh and make you cry out in agonizing pain. That is an idol. That is a false image and a false idea about God. There was a lot of that going on in the midst of the Church in Pergamos. Pergamos—fortified; a tower; a castle. A fitting name—a castle fortified with all of those ghoulish figures, false images, idols.

What can we do about these idols? First of all, we must fill our mind with the truth about the finished work of Calvary, and as a result, there will be some things that are cast down and brought into captivity within our lives. In the past, we thought we were fighting something outside of ourselves, and we were warring with flesh and blood, with carnal weapons. All this time, we were using the word of God and we thought we were using it the right way. We thought "the devil is so strong," like God was having a wrestling match with the devil. Many in the Church preach such a powerful devil. All I want to minister is a great big God, a defeated devil, and a dead old man. When we really see that, and fill our mind with that truth, then something is going to happen. Look at 2 Corinthians 10:3-5:

> For though we walk in the flesh, we do not war after the flesh: (For the weapons of our warfare are not carnal. but mighty through God to the pulling down of strong holds;) casting down imaginations, and every high thing that exalteth itself against the knowledge of God and bringing into captivity every thought to the obedience of Christ;

Where verse 3 refers to "though we walk in the flesh," it means that we are in the body. It is not talking about walking in the flesh as opposed to walking in the spirit. Romans 8:9 tells us we are not in the flesh, but we are in the spirit. Here, the text is saying "though we walk in the body, we do not war after the flesh." Our war is not a natural war, as we see in verse 4. He says the weapons of our warfare are mighty. How? Through God. If we are going to pull down strong holds *through God*, how are we going to do it? By binding and losing? I know there was a day and a realm for that and we all benefited from that. But in the Amplified version of Matthew 16:19, when Jesus told Peter he was going to give him the keys of the kingdom, he said that whatever we bind on earth must be what is already bound in heaven and whatever we loose on earth must be what is already loosed in heaven. He is telling us that what is already bound or loosed in the realm of the spirit, because of the cross, is going to be bound or loosed in earth, as we renew our minds. Through Calvary, some things were bound (became illegal), and some things were loosed (became legal).

Notice, all of the things in 2 Corinthians 10:5, is a veil that has to be taken away in our minds. Where are imaginations? In our minds. Where are those high things that exalt themselves against the knowledge of God? Where is knowledge? In our minds. Where are the thoughts that we are to bring into captivity? They are, of course, in our minds.

But notice, it says that our weapons are mighty *through God*. As Zechariah said to Zerubbabel, it is "not by might or by power, but by the Spirit." But we did this by might and power for many years. Now, when we renew our minds to the fact that it is a done deal, that it is already finished, then we are empowered, and that renewing of the mind will cause those imaginations to be cast down, the strong holds to be pulled down and the thoughts to be brought into captivity to the obedience of Christ.

One of the last things Jesus talked to Pergamos about is the doctrine of the Nicolaitanes and he says that he hates it! "Nicolaitanes" means "victorious over the people." What has ruled the world—including the Church world—since the "prince of this world" came on the scene? Religion, the great Satan. Are you getting the message?

Thyatira—Female Woman

The Church in Thyatira is addressed in Revelation 2:18-20:

> And unto the angel of the church in Thyatira write; 'These things saith the Son of God, who hath his eyes like unto a flame of fire, and his feet are like fine brass; I know thy works, and charity, and service, and faith, and thy patience, and thy works; and the last to be more than the first. Notwithstanding, I have a few things against thee, because thou sufferest that woman Jezebel, which calleth herself a prophetess, to teach and to seduce my servants to commit fornication, and to eat things sacrificed unto idols.

Again, we see the pattern in verse 18, as he first tells them an aspect about himself and the finished work before he tells them what is required of them. Then he tells us "his eyes are like a flame of fire." Fire speaks of cleansing. There is a purifying taking place as we view the person and the work of Christ. He tells us in the symbolic language of "his feet are like fine brass," that his judgment was our judgment.

We discussed this when we talked about Old Testament history and the seven Churches. But what can this mean to us today? The meaning of the name "Thyatira" is "female woman." The Greek for the word "soul" is in the feminine gender. Many times when we see the word "woman" in scripture, it is referring to the soul. That is why David said, "My soul shall make *her* boast in the Lord." Our soul is our woman. What the spirit is saying to the Churches today is that our soul should not be in the driver's seat. The scripture in 1 Corinthians 14:34 has been abused so badly in the Church: "Let your women keep silence in the Churches: for it is not permitted unto them to speak ..." A man, in gender, in the natural, could be standing in the Church with his "woman" speaking if he is ministering out of his soul instead of ministering in the Spirit.

Psalm 27:4 tells us that our soul (our woman) needs to stay at home. The word "soul" is not used, although the yearning, the desire, the emotions David expresses in this passage all comes from the soul. In other words, we must draw our thoughts from the spirit inside. Spirit must flow through soul. Spirit must flow through mind. The Greek word for "spirit" is in the masculine gender. Paul refers to our spirit as our inner man. Spirit, the masculine part of us, needs to flow through soul so that we are not speaking from our feminine part, the soul. Thank God this is changing, but we still have a lot of "women" that are preaching and teaching, as 1 Corinthians refers to, and they are not keeping silent. Spirit and soul must become one. The spirit is the initiator and the soul is just the projector—just as a man deposits seed into a woman and nine months later, the womb (soul) projects it out. We have The Seed of God in our spirit and it is impregnated into the womb of our mind. When we speak with our mouth, we project it out, and we are not just speaking from our natural mind.

So, Thyatira means a female woman. Obviously, this was happening in the natural. There was a woman in the natural, during this time, who was saying that she was a prophetess, supporting Baal worship and prostitution. There is still *spiritual* prostitution in the midst of Church today. The name "Jezebel" means "unchaste dwelling." Our *soul* can be unchaste if we fill it with false ideas about God. Jezebel's teaching causes the people to eat things sacrificed to idols. An idol is a false idea about God. In today's Church, Jezebel's teachings are things about the sacrifice of Christ that are false. For example: teaching that Jesus did not become sin, die spiritually, and go into hell as us. Jezebel teaches that his finished work was not really finished and we still have works to do to add to our righteousness. She teaches that Jesus defeated Satan, yet we are still "fighting a defeated devil." She teaches that Jesus, who suffered and was wounded for our healing, will turn around and put sickness and disease and plagues and tribulation back on us if we don't do what she thinks we should do. These are *imagi*-nations! These are false *images* of God (2 Corinthians 10:5). In this study of the book of Revelation, we are going to find that in some places, "the nations" are symbolic of imagi*nations* like these just mentioned.

Chapter Three

Sardis—A Gem

Look at Sardis in Revelation 3:1-6:

> And unto the angel of the church in Sardis write; 'These things saith he that hath the seven Spirits of God, and the seven stars; I know thy works, that thou hast a name that thou livest, and art dead. Be watchful, and strengthen the things which remain, that are ready to die; for I have not found thy works perfect before God. Remember therefore how thou hast received and heard, and hold fast, and repent. If therefore thou shalt not watch, I will come on thee as a thief, and thou shalt not know what hour I will come upon thee. Thou hast a few names even in Sardis which have not defiled their garments; and they shall walk with me in white: for they are worthy. He that overcometh, the same shall be clothed in white raiment; and I will not blot his name out of the book of life, but I will confess his name before my Father, and before his angels.

When we discussed Old Testament history and the seven Churches, we saw a spiritual people, a carnal people, and a dead people. Right in the midst of the Church today, we can see a heavenly people (spiritual), a people on land (carnal), and a people in the sea (dead).

Sardis means "a gem." Look at Isaiah 62:1-4:

> For Zion's sake will I not hold my peace, and for Jerusalem's sake I will not rest, until the righteousness thereof go forth as brightness, and the salvation thereof as a lamp that burneth. And the Gentiles shall see thy righteousness, and all kings thy glory: and thou shalt be called by a new name, which the mouth of the Lord shall name. Thou shalt be a crown of glory in the hand of the Lord, and *a royal diadem* in the hand of thy God. Thou shalt no more be termed Forsaken; neither shall thy land any more be termed Desolate: but thou shalt be called Hephzibah, and thy land Beulah: for the Lord delighteth in thee, and thy land shall be married (emphasis added).

God is saying in verse 1, "I am not going to hold my peace." The book of Matthew says the kingdom will be preached and then the end will come. God is not going to hold his peace until a people go forth ministering the righteousness of God. The bread and the wine must be ministered—the death, burial, and resurrection.

The remainder of this passage in Isaiah is a beautiful picture of what we are after in our lives—to fill our minds with the finished work, like the little Shulamite. She thought there was no way she could become one with the king. She thought she was black like the tents of Kedar. When he took her up to the mountain of Bether and showed her that her spots were done away with at the cross of Calvary, in type, then she was released to have a love relationship.

As we hear the truth about the finished work and understand that we are seated in the Most Holy Place, we are going to experience a union and we are going to birth something. We are not going to be called "Forsaken" anymore. We are going to be called "Hephzibah," a delight to the Lord. We will no longer be called "Desolate," but we will be called "Beulah" because we are married to him in experience.

Look at Isaiah 28:5: "In that day shall the Lord of hosts be for a crown of glory, and for a diadem of beauty, unto the residue of his people." It is not *us* that is a gem or a royal diadem, it is him—in us. He is the royal diadem and as he stands up in us, he becomes that to us and through us. That word "residue" in Isaiah 28:5 is "remnant." Mark 16:13 also speaks of a residue, but they are a residue of unbelievers. Then the book of Acts speaks of a residue of men that will seek the Lord after the Tabernacle of David has been rebuilt (Acts 15:13-18). In the Old Testament, the Tabernacle of David was the only Tabernacle that had no veil. It represents a people of maturity. The New Testament Tabernacle of David is a people in whom the veil has been taken away. Because of this Tabernacle of David—a people expressing the very nature of Jesus Christ—all those who do not know the Lord will come to him. And in *This Day* shall the Lord of hosts be for a crown of glory, and for a diadem of beauty, unto the residue of his people!

Philadelphia—Brotherly Love

The name of the Church Philadelphia, in Revelation 3:7, means "fond of the brethren." There were not many negative things said about this Church.

> And to the angel of the church in Philadelphia write: 'These things saith he that is holy, he that is true, he that hath the key of David, he that openeth, and no man shutteth, and shutteth, and no man openeth; I know thy works: behold I have set before thee an open door, and no man can shut it: for thou hast a little strength, and hast kept my word, and hast not denied my name. Behold, I will make them of the synagogue of Satan, which say they are Jews, and are not, but do lie; behold, I will make them to come and worship before thy feet, and to know that I have loved thee.

There is a people who know and perceive that we abide in the presence of the Lord and that we have an ongoing, intimate relationship with him. The word says that all nations are going to flow to Mt. Zion because they see something flowing out of our lives that they do not have—and they are going to want what they see. Mt. Zion represents a people.

This is the Church of brotherly love. We can preach to people every Sunday, beating them over the head with "love your neighbor!" and they may *act* like they love their neighbor, but only the Holy Spirit can work in us the kind of love John writes about in 1 John 4:7-10:

> Beloved, let us love one another: for love is of God; and every one that loveth is born of God, and knoweth God. He that loveth not knoweth not God; for God is love, In this was manifested the love of God toward us, because that God sent his only begotten son into the world, that we might live through him. Herein is love, not that we loved God, but that he loved us, and sent his son to be the propitiation for our sins.

This is not talking about *phileo* love. It refers to *agape* love, the highest form of love. We can love in other ways, like, "You scratch my back and I'll scratch yours," but there is the type of love that loves even our enemies, the *agape* love of God. We cannot have the *agape* love of God flow through us until we see his love for us first. John says God sent his son into the world that we might *live* through him. It is not that we loved God, but he loved us, and sent his son to be the atonement for our sins. In verse 10, he connects this level of love with the cross. God sent his son to be the propitiation for our sins. That understanding will develop and release the love of God. John 15:13 tells us that there can be no greater love than a man laying down his life for his friends. Jesus did that at Calvary. Romans 5:8 also connects his love with dying for us. It says, "But God commendeth his love toward us, in that, while we were yet sinners, Christ died for us." We can try to "work it up," we can try to "call it down," but when we get an impartation of understanding from spirit to mind—not just head knowledge or information—then the love of God will be birthed out of us. And it is like a birthing. It is birthing the manchild—there is something that has to take place—the veil has to be taken away and then Christ will appear! All Christ can do is love with the agape love of God!

This Church who loves people has "a little strength," he says in verse 8. "Little" is the Greek *mikros,* and it means "small in size, quantity, number." The word "strength" is the Greek *dunamis,* meaning "miracle working power, ability, might, and strength." Little strength. How much dynamite do we need? Well, Jesus said if you have faith as a grain of mustard seed, you could transplant fruit bearing trees from the kingdom of God into the sea of humanity (Luke 17:6)! He said to the Church who loves, if you take this little mustard seed and sow it in the field of the world, it is the tiniest seed of all, but when it is grown, it is the greatest among the herbs, and it will become a fruit tree so that all heavenly people can come and live in it and eat the fruit that love grew! You say, "But Jesus was talking about faith, not love." Even better! Faith, hope, and love—all three live together, but the greatest of these is love. How much dynamite do we need? A little love, God's love, goes a long way. So what do you suppose, even in your *daringest* dreams, would happen if the Church got the message? The Lord would receive the nations for his inheritance and the uttermost parts of the earth for his possession—in manifestation!

Laodicea—A People

It does not matter that there are a majority who are caught in the middle and lukewarm. God is going to have a people who experience fullness! He has always had a people, he is always going to have a people. He always has a firstfruit company. Even those who want to remain in the middle, in the Holy Place realm, will eventually want what we who are the remnant have. When they see the glory of the Lord, the nature of God being manifested, they will flow to Mt. Zion.

Notice what it says in Revelation 3:14-15:

> And unto the angel of the church of the Laodiceans write; 'These things saith the Amen, the faithful and true witness, the beginning of the creation of God; I know thy works, that thou art neither cold nor hot: I

would thou wert cold or hot.

In verse 14, he reveals something about the person and the work of Jesus. Then in verse 15, he tells this Church that their experience is neither in the Outer Court nor in the Most Holy Place. Then he says "I wish you were either cold or hot; I don't want you stuck in the middle." There is nothing wrong with the middle. I'm learning more and more that to be good parents, we must minister to people where they are in their experience, whether that is the Outer Court, the Holy Place, or the Most Holy Place. We can do that and not compromise the word. But the problem is; even though there is nothing wrong with the Middle Court, when that has been your experience for twenty, thirty, or forty years, God says "I want to spit," because he does not want us to stay in the "courting" area experientially.

In Ephesians, Paul says that the baptism of the Holy Spirit is an earnest, or a down payment. It is the Greek word that has to do with an engagement ring. First there are the courting days, and then the engagement time. The Holy Place or the gift realm is the engagement time. It is not the marriage. God is saying "I don't want you to stay in that Middle Court. I'd rather you be cold or hot, but don't just stay in the middle for most of your life."

We're going to find that John hears a voice that says, "Come up hither," and it is not talking about a literal rapture as the Church has taught. It is talking about coming out of the Holy Place realm in your experience, and experiencing the Most Holy Place. As previously discussed, in chapter 1 of Revelation the word "candlestick" is used in the dialogue of the seven Churches, and the candlestick is in the Holy Place. The people here are born-again and spirit-filled, but they need to come up higher. They need to come out of the middle court, the engagement area. They need to come into a place in their experience where they become one, consummate the marriage, and bring about a birthing.

We are already seated in the Most Holy Place in spirit, but now we need to look around and see what is in the Most Holy Place. God is raising our sight through the Spirit so that we can experience the consummation of the marriage. We are also taking a look *from* the Most Holy Place, *through* the Holy Place, and all the way out to the Outer Court, *to see how we got to* the Most Holy Place. That causes us to mature. We are no longer just a teenager who knows everything, telling everyone else how much we know. People who are caught in the Holy Place realm think they know everything and they think "You guys have to know what we know!" I remember those days well. Now we are at rest. Now we know who needs to hear what. Now we minister in all realms, a word of great grace—not condescending, not condoning—great grace—the power that disarms.

God is bringing us "up hither" as our minds are being renewed by the Spirit, to experience the dimension beyond the "in part" realm. We are experiencing, as the little Shulamite, a union, a marriage. We are going into the green room, the living room, the loving room, as the Shulamite said. In Revelation chapter 4, there was a rainbow round about the throne, green like an emerald. Green. Life. He is taking us into the green room in experience, where there can be conception, where there can be a birthing, a manifestation.

Paradigm Lift

Revelation chapter 4 is the chapter that most people reference when teaching a literal, physical rapture. What they say is that between the end of chapter 3 and the beginning of chapter 4, the literal rapture of the Church takes place because John finds an open door and a voice is saying, "Come up hither." They teach that whether it is "pre-trib," "mid-trib," or "post-trib," a literal rapture is going to take place, and then the Holy Spirit is going to be taken from the earth. Then there will be a seven year tribulation and the sacrificing of the blood of bulls and goats will be re-instituted in Israel.

Then they say that as a result of the literal rapture, people will be saved through the preaching of 144,000 Jewish preachers who realized that Jesus was truly the Messiah, after the physical rapture has taken place. And, of course, they use the book of Revelation to try to prove this theory.

In this study, we will find out what the Spirit is really saying to the Church. And one of the things the Spirit is saying to the Church is this: "Get rid of the notion of 'the great escape.' Sweep out the idea that you do not have to grow up because 'the Lord is coming to get us out of here.' Get on with the business of maturity and growing up into him in all things who is the head, even Christ—and you are his body. A head must have a body in order to live and move and have being. In this is the appearing of the Lord in the earth—when you realize that Christ is the head and you are his body. Yes, the Lord is coming. He's coming in clouds. He's coming in glory. He's coming to *grow* us up out of 'here.' It is a paradigm *lift!*" Let's take a look at what Revelation chapter 4 is really teaching.

The Three Feasts Of The Lord And Where They Take Place

Passover—The Outer Court

Passover represents the repeated phrase in Revelation chapters 2 and 3, "To him that overcomes." We overcome by the blood of the Lamb and by the word of our testimony, the word of our martyrdom, and we love not our life unto death. We are not trying to resurrect an old man that was crucified. But to love not our life unto death means that we do not think we can reform our old man. Only those who enter the Ark of Jesus Christ will live. God did not want to save the human race. The wages of sin is death and they were paid in full at the cross, where all in Adam died. But because God so loved the world, he gave his only begotten Son, that whosoever believeth in him should not perish, but have everlasting life. That is how we enter the Ark—through believing.

When the children of Israel came out of Egypt and observed the second part of Passover, they were to sweep the leaven and the dirt out of their homes. We symbolically see the second part of Passover, which is Unleavened Bread, in Revelation chapters 2 and 3. Jesus told them *how* to get the leaven out of their lives and it was by seeing the different aspects of the finished work of the cross, because that is how *we* overcome. The unleavened bread typifies Jesus, who knew no sin. He had no leaven in his life and that qualified him to go to the cross. He went to the cross of Calvary and became sin. He became who we were.

During Passover, on the Feast of Firstfruits, the people of Israel took a firstfruit of barley and presented it unto the Lord. Barley speaks of resurrection life. This is what we see in Revelation chapters 4 and 5. In Revelation chapter 4, we see some activity around the throne, and John is just beginning to get revelation of something that is going to happen afterwards.

As we know, if we look at the furniture in the tabernacle of Moses, we see the shape of a cross. If we superimpose Jesus on that cross, he would have a head of gold (the Ark was overlaid with gold on the inside and the outside). His feet would be in the brazen altar (brass speaks of judgment). This represents everything that was involved in the person and the work of Christ. Each piece of furniture in Moses' tabernacle depicts the bleeding spots inflicted upon the Lord Jesus Christ when he went to Calvary's cross.

Pentecost—The Holy Place

In Revelation chapter 1, we see where the Church was. They were not in the Outer Court. The Church in Revelation chapter 1 was in the Holy Place, because the candlestick, in the tabernacle of Moses was in the Holy Place dimension. There is nothing wrong at all with the Holy Place dimension. But we see in chapters 2 and 3 of Revelation that the Lord is rebuking them for *staying* in that dimension of the Holy Place and not moving on in God.

Let's look at this same situation in the book of Ruth, where Boaz represents the Lord Jesus Christ. Ruth is a type of the Church. We saw in chapter 1 of Revelation that Jesus' feet were like fine brass. Feet are associated with the body (the Church) because feet are part of the body. His feet were brass. Brass is a metal that speaks of judgment. That simply tells us that his judgment was our judgment. What we need to do, and what we *are* doing here, is uncovering his feet, as Ruth did (Ruth 3:7). As we uncover his feet, we are going to be able to come into an intimate relationship with the Lord Jesus Christ.

In Song Of Solomon chapter 1, the little Shulamite said "I want his kisses more than wine." Here, wine speaks of the Holy Place dimension, the gift realm. In other places, wine speaks of the death of Christ. But in chapter 1 of the Song Of Solomon, the wine was referring to the Holy Place dimension. In Revelation chapter 4, a people are in the Holy Place dimension but God is saying, "I want you to come up higher." We must go on to experience the manifestation of that resurrection. It is not just Christ *in* us, the hope of glory. He must become Christ, the manifestation and the expression of glory. The more we uncover his feet, the more the veil that was done away at the cross is going to be taken away from our minds, and that which has been hidden will be unveiled and uncovered, which is what "revelation" means!

As we do what Ruth did, we are going to experience an intimate union. We are going to experience his kisses. We are going to experience intimacy like we've never experienced it before, and there is going to be an unveiling of the Christ *from* spirit *to* soul, and out of our bodies. As this takes place, our bodies are going to be quickened to life. It is going to be *more* than healing! The very cells of our bodies are going to be quickened with the quickening life of God.

In the book of Ruth, we want to see first of all, where Boaz is. Ruth's mother-in-law, Naomi, tells her to go out and find him and she finds him at the threshing floor. And look what it says there, in Ruth 3:2:

> And now is not Boaz of our kindred, with whose maidens thou wast? Behold, he winnoeth barley to night in the threshing floor.

The threshing floor is where the lifeless part of the grain, the chaff, is removed. This is where the wheat and barley, which has been gleaned, is taking on life. The wind of the Spirit is winnowing or removing chaff from our minds as we learn of the death and resurrection! Ruth (who represents the Church), like the little Shulamite, was not just satisfied with wine (the Holy Place dimension), she wanted his kisses. She wanted intimacy with him. This is what we see happening in Revelation chapter 4. It is more than just knowing that we have the resurrected Christ within us. It is coming up higher, out of the Holy Place experience, into the Most Holy Place experience. Now look at Ruth 3:7:

> And when Boaz had eaten and drunk, and his heart was merry, he went to lie down at the end of the heap of corn: and she came softly, and uncovered his feet, and laid her down.

In John 12:24, Jesus talked about a corn of wheat and he said, "Except a corn of wheat fall into the ground and die, it abideth alone: but if it die, it bringeth forth much fruit." So we see from this that the heap of corn that Boaz rested at or laid at represents the death of Jesus. Then Ruth came softly, and uncovered his feet, and lay down also. Lying down speaks of rest. How will the Church come into rest? By uncovering his feet. In Revelation chapter 1, his feet are brass, which speaks of judgment. When we come to understand that his judgment was our judgment, we can enter into rest. We already partook of that in the Holy Place, where across from the golden candelabrum, was the table of shewbread that had on it bread and wine. When the book of Revelation talks of the seven vials or bowls of blood poured out upon a people in chapter 16, it is referring us to the wine that is in the cup on the table of shewbread.

Right now, what are we doing? We are uncovering his feet. We are eating the bread, drinking the cup, and showing forth his death until that which has been hidden appears. As the veil is taken away from our minds we are going to experience that happening simultaneously.

The writer of Hebrews talks about this rest in chapter 4, verses 9-12:

> There remaineth therefore a rest to the people of God. For he that is entered into his rest, he also hath ceased from his own works, as God did from His. Let us therefore labor to enter into that rest, lest any man fall after the same example of unbelief. For the word of God is quick, and powerful, and sharper than any twoedged sword, piercing even to the dividing asunder of soul and spirit, and of the joints and marrow, and is a discerner of the thoughts and the intents of the heart.

He tells us how we are to enter into this rest. We are to labor to enter into rest and that labor is not our own energy and works of the flesh, but that labor is filling our minds with the finished work of Calvary. That labor is uncovering his feet like Ruth did. That labor is eating of the bread on the table of shewbread and drinking of the wine on that table. Renewing the mind with the truth of the finished work of Calvary will bring us into rest. It will take away the veil that darkens the understanding of our minds, just like it was done away at the cross, over 2000 years ago. When the veil is taken away, there is nothing to stop the appearing, the expression of the Lord!

I am not talking about "positive thinking," I am not talking about "mind over matter," I am talking about the Spirit of wisdom and revelation in the knowledge of him, and the eyes of our understanding being enlightened. That is a lot different than just head knowledge. Head knowledge will puff us up. With head knowledge, we get the idea and the attitude that we have more than the other Church down the road. That is not what we're after. I do not want to fill heads with knowledge and information that puffs them up until they think "We've got a corner on the market somewhere. We've got a monopoly on God. We've got something that no one else has." Listen, to whom much is given, much is required. If we are given this, we are given it for one reason: that we might express the Lord, feeding others with bread and wine.

Revelation—A Book Of Transition

When we were in the Holy Place, or the gift realm, we thought "everyone should know what we know!" There are a lot of people in the Holy Place realm that have pitched their tent around the gifts and when you get around them, and all they want to do is rattle off at the mouth and tell you what they think you ought to know. That is the teenage realm. If you have raised any teenagers, you already are aware that they know everything. They know more than Mom and Dad. When I was young, I thought my parents were the dumbest people on the earth—until I had a few kids of my own.

In the Holy Place realm, the teenage realm, you have just enough power to be dangerous because there is still an immaturity. We are going to see in this study of Revelation, that God's purpose is to take us from one realm of glory to another realm of glory. The book of Revelation is about a transition from the Holy Place experience to the Most Holy Place experience. And it is going to happen as we uncover his feet and fill our minds with the spirit of wisdom and understanding. Then we are going to see that veil taken away and the appearing of the Lord through a people.

We are entering into rest. In Hebrews 4:12, we see the flaming sword from the Garden of Eden—the sword is the word; the flame is recognizing that his judgment was our judgment. That brings a true cleansing of our minds ("fire" also speaks of cleansing). This is the only thing that is going to take away the veil that remains in our minds, that was done away at the cross of Calvary. This is the only thing that is going to cause the Christ who has been hidden, to come forth and manifest himself on a consistent basis.

In Revelation chapter 1, John is addressing the Church in the Holy Place realm. The candlestick is not just some pretty piece of furniture just inside the eastern gate. It is not just something for us to look at and admire. It is something symbolic that we need to understand spiritually today.

Many today are confused because they are eating a mixed diet. But people are beginning to realize that and seek for truth without mixture. We are going to have baked bread that we can minister to them and show them what they should partake of that will bring them into a dimension in God that we are experiencing. Romans chapter 8 says that the manifested sons of God are going to redeem the groaning creation and bring them into the same glory. And it is not going to be as some have taught from the book of Revelation, that a people will shepherd the nations from some exalted place while others are under them in some carnal dictatorship sense. It is not going to be that way in the kingdom.

Cold (Outer Court), Lukewarm (Holy Place), or Hot (Most Holy Place)

Revelation 3:15-16:

> I know thy works, that thou art neither cold nor hot: I would that thou wert cold or hot. So then because thou art lukewarm, and neither cold nor hot, I will spue thee out of my mouth.

This is the Church of Laodicea. The "cold" that he is referring to here is the Outer Court, and "hot" is the Most Holy Place. He says you are not cold, you are not in the Outer Court in your experience, and you are not hot, or you are not in the Most Holy Place in your experience. He says "I would that thou wert cold *or* hot."

Listen to what he says next: "So then because thou art lukewarm, and neither cold nor hot, I will spue thee out of my mouth." In other words, because you are not in the Outer Court (the realm of coldness), and because you are not in the Most Holy Place (the realm intimacy), but because you are caught somewhere in the middle and not progressing on into the Most Holy Place, God says, "I just want to vomit."

So if you are "cold," you are not moving beyond the Outer Court experience and you're getting cold as a result. But they were not "hot" either. Even though they were positionally seated in the Most Holy, they were not experiencing real intimacy. Then he said that he'd rather have them cold or hot than lukewarm (caught somewhere in the middle). The sense is that lukewarmness makes him sick.

There is nothing wrong with being in the middle, but there is something wrong with being *caught* in the middle. Even though we are seated positionally in the Most Holy Place, if we have only been experiencing the Holy Place and have not gone any further than just the gift realm, and we have been caught there for years, God says it just makes him sick. That is what he is saying here: "I don't want you to be caught in that dimension. I want you to come up higher. I want you to *experience* the Most Holy Place. I don't want you to be in the Outer Court and be cold, I would rather have you in the Holy Of Holies, in the intimate realm, but if you are just caught in the middle, in the lukewarm realm, I'm not too happy about that."

Continuing with Revelation 3:17:

> Because thou sayest, "I am rich, and increased with goods, and have need of nothing;" and knowest not that thou art wretched, and miserable, and poor, and blind, and naked:

It is hard for a rich man to enter into the kingdom. This is not talking about financial wealth. It is talking about people who say, "I don't need anything. I am here in the Holy Place and I'm born again and filled with the spirit and I have need of nothing. I'm happy just waiting on a literal rapture to take place, or waiting on the glory train, or waiting to die, or waiting for my ministry to grow."

But look at the rest of the verse: "and knowest not that thou art wretched, and miserable, and poor, and blind, and naked." In other words, "Don't you know that if you've been caught in the middle and you've been there for most of your life, thinking you have no need of maturing, in reality you are wretched, miserable, poor, blind, and naked?" And many in the Holy Place realm have this mentality as if to say, "We don't need anything more. We operate in all the gifts of the Spirit. We speak in tongues more than ye all. Why do we need to come up higher? Why do we need to experience the Most Holy Place?" And the Lord says "You're pitiful. You're naked. You're wretched, you're miserable, you're spiritually bankrupt, spiritually blind—and you don't even know it!"

Trial Of The Ages

Here is the remedy—Revelation 3:18:

> I counsel thee to buy of me gold tried in the fire, that thou mayest be rich; and white raiment, that thou mayest be clothed, and that the shame of thy nakedness do not appear; and anoint thine eyes with eyesalve, that thou mayest see.

In this passage, the Lord is not telling us to ask him to pour on us all the fiery trials that he can. A lot of people believe that "the more we suffer, the more we are going to be purified," misinterpreting the scripture that tells us if we suffer with him, we will reign with him.

But listen: he is saying "I counsel thee to buy of me gold tried in the fire." Gold represents the divine nature of God. Where did we get divine nature? When did we get divine nature? The answer to both questions—at the cross of Calvary. Being "tried in the fire" is the cleansing we receive from the word concerning our divine nature (gold) and how and where we received that nature.

Continuing in verse 18 he goes on to say, "that thou mayest be rich," spiritually rich, "and white raiment, that thou mayest be clothed" with righteousness, "and that the shame of thy nakedness do not appear; and anoint thine eyes with eyesalve, that thou mayest see." What will cause us to *really* see? When we understand the person and the work of Christ, we will really see. That is the wisdom of God, which is the power of God. Paul said he was determined to know nothing except Christ and him crucified. The thing that is going to anoint our eyes with eyesalve so we may really see is coming to understand the person and the work of Christ. When we realize that Tabernacles is a second look at Passover, and it is not by works that we are saved or mature, it will really open up our spiritual eyes. When we see that the works that we do are done because we *already are* righteous, not because we're trying to *get* righteous, it changes our vision!

Tabernacles—The Most Holy Place

Look what he goes on to say in Revelation 3:20:

> Behold, I stand at the door, and knock: if any man hear my voice, and open the door, I will come in to him, and will sup with him, and he with me.

He did not say "I will come in and have breakfast with him in the Outer Court." He did not say "I will come in and have lunch with him in the Holy Place." May I paraphrase? "If you'll open the door, I'll come in and have supper with you. But you've got to open the door." The largest meal in Israel is "supper time". God is saying, "If you'll open up the door, I'll come in and we will sup with one another and you will experience a dimension in me that you have never experienced before." Guess what he is feeding us at supper time. Lamb. Bread and wine. Marriage supper of the Lamb. We are already supping with him. We are already partaking of Benjamin's mess that was five more times than the rest of Joseph's brothers. Five speaks of grace. Benjamin speaks of sons of the right hand—ruling and reigning. We're coming to understand the grace of God, fully and completely, and that constitutes ruling and reigning. It is not about "what I suffer in this realm." It is about understanding that I already suffered with him at the cross of Calvary over 2000 years ago. Then we are going to experience throne realm dominion, throne realm ruling and reigning.

If our eye be single, our whole body will be filled with light. David said in Psalm 27:4, "One thing have I desired." We've had so many things. Our eye needs to become single. We need to realize there is only one power, because the enemy's power was done away with. When we see that, there will be an uncovering and there will be something expressed out of our lives. Look at Matthew 6:22:

> The light of the body is the eye: if therefore thine eye be single, the whole body shall be full of light.

We have to have an eye for Jesus. The Holy Spirit's ministry does not speak of himself, but he glorifies the son. If he is going to glorify the son, he is going to be speaking concerning the person and the work of Christ.

The book of Revelation is a hand-delivered letter from the Lord telling us that if we will open up the door he will come in and sup with us. He will feed us of this great Feast of Tabernacles. He will feed us with this great supper at the end of the day, at the end of the age.

We have to realize that the Holy Place dimension is the teenage realm. The teenage realm is not the grown up realm. The letter to the Ephesians tells us that the Holy Spirit is a down payment. It is the Greek word *arrhabon*, which means an engagement. That is the baptism of the Holy Spirit, and it is an earnest, or a down payment. An earnest, or a down payment means there is more to come, it's not the end of the story.

Leave Old Ministry

When Elisha received the mantle from Elijah, he was plowing in the field with twelve yoke of oxen. The mantle came upon Elisha and he said to Elijah, "Let me go back and kiss my father and my mother first, before I follow you." And Elijah said "What in the world have I done to you?" So Elisha went back and kissed his father and mother and he took the oxen and he sacrificed them and fed the people. The oxen speak of ministry, as it does in 1 Timothy 5:18, where Paul says, "Thou shalt not muzzle the ox that treadeth out the corn; and, The laborer is worthy of his reward." Oxen are symbolic of ministry. So, what did Elisha do? He sacrificed his ministry that he might go on and follow Elijah. He laid down the ministry of the Holy Place dimension that he might take on the ministry of the Most Holy Place dimension.

That is where we are. I can remember when God called me to lay down what I thought was the ultimate ministry, because I was operating in the gifts of the Spirit. It feels real good to experience the anointing and the power! But God is resurrecting that ministry within us, and it is going to be a greater ministry than we've ever experienced. It is not going to be an in-part ministry, but it is going to be the full release of the anointing and the full power of God. Why? The power of God is the preaching of the cross! When our mind is filled and the veil is taken away—talk about power and anointing! And it's is only going to intensify!

When we, like Elisha, can sacrifice the ox, we're going to go somewhere in God. It is not laying it down, as in "no longer operating in that." It is laying it down as "having God resurrect it in his way and in his time, without a mixture." This will bring forth the Spirit of wisdom and knowledge and might and power. There is no mixture. We will not be speaking partly by God and partly by flesh. When we speak, it is a river of living water flowing out of us, and everything that comes in contact with it shall live! We see in Revelation that out of the city flows a river that is clear as crystal. No debris, no dogma, no traditions and doctrines of men. It is a pure river straight from the throne of God, the Most Holy Place.

A Certain Man

In Luke 14, we read about a *certain* man who made a great supper and sent his servant *at suppertime* to say to them that were bidden, "Come; for all things are now ready." We will study the living creatures in Revelation chapter 6, who keep saying, "Come and see." That is not referring to seeing with our natural eye, but with the eye of our understanding, with the eye of our spirit. Come and see the death of Christ and how you were involved in that.

Come and see the resurrection, and the seating and how you are involved in that. Come, for all things are now ready. Come to the super supper that says "It is finished."

We have a hand-delivered invitation from this certain man, to come to his "super supper" if we will open the door. "Opening the door" in Revelation chapter 4 is not talking about the born-again experience. It says there in chapter 4, that the door was already opened, so obviously, someone opened the door and something happened. Let's read Luke 14:16-20:

> Then said he unto him, "A certain man made a great supper, and bade many: and sent his servant at supper time to say to them that were bidden, 'Come; for all things are now ready.' And they all with one consent began to make excuse. The first said unto him, 'I have bought a piece of ground, I must needs go see it: I pray thee have me excused.' And another said, 'I have bought five yoke of oxen, and I go to prove them: I pray thee have me excused.' And another said, 'I have married a wife, and therefore I cannot come.'

This certain man made a great supper and people made excuses. We find the same story in Revelation 3:20. Jesus speaks the same thing again! "Open the door and I will come in and sup with you." Jesus is saying "I've already prepared this super supper for you and if you'll just open the door, I will come in and we will sit down and eat."

Those who are not making excuses are partaking of this super supper right now. It's Lamb. It's bread and wine. It is the marriage supper of the Lamb and it is not out there on some planet that we have called heaven. He has set eternity in the hearts and the minds of men, as the Amplified version of Ecclesiastes 3:11 tells us. The marriage supper is taking place within us, as spirit and soul become one. The seals on the backside are broken so the life of the Lamb can flow out. We are growing up into the stature of the fullness of Christ. We are a maturing by *viewing*, not by *doing*. We are putting a scarlet thread in the window of our soul by seeing what happened over 2000 years ago and how we are identified with it. But in the gospel, Jesus told this story and he said that people made excuses. Listen to the excuses!

I Bought A Piece Of Ground

I have never heard of someone buying a piece of ground that they have never seen before! As a matter of fact, the virtuous woman considers a field before she buys it and she, like little Ruth understands that Boaz owns the whole field! The whole earth is the Lord's and the fullness thereof! This character in the parable represents those who spend their lives working for things to satisfy the flesh—"the American dream," if you will. They spend all their time in the field of medicine, the field of science, the field of business, the field of religion, even the field of eschatology. Not that there is anything inherently wrong with these fields, but why are you in those fields? Is it for personal gain, or did God send you there? Are you shepherding yourself on the sheep (Ezekiel 34)? That is the reason we have denominations, separation, and luxation in the body of Christ—shepherds who shepherd themselves on the sheep. If you are in a field because you have been sent there by God, do you live in his presence or just in your field? If you live in his presence, *your* field will be *his* field and his field is always fruitful.

We can see the same thing in the book of Ruth, where Boaz said, "I want you to stay in my field and I have commanded the reapers to leave a little for you to glean. Don't go over into another field." A lot of times, the grass looks greener on the other side, where they have numbers and music and programs. But God is telling us today that we need to stay in the field of Boaz. Stay in the field because later on, as did Ruth, we will receive bread and wine. Ruth took one measure (an ephah), and beat it out. She had just begun gleaning. This typifies that she had just begun to eat of the finished work. Then she took six measures full of grain (crucified, died, buried, quickened, raised, and seated) to her mother-in-law—because she stayed in Boaz's field. If she beat out one measure, how much more should we beat out all six? And if we beat out all six measures, we will come to have twelve measures (crucified with, died with, buried with, quickened with, raised with, and seated with).

So, Boaz told little Ruth to glean only from his field and not go over into another field. Ruth obeyed, and ended up marrying the one who owned the whole field! Boaz, like Melchisedec, fed Ruth bread and wine—broken body, shed blood (Ruth 2:14). It is very important that we partake of bread and wine from a Melchisedec ministry. And it is very important that we sit under a shepherd that abides in a tent, as Solomon told the little Shulamite. A tent is movable. When the Lord leads you into another realm, the tent collapses, folds up, and makes the journey with you. A shepherd who abides in a tent is one who goes from realm to realm and from glory to glory—not one who has been preaching the same thing for years, from a permanent structure called Pentecost. God did not say that he was going to rebuild Solomon's Temple. That is a permanent structure. He said that he was going to rebuild the Tabernacle of David which was a *tent* with *no veil!* We must sit under a ministry and be fed where the word will take us from realm to realm and from glory to glory.

I Bought Five Yoke Of Oxen

Look at the next excuse: "I have bought five yoke of oxen." This is the five-fold ministry excuse. Many ministers have said, when presented with truth that is beyond the Holy Place mentality, "There is no way that I can minister that, after all, we have a building to pay for! There is no way I can sacrifice my ministry and teach a word out of the Most Holy Place. People will leave! I've built my ministry for twenty years, I've perfected the gifts, and I have to sacrifice this now?" This is a perfect example of a shepherd who abides in a building, a permanent structure—not in a tent. Just lay it down and sacrifice it unto the Lord, and God will raise it up to a greater degree than it was before, "That the residue of men might seek after the Lord, and all nations, upon whom my name is called, saith the Lord who doeth all these things."

I Have Married A Wife

Then another said "I have married a wife." This person was in covenant with the wrong one. He could not wait on the lover of his soul. So instead of waiting for the lover of his soul, he became married to his denomination, or to his own ministry, his own kingdom. He was in covenant with something else when he should have been in covenant with the Lord. We, like the children of Israel, must move with the cloud by day and the pillar of fire by night. We must be willing to submit it all. And I know that it is easier said than done. We must realize that we don't lay anything down in comparison to what we lay hold of. We must realize that God will resurrect whatever we lay down and raise up something that is all him, and not a mixture. It will be more than a *gift* of the word of knowledge, more than just a fragmentary part of the knowledge of God for any given situation, but it will be the *Spirit* of knowledge! Then, what comes out of our mouths will be a pure word with the power to effect change.

So, if we are going to partake of this super supper at the end of the day, we have to:

1. Stay in Boaz's field and feast on bread and wine.
2. Sacrifice the ox, and leave one realm of ministry for another.
3. Be in covenant with the right one.

We are already beginning to realize these dynamics. We are in Boaz's field; he is feeding us bread and wine. We have sacrificed all to experience the Most Holy Place. We realize that the only Covenant is the blood of Jesus. We are eating the super supper this certain man, Jesus, has prepared and we're entering into a real Covenant relationship. We are partaking of the marriage supper of the Lamb that has been roasted with fire.

After This

The first two words of Revelation chapter 4 are "after this." After what? After everything that I've said in chapters 1 through 3. He's saying "I want you to sweep out the leaven." And the only way you can do that is by understanding everything that he said to each of those seven Churches about himself. And he said "I want you to repent," or I want you to change your mind about the way you've thought, and as you do that, this door in Revelation 4, is going to be opened and you're going to behold something. The word "pent" is where we get the word "penthouse" and "pinnacle," a high place. To "re-pent" means to draw your thoughts from the realm of spirit. Let's read this passage in Revelation 4:1:

> After this I looked, and behold, a door was opened in heaven: and the first voice which I heard was as it were of a trumpet talking with me, which said, "Come up hither, and I will shew thee things which must be hereafter."

Until this time, most in the Church have taught this as a literal rapture. Remember the principle of hermeneutics. We won't get the message if we are double-minded, interpreting one verse literally and another verse spiritually. This call to come up higher is a call to spiritual maturity. It is a call to go beyond the veil of the flesh into the realm of Spirit. It is a call to go beyond the anointed flesh realm into maturity. Here he says, not to the unbeliever, but to the born again and spirit-filled, "If you'll open up the door, you can come into this throne room dimension and you can rule and reign from the position that you are already seated in."

With every clear sounding word that you hear and understand, the Lord is going to descend in you from spirit to soul and there is going to be a vibration of life out through your body. The more understanding we gain—not just head knowledge—not just information—but the more understanding of truth we gain, the more the trumpet sounds from within us. As the trumpet sounds within us, the Lord descends from spirit to soul, and we ascend, being raptured into the realm of Spirit. The last trump is sounding right now. In 1 Corinthians 15:52, it says when the last trump sounds, we are changed in a moment, in the twinkling of an eye. One definition of "twinkling of an eye" is, "the upward sweep of revelation." *It is not a future event!* It will intensify with time, but it is something that is happening right here and right now.

Notice what the trumpet is saying in Revelation 4:1: "Come up hither, and I will shew thee things which must be hereafter." In other words, this trumpet is saying, "I want you to come out of the

Holy Place experience of the gift realm and into the Most Holy Place experience, where you really already are seated. I want you to come from one dimension to another dimension. I want you to lay down the ministry of the Holy Place and come up higher because I want to experience a covenant relationship with you where I can reproduce myself through you. "

Not A Fat Baby With Wings

This trumpeter is not a "fat baby cherub with wings" that will step out on an atmospheric cloud and blow a horn some day, as some have taught. This trumpet began to sound and it was a prophetic voice, a prophetic word, which spoke to him and said, "Come up hither." A trumpet is a clear sounding word. That trumpet is getting clearer in its sound in This Day. The sounding of the trumpet, particularly the sounding of the last trumpet, is going to bring the coming of the Lord. Look at 1 Thessalonians 4:16-17:

> For the Lord himself shall descend from heaven with a shout, with the voice of the archangel, and with the trump of God: and the dead in Christ shall rise first: then we which are alive, and remain, shall be caught up together with them in the clouds, to meet the Lord in the air: and so shall we ever be with the Lord.

Some teachers have used this scripture also, as a literal, physical rapture. The word "caught" is the Greek word *harpazo*, and it comes from the Hebrew word "nasa" or "nacha," that means "to love with a love embrace," or "to marry." Isn't that what happened to Ruth when she partook of enough bread and wine? Isn't that what happened to Paul when he was "caught up?" Yet he remained on the earth not only to tell about his experience, but to preach from the throne. The Greek word for "caught" in 1 Thessalonians 4:17 is also the same Greek word used in Acts 8:39, where Philip was caught up, and again, he was here on earth ministering the Lord Jesus. God has a people who are experiencing this love embrace in the here and now. Where is the loving room of the living room of

God? It is in the Most Holy Place, in an intimate love relationship with the Lord where his very nature is being reproduced out of our lives. In this place, our soul is enraptured in his presence on a consistent basis that steadily intensifies as we mature.

Trumpeting A Clarion Word

The Young's Literal Translation says it this way:

> For the Lord himself will descend from heaven *in* the shout, *in* the voice of the chief messenger, and *in* the trump of God (emphasis added).

In the shout, not just with a shout. *In* the voice, not just with the voice. *In* the trump of God, not just with the trump of God. All of these trumpets speak of a clear sounding word about the person and the work of Christ. As we come to understand that, there is going to be a descending of the Lord himself. He descends from spirit to soul, as soul is *lower* than spirit, (spirit, soul, and body). As we hear a clear sounding word, as we feast on the bread and the wine, the Lord himself descends from our spirit to our soul and is expressed through our body, *in* the shout, *in* the voice of the chief messenger, *in* the clear sounding word. *That* is the coming of the Lord.

With every trumpet sound that becomes clearer, and with the understanding of that clarion word, there is a greater descending of the Lord from spirit to soul. And there is a greater experience of ascension for us into the air, which is the realm of spirit. We'll be caught up a little higher in every trumpet sound!

The Last Trump

Finally, in the last trump, we'll be totally changed. We find the last trump in the book of Revelation when the seven vials of blood are poured upon our heads. With each trump, there is a little more understanding that comes concerning the death of Christ. With each trump, there is a little more clarity brought concerning the person and the work of Christ. With each trump, he comes in the shout, in the voice, in the trump. It is not something in the sweet by and by. It is not something in the future as in two years down the road! It is right now! It is beginning to happen right now as we eat Lamb that is not soddened down with water, but roasted with fire. It is happening as we partake of bread and wine. We can also read about the last trump in 1 Corinthians 15:51-57:

> Behold, I shew you a mystery; We shall not all sleep, but we shall all be changed, in a moment, in the twinkling of an eye, at the last trump: for the trumpet shall sound, and the dead shall be raised incorruptible, and we shall be changed. For this corruptible must put on incorruption, and this mortal must put on immortality. So when this corruptible shall have put on incorruption, and this mortal shall have put on immortality, then shall be brought to pass the saying that is written, 'Death is swallowed up in victory.' 'O death, where is thy sting? O grave, where is thy victory?' The sting of death is sin; and the strength of sin is the law. But thanks be to God, which giveth us the victory through our Lord Jesus Christ.

The phrase "in the twinkling of an eye" does not mean the blinking or batting of an eye. The thing that makes our eyes twinkle is light! Another meaning of this phrase is "the upward sweep of revelation." The revelation of Jesus Christ! Hear what the trumpets are really saying!

The text goes on to say "at the last trump." When the vials of blood are all poured on us, the last trump in the book of Revelation, what is going to happen? The last trumpet shall sound, and the dead shall be raised incorruptible, and we shall be changed. For this corruptible must put on incorruption.

Right now, any veil that is not taken away from our minds is corruption. Corruption here, does not talk about the physical body. "Corruption" and "incorruption" has to do with the mind, whereas "mortal" and "immortality" has to do with the physical body. But when we get rid of the veil, the residue of Adam, that was done away but is yet to be taken away, we are going to put on incorruption in our minds as we fill our minds with the person and the work of Christ. Then automatically, this mortal must put on immortality. It will not have any choice in the matter. When the veil is taken away from our minds, that is the Lord descending. That is the last trump. That is the upward sweep of Revelation. That is the vials of blood being poured upon our heads.

Just as John 3:7 says, "ye *must* be born again," so as a people put on incorruption, their bodies must respond. Our bodies are going to automatically respond and there is going to be quickening life—more than just healing—there is going to be quickening life take place in the very atoms and the molecular structure of the cells of our bodies. Jesus, in his resurrected body appeared to the disciples, walked through walls, and let Thomas put his hand in his wounds. But that is not the issue and we are not to make that our focus. The person and the work of Christ is the issue. He is our only focus. The nature of Jesus Christ is walking through walls today—walls of defense erected by hurting people who have been kicked out of the religious system because they were deemed "disqualified" by the law. The nature of Jesus Christ is breaking down the middle wall of partition in the religious Church, smashing it to Kingdom come!

The text in 1 Corinthians 15 continues, "Then shall be brought to pass the saying that is written, 'Death is swallowed up in victory.' 'O death, where is thy sting? O grave, where is thy victory?' The sting of death is sin; and the strength of sin is the law." When Adam sinned, we were dead in sins and trespasses. The wages of sin is death. We got what we deserved. The judgment of God was executed against us at the cross of Calvary. My paraphrase is: The sting of death is sin and the strength of sin is thinking that you can add one cubit to your stature by your works! If you are still living in a religious system of legalism, you will have sin to deal with because law gives sin its strength. By grace are ye saved, through faith; and neither the grace nor the faith comes from yourselves, it is a gift of God—not of works, lest any man should boast.

The strength of sin is the law, even though it was fulfilled at the cross of Calvary. If we think that we are to be involved in a works salvation and that whatever we do, we can become more righteous or get brownie points with God, we put ourselves right back into the realm of death. But when we come to understand that we can't add one cubit to our stature, then like the lily, we will grow. The work was accomplished over 2000 years ago. When we come to understand that, and how it all happened, there will be some changes. This corruptible mind is going to receive incorruption. The veil will be taken away, and the body *has* to respond—it will have no choice in the matter.

The upward sweep of revelation, the last trump, partaking of the bread and the wine, staying in Boaz's field and uncovering his feet—these are some of the ways the Lord brings us into a love relationship with him.

Chambers—Courts, Courts, Courts

Chapter 1 of the Song Of Solomon begins with a woman taking her walk in the Outer Court. She sees "chambers" (plural) or "courts." She says "I'm totally smitten with the king, but my problem out here in the Outer Court is that I think I'm as black as the tents of Kedar." The little Shulamite thought there was no way that the king could love her because she was black. That has nothing to do with the color of the skin. The word "Kedar" means "the second son of Ishmael." She was saying, "There is no way that I can come into union with the king because I am a son of the flesh." Look at Song Of Solomon 1:5:

> I am black, but comely, O ye daughters of Jerusalem,
> like the tents of Kedar, like the curtains of Solomon.

She had the mindset that she was a son of the flesh. She sees herself in Ishmael (the flesh,) and not in Isaac (the supernatural birth). She sees herself in Adam, not in Christ. But look what the king says to her in verse 15:

> Behold, thou art fair, my love; behold, thou art fair;
> thou hast dove's eyes.

She says "I'm just black as the tents of Kedar, there is no way you're going to want to have union with me." And at the end of chapter 2, he takes her to the mountain of Bether, which means "the mountain of suffering," The word "Bether" in the Strong's Concordance is #1336, which refers to #1335 and #1334, which means "to chop up," "to divide." God cut covenant with himself at Calvary, the mountain of suffering. It is here that the king shows her that her blackness was done away with, her spots were done away with, and that is what released her to come into a love relationship with him!

Now he is teaching her that she is as beautiful or as comely as the curtains of Solomon. The Lord is saying, "Don't you know that you are fair and pleasant?" And our response has been "Lord, I don't believe that." To which the Lord responds, "And that's why you're still acting like you are black, and like you still have spots." The Lord is saying, "If you think you still have spots and blemishes, then you are going to *act* like you still have spots and blemishes. If you think you are the son of Ishamael, then you need to come to the mountain of Bether, the mountain of suffering, and see that my suffering was your suffering, and I did away with all your blackness. Now you are a new creation." That will release us to come into a love relationship with the King.

The Song Of Songs, Which Is Solomon's—
Let's Take It Up An Octave!

We live our lives from the outside looking in. We go to Church, and we think that if we sing the right praise songs, and perform in worship, we will appeased some "god" that will come from some outside heaven and visit us. Then we say, "The Lord is in this place." I guess that's why the New Testament refers to us as Greeks—we think and live just like they did if we have this mindset. I love to praise and worship God! But I think we've done it for the wrong reasons in the past, and some people are still worshipping for the wrong reasons. God is omnipresent. He is everywhere! But could it be that the Lord is *manifestly* in this place because *we* are in this place? He showed up from the inside of us, not from the outside of us. We live our lives from the outside (Outer Court) looking in. We're outside in. We need to live from the inside (Most Holy Place) looking out. We need to be inside out! Then, the Christ that's inside us will manifest!

Let's take it up an octave and sing a new song! We love to praise and worship the Lord, but what does the Lord love? Jesus said, "This people draweth near unto me with their mouth, and honoreth me with their lips, but their heart is far from me. But in vain they do worship me, teaching for doctrines the commandments of men." Then he said, "But the hour cometh, and now is, when the true worshippers shall worship the Father in spirit and in truth; for the Father seeketh such to worship him." Vain worship or true worship—the choice is ours. He wants us to *be* a people for a name, he wants us to *be* a praise and a worship and a glory (Isaiah 62:7, Jeremiah 13:11, Zephaniah 3:20)! So, if we think praise and worship is something we *do,* instead of something we *are,* the Lord is missing out on a blessing! The best of songs, which is the Lord's—is a people! The Lord, our God rejoices over us with singing (Zephaniah 3:17)!

Off With The Veil—Let's Raise The Roof!

Where there is a veil, the Lord cannot appear. The veil must be taken away. The veil was done away in Christ, but yet the veil must be taken away from our minds (2 Corinthians 3:14). When that happens, our corrupted thinking becomes incorruptible and immortality (Christ) follows suit. Talk about holy, pure, and true thanksgiving, praise, and worship—we'll raise the roof! The veil is taken away by feasting on as much as we can of the roasted Lamb, unleavened bread, and wine. We must like Ruth, uncover his feet and then we will enter into rest. The trumpets say, "Come up hither. Don't stay in the candlestick realm, but come up hither." It is not a literal, physical rapture. It is a spiritual rapture. It is time to experience the married life. The Church has made a doctrine of a literal rapture the focus, while the Word of God has been trumpeting for over 6000 years, "Behold the Lamb!" The person and the work of Christ is our only focus.

Jasper—Reuben—Behold, a Son

Let's read about what happens next in Revelation 4:2-3:

> And immediately I was in the Spirit: and behold, a throne was set in heaven, and one sat on the throne. And he that sat was to look upon like a jasper and a sardine stone: and there was a rainbow round about the throne, in sight like unto an emerald.

Let's look first at the word "jasper." The jasper stone was the stone of Reuben. The name "Reuben" means "behold, a son!" That is what we are beholding as we read this verse. We are beholding the son, the person and the work of Christ. So, what did he see here in the throne but a vision of the son, the person and the work of Christ? The sardine stone is red in color and was the stone of Judah, which again, speaks of Christ.

Emerald Rainbow

Then, in Revelation 4:2-3, John saw a rainbow round about the throne, in sight like an emerald:

> And immediately I was in the Spirit: and behold, a throne was set in heaven, and one sat on the throne. And he that sat was to look upon like a jasper and a sardine stone: and there was a rainbow round about the throne, in sight like unto an emerald.

An emerald is green, the color which symbolizes life throughout the scriptures. When we talk about the rainbow, we are dealing with covenant. God made covenant with Noah by the sign of a rainbow in the heavens. "Noah" means "rest and grace." Noah is a picture of a people who come out of an old world dominated by the curse and sin, and into a new world. They did this by coming into an Ark. "Ark" is always a type of Jesus Christ. Noah and his family got into this Ark. They did not escape judgment. They heard the winds and the waters beating on that Ark. We are in the Ark. When we realize that we are *in* Christ Jesus, we realize that his judgment was our judgment. They did not escape judgment—they were right in the midst of it! But they were safe. Isn't it good that we can get in a vehicle called Christ, leave a world that is dominated by sin and giants, and come into a new world of righteousness?

Our new world begins when we accept Jesus as savior, but we really come into a new beginning when we see that it was not just one man who hung on the cross, but we were there too. His death was our death, His crucifixion was our crucifixion. His burial was our burial. When we, the eagles, gather round the carcass, the death, we will see that there are treasures in darkness, there are treasures in the death. When we answer the riddle of the ages, it will change our lives completely. Something will come from within to without, from invisible to visible, from heaven to earth in manifestation, and the knowledge of the glory of the Lord will fill the earth like the waters cover the sea!

So, the rainbow speaks of covenant. When we accept Jesus as savior, we enter into a contract or a covenant that was settled forever, before the foundations when Jesus shed his blood (Revelation 13:8). When a person gets married in the natural, they enter into a covenant. Now I know we are in union with him. I understand we were married to him, but to really experience the covenant in the full sense of the word is when we come, in our experience, out of the Holy Place into the Holy of Holies and he can reproduce himself through us. That is what happened in the book of Ruth. That is what happened in the Song Of Solomon. This is a paradoxical truth. We were married to the Lord at our initial salvation, but we did not know it by experience. Our experience must go through the protocol.

In the Ark of Noah, the window was on the roof. They were to look up. We are to look up—not directionally, but dimensionally—for our redemption draweth nigh. Noah's Ark represents a people who understand that his judgment was their judgment. They were *in* the Ark, and we are *in* Christ. We were in him before the foundations of the world, and we were in him at the cross of Calvary. The full judgment of God beat upon him and he took the totality of God's judgment *as us*. We that are in him received the judgment of God at the cross of Calvary. And God's judgment was executed at Calvary's cross. When we understand what took place and we look up and see what happened at the cross, we are going to see as we've never seen before. We will anoint our eyes with eyesalve. The preaching of the cross is the wisdom of God. It is the power of God. Paul determined to know nothing, save Christ and him crucified.

When we look up *and behind* dimensionally, as did John, and see what happened at the cross, we will begin to see as we've never seen before. We're going to see differently. When our eye is single, our whole body will be full of light. We will see the big picture. We will see that the Bible is about redemption! It is the revelation of Jesus Christ!

E. W. Bullinger writes in his book, <u>Number in Scripture</u>[25]:

> When the waters abated, it was Noah, "the eighth person" (2 Peter 2:5) who stepped out on to a new earth to commence a new order of things. "Eight souls" (1 Peter 3:20) passed through it with him to the new or regenerated world.

Eight is the number of new beginnings. Eight is the dominical number. It is the number of his name, Jesus (888)[26]. 888: 8 (body) 8 (soul) 8 (spirit). He was *fully* Jesus.

Mt. Ararat—The Curse Reversed

When the waters receded, they were landed on Mt. Ararat, which means "the curse is reversed." In light of this, let's read Genesis 6:14:

> Make thee an ark of gopher wood; rooms shalt thou make in the ark, and shalt pitch it within and without with pitch. And this is the fashion which thou shalt make it of: The length of the ark shall be three hundred cubits, the breadth of it fifty cubits, and the height of it thirty cubits. A window shalt thou make to the ark, and in a cubit shalt thou finish it above; and the door of the ark, shalt thou set in the side thereof: with lower, second, and third stories shalt thou make it.

If Noah is to make an Ark of gopher wood, he is going to have to cut down a tree. Right there is a death, because the tree is cut off from its life source. Wood speaks of humanity. Jesus was cut off out of the land of the living to become our Ark. Then Noah is to make rooms in the Ark and pitch it within and without with pitch. That word "pitch," in Hebrew is "atonement." In type, what spiritually sealed this Ark was the precious blood of Jesus.

In verse 15, the length of the Ark is three hundred cubits—the number of complete deliverance. The breadth is fifty cubits—Pentecost and Jubilee. The height is thirty cubits—maturity.

In verse 16, we see that there are three levels in this boat—Outer Court, Holy Place, and Holy of Holies. Notice, the window was not just on the third story, it was on top, on the roof above, meaning: "Look up for your redemption draweth nigh." It is not looking up directionally, but looking up dimensionally. Noah is to make a door in this Ark. There is only one door! There is only one way into this Ark, and it is through The Door, Jesus Christ.

In Genesis chapter 8, Noah first sent out a raven which went forth to and fro, until the waters were dried up from the face of the earth. There are some glorious liberties that we are going to find when we study this further. But for now, let me say that the raven is seen in the book of Revelation and it represents unclean thoughts. When we study Revelation 18, we will see that Babylon has become the habitation of every foul spirit, and a cage of every unclean and hateful bird.

Then Noah sent forth a dove to see if the waters were abated from off the face of the earth. The first time he sent the dove out, it came back. The second time (seven days later,) he sent the dove out and it came back with an olive leaf in its mouth. The third time (another seven days,) he sent the dove out it did not return. The dove, which is a symbol of the Holy Spirit, is connected with a new world. As Lynn Hiles says, "The dove goes all the way from Genesis chapter 8, to Matthew chapter 3, looking for an olive branch—and it finds Jesus in the river Jordan! John the Baptist understood that where the Spirit descends as a dove is where the new world is—and the dove landed on Jesus being baptized in the Jordan River! *He* is where the new world is. *He* is the new creation! *He* is the Ark. *He* is where the curse is reversed. *He* is the New Man and the Jordan River is where you identify with him because if you go down with him in the waters of baptism, what you're saying is, 'His death was my death!'"

Rainbow—Different Levels Of Light Through Three-Sided Vessel

There are numerous truths about the rainbow in Revelation chapter 4. We see a rainbow when we bend light through a three-sided prism. We are a three-part being—spirit, soul, and body. There are three dimensions to the Tabernacle; Outer Court, Holy Place, and Most Holy Place. We are the temple of God—Outer Court (body), Holy Place (soul), Holy of Holies (spirit). We are made in the image of our triune God—Father, Son and Holy Ghost. To get this rainbow, light is sent through a three-dimensional prism, which we are. As our soul receives the understanding that is in our spirit, we are going to have that quickening light vibrate through our body. This rainbow shows us the different dimensions that we experience in the light of God flowing through our three-sided prism.

The rainbow round about the throne was green, like an emerald. Green speaks of life. Planted in his death, a lily comes to life. If we want to have the book on the inside of us unsealed, and the life of the Lamb flow out, then we've got to understand some things about the book of Revelation. As we unlock the truths in the book of Revelation, we are going to experience more manifestation of the life of Jesus coming from our spirit to our soul and out through our mouths, and in our lives, than we have ever experienced before. When the revelation of Jesus Christ is a revelation to you, it will walk itself out! God wants to take us to the green room. The Most Holy Place is the green room of God. After the little Shulamite says to the king, "You're not going to want me because I'm black as the tents of Kedar. I am in the flesh," he comes to her in the end of chapter 1, and in verse 15 he says:

> Behold, thou art fair, my love; behold, thou art fair;
> thou hast doves' eyes.

He tells her she is not black as she thought, she is not of the flesh. Twice he tells her that she is fair, speaking of her spirit. Now look at what he says to her in verse 16:

> Behold, thou art fair, my beloved, yea pleasant: also
> our bed is green.

At this point she sees that *he* is fair, but does not see herself that way. That's too much for her to grasp. Notice that she called the bed *our* bed. This points to the fact that his place of rest is also our place of rest. She also calls *him* pleasant here, but she becomes pleasant by the time we get to chapter 7, verse 6. It takes her a while to realize who she is.

In chapter 2 of Song Of Solomon, the Shulamite is still in the "dating game" Holy Place realm. Look at verses 4 and 5:

> He brought me to the banqueting house, and his
> banner over me was love. Stay me with flagons,
> comfort me with apples: for I am sick of love.

There is nothing wrong with the gift realm, but that is the dating realm. That is the courting realm. But we cannot stay in that realm. We've got to move beyond that dimension. Notice the word, "banqueting." It is the Hebrew word "effervescent." It is like a bottle of champagne. You shake it up and pop the cork. That is what happened when we received the baptism of the Holy Spirit. Someone laid their hands upon us, shook us up, popped the cork, and we began to speak in tongues. Something that was already in us, came out!

Today he is saying "I want to take you into the green room. I want you to experience *more than* the Holy Place realm. I want to do more than just court you. I want to marry you. I don't want to take you home after the date is over." Today he wants us to experience the green room. The "our bed" of 1:16 became "her bed" in 3:1, and then "his bed" in 3:7—we finally enter his rest. The Lord is saying, "Our bed is green." He wants to birth something. He wants to reproduce himself through her. The only way that can happen is for her to realize that he has made her worthy and that she is not black like the tents of Kedar. Her self image was marred because she saw herself in the image of the flesh, not in the image of the new creation she had become in Christ. This is an imagination (2 Corinthians 10:5). Some of the "nations" mentioned in the book of Revelation are not Iraq and Iran, or Russia. They are condem-nations, imagi-nations, denomi-nations. It is condemnation that has kept us from realizing that *he is* our worthiness! We are worthy to become one in union experientially with him, and birth something. We are worthy not because of self-righteousness, but because of what happened at the cross of Calvary over 2000 years ago.

Then, in Song Of Solomon 4:12 the king says to her:

> A garden inclosed is my sister, my spouse; a spring shut up, a fountain sealed.

This Shulamite did not stay a garden inclosed for long! As soon as she was taken to the mountain of Bether, he opened her up. Every woman in the Old Testament that typifies the bride was barren. They were fountains inclosed. It wasn't long before the Shulamite bride was opened up and was no longer a garden inclosed or a spring shut up, or a fountain sealed. She became *unsealed,* as we find in Song Of Solomon 4:13-16:

> Thy plants are an orchard of pomegranates, with pleasant fruits; camphire, with spikenard, spikenard and saffron; calamus and cinnamon, with all trees of frankincense; myrrh and aloes, with all the chief spices: A fountain of gardens, a well of living waters, and streams from Lebanon. Awake, O north wind; and come, thou south; blow upon my garden, that the spices thereof may flow out. Let my beloved come into his garden, and eat his pleasant fruits.

This is just like the passage in Revelation chapter 5 where we read of the book within, sealed on the backside with seven seals. As we come to understand the horses in relation to Jesus Christ, every seal is going to be broken, and out of us is going to flow the Lord Jesus Christ.

Now compare Song Of Solomon 4:11 with Song Of Solomon 5:1:

> Thy lips, O my spouse, drop as the honeycomb: honey and milk are under thy tongue; and the smell of thy garments is like the smell of Lebanon.
> I am come into my garden, my sister, my spouse: I have gathered my myrrh with my spice; I have eaten my honeycomb with my honey; I have drunk my wine with my milk ...

Where did he get the honey and the milk? This is a natural picture of something spiritual. We must be mature enough to understand what is going on. He got the honey and the milk from under her tongue, during an intimate relationship. That speaks of union and intimacy that went beyond the "dating game." That speaks of her praise and worship. She is loving and enjoying her husband. In chapter 4, verse 16, when he "eats his pleasant fruits," he is enjoying his inheritance of the fruitful saints! 1 Corinthians 3:9 speaks of this kind of relationship with God. The King James Version says that we are his *husbandry*. The Amplified version says "For we are fellow workmen (joint promoters, laborers together) with and for God; you are God's garden and vineyard and field under cultivation, [you are] God's building."

In the New Testament, our mind is compared to a womb (Luke 12:35, Ephesians 6:14, 1 Peter 1:13). Our woman, the soul, is our mind, our will, and our emotions—the womb of our mind. When we are born again we receive the Incorruptible Seed of God in our spirit, our inner man. Now our spirit is wall to wall Jesus. The Holy Spirit wants to impregnate the womb of our mind with this Incorruptible Seed. Another way of saying it is: he wants to get the salvation that is in our spirit into our soul so the veil can be taken away, that was done away with at the cross. In doing this, he will be reproduced through our lives. He will appear.

In Revelation chapter 4, we just begin to see what God wants to do and where he wants to take us. It speaks of firstfruit in the Feast of Passover, or resurrection, but it is just a vision. The door was opened and John sees a vision. We experience Tabernacles by taking a second look at Passover. So, John has a vision of resurrection experienced and then immediately *sees* the throne realm. When he saw the twenty-four elders, they were not seated *in* the throne, but *around* the throne. Here, we see that there is a progression in understanding the death of Christ. Once we understand that we were resurrected with him then we will understand that we are seated with him. But we really don't see that *fulfilled* until later in the book of Revelation.

What else do we know about the color green in the word of God? Let's look at the passage in Psalm 23:1-3

> The Lord is my shepherd; I shall not want. He maketh me to lie down in green pastures; He leadeth me beside the still waters. He restoreth my soul.

He maketh me to lie down in *green* pastures. Then in verse 3, he *restores* my *soul*. When we come out of the dating place, or the Holy Place, and are led into the green room, when we sacrifice that which is known as "ministry," and begin to partake of bread and wine from the throne, from the green room, our soul is going to be restored. We get some of this restoration in the Holy Place, but we get a progressive restoration of the womb, and we can birth something when we hear a word from the Most Holy Place, from the throne.

No Wedding, No Intimacy

The rainbow represents covenant relationship. We're not believing Jezebel's lies. The truth is—no wedding, no intimacy. If you are not going to enter into this aspect of the covenant where you come into union *in experience* with him, there is not going to be anything reproduced out of your life. We're coming into a new aspect of the covenant of God as we come into this union experientially. We must leave that Holy Place dimension and come into the Most Holy Place dimension in our experience.

When we see this word "rainbow," it has to do with a people that have understanding of the covenant—who we were has been done away with at Calvary. The only thing that is keeping us from experiencing the Most Holy Place dimension is the fact that we think, like the little Shulamite, that we have black spots. If you think that you're Adam, if you think you have black spots, if you think you are as black as the tents of Kedar—which is another way of saying that you think you have two natures—you think with duality. James said that a double-minded man is unstable in all his ways. If this describes you, then you have a veil that has been untaken away from between your ears, and it is preventing you from experiencing the secret place.

The rainbow has seven colors and we see seven colors from the rainbow in Noah's day to the rainbow around the throne. The rainbow speaks of covenant and there are different levels of that covenant. In this seventh day, we are coming into the highest level of the covenant. There are seven feasts of the Lord. There are seven pieces of furniture in Moses' tabernacle. The rainbow that was round about the throne can also speak of praise and worship. The stone of Judah on the breastplate of the high priest was the emerald. Judah represents praise and worship. The only way we have true praise and worship going on in our midst, is as we see the death of Christ. Appropriating the principle of first mention, the first time we see worship mentioned in the Bible is when Abraham takes Isaac up the mountain to sacrifice him. When we have true praise and worship from an understanding of the sacrifice, it will release throne room operation within our life.

Feast Of Firstfruits

So, in Revelation chapter 4, we see Firstfruits, and the beginning of resurrection. He is not just seeing Passover and Unleavened Bread here, but Firstfruits or resurrection, the sheaf of firstfruit. Look at verses 2 and 3 again:

> And immediately I was in the Spirit: and behold, a throne was set in heaven, and one sat on the throne. And he that sat was to look upon like a jasper and a sardine stone: and there was a rainbow round about the throne, in sight like unto an emerald.

One sat on the throne and he looked like a jasper and a sardius stone, and there was an emerald rainbow around the throne. John is seeing the resurrection of Jesus and him seated on the throne. He also sees a many-membered people resurrected. John said, "And he that sat was to look upon like a jasper and a sardine stone." Jasper is the stone of Benjamin. The name "Benjamin" means "Son of the right hand." Sardius is the stone of Reuben. "Reuben" means "Behold a son." In the book of Genesis, the order of the tribes of Reuben and Benjamin is first and last, respectively[27]. So John was seeing the Son, the First and the Last, in verses 2 and 3. John was seeing the resurrection. Look at Revelation 4:4:

> And round about the throne were four and twenty seats: and upon the seats I saw four and twenty elders sitting, clothed in white raiment; and they had on their heads crowns of gold.

The twenty-four elders are indicative of the tabernacle of Moses, where there were twenty-four courses of priests that served in the tabernacle. There were twenty-four courses of singers in Solomon's temple. David also set up twenty-four courses of priests and singers in his tent. This passage in Revelation is not referring to king-priest ministers yet, these are just people that are *around* the throne. This typifies resurrection. These seats were *round about* the throne. They are not yet *seated in and on* the throne. This is resurrection, not seating. There were twenty-four elders with white raiment. These were not yet kings and priests fully manifested because the seats were still *around* the throne. They have the righteousness of God. We have the righteousness of God even as a new born Christian. These are not ruling and reigning yet—they're just coming to understand something about the sheaf of firstfruit. Let's continue with Revelation 4:5-6:

> And out of the throne proceeded lightnings and thunderings and voices: and there were seven lamps of fire burning before the throne, which are the seven Spirits of God. And before the throne there was a sea of glass like unto crystal: and in the midst of the throne, and round about the throne, were four

beasts full of eyes before and behind.

Here, we see Outer Court, Holy Place, and Most Holy Place. Notice the sea of glass in verse 6. This typifies the molten sea in Solomon's temple and the brazen laver in Moses' tabernacle, which was in the Outer Court. The seven lamps of fire in verse 5 typify the Holy Place. The lightnings and thunderings in verse 5 proceeded out of the throne—the Most Holy Place. First, lightening—illumination—comes from the throne, and then thunderings—a trumpeting or a thundering out—the voice of God.[28]

The Four Living Creatures

The four beasts in verse 6 are not the same beasts in Revelation chapter 13, which are wild beasts. These four beasts in verse 6 represent creatures expressing life. The number 4 means "universal." North, south, east, and west. This speaks of people expressing life, who are full of eyes—perfection of perception. To be a creature full of eyes before and behind, means that we can go into any realm and minister to people. For example: we can be good parents who get down and play with the children and their toys to win their hearts. When we minister to people who are not yet in the deeper life, we do not zap them with the lightnings and speak to them with thunder. We minister to them on their level, with grace and mercy, just as our Father does with each one of us. We can be good parents when we model our lives after the greatest parent, Father God. This does not mean compromising the word, it means feeding them what they are ready to eat. Paul said, "I wanted to speak spiritual things to you, but I had to speak carnally because you were still babes in Christ. I fed you with milk and not solid food because you were not able to bear it." The word talks about "the controversy of Zion" and these things are controversial, so we need to be able to deal with people where they are.

Now, in Revelation 4:7, we read:

> And the first beast was like a lion, and the second beast like a calf, and the third beast had a face as a man, and the fourth beast was like a flying eagle.

The lion, the calf, the man and the eagle were the banners that were over the twelve tribes of the Israelites. When they were at rest, there were three tribes in each four directions, north, south, east, and west, forming a cross. We also see a cross when we look at the placement of the furniture in Moses' tabernacle. If we had an aerial view, we could see a cross within a cross. His death was our death. We see the same picture in the exodus with the blood on the door posts and on the side posts—a double cross: meaning that his cross was our cross. What does the scripture mean "take up your cross and follow him?" It does not mean that we are to trudge along and just let anything come into our lives and forget about renewing our minds. It does not mean that we are to just accept everything as coming from God. Taking up our cross and following the Lord means to fill our minds with the fact that he already took up the cross over 2000 years ago, and so did we. Because he was crucified for all, all were crucified, because he died for all, then were all dead (2 Corinthians 5:14). It does not mean "If I'm poor, I've got to stay poor and that is bearing my cross." That is not at all the sense that God wants to convey to us. To bear the cross of the Lord Jesus Christ, even to bear the marks of the Lord Jesus, is to see that his suffering was our suffering at Calvary—the double cross. A cross within a cross—realizing it already happened and if we suffer with him, we will reign with him.

So, the first beast was like a lion, the second beast like a calf, the third beast had a face as a man, and the fourth beast was like a flying eagle. In Ezekiel chapter 1, verse 10, again we see that the book of Revelation is a "carbon copy" of the book of Ezekiel. In the end of the book of Ezekiel we see a people who are called "the Lord is there." In the end of Revelation, we see the Lord in the midst of the city—the same thing. John's revelation was not at all strange to those of his day who knew the scriptures. John used the phrase "the son of man." Over eighty times, Ezekiel is called "the son of man." John saw colored horses; Zechariah saw colored *and* spotted horses. John's revelation was understood by the people of that era. Look what Ezekiel saw in chapter 1, verse 10:

> As for the likeness of their faces, they four had the
> face of a man, and the face of a lion, on the right

> side: and they four had the face of an ox on the left side; they four also had the face of an eagle.

Each of these animals is a king in their own domain. Man is God's crowning glory (Isaiah 62, Jeremiah 13:11, Hebrews 2:9-10). The lion is the king of beasts. The ox is the king of the burden-bearing animals. The eagle is the king of the heavens and the earth. Each of these animals is portrayed in the gospels as an aspect of the nature of Jesus. Matthew wrote to the Jews and revealed the "lion" nature of Jesus (Zechariah 9:9). The book of Mark, written to the Romans, portrays the "ox," or the servant nature of Jesus (Isaiah 42:1). Luke wrote to the Greeks about the "man" nature of Jesus (Zechariah 6:12). And John wrote to us all, showing us the "eagle" nature of Jesus (Isaiah 40:9). The gospels declare the historical surroundings of the life, death, burial, and resurrection of Jesus.

In Exodus chapters 30 and 37 holy anointing oil was mixed according to the art of the apothecary, to anoint the prophet, the priest, and the king. This anointing oil had four ingredients that portray the Christ of the four gospels, namely myrrh, cinnamon, calamus and cassia. A fifth ingredient, a hin of oil, speaks of the book of Acts where the promise of the Spirit was poured out. What does this mean to us? It is going to take the understanding of the gospel—Matthew, Mark, Luke, John, Acts, the epistles, for us to be brought to a place where the anointing is released, where Christ can be expressed and where he can be seen—the revelation of Jesus Christ.

In Revelation chapter 3, the Lord said that if we'd open the door, he would come in and have a super supper with us. In Revelation chapter 4, the door is opened and the Lord says, "Come up higher." Come out of the Holy Place dimension. Lay the ministry down. Sacrifice the ox. Come up higher! When John did that, what did he see? He saw a people in resurrection—firstfruit. He saw a people come to understand not just the death and the burial, but the resurrection. Following chapter 4, we are going to see some things really begin to happen!

In chapter 5 is the book within that is sealed on the backside with seven seals. It is not talking about the Bible being sealed. It is not talking about the book of Revelation being sealed, even though it has been sealed. It is talking about the book *within* that has been sealed, like the little Shulamite that was a fountain sealed. It is talking about us coming to an understanding of the death, burial, and resurrection and our identification with it. That is going to break the seven seals on the backside that have kept Christ from being revealed on a consistent basis.

When we come into chapter 6, we see all the horses—the white horse (the righteous earth walk of Jesus), the red horse (Jesus becoming sin), the black horse (Jesus dying spiritually), and the pale horse (Jesus going into hell). In the fifth seal, we see the souls under the altar. Right now, we are a soul under the altar because we are losing the residue of the Adamic thinking and we are putting on the mind of Christ. Then we see an earthquake, which speaks of resurrection.

With the seventh seal, there is silence in heaven about a half an hour—selah. That is what will happen when we come to understand that it is not by works. When we understand that it is by the grace of God, it happened at the cross, and we were there, there is going to be some silence. We will not be trying to work up things in the energy of the flesh. We will no longer have the thinking that we can add anything to our righteousness. We are going to realize that we can't add anything to our stature. There is nothing we can say, there is nothing we can do. When we come to realize there is nothing we can say and there is nothing we can do—that is rest! That is where we are headed. In volume 2 we will look further into the silence of the seventh seal.

As we progressively understand the book of Revelation, there's going to be a greater unsealing and a greater expression of the Lord, on a consistent basis. And this is not limited to the book of Revelation, but the entire Bible. When it is a true revelation, the revelation will walk itself out in our every day lives. It won't just be head knowledge. It won't just be information. But it will be something that will be quickened. It will be the spirit of wisdom and revelation in the knowledge of him. When incorruption comes, something is going to happen. It's going to be the unveiling of Christ to the extent that the very molecular structure of our bodies will be changed!

That is what we must see. We have to see the appearing of the Lord. That is what the book of Revelation is about—the person and the work of Christ. It is about having vials of blood poured upon our heads so that our minds are fully and completely renewed. Then we can experience Romans 12:2—a transformation. We are living in the time for God to reveal the book of Revelation. It is being revealed by the spirit. We are coming to understand that it is nothing more and it is nothing less than the revelation of Jesus Christ! We are understanding the signs and symbols, written in redemptive terms.

When Maturity Comes The "In Part" Shall Be Done Away

At the time of the writing of the book of Revelation, the Church was experiencing the Holy Place dimension (Revelation 1:12 and 3:15-16). There comes a time when we have to sacrifice that realm and ministry and trust the Lord to resurrect it in his way and in his time. Paul called the "gift" realm an "in part" realm, not the fullness. Once Elisha kissed his former ministry good-bye, he sacrificed the oxen. We must take the ministry that we have been involved in that we have *thought* was the fullness, but was really the "in part" or the "gift" realm, or the Holy Place dimension, and sacrifice it as Elisha did. We must lay it down and allow God to raise it up in his way and in his time. Then it will be greater than just an "in part" manifestation.

Paul said, "But when that which is perfect is come, then that which is in part shall be done away." The Greek word "perfect" in this scripture means "complete in growth, in mental and moral character; of full age." This speaks of maturity. The word "perfect" in this scripture also means "man" and "perfect." In Ephesians 4:13, Paul wrote, "Till *we all* come in the *unity* of the faith, and of the knowledge of the son of God, unto *a perfect man,* unto the *measure* of the *stature* of the *fullness of Christ"* (emphasis added). We, the full grown, mature body of Christ = a perfect man which is Christ the Lord. This is not referring to separate, individual places of worship or to separate denominations or to any religion. It is referring to the body of Christ—every Church in every city, in every state, in every nation in which the Lord Jesus Christ is the Head.

That is what the Lord is telling the Church in Revelation 3:15. If you stay in an "in part" realm when God wants you to move on, you become lukewarm. You lose that first love. If you won't sacrifice the ministry and go into the place of Revelation 4:1, and come up to the Most Holy Place experience, there will be a lukewarmness that will settle over you.

There was a time in my life when I thought I was in the ultimate ministry. I did not want to leave that ministry, but God was dealing with me. I did not want to lay it down, but I sensed within my spiritual life a lukewarmness, until I finally made the decision to lay it down and go into the ministry that proceeds out of the Most Holy Place. I did not know what God was doing at that time though.

When God wants us to move from one realm to the next, but we are satisfied with just being stuck in the middle, we are saying that we are rich and increased with goods and have need of nothing. When God wants us to move on with him but we are satisfied right where we are, we are saying, "We have numbers, we have money, we have programs, and we have a ministry." And God is saying, "Don't you know that you are wretched, miserable, poor, blind, and naked?"

Then in Revelation 3:18 the Lord tells them, "I counsel thee to buy of me gold tried in the fire, that thou mayest be rich; and white raiment, that thou mayest be clothed, and that the shame of thy nakedness do not appear; and anoint thine eyes with eyesalve, that thou mayest see." Isaiah 55:1 says that we are to buy without money and without price—without works of the flesh. We buy with our hunger for him. And only because of his grace, do we receive his gold (divine nature), his raiment of righteousness, and his ability to see spiritual things.

In Revelation 5, John was weeping because no man could open the book. No man can open the book, and no amount of "what we go through" can open the book. No works can open the book. Nothing we do can open the book within and cause the life of the Lamb and the rivers of living water to flow out of our innermost being. If we suffer with him we reign with him, and we suffered at the cross of Calvary. That is what he is saying when he says, "I counsel you to buy of me gold tried in the fire." Jesus experienced a fire, a judgment, a bitter cup, at the cross over 2000 years ago. At first, he didn't even want to drink it. Then he said, "Not my will but thine, be done." And that is when his fire began to become our fire. His suffering became our suffering. No man can open the book. No matter what we do, we cannot open the book. Only when you receive the Lamb that was slain can the book be opened.

In Revelation 3:20, the Lord said that if we'd open the door, he would come in and sup. The biggest meal is at the end of the day. For over 2000 years we've been at the end of the age of the Mosaic Law, but blinded from that truth by the god of this world. God has given us a hand-written invitation to come to this super supper he has prepared. We've opened the door and we are beginning to partake. We have "come up hither." Jesus is more than life itself. He is more than the necessary food that we eat. Jesus is more than anything! He's everything!

To have the book of life that is within us unsealed on the backside—crucified, died, buried—means that out of us, can flow the life of the Lamb—quickened, raised, and seated. That is why we were created in the first place. We were made to become a praise and a worship unto him. We were created to have him, the rivers of living waters, reproduced out of us. When we understand the book of Revelation there is going to be a great outflowing coming from all of us.

There have been so many things that have come against the body of Christ that unless we can grab a hold of this spiritual understanding that it is not what we must suffer, but what we have *already* suffered, we will not begin to reign with him in the throne. I'm so convinced of this that I'm angry. The word tells us to be angry and sin not. Anger is just a sign that tells us that we need to move forward to confront those things that have come against us. Unless we grab a hold of this, Matthew 21:43 says that the kingdom will be given to another nation. It could be given to a people who are only experiencing the Holy Place at this time. A people who are hungry. A people who are desperate. A people who know that there is more than the baptism of the Holy Spirit, there is more than the gift realm, and they are crying out from the Holy Place to find it.

But there is a people here and now, that are walking in the kingdom. There is a people in the deeper life experience of the Most Holy Place that are experiencing throne realm dominion. The Lord has brought this word for that purpose. We are walking in the kingdom and *experiencing* the place that we are *already* seated in. We are no longer trying to get into a chair that we are already seated in. We're living it more and more with each passing day! It is naturally supernaturally walking itself out, through the self-fulfilling power of his word (Isaiah 61:11 Amplified Bible)!

Right now, we are coming out of the Most Holy Place to see how we got there. And as we do, we are filling our mind with the knowledge and the understanding of how we got there—which is the death, the burial, and the resurrection of Jesus Christ. We are not eating the lamb in haste as the Israelites did when they came out of Egypt. We are enjoying the marriage supper of the Lamb with our feet underneath his table. In this kingdom age we will not go out with haste, *nor by flight;* for the Lord has gone before us, and the God of Israel is our rear guard (Isaiah 52:12). When we experienced initial salvation we ate the Lamb with haste in our first look at the cross. But as we take a second look we are savoring every detail of the finished work of Calvary.

Revelation—A Carbon Copy of Ezekiel

The book of Revelation is a carbon copy of the book of Ezekiel. Look at Ezekiel 1:1-14:

> 1. Now it came to pass in the thirtieth year, in the fourth month, in the fifth day of the month, as I was among the captives by the river of Chebar, that the heavens were opened, and I saw visions of God. 2. In the fifth day of the month, which was the fifth year of king Jehoiachin's captivity, 3. The word of the Lord came expressly unto Ezekiel the priest, the son of Buzi, in the land of the Chaldeans by the river Chebar; and the hand of the Lord was there upon him. 4. And I looked, and, behold, a whirlwind came out of the north, a great cloud, and a fire infolding itself, and a brightness was about it, and out of the midst thereof as the color of amber, out of the midst of the fire. 5. Also out of the midst thereof came the likeness of four living creatures. And this was their appearance; they had the likeness of a man. 6. And every one had four faces, and every one had four wings. 7. And their feet were straight feet; and the

sole of their feet was like the sole of a calf's foot: and they sparkled like the color of burnished brass. 8. And they had the hands of a man under their wings on their four sides; and they four had their faces and their wings. 9. Their wings were joined one to another; they turned not when they went; they went every one straight forward. 10. As for the likeness of their faces, they four had the face of a man, and the face of a lion, on the right side: and they four had the face of an ox on the left side; they four also had the face of an eagle. 11. Thus were their faces: and their wings were stretched upward; two wings of every one were joined one to another, and two covered their bodies. 12. And they went every one straight forward: whither the spirit was to go, they went; and they turned not when they went. 13. As for the likeness of the living creatures, their appearance was like burning coals of fire, and like the appearance of lamps: it went up and down among the living creatures; and the fire was bright, and out of the fire went forth lightning. 14. And the living creatures ran and returned as the appearance of a flash of lightning.

In verse 1 of this passage, "thirty" speaks of maturity, "four" speaks of universality, and "five" speaks of grace. "Chebar" is Babylon. In other words, it does not matter how much confusion you are in the midst of, God will still give you visions of himself. Even though you are in the midst of total confusion, if you desire to see him, the heavens will open and you will have visions of God. He will gather what he has scattered and form his kingdom. In his kingdom, all (4) will come to maturity (30) by his grace (5).

In verse 3, the word of the Lord came "expressly" or clearly. This is like the trumpets in Revelation, a clear sounding word that gives clarity to the word. In verse 4, we read a description that sounds like something out of the book of Revelation again. "Amber" means "bronze or polished metal," and "fire" speaks of judgment. In Revelation 1:15, Jesus' feet were like fine bronze, as if they burned in a furnace. Verses 5 and 6 are similar to Revelation 4:6b-8 in describing the living creatures.

Then in verse 7 of Ezekiel chapter 1, we read, "And their feet were straight feet." Our walk is a walk that is straight. It is a walk of holiness. It is a walk of righteousness. And it is obtained by understanding that we are the righteousness of God in Christ. We, the people that Revelation refers to, are walking a holy walk. We are walking the street of gold, which means our walk is a walk of divine nature. This is a people who are not in any way condoning sin, but are awakening to righteousness and finding out that sin is not even an issue! We do not develop a righteous walk by preaching about, thus magnifying, sin. We develop a righteous walk by seeing what happened at the cross of Calvary. We come into union and he is birthed through us when we see that our spots were taken care of at the cross! It is not the other way around. When the Shulamite was taken to the mountain of Bether, the mountain of suffering, is when she was released to come into a love relationship with the king, and not before that.

Then, in Ezekiel 1:7, it goes on to say that the sole of their feet was like the sole of a calf's foot. The phrase "calf's foot" means "almost mature." So, he is seeing a people who are on their way, moving out of the Holy Place experience and into the Most Holy Place. They are almost matured. Our spirit is saved in the Outer Court experience. Our soul begins it's salvation in the Holy Place. But when we come into the experience of the Most Holy, and are hearing a word from the throne, our soul will be *completely* saved. The salvation in our spirit will come to our soul (our mind, our will, and our emotions) and that veil will be taken away.

At the end of verse 7 we find that *their feet* sparkled like the color of burnished brass too! Why? Because they understood that his judgment was their judgment. He continues to describe the living creatures in verse 8.

Verse 9 says they were joined to one another and they turned not when they went, and they all went straight forward. They were in unity. They kept rank. They were not involved in some ministry off to the side that they are not even called to. Their walk was straight and they all went straight forward. They were all progressing in God.

Verse 10 is a picture of the four gospels. In Exodus chapters 30 and 37, holy anointing oil was mixed according to the art of the apothecary, to anoint the prophet, priest, and king. This anointing oil had four ingredients that portray the Christ of the four gospels, namely, myrrh (meekness), cinnamon (goodness), calamus (gentleness), and cassia (humility). These spices speak of the death of Christ. A fifth ingredient, a hin of oil, speaks of the book of Acts where the promise of the Spirit was poured out. What does this mean to us? Only when we follow him in death will we come to the full possession of the promise, the anointing of the Most Holy—Jesus Christ. And it is going to take the understanding of the gospel—Matthew, Mark, Luke, John—as well as Acts, the epistles, and Revelation, for us to be brought to a place where the anointing is released, where Christ can be expressed and where he can be seen.

In Ezekiel 1:12, they went wherever the spirit was to go. This is just like the passage in Revelation 14:14 which says that we follow the Lamb wherever he goes. Again we see the living creatures in Ezekiel 1:13. In Revelation, these living creatures are the four beasts mentioned in chapters 4 and 6. Ezekiel tells us that their appearance was like burning coals of fire.

From "Woe" To "Holy"

In Isaiah chapter 6, Isaiah cried, "Woe, woe, woe," but he heard the angels crying, "Holy, holy, holy." This is where Isaiah received the vision of what happened at the cross of Calvary and a coal was taken from the altar to touch his mouth. The coals that burned the incense on the golden altar came from the coals on the brazen altar in the Outer Court which represents the death. Let's read Isaiah 6:1-8:

> In the year that king Uzziah died I saw also the Lord sitting upon a throne, high and lifted up, and his train filled the temple. Above it stood the seraphims: each one had six wings; with twain he covered his face, and with twain he covered his feet, and with twain he did fly. And one cried unto another, and said, Holy, holy, holy, is the Lord of hosts: the whole earth is full of his glory. And the posts of the door moved at the voice of him that cried, and the house

> was filled with smoke. Then said I, Woe is me! for I am undone; because I am a man of unclean lips, and I dwell in the midst of a people of unclean lips: for mine eyes have seen the King, the Lord of hosts. Then flew one of the seraphims unto me, having a live coal in his hand, which he had taken with the tongs from off the altar: And he laid it upon my mouth, and said, Lo, this hath touched thy lips; and thine iniquity is taken away, and thy sin purged. Also I heard the voice of the Lord saying, "Whom shall I send, and who will go for Us?" Then said I, "Here am I; send me."

King Uzziah typifies the Adamic nature. You may be thinking, "But Uzziah was a good king." Yes, Adam can be good. He can even memorize scripture and preach from a pulpit. But when Isaiah saw in type, that our old man was crucified, dead, and buried, something began to take place. He went from crying "Woe, woe, woe," to crying "Holy, holy, holy." Then one of the Seraphim touched his lips and Isaiah said, "Lord, I'll go, send me." Why? Because his mouth had been touched with a coal from the brazen altar. He began to understand what happened at the cross of Calvary in type, and he went from crying "Woe, woe, woe" in chapter 5, to hearing a cry from the throne, which was very different! It was a cry of "Holy, holy, holy, is the Lord of hosts: the *whole earth* is full of his glory!" When we understand the death of Christ our testimony changes from "Woe" to "Holy!" It is a drastic change when our "Woe is me" mentality is exchanged for the "I am the righteousness of God in Jesus Christ" mentality. It is time to cry "Holy," messengers of God!

We have the same story in Revelation 4:7-11:

> And the first beast was like a lion, and the second beast like a calf, and the third beast had a face as a man, and the fourth beast was like a flying eagle. And the four beasts had each of them six wings about him; and they were full of eyes within: and they rest not day and night, saying, Holy, holy, holy, Lord God Almighty, which was, and is, and is to

> come. And when those beasts give glory and honor and thanks to him that sat on the throne, who liveth for ever and ever, The four and twenty elders fall down before him that sat on the throne, and worship him that liveth for ever and ever, and cast their crowns before the throne, saying, Thou art worthy, O Lord, to receive glory and honor and power: for thou hast created all things, and for thy pleasure they are and were created.

The living beasts are creatures expressing life. These are not the same as the beast in Revelation 13. We will find that in chapter 6 these living beasts say, "Come and see." That is what we are saying. That is the message of the Melchisedec priesthood. These living creatures expressing life are going to declare the decree (Psalm 2:7) —"Bread and wine! Come and see. Come and eat. Come and understand something about the death of Christ." The only way we can ever declare that message is when we, like Paul, are gripped by the cross and we realize that the Bible is not many different messages, but it is one little book, as Revelation declares. Every message has been condensed into one. We are now ministering nothing but Jesus Christ and him crucified, and our identification with him in his death, burial, and resurrection. When we begin to move in that, and get gripped by the death of Christ, it is going to change our lives completely. It may not happen over night, but it will happen. We will begin to SEE as never before.

We then, will begin to speak from the throne as a Melchisedec ministry and we will give nothing but bread and wine, or Lamb. It won't be soddened with water, but roasted with fire. We will tell the *whole* story! Jesus became sin, died spiritually and went into hell. He wasn't just a sin offering that just *covered* our sin. *He became sin.* He drank the bitter cup. He took it into himself. The priest in the Old Testament was to eat the sin offering. He was to take it into himself. Jesus *became* sin; otherwise we are just forgiven sinners. But we are not *only* forgiven! We are new creations in Christ Jesus. If this were not true, he could not be the firstbegotten of the dead. There were others that were physically raised from the dead before Jesus was raised from the dead. He was the first one born from death unto life because he died spiritually. One translation says that Jesus had to be born again—not because he sinned—but because God was not going to raise who he had become. God is not saving Adam.

Revelation 4:9-11 illustrates that John is seeing one in the throne. He is seeing the beginning of resurrection life. He is beginning to see glimpses of what is going to happen as people begin to understand what happened in the death of Christ. This understanding will take away the veil that has already been done away in Christ.

The Book Within

The book of Revelation has not been understood because it has been interpreted from a natural, literal perspective. If we try to interpret this book by outer events, the outer events always change, leaving us with an unstable interpretation that changes with every wind of doctrine. For example, many years ago, they taught us that the antichrist was Henry Kissinger. Then it was Ronald Reagan because all his names had six letters. Then it was Sadam Heussein. The interpretation always changed because it was controlled by current events. Those things are not what the book of Revelation is about. John understood that the revelation of Jesus Christ had nothing to do with current events, or with what may be happening in the Middle East or with Russia or Iraq or Afghanistan. John got it, and we can too. This is the revelation of Jesus Christ. There are truths that we have not yet received from the book of Revelation and this is the time to unveil it, if we have an ear to hear.

There are two reasons why people do not understand the book of Revelation. First, they do not understand that it is written in the language of spirit. God signified it by his angel unto John. "Signified" is a word that means sign and symbol. When horses are mentioned, they are not literal horses. If they were literal horses, the pale or green horse is inconsistent, even with our language, not to mention being inconsistent with reality. It is written in the language of spirit—a redemptive language. It is a code book, if you will. And the code is not cracked by a computer. The code is cracked by the Holy Spirit.

The second reason people do not understand this book is that they do not realize that John heard a voice, and he turned to see the voice not up in front of him, but behind him. The things John was to write had nothing to do with future events that were to be interpreted with things that happen outside in the world. But he turned to see the voice behind him—the crucifixion, the death, the burial, and the resurrection. The religious system has looked at the Revelation as things that have to do with external events. The spiritual interpretation of the book of Revelation is not based on some isolated verses of scripture that we hold to. We are seeing the big picture as we let the Bible interpret the Bible. When we see the redemptive theme of the Bible that reveals Jesus Christ from Genesis to Revelation, we see the whole masterpiece and we are able to teach every chapter redemptively. We can teach the tabernacle of Moses, Noah's Ark, the exodus, the wilderness wanderings, and everything else, when we see the theme. As we look behind us, we'll see that a scarlet thread runs through every page.

Revelation chapter 5 talks about "the book within." Let's read the entire chapter:

> And I saw in the right hand of him that sat on the throne a book written within and on the backside, sealed with seven seals. And I saw a strong angel proclaiming with a loud voice, Who is worthy to open the book, and to loose the seals thereof? And no man in heaven, nor in earth, neither under the earth, was able to open the book, neither to look thereon. And I wept much, because no man was found worthy to open and to read the book, neither to look thereon. And one of the elders saith unto me, Weep not: behold, the Lion of the tribe of Judah, the Root of David, hath prevailed to open the book, and to loose the seven seals thereof. And I beheld, and, lo, in the midst of the throne and of the four beasts, and in the midst of the elders, stood a Lamb as it had been slain, having seven horns and seven eyes, which are the seven Spirits of God sent forth into all the earth. And he came and took the book out of the right hand of him that sat upon the throne. And when he had taken the book, the four beasts and four and

twenty elders fell down before the Lamb, having every one of them harps, and golden vials full of odours, which are the prayers of saints. And they sung a new song, saying, Thou art worthy to take the book, and to open the seals thereof: for thou wast slain, and hast redeemed us to God by thy blood out of every kindred, and tongue, and people, and nation; And hast made us unto our God kings and priests: and we shall reign on the earth. And I beheld, and I heard the voice of many angels round about the throne and the beasts and the elders: and the number of them was ten thousand times ten thousand, and thousands of thousands; Saying with a loud voice, Worthy is the Lamb that was slain to receive power, and riches, and wisdom, and strength, and honor, and glory, and blessing. And every creature which is in heaven, and on the earth, and under the earth, and such as are in the sea, and all that are in them, heard I saying, Blessing, and honor, and glory, and power, be unto him that sitteth upon the throne, and unto the Lamb for ever and ever. And the four beasts said, Amen. And the four and twenty elders fell down and worshipped him that liveth for ever and ever.

In Revelation 5:1, when John talks of a book written within that is sealed on the backside with seven seals, he is not talking about the Bible. He is not even talking about the book of Revelation, as we see in Revelation 22:10. There are <u>six reasons</u> why "the book written within" first mentioned in Revelation chapter 5, is not a Bible that we can hold in our hands.

The First Reason We Are The Book Within

Look at Revelation 22:10:

And he said unto me, "Seal not the sayings of the prophecy of this book; for the time is at hand.

If we'd had our ear nailed to the door and we lived in the time that John was living in, we could have received the same revelation. The understanding of the book of Revelation *does* need to be opened unto those who have not had their ear nailed to the door, but as this scripture shows, the book of Revelation is not the book that is sealed in Revelation 5:1. Many people are interpreting the book of Revelation according to outer events, or current events, that are constantly changing. The book of Revelation cannot be interpreted on a foundation of shifting sand because if it is, the interpretation will always change. This is the Revelation of Jesus Christ the solid Rock, who is the same yesterday, today, and forever (Hebrews 13:8). People will not be established in what the book of Revelation is about if we are always changing the meaning. That is why people, even preachers today, say that we are never going to understand the book of Revelation so we might as well just stay out of it. But we're not staying out. We're going all the way in, past the veil, into Jesus, the Holy of Holies!

In general, because we are at the end of the Church age and have stepped into the Kingdom realm, the book of Revelation is being opened up more and we are understanding the coming of the Lord. God has a time, and there is a progression of maturing and growing, and if our ear is nailed to the door, we will understand the things of the Spirit. The purpose of the Lord for us who live in such a time as this, the fullness of times, is to gather together in one, all things in Christ, both which are in heaven and which are on earth, even in Him—to the praise of his glory, forever.

This is the revelation of Jesus Christ, and when we understand that it was written in sign and symbol, and that John looked behind him, we will not teach this in terms of future events, but as something that *already happened.* The more understanding, the more the spirit of wisdom and revelation in the knowledge of him comes to us—to our mind—the more the veil is going to be taken away. The "old woman" will be taken away and there will be an appearing of Jesus Christ. If there were a veil between you and someone, you would not be able to see them. You may hear them, but you could not see them. The veil was done away (2 Corinthians 3:14). But when the veil that is over our mind, is taken away, Jesus is going to appear! We will no longer be as the little Shulamite, a garden inclosed, a spring shut up, a fountain sealed. We are going to be opened up and the king can then reproduce himself through us as he comes from spirit to soul. Then there will be a reproduction of the life and the nature of God on a consistent basis.

So, the Bible, the outer book, is not the book *within* that is sealed with seven seals which need to be broken. It is the book within, the book of spirit that has been sealed. We saw in Revelation 22:10 that the book of Revelation is not sealed, and this was written nearly 2000 years ago. It has not been sealed, although many have not understood it. Even though it is being opened up to our understanding more at this time, we could have understood it if we'd had our ear nailed to the door. Even though there is a time to open this, God always has forerunners who see it before the time.

The book within is the body of Christ. We've been sealed up on the backside with seven seals. Not seven literal seals, but we were fully sealed up when we received the baptism of the Holy Spirit, until the redemption of the purchased possession (Ephesians 1:10-14). We have been, like the little Shulamite—a garden inclosed, a spring shut up, a fountain sealed. Even though we received the baptism of the Holy Spirit, we have been sealed. The down payment, the earnest, the engagement ring, was just a sign that there is more to come. Even though we had the baptism of the Holy Spirit, operated in the nine gifts of the Spirit, and spoke in tongues, we were still a fountain sealed ... that is, until the day of our full release, or our full redemption, because the Holy Spirit is the seal. So, what now? We loose the Holy Spirit on earth as it has already been loosed in heaven!

The book that is sealed is not the Bible that you hold in your lap—it is a people! There is a people who are growing up into the fullness of Christ. Jesus was the word made flesh. If we are growing up into the head in all things, he is going to become the word made flesh—through our flesh. Ephesians 4:12-13 says, "For the perfecting of the saints, for the work of the ministry, for the edifying of the body of Christ: till we all come in the unity of the faith, and of the knowledge of the Son of God, unto a perfect man, unto the measure of the stature of the fullness of Christ." When we understand what John saw on the backside, the crucifixion, the death, the burial, and when we grow up into the full measure of the stature of Christ, the seals of our book will have been broken, and out of us will flow the life of the Lamb.

This book within that is sealed on the backside with seven seals is not speaking of the Bible it is not speaking of the book of Revelation. It is speaking about a people. We are a book. We are a love letter from God to the world. But the letter has been sealed. We've been like the little Shulamite, a garden inclosed, a spring shut up, a fountain sealed—even with the baptism of the Holy Spirit. Ephesians tells us that the baptism of the Holy Spirit, the promise of the Father, is a seal until the day of full redemption. When is the day of full redemption? When the veil is taken away from our mind we are going to experience the day of full redemption. God, by his spirit, has already broken the seals at the cross of Calvary and now, as we come to understand that, they are going to be broken off in *experience,* in our lives.

If we are growing up into Jesus, then he, through our flesh (our lives), is becoming the word made flesh *the second time* (Hebrews 9:28). We are becoming an open revelation. We are becoming the book unsealed. This will only happen corporately as it happens individually, so let me make this personal. Once these horses gallop through your mind and imprint the true revelation of the white horse, the red horse, the black horse, the pale horse and what they represent, then the fifth seal is opened, and your soul is going to be under the altar. When your soul goes under the altar, you lose your mind and take on the mind of Christ. The veil is going to be taken away from your mind and an anointing is going to gallop out of you. The Christ *in* you is going to gallop out of you!

When Jesus said, "Out of your bellies shall flow rivers of living waters," it was the *last day,* the great day of the feast, referring to the Feast of Tabernacles. Jesus was connecting Tabernacles with the fullness of the Spirit. As we mature and experience the Feast of Tabernacles, out of us will flow the Spirit without measure (John 3:34-36). Ezekiel 47 speaks of water ankle deep, knee deep, loin deep, and then waters to swim in. The waters to swim in denote the fullness of the Holy Spirit flowing out of the sanctuary. This is the open book! The seals have been broken! Out of us flow rivers of living water. We are no longer a garden inclosed, a spring shut up, a fountain sealed! We are now opened up and have become one with Jesus Christ our Lord experientially.

The reason that we believe what we believe is not just because of some isolated scriptures taken out of context in an attempt to explain spiritual things with a carnal mind. People can take scriptures out of the Bible and wrest them unto their own destruction, making them say about anything they want them to say. We believe what we believe and we're teaching what we're teaching because we are beginning to see the big picture. We are beginning to see that the theme of the entire Bible is redemption. When we begin to see the big picture, then we can teach the death, burial, and resurrection out of every chapter. We can teach it from the tabernacle of Moses. We can teach it from David's tent. We can teach it from Solomon's temple. We can teach it from the garments of the high priest. We can teach it from Ruth. We can teach it from the Song Of Solomon. We see it everywhere once we see the big picture and the theme of the Bible, which is redemption to mankind—by, in, and through the death, burial, and resurrection of Jesus Christ, and the Church's identification with that. The entire word of God is like apples of gold in pictures of silver (Proverbs 25:11). An apple is a fruit, a life-giving food. An apple of gold is divine food that ministers life to the spirit, soul, and body. Pictures of silver are pictures of redemption. The divine word of God ministers life to our total being with pictures of *redemption*—not with pictures of wrath and judgment and gloom and doom and tribulation and a mean, angry Father who is just waiting for us to mess up so he can beat us up or withdraw his presence from us. That picture only ministers death and it is *not fit* to be spoken. But a word *fitly* spoken is like apples of gold in pictures of silver.

The Second Reason We Are The Book Within

The second reason why "the book written within" first mentioned in Revelation chapter 5, is not a literal book, is found in John 1:14:

> And the Word was made flesh, and dwelt among us
> (and we beheld his glory, the glory as of the only
> begotten of the Father), full of grace and truth.

That was said about Jesus primarily, but now it is being said about the whole body of Christ. For three and a half years, Jesus was the book opened in crystal clear terms and full manifestation because Jesus said, "When you've seen me, you've seen the Father." He was the opened book and he is going to have a people who become living epistles read by everyone.

The Amplified Bible says, "You show and make obvious that you are a letter from Christ delivered by us, not written with ink but with [the] Spirit of [the] living God, not on tablets of stone but on tablets of human hearts" (2 Corinthians 3:3). The seals will be broken, and we come into the full manifestation, the full salvation—not just the down payment—the fullness.

Look at Hebrews 10:5, 7:

> Wherefore when he cometh into the world, he saith, "Sacrifice and offering thou wouldest not, but *a body* hast thou prepared me:
> Then said I, Lo, I come *(in the volume of the book it is written of me)* to do thy will, O God." (Emphasis added).

First he says in verse 5, "A body hast thou prepared me." That is primarily talking about Jesus' human body. Secondarily, it is talking about us, the body of Christ. After he acknowledges that Father God gave him a body, he says "*Then* said I, Lo, I come (in the volume of the book it is written of me) to do thy will, O God." If Jesus was the word made flesh, and we are growing up into him in all things, then we become the word, the book within, in Revelation 5:1. He is the open revelation, the open book. He is the book in Revelation 5:1. He is the head, and we are the body. The body is the book. For years, we've been so concerned about the inheritance *we* are going to get. Thank God that is changing. Now we are concerned about the inheritance *he* is going to get. He is going to get an inheritance when we have our mind renewed and the total transformation has taken place. We become *his* inheritance. He is going to get his inheritance. He has always had a people, he is always going to have a people, and he is going to get his inheritance, which is a people (Ephesians 1:18).

So *after* Jesus received a body he said, "Lo, I come (in the volume of the book it is written of me) to do thy will, O God." It is also written in the volume of the book in our spirit, the book of life. It is written in our spirit to do God's will, now that we are the body of Christ. It is written of us, in the book of spirit. It is like a script that was written from before the foundations. I believe there was a script that was written about you and me from before the foundations. In that script, it said you are going to do God's will. Once we got a body, it began to walk itself out. This is happening individually and corporately. God is preparing Jesus' body, the body of Christ, the Church. The many-membered body joined and knit together by what every joint supplies, is rising up in the earth today saying, "Lo, I come (in the volume of the book it is written of me) to do thy will, O God!"

Now look at Hebrews 10:16:

> This is the covenant that I will make with them after those days, saith the Lord; I will put my laws into their *hearts,* and in their *minds* will I *write* them (emphasis added).

Because the book within is the body of Christ and not the Bible that we hold in our hands, then as the seals are broken, out of us will come forth a manifestation of him. When we read about "the book within" in Revelation chapter 5, we are not talking about a piece of paper. We are not talking about anything that is written with ink. We are not even talking about rote memorization of scripture and being able to quote it. We are talking about the Holy Spirit of understanding and revelation causing us to become one with the word so that the word becomes flesh and dwells among us. He is the word. We are his body. We are talking about rivers of living water flowing out of us, and as Ezekiel said, everything we come in contact with is going to receive life.

What the world needs is life! And they are going to get it as we preach and teach and explain about *the death.* Beyond preaching and teaching, beyond proclaiming, we are going to *explain* to them about the death. When we explain to them the death, and show them that they were crucified, they are dead, and they were buried, the subsequent result is going to be life! People are living a debilitated life because of an absence of *true* life. He who has the Son, has life! There is a people today coming to understand that they are the book within, they understand the four horses of Revelation, they understand the death of Christ, and out of them is flowing the rivers of living water, bringing life to the nations of the world.

When we talk about the book in Revelation 5:1, we are not talking about pieces of paper. We are not talking about letters written on parchment. Those do not change us at all. The Bible will not change you at all. It can be just like any other book to you—until the spirit reveals it unto you! When the spirit reveals it unto you and brings it from spirit to soul, the veil is taken away and there will be changes. There is going to be a *revolution* within our lives.

To see another example that we are living epistles, let's read 2 Corinthians 3:2-3:

> Ye are our epistle written in our hearts, known and read of all men: for as much as ye are manifestly declared to be the epistle of Christ ministered by us, written not with ink, but with the Spirit of the living God; not in tables of stone, but in fleshy tables of the heart.

An epistle is something that is written; a letter or a document. When the garden is *un*closed, when the fountain is *un*sealed, and the rivers of living water begin to flow out of us on a consistent basis, then it can be said in the full sense of the word, that we are the epistles of God, known and read of all men. People want to read your book! They *are* reading your book. But they are *really* going to want to read our book when the veil is completely taken away that has been over our mind. Thank God, it is just about gone! We really do not have that far to go!

This is the Day of Jubilee and there are going to be some drastic changes in this day! This is the time of Jubilee. Jesus is the Jubilee. The people that are really going to experience Jubilee will be those who are hearing the long, loud blast of a ram's horn. Where do we get a ram's horn? From a sacrificial, dead, male lamb. When we hear that, it is going to bring change. It is going to bring revolution. We will no longer be a fountain sealed.

In the Song Of Solomon, the little Shulamite said, "I am sick of love," which means that she was love sick. She was madly in love with the king. She thought that the king was never going to love her because she was in the flesh. So he takes her to the mountain of Bether, the mountain of suffering, and shows her that her spots were removed at the cross of Calvary, in type. That is what released her to have a love relationship with him to the place that he could reproduce himself through her—*and not before then.* She had to realize that she was fair and that she was pleasant. In fact, she said before she even received the baptism of the Holy Spirit, in type, "Our bed is green." In other words, what he had revealed to her is, "What I want for you and for me is to come into a relationship, into such a dimension in me that I can reproduce myself through you." He told her that, even before she received the baptism of the Holy Spirit, in type. Then he wined her and dined her and took her to the banqueting house where she in type, received the baptism of the Holy Spirit. Remember, the word "banqueting" means "effervescent," like a bottle of champagne. When you shake it up and pop the cork, out comes all the champagne. That's what happened to us when we received the baptism of the Holy Spirit. Someone laid hands on us, shook us up, and we bubbled all over the place.

The same thing happened with little Ruth. Boaz represents Christ; Ruth represents the body of Christ, the bride (our soul). She had to uncover his feet, which are brass in Revelation chapter 1. When she uncovered his feet, she could lay down at rest. When we come into rest something is going to happen. Through intimacy Boaz placed his seed in the womb of Ruth. That is what is happening today. A conception is taking place in the womb of our mind. We are being impregnated by the King. As the veil is being taken away, the salvation that is in our spirit is impregnating the womb of our mind and we are birthing the Lord Jesus through our lives. As in the natural; so in the spiritual (1 Corinthians 15:46,47).

2 Corinthians 3:3 says, "For as much as ye are manifestly declared to be the epistle of Christ ministered by us, written not with ink, but with the Spirit of the living God; not in tables of stone, but in fleshy tables of the heart." So, here we are called epistles of Christ. In Revelation 5:1, John did not see a scroll that was written with ink. He saw in God's right hand, a scroll in the hearts of the

people that was written by the Spirit of God. We are love letters from God. But the problem is; the love letter has been sealed. You have to unseal a letter to get the contents of the letter out. As we fill our mind with bread and wine, as we eat Lamb that is not soddened down with water, but roasted with fire—seeing every aspect of the finished work of Calvary—the veil is taken away. In other words, once the letter is unsealed, out of us flows the life of the Lamb.

James wrote about the engrafted word. The word is not engrafted on pages of parchment. The word can only be engrafted in a people's heart. Within us is the engrafted word. The book *within* is the engrafted word, not a Bible that we hold in our hands. Look what he says in James 1:21:

> Wherefore lay apart all filthiness and superfluity of naughtiness, and receive with meekness the engrafted word, which is able to save your souls.

When James refers to the engrafted word which is able to save our *souls,* he says the same thing John says in Revelation chapter 4 when he talks about the emerald rainbow round about the throne—the green room. We likened it to the green room that the king wanted to take the Shulamite into. We likened it to the green pastures of Psalm 23, where our soul is restored. Every woman in the Old Testament that represents the bride of Christ was barren. They had to have their soul restored. To them, it was a *natural* restoration of the womb. Today, the womb speaks of the womb of our mind, a *spiritual* womb. Our soul is being restored as we are eating in green pastures—as we are coming to see that we are already in the throne realm, which is green. We are already in the green room and something in the green room is beginning to happen as never before, so that we can reproduce the king.

James said, "You're to receive with meekness the engrafted word." That word "meekness" means "teachableness." Be teachable. You are to receive with meekness the engrafted word, which is able to restore your womb. Another way of saying what Brother James said is, "Receive with meekness the engrafted word, which is able to get rid of the veil between your ears (in your mind). Receive the engrafted word that is in your spirit." The engrafted word is the word that is quickened to our hearts, written upon our minds, so that the veil that was done away in Christ can be taken away from our minds. When that veil is taken away, Christ can appear. When the veil is taken away, there can be an expression of the life of God. I could minister the word to you until I am blue in the face, but unless the spirit of wisdom and revelation in the knowledge of him reveals it unto you, it will not change you. That happens as the engrafted word, which is written with the spirit upon your mind, comes into your soul, taking the veil away, so that the Christ in you can make his appearance and expresses himself through your life.

When the horses of Revelation chapter 6 get finished riding through your mind leaving hoof prints between your ears, something is going to happen. The fifth seal will be opened and your soul will be under the altar. Notice, in Revelation 6:9 John does not say that *people* are under the altar, but *souls* are under the altar. Right now, our souls are being beheaded. That old woman is being beheaded under the brazen altar as we come to understand that the brazen altar speaks of the death of Christ and our identification with that.

Hebrews 8:10-11 tells us how this is being done:

> For this is the covenant that I will make with the house of Israel after those days, saith the Lord; I will put my laws into their mind, and write them in their hearts: and I will be to them a God, and they shall be to me a people: and they shall not teach every man his neighbor, and every man his brother, saying, Know the Lord: for all shall know me, from the least to the greatest.

Hallelujah! How is everyone going to know him? Because every eye is going to see him! They are going to see the expression of Christ. They are going to see a people that are no longer a garden inclosed, a spring shut up, and a fountain sealed. They are going to see these horses galloping out of a people. They are going to see the life of the Lamb coming forth in manifestation from a people on a consistent basis. This is how God is writing this word upon our hearts and upon our minds. The word "heart" there, is the same word as "mind." He is not talking about spirit there, but he is writing *with the Spirit* upon our mind. Both of those words, "mind" and "heart," refer to the soul. The script is already written in our spirit. The book within is already there.

People say, "To experience the Most Holy Place, we must have 'more of Jesus.'" We already have every bit of his character and all of his nature in our spirit. We do not need one ounce "more of Jesus." What we need is less of us! How we get less of us is not in crucifying and dying to self, but waking up to the fact that the old man is already dead. That will take away the veil so Jesus can appear.

When the children of Israel went into the Promised Land, they did not get victory by taking things *into* the Promised Land. We are not going to experience the Promised Land by getting "more of Jesus." Jesus *is* the Promised Land. They got the victory by kicking some things out. There were "ites" there. They had to get rid of the "ites." That is a picture showing us that we do not need "more of Jesus." He *is* the Promised Land. We've got all of his nature, all of his character, all of his ability and power within our spirit. But what we need to do to inherit the Promised Land in manifestation, is kick something out. That "something" is the veil that is untaken away from our mind. As he writes the word upon our mind, that veil is being taken away and we are kicking out principalities and arguments and reasonings and every proud and lofty thing that sets itself up against the true knowledge of God. And we are coming into the manifestation of the Promised Land Man. Then *Jesus* can get *his* inheritance!

The seals on the backside are being broken so that out of us can flow the rivers of living water. Jesus stood, on the great day of the feast and said, "Out of your bellies shall flow rivers of living water." Many people teach that as the baptism of the Holy Spirit. But it was the last day—the great day of the feast—the Feast of Tabernacles. Tabernacles is the second look at Passover. As God tabernacles in us, the rivers of living water are going to flow out of us (Zechariah 14). As Ezekiel said, everything that comes in contact with that river of living water is going to live. When we study Revelation chapters 21 and 22 that is what we will see. We will see a City, which speaks of the soul (our woman). We see a bride, a City, and out of her is flowing a river as clear as crystal with no debris whatsoever. That which flows out has no taint of Adam's mentality, no residue of Adam whatsoever.

With this in mind, let's read 2 Corinthians 3:2 again. "Ye are our epistle written in our hearts, known and read of all men." Paul is using spiritual terminology. Revelation 1:7 tells us that every eye is going to see him, as he comes in clouds. What are the clouds? The clouds represent people, not atmospheric clouds. It is written in the language of the Spirit. Paul is saying the same thing, using different terminology, in this passage when he says we are epistles known and read of all men. 2 Corinthians 3:3 says, "For as much as ye are manifestly declared to be the epistle of Christ, ministered by us, written not with ink, but with the Spirit of the living God; not in tables of stone, but in fleshy tables of the heart." This is the second reason "the book within" is the body of Christ and not a literal book. The book within is a people who come to understand the death, burial, and resurrection, and because of that they become in expression, living epistles, known and read of all men.

When the horses of Revelation 6 finish riding through our mind, we are going to see souls that were beheaded in the fifth seal. Notice Revelation 6:9 does not say *bodies* were slain, it says *souls* were slain. These are the same souls that are beheaded in Revelation 20:4. In other words, the residue that is left in our mind is taken away—beheaded—the old woman is done away with. The old man was crucified, but we still have some residue of Adamic thinking—that is the old woman, the soul, the unrenewed mind, will, and emotions. The old woman has to be beheaded. The veil has to be taken away from our mind. The old woman has listened to Adam and still has a residue of Adam between her ears. The old woman is going to have her mind, her soul, under the altar until she no longer thinks the thoughts of Adam, but has the mind of Christ. We will discover this when we study Revelation chapter 16.

With this in mind, let's look at Hebrews 8:8-10 again:

> For finding fault with them, he saith, "Behold, the days come, saith the Lord, when I will make a new covenant with the house of Israel and with the house of Judah: Not according to the covenant that I made with their fathers in the day when I took them by the

hand to lead them out of the land of Egypt; because they continued not in my covenant, and I regarded them not, saith the Lord. For this is the covenant that I will make with the house of Israel after those days, saith the Lord; I will put my laws into their mind, and write them in their hearts: and I will be to them a God, and they shall be to me a people."

Verse 10 contains the New Covenant. Notice, it is not in doing. It is in viewing. This New Covenant, this book, is opened in Revelation 5. It is the book within, and it was in the right hand of him that sat on the throne. "Benjamin" means "son of the right hand." Benjamin speaks of ruling and reigning. Joseph is a type of Christ. Benjamin represents the body of Christ. What was it that Benjamin had that none of his brothers had? He had a silver cup. Silver speaks of redemption. The silver cup was empty. The right hand refers to a people who are in God's right hand. These sons of the right hand have a silver, redemptive cup. These people understand that Jesus drank the bitter cup. That is the death of Christ. So Benjamin, son of the right hand, speaks of our ruling and reigning with Christ. We are a people all over the world—four living creatures—expressing life. The seals have been broken on the *backside,* meaning we understand what's *behind* us. When we understand the death of Christ, the seals on the backside will be unsealed, and out of us will flow the rivers of living water.

The book within is the body of Christ. We are love letters from God to the world! Epistles of Christ, written not with ink, but written by the Spirit upon our hearts and upon our mind. As this revelation comes, it will walk itself out. As the correct revelation comes, as we partake of bread and wine from a Melchisedec ministry, as we eat Lamb, we will experience the contract, the marriage, the New Covenant in the fullest sense, so something can be birthed out of our lives.

Of what use is it to be a Christian and to be spirit-filled, operating in all the gifts of the Spirit, as good and wonderful as they are, if the full purpose of God is not manifested in our lives? And the full purpose of God is to reproduce Christ on a consistent basis. That for which we were created is beginning to come into its own as we come to understand the death of Christ which breaks the seals on the backside, releasing from us a an ever-flowing river of the nature of Jesus Christ the Lord.

At the end of the Song Of Solomon, Solomon and the Shulamite birthed something. At the end of the book of Ruth, Boaz and Ruth birth something. How did Ruth find that place of intimacy? Before she could enter into rest, she uncovered his feet—and his feet are brass in Revelation 1. She came to understand that his judgment was her judgment. That is the thing that will bring us into rest. This rest comes as we realize that it is not in doing, but in viewing— seeing that his judgment was our judgment. No amount of doing, no amount of what we suffer, no amount of the might and power of man can open the book. Only Christ can open the book as the Spirit brings the revelation of the death, the burial, and the resurrection.

The book within, in Revelation 5:1 is not the book of Revelation and it is not the Bible. Scripture talks about a people growing up into the full measure of the stature of Christ. If you have grown to the full measure of the stature of Jesus Christ, wouldn't you think that you would be the letter unsealed? When we are mature we are really living epistles known and read of all men. People see the fruit manifested when we are mature. Wouldn't you think that you would no longer be a garden inclosed, a spring shut up, or a fountain sealed? You would be an open revelation of the Christ in you. And Christ in you would be an open revelation as he flows out of you. The book within that is sealed with seven seals is the body of Christ. Look at Ephesians 4:11-16:

> And he gave some, apostles; and some, prophets; and some, evangelists; and some, pastors and teachers; for the perfecting of the saints, for the work of the ministry, for the edifying of the body of Christ: till we all come in the unity of the faith, and of the knowledge of the Son of God, unto a perfect man, unto the measure of the stature of the fullness of Christ; that we henceforth be no more children, tossed to and fro, and carried about with every wind of doctrine, by the sleight of men, and cunning craftiness, whereby they lie in wait to deceive; but

> speaking the truth in love, may grow up into him in all things, which is the head, even Christ: from whom the whole body fitly joined together and compacted by that which every joint supplieth, according to the effectual working in the measure of every part, maketh increase of the body unto the edifying of itself in love.

The word "perfecting" in verse 12, is "maturing." Then we see the word "edifying" in the same verse. We (the body of Christ) are coming into unity of faith in the knowledge of Christ unto *a perfect man.* Christ is the head and we are his body. We are *growing up into him.* The whole body of Christ is fitly joined together and compacted and every joint supplies and is effective. This makes the body increase unto the edifying of itself *in love!*

Then we come to the book of Revelation, where John was in prison on Patmos Island, and he was sending this letter (Revelation) *to encourage people.* He wrote "blessed is he that readeth, and they that hear the words of this prophecy, and keep those things which are written therein." One translation uses the word "happy" along with the word "blessed." How happy could you be unless this book encouraged and edified? How happy could you be if it talks about a seven year tribulation that you have to go through? But when you see that it is the revelation of Jesus Christ, you're blessed. We are a blessed people!

We are being brought to a place where there is a process of elimination going on. We are not swayed by teaching just because they call it "deep" and say it's God. I want to hear a pure word. We are going to have to get to the place that we do not just listen to anything. There must come a time in our lives where we begin to discern a little more. It is okay to read and listen to others, if you can rightly divide and discern it. But there is so much being said in the midst of the Church today that requires "rightly dividing." There has to be some separation. We should not be a people that just eat anything—especially not food that is sacrificed to idols. This is why people today have health problems in the natural—because they do not eat right. They eat too much junk food. In the same way, we can eat spiritual junk food and get hardening of the arteries and a hard heart and not mature and grow in God as we could. I do not want to chew and spit out the bones just to be able to eat the meat any more. I'm getting more particular. I want to hear a pure word that comes from the throne. There are enough people ministering this message that we can do that. This message is beginning to be ministered all over the world.

There is a people that are growing up into the measure of the stature of the fullness of Christ as they partake of bread and wine and hear a pure word that comes from the throne. In John chapter 1, we understand that Jesus was the word made flesh. If we are growing up into him in all things, we are becoming the word made flesh, or the book within. We are the book written within in God's right hand—the Church. And we are experiencing more and more, the loosing of these seals, so that the life of the Lamb can flow out of us. We need his nature to flow out of us on a consistent basis.

The Third Reason We Are The Book Within

The third reason why the book within that is sealed with seven seals is not a literal book, but is the body of Christ, is that throughout the book of Revelation, we see pictures that liken the body of Christ to the Word. One thing we found out is that no man can open this book. Martin Luther could not open it. Smith Wigglesworth couldn't open it. I can't open it. No amount of suffering that we go through will open the book. Nothing can open the book except the Lamb slain. An understanding of the death of Christ and everything that was accomplished in his crucifixion, his death, and his burial is what breaks the seals and opens the book. We are going to see that on the back side it is sealed with seven seals. "Seven seals" typify that the body of Christ is *fully* sealed with the Holy Spirit. We're sealed on the backside—behind us—where Jesus was crucified, dead and buried. And now we understand that we are crucified with, dead with, and buried with him. But on the *inside* of us, the book, we see Jesus quickened, raised, and seated—and we are in him! So we are quickened with, raised with, and seated with him. These are the twelve redemptive aspects that govern the opening of the seven seals. So, this book that is sealed on the backside, where Jesus was crucified, dead, and buried and we with him, is closed. It is sealed. It is fully sealed with the Holy Spirit. It is finished. Adam is totally dead. But if someone could open this book, what would be on the *inside* of the book? The quickening, the raising and the seating of Christ—and we are alive in him! We are quickened, raised and seated with him! And in this day, the book of life is being opened by the only one who is worthy to open us up—the Lamb slain—understanding the death of Christ.

All the way throughout Revelation, the Church is likened to the word. We see it in Revelation 1:20:

> The mystery of the seven stars which thou sawest in
> my right hand, and the seven golden candlesticks.
> The seven stars are the angels of the seven churches:
> and the seven candlesticks which thou sawest are the
> seven churches.

So the candlesticks, or the body of Christ, are likened to the word. Exodus chapter 25 gives us the details of the candlestick. Jesus represents the central shaft of the candlestick. On the central shaft, there were four sets of ornaments with three ornaments in each set for a total of twelve ornaments. The six branches had a total of fifty-four ornaments. When the twelve ornaments on the central shaft are added to the fifty-four ornaments on the branches, there is a total of sixty-six ornaments. And there are sixty-six books in the Bible. If the Church is likened to a candlestick, with the central shaft representing Jesus and the branches representing the body of Christ, the whole representing the light of the word (Psalm 119:105), we can see how the body of Christ is called the word of God.

Remember, the literal letter kills but the Spirit gives life (2 Corinthians 3:6, Romans 7:6). Revelation chapter 19 has been taught as a literal, physical coming of the Lord. Many people believe that they are going to be "up there" having a good time while people on earth are left behind to go through literal hell. Many "teachers" teach that they are going to be literally raptured and then the Holy Spirit will be taken off of the earth and the world will be hurled into a seven year tribulation. The book of Revelation does not teach that.

In Revelation chapter 19:11-13, we read about the coming of the Lord:

> And I saw heaven opened, and behold, a white horse; and he that sat upon him was called faithful and true, and in righteousness he doth judge and make war. His eyes were as a flame of fire, and on his head were many crowns; and he had a name written, that no man knew, but he himself. And he was clothed with a vesture dipped in blood: and his name is called the word of God.

John saw a white horse "and he that sat upon him was called faithful and true, and in righteousness he doth judge and make war." The prophet Joel saw the very same thing in chapter 2. He saw today's army of God. Their appearance was as horses and horsemen and he couldn't tell where the horses began and where the horsemen ended—because they were one.

The phrase in verse 12, "on his head were many crowns," denotes a many-membered coming of the Lord. The last phrase in verse 12 says, "and he had a name written, that no man knew, but he himself." No one but God knows the names of all the myriads of people who make up the body of Christ! Notice verse 13; "And he was clothed with a vesture dipped in blood: and his name is called the word of God." Jesus is our vesture, he is our prayer covering, he is our garment. We are arrayed in his righteousness, purchased with his own blood.

Revelation chapter 19 shows us an in-Christed people and the coming of the Lord through a people—and his name is called the word of God. This is what Paul writes to us concerning this in Colossians 2:9-10 (Amplified Bible):

> For in Him the whole fullness of Deity (the Godhead) continues to dwell in bodily form [giving complete expression of the divine nature]. And you are in Him, made full and having come to fullness of life [in Christ you too are filled with the Godhead—Father, Son, and Holy Spirit—and reach full spiritual stature]. And He is the Head of all rule and authority [of every angelic principality and power].

The Fourth Reason We Are The Book Within

Fourth, in Revelation 5:1, the book is in the *right hand* of him that sat on the throne. As we said earlier, Joseph is a type of Christ and his only full brother was Benjamin, the son of the *right hand*. "Benjamin" speaks of the position we are seated in—ruling and reigning in the Most Holy Place. The book is in the right hand. There is one thing that Benjamin had that the rest of his brothers did not have—a silver cup. Silver speaks of redemption—and that cup was empty. It was empty because it symbolizes the cup that Jesus drank. Jesus drank the bitter cup, took it into himself, became sin, died spiritually, and went into hell. Jesus drank all of that bitter cup.

We know that when Joseph had the meal prepared for his brothers, Benjamin was the one that received five more messes than the rest. Joseph represents Jesus. The rest of the brothers represent the Church. Benjamin represents a firstfruit company—sons of the right hand—who are ruling and reigning and who receive five more messes than the rest. Benjamin is the one that had Joseph's silver cup, which speaks of redemption, and it was an empty cup. This silver cup differentiates between the teaching of true redemption by grace and the teaching of the religious system in Revelation 17, which is a *golden cup* full of self righteous works.

The sack where the silver cup was found represents the word of God. It was a sack full of corn. The Hebrew word for "corn" in the Strong's is #1250, and is rendered "wheat." Wheat speaks of death (a corn of wheat—John 12:24). "Corn" refers to the word. So the corns of wheat in this sack represent the word of Christ's death. As we come to understand redemption, we see that we have to go through the cup before we can get to the corn. If we are going to understand the word, we will understand that this book is a book about redemption—period. So, the fourth reason the sealed book is the body of Christ and not the Bible, is that the book is in the right hand—which speaks of Benjamin. It speaks of a people who understand that Jesus drank all of the bitter cup and who also understand all that it means.

The Fifth Reason We Are The Book Within

The fifth reason that the "book written within" is not the book of Revelation or the Bible itself is found in the story of the little Shulamite. The Shulamite represents the bride of Christ, the Church, and she was a garden *inclosed,* a spring *shut up,* and a fountain *sealed.* She was madly in love with the king but she thought that he could never love her because she was full of spots and black as the tents of Kedar. He took her to the mountain of suffering to show her that her spots were done away with. He told her that she was fair and she was pleasant. That is what the Lord is telling us. We are not unworthy. His worthiness is our worthiness. We are worthy because he is our worthiness. We *can* have this union in him. We *can* reproduce his nature. We don't have to shy away from that. We can come boldly to the throne because we are already seated *in* the throne. We can pray out of this realm. We can speak out of this realm. We have authority in this realm. It is not fully manifested while there is a residue of Adam left in our mind, but we are being quickly brought to a place where we will no longer be a garden inclosed, and the river of life will flow out of us on a consistent basis. Look at Song Of Solomon 4:12:

> A garden inclosed is my sister, my spouse; a spring shut up, a fountain sealed.

As the seals are broken, we are opened up and out of us flows Christ. The prophet Isaiah spoke of Mt. Zion, which is a people, and in chapter 41, verse 18, he said that out of them is going to flow rivers of living water. We become open rivers in the high places, and all men are going to flow to Mt. Zion. Why? Because the invisible Christ is now being made visible! Heaven is now manifesting in the earth. The kingdom of God is manifesting in the earth. Something that has not been seen from heaven is now coming from spirit to soul and out through our bodies. We are living in that time because we are hearing a word of bread and wine that is causing that to take place. We are on the right path. I am hearing from people all over the world who are beginning to realize that there is something more and that there is something they've missed and they are beginning to hear what it is.

So, the book within was sealed on the backside. The Shulamite represents the Church and she is *unsealed*—no longer a garden inclosed, a spring shut up, or a fountain sealed. She is opened up and out of her is flowing rivers of living water—the Feast of Tabernacles—rivers of living water are flowing out of our bellies, or out of our innermost being.

The Sixth Reason We Are The Book Within

The sixth reason that the sealed book is the body of Christ and not the Bible is found in Ephesians 1:12-14. Here, we see a picture of the purchased possession, which we are:

> That we should be to the praise of his glory, who first trusted in Christ. In whom ye also trusted, after that ye heard the word of truth, the gospel of your salvation: in whom also after that ye believed, ye were sealed with that Holy Spirit of promise, which is the earnest of our inheritance until the redemption of the purchased possession, unto the praise of his glory.

Paul writes about the gospel of your salvation, which is the death, burial, and the resurrection. Then he tells us that we were *sealed* with the Holy Spirit of promise. In other words, you can be born again, filled with the Holy Spirit, operate in all nine gifts of the Holy Spirit, and still be a fountain sealed. It is possible to have all of that and still not be an expression of the nature of God. The gifts and the callings of God are without repentance, or without maturity. Repentance means to change your mind, or more accurately, *exchange* your mind for the mind of Christ. This is the only way we can mature and grow up into him in all things. So, it is possible to operate in the gifts of the spirit and not be mature, or not manifest the fruit. You can be in that "in part" dimension and flow in that, and there is nothing wrong with that realm—unless you are stuck there and not maturing. We are not doing away with the gifts or the Holy Place realm. But you can have all of that and still be sealed up as far as the King reproducing himself through you.

Then he says in verse 14, "Which is the earnest of our inheritance *until the redemption* of the purchased possession, unto the praise of his glory." May I paraphrase? "Which is a measure of our inheritance, until the *full* redemption of the *purchased possession*, unto the praise of his glory." Who is this purchased possession? The purchased possession is the body of Christ and we have been sealed with the Holy Spirit of promise until the day of full redemption.

Let's look at this historically. We find this in the Amplified version of Jeremiah 32:10-11, 14:

> And I signed the deed and sealed it, called witnesses, and weighed out for him the money on the scales. So I took the deed of the purchase—both that which was sealed, containing the terms and conditions, and the copy which was unsealed ... Thus says the Lord of hosts, the God of Israel: Take these deeds, both this purchase deed which is sealed and this unsealed deed, and *put them in an earthen vessel*, that they may last a long time (emphasis added).

The scroll that John saw in Revelation chapter 5 is likened to a deed to a piece of property. We are his property. We are his purchased possession. This scroll was rolled up as a deed as if it was property that had been foreclosed. And every generation of the past had signed the backside as a testimony against this property, so that no man could redeem it. But someone came and took the scroll, redeemed it, and broke the seals so that he could receive his inheritance. That is the proof of ownership. The proof of ownership and Jesus getting his inheritance is *not* our receiving the baptism of the Holy Spirit, as great and miraculous as that is! The proof of his inheritance, the proof that he owns the property is when the full redemption begins to come forth and be manifested—when the seals are broken.

In Hebrew custom, if you defaulted on a piece of land that you bought, you could not sell it through the courthouse to the highest bidder. It had to be sold to a near-kinsman redeemer and only until the year of Jubilee. We can read more about the near-kinsman redeemer in the book of Ruth than in any other book. We needed a near-kinsman redeemer. Our near-kinsman redeemer came more than 2000 years ago and broke the seals! As we come to understand that and fill our mind with bread and wine, the evidence or the proof that we are his purchased possession is going to come forth manifested! *Then Jesus will get his inheritance—which is us!*

As in the natural; so in the spiritual. We needed to be redeemed! Now look at Jeremiah 32:36-44:

> And now therefore thus saith the LORD, the God of Israel, concerning this city, whereof ye say, It shall be delivered into the hand of the king of Babylon by the sword, and by the famine, and by the pestilence; Behold, I will gather them out of all countries, whither I have driven them in mine anger, and in my fury, and in great wrath; and I will bring them again unto this place, and I will cause them to dwell safely: And they shall be my people, and I will be their God: And I will give them one heart, and one way, that they may fear me for ever, for the good of them, and of their children after them: And I will make an everlasting covenant with them, that I will not turn away from them, to do them good; but I will put my fear in their hearts, that they shall not depart from me. Yea, I will rejoice over them to do them good, and I will plant them in this land assuredly with my whole heart and with my whole soul. For thus saith the Lord; Like as I have brought all this great evil upon this people, so will I bring upon them all the good that I have promised them. And fields shall be bought in this land, whereof ye say, It is desolate without man or beast; it is given into the hand of the Chaldeans. Men shall buy fields for money, and subscribe evidences, and seal them, and take witnesses in the land of Benjamin, and in the places about Jerusalem, and in the cities of Judah, and in the cities of the mountains, and in the cities of the valley, and in the cities of the south: for I will cause their captivity to return, saith the Lord.

This all happened over 2000 years ago when Jesus established the New Covenant, and we are becoming the performance of the New Covenant as the seals are loosed.

In verse 4 of Revelation chapter 5, John wept because no man could take the book and stop the foreclosure procedures. No one could redeem us. But behold! The Lion of the tribe of Judah, the Lamb slain, is worthy to take the book and loose the seals! The understanding of the death, burial, and resurrection, and our identification with it, is going to bring forth the evidence or the *proof* that we are his purchased possession!

In Jeremiah chapter 32, when the seal was broken it gave proof that the person who broke the seal owned that piece of property. When the seals are broken on the backside of the book within that gives *evidence* or *proof* that Jesus owns the whole City, the New Jerusalem, the bride.

When this book of life (which we are) is opened and the seals are broken, we are no longer inclosed, but Jesus is flowing out. This is the book of life that is opened in Revelation chapter 20. Let's see what John says in verses 12-15:

> And I saw the dead, small and great, stand before God; and the books were opened: and another book was opened, which is the book of life: and the dead were judged out of those things which were written in the books, according to their works. And the sea gave up the dead which were in it; and death and hell delivered up the dead which were in them: and they were judged every man according to their works. And death and hell were cast into the lake of fire. This is the second death. And whosoever was not found written in the book of life was cast into the lake of fire.

In verse 12, the dead stood before God and the books were opened. Their *lives* were opened. Then the book of life was opened. That's us. The Church is the book of life. And the dead, the people who are not born again who are dead in sins and trespasses, are judged out of those things which are written in us.

In verse 12, when John saw the dead, small and great, he was seeing men of insignificance and also men who have great power. When we are opened up—the book of life, which is the Church (we are living epistles or living books)—these people are going to be judged out of what is written in our book. The deeds that they have done are going to be judged, but they are going to be judged out of things that are written in *our book*. What is written in our book had better not be "Good old Adam." What is written in our book had better not be "I'm saved by my works. I merited salvation." Because, if that's what is written in our book, those thoughts have to be cast into the lake of fire and we must go through the second death.

When the book of life is opened and a people like the Shulamite reproduce the Lord, which is going to open up the lives of those dead in sins and trespasses. Then they will be judged according to their works and what they thought about their works. That judging is going to come out of the book of life that is opened up, and what we are going to tell them is: God is not mad at you. Now, what you need to do is get *your* works lined up with *his* works and realize that it is not even about your works, it is not about your good deeds, it is about what Jesus *has done!*

This world is a better place because of "good" people, philanthropists, volunteers, people who do good works, for sure. I'm not taking away from that. I would rather be around a good Adam than an evil Adam. The world is a better place, in the natural, because of the good things that people do for one another. But God is not saving Adam. If we are the book of life, then they are books too, and something is written in them. Those works, no matter how good a person has been, when their book is opened, the things that are written in them are going to have to line up with the things that are written in us, the book of life. That is when we go forth and share with them that God is not mad at them. He is not condoning what they've done, but they are not going to be saved by their good works either. That is when we bring judgment to them. A people to whom judgment has been given, brings judgment to them because our book of life has been opened and the things that are written in our book of life correspond with the work that took place at the cross of Calvary more than 2000 years ago. Does that mean we're soft on sin? No, it means we are magnifying righteousness. We do not condone sin. Neither do we magnify it by preaching a sin-conscious message. We minister and magnify Jesus Christ and him crucified, because what we magnify is what is going to manifest in the earth.

This righteous judgment will then cause their works to be cast into the lake of fire. What is a lake? A lake is a body of water. What is a lake of fire? It is a body of people who are one with him *who is a consuming fire*. When our book is opened up, their books will be opened up and their works will be judged. We can already see it happening. When we come into contact with immature Christians who are born again and spirit filled, but are stuck in believing that all their good works is what is going to get them to heaven or bring them into maturity, their works are being judged by the true book of life that is a living body of Melchisedec priests. "Goody-two-shoes" is not going to get us there. My doing must be cast into his doing. What is written on the pages of the body are *his works!* *"In him"* is going to get us there as we understand that he paid the price. We owed a debt we could not pay. He paid a debt he did not owe. We needed *someone* to wash away our sin. And not only wash away our sin and forgive us, *but make us a brand new creation in Christ Jesus.*

Now, Revelation 5:3:

> And no man in heaven, nor in earth, neither under the earth, was able to open the book, neither to look thereon. And I wept much because no man was found worthy to open and to read the book, neither to look thereon.

No man in heaven, no amount of works, no amount of suffering that we go through as far as the suffering that Jesus took at the cross, is able to open the book. Realizing that his suffering was our suffering is how we suffer with him. If we suffer with him, we reign with him. If we suffer with him, the seals will be broken. We bear in our bodies the marks of the dying of the Lord Jesus Christ, which means that we understand—we bear in our understanding the marks of the dying of the Lord Jesus because we were in him at the cross of Calvary.

John wept much because no man was worthy to open the book.

No matter how anointed a teacher or preacher is, no man can open the seals of your book. Only as you identify with the Lion and the Lamb will your book be opened. The Lion—the righteous earth-walk of Jesus Christ, who knew no sin. The Lamb—the sinless Lamb slain for us, as us. The Lion and The Lamb—he, who knew no sin, was made to be sin for us, that we might be made the righteousness of God in Him. In Revelation 5:5 he says:

> And one of the elders saith unto me, Weep not: behold, the Lion of the tribe of Judah, the Root of David, hath prevailed to open the book, and to loose the seven seals thereof.

Now look at Revelation 5:6-10 and you will see the glory of Jesus' sacrifice—when John looked to see the Lion, he saw a Lamb instead:

> And I beheld, and, lo, in the midst of the throne and of the four beasts, and in the midst of the elders, stood a Lamb as it had been slain, having seven horns and seven eyes, which are the seven Spirits of God sent forth into all the earth. And he came and took the book out of the right hand of him that sat upon the throne. And when he had taken the book, the four beasts and four and twenty elders fell down before the Lamb, having every one of them harps, and golden vials full of odours, which are the prayers of saints. And they sung a new song, saying, Thou art worthy to take the book, and to open the seals thereof: for thou wast slain, and hast redeemed us to God by thy blood out of every kindred, and tongue, and people, and nation; And hast made us unto our God kings and priests: and we shall reign on the earth.

The book in Revelation 5:1 is a people. We are a people who eat the bread and drink the wine. We are a people who can answer the riddle of the ages as we, the eagles, gather around the carcass and understand the treasures in darkness, as Isaiah chapter 45 says.

There are treasures in the death of Jesus Christ. As we come to fully receive the spirit of wisdom and revelation in the knowledge of him, and our mind is illuminated with understanding—not just knowledge or information—but as the spirit writes upon the tablets of our hearts and our minds, the veil is taken away. We then realize that we are no longer as black as the tents of Kedar, but we were taken to the mountain of Bether and we saw that his suffering was our suffering. Now we are in the green room and are beginning to *experience* that dimension as the life of the Lamb begins to flow out of us. As we see the Lamb slain, the seals are broken. This is what the world is looking for, *including the Church world.*

Many in the Church world know that what they have had for years has not been enough to mature them. They are beginning to realize, as it is written in Revelation chapter 12, that the woman, the Church, is in the wilderness—and the wilderness is not some place like Petra in the Middle East, as some believe. The Church is hungry. She is in the wilderness. She realizes that what she's heard for the most part has not brought the maturity. Why? Because she's heard a lot of works and legalism and "doing." That doctrine of works is wearing out the saints of the Most High, as Daniel prophesied and as John exclaims—and both use the same reference of time. The Church is in the wilderness and she is nourished by the manchild. What is the manchild? One that is birthed of the Lord into maturity.

I once heard someone say that the word "Busy" is an acronym for B-eing U-nder S-atan's Y-oke. The answer is not in doing. It is in viewing. We will find out in Revelation chapter 6, that the four living creatures say, "Come and see." Not "Come and do," but "Come and view." That is what happened in the wilderness when God told Moses to take a fiery serpent and put it on a pole—they lived for a look. They lived by seeing something. They lived when they beheld all that was accomplished in his death. And we are being consecrated, as the priests, not by *doing* something, but by *seeing* something—seeing the sacrifice, and having bread and wine laid in our hands—broken body, shed blood. That is what is taking away the veil. That is what is breaking the seals on the backside. That is what is causing the life of the Lamb to flow out on a consistent basis.

It Is Not A Future Event—But It Will Change The Events Of The Future!

I am familiar with the teaching of the futuristic view of the book of Revelation. I have also familiarized myself with the preterist view of the book of Revelation. But when we see that it is the revelation of Jesus Christ, it encompasses the whole—past, present, and future. Not "future," in the way the futuristic view has been taught, as a literal seven year tribulation and literal vials of wrath being poured out and an literal beast in the Middle East. I'm not talking about the futuristic view in that manner. But as we come to understand what John saw behind him, the "was," then we are going to understand the "is"—what is true of us because of what was. Then as time goes on, and the more we fill our minds with what was and what is, we are going to experience "that which is to come," which is the full manifestation of Christ revealed in and through his body, the Church. That is the product of our coming to understand what is true of us because of what happened at the cross of Calvary.

The *residue* of Adam that is still hanging over our mind, the *veil* that was done away in Christ, that has yet to be taken away from our mind, we call "the old woman." We are not going to get rid of the veil, the old woman, the residue of the thoughts of Adam by showing her the *new* man. We are going to get rid of the old woman, the residue of Adamic thinking that is in our mind, by showing her the *old man,* where he is now, and what happened to him. We must show people that they were widowed over 2000 years ago, at the cross of Calvary. People will not walk into this dimension by showing them the new man. They will walk into this dimension by showing them what happen to the old man—and that only leaves one other man—the Lord Jesus Christ. That is why Paul said, "For I am determined not to know anything among you, save Jesus Christ, and him crucified." Otherwise, people get the idea that we are trying to save Adam, or that we are trying to transform Adam.

Many times they use the butterfly as an example. You know the story. There was a little worm that crawled on the earth for a while, and then he formed a silk cocoon and waited there in the cocoon, passing through the pupal stage until the adult butterfly emerged. The worm underwent a metamorphosis and was transformed into a butterfly. He grew up. We can use that as an example for a maturing process. The caterpillar is changed just like we are changed—from one glory to another glory—as our mind is renewed to the finished work of Calvary (2 Corinthians 3:18). But we cannot use the butterfly as an example of initial salvation, because God is not saving the worm. God is not saving Adam. He has done away with Adam and the new creation is being developed and matured—with unveiled face.

We are not going to get rid of the old woman (the residue of Adam in our mind) by showing her the new creation. We are going to get rid of the old woman by showing her the death of the old man. The Cherubim looked down upon the blood sprinkled on the mercy seat on the Ark of the Covenant. That is where the glory of God is. When we find out where the old man is and what happened to him, then we can put on our new identity. Paul explained how this occurs in the book of Ephesians. First look at Ephesians 4:22 and 24 (Amplified Bible):

> Strip yourselves of your former nature [put off and discard your old unrenewed self] which characterized your previous manner of life and becomes corrupt through lusts and desires that spring from delusion; And put on the new nature (the regenerate self) created in God's image, [Godlike] in true righteousness and holiness.

But the key to doing this lies between these two verses, in Ephesians 4:23:

> And be constantly renewed in the spirit of your mind [having a fresh mental and spiritual attitude].

We must have our mind renewed to the fact that we were crucified with Christ. For years the Church has tried to present Christ without showing the death. Babylon is destroyed by seeing the death (Revelation 18:7)! The teachings of man, the enemy, can take away from what you believe, if you do not know *how* you became seated with Christ. But when we come to understand *how* the old man was crucified, when we come to understand *how and when* we were quickened, raised, and seated, then we have a foundation to stand upon and we will not be soon shaken. When people, or the dogmas of man, or the even the enemy of our own soul would try to say, "Who do you think you are? You're not the righteousness of God in Christ Jesus," we will be able to stand on the rock of the revelation of who Jesus is and who we are in him.

A perfect example of this is the little Shulamite who said in her carnal mind, "I'm black, but comely ..." she was double-minded. She was saying, "I'm a sinner, but I'm saved. I have spots, but I'm a new creation." She thought she had two natures. So when the enemy of your mind comes, or when any false teaching comes along that teaches you that you have two natures, you have no defense against that unless you can say, "But I know *how* I got to be the righteousness of God." When you can say that, then you have a defense against false teaching. You will fill your mind with truth and the enemy of your soul will have absolutely no ground to stand on.

Jesus Was A Fountain Sealed

We need to understand every detail of the finished work of Calvary—not sodden the lamb down with water, but roast it with fire. To roast it with fire means that we look at every little detail as the word declares it and as the spirit reveals it to us. For example, Jesus wore the crown of thorns. Thorns are a result of the curse. The crown of thorns symbolically represents that Jesus identified with our cursed thinking so that we could have the mind of Christ. Everything that Adam brought upon us, Jesus took upon himself. Jesus knew why he came. He knew the purpose of his life. He said "To this end was I born, and for this cause came I into the world, that I should bear witness unto the truth." But then, when he hung dying on the cross, he said "My God, my God, why hast thou forsaken me?" In other words, he entered into confusion and he identified with our confusion, that we might be sound in our thinking.

We are the book within, sealed on the backside with seven seals. The woman in the Song Of Solomon was a garden inclosed, a spring shut up, and a fountain sealed. Even though we are born again and have received the baptism of the Holy Spirit, we are still sealed up until the day of redemption. Another way of saying that is, we are sealed up until the year of Jubilee, or we are sealed up until we hear a long, loud blast of a ram's horn. Then, Christ which is within us is no longer just a hope of a manifestation, but he begins to be manifested. As the truth comes, it takes away the veil that remains in our mind, and Jesus can appear.

Psalm 88, like Psalm 22, is a prophetic Psalm of the cross of Jesus Christ. During the crucifixion, death, and burial, Jesus experienced being sealed up. He was a garden inclosed, a spring shut up, and a fountain sealed. We see this in Psalm 88:8:

> Thou hast put away mine acquaintance far from me; thou hast made me an abomination unto them: *I am shut up, and I cannot come forth* (emphasis added).

Jesus experienced exactly what we experience. Even though we are born again and spirit-filled, we are still a garden inclosed until we are mature in God. The release of the life of our Lord Jesus Christ has not fully and completely come out of us yet. That is what we must see. What the world needs is life! They need to see the life of the Lamb flow out of a people! And it is going to flow out of a people, not as we show them another man, but as we show them what has happened to the old man, Adam—he is crucified, dead, and buried. Then they will see that not only was the old man crucified, but through Jesus' crown of thorns the residue of the old man (the old woman) was done away with too. The veil was done away with at the cross and now it is being taken away from our mind. So at Calvary, Jesus also became a garden inclosed, a spring shut up, and a fountain sealed.

In Revelation chapter 5, there is a book that is sealed and it is not the Bible. And even though the book of Revelation needs to be revealed more and more, and is being revealed more and more, the book that is sealed is not the book of Revelation. The book that is sealed is *us*. In Revelation 5:1, John saw in the right hand of *him that is seated on the throne* a book written within and on the backside, sealed with seven seals. Who is the one that is seated on the throne? The Lord Jesus is seated on the throne—he and the Father are one. The book within is a people, it is the body of Christ.

Let's recap the six reasons that "the book within" in Revelation 5:1 is the body of Christ. First, we know that the book within is the body of Christ. In Ephesians chapter 4, we read about a people who are growing up into the head in all things unto a perfect man, unto the measure of the stature of the fullness of Christ. In the three and one half years of Jesus' earthly ministry, Jesus was the word made flesh. If we are growing up into the head in all things, of he who was the word made flesh, then we are becoming the word—the book within—unsealed, or made flesh. We become a manifestation of Christ, an open revelation in crystal clear terms. When we study the city in Revelation, we will see that the word "city" is written in the feminine gender. Out of this city or out of the soul, comes forth a river that is clear as crystal and everything that comes in contact with it lives.

Second, we are called epistles of Christ in 2 Corinthians 3:2-3. One translation says we are letters from God. We are love letters from God to the world. But the problem is, the letter has been sealed up. Jesus was also shut up and he bore that—being sealed up like we have been sealed up. The life of Jesus will flow out of us when we are no longer sealed up, no longer inclosed, but every eye will see him as he flows out of his people! Every eye shall see him as he comes in the cloud of his people, clouds of his glory, when he is no longer hidden inside earthen vessels, but shining all the way through them in *ephiphaneia!* You can't be a cloud if you're not "caught up." Otherwise, you're just a fog, seeing through a glass darkly.

Remember Gideon's army? 32,000 men were reduced to just 300 (the number of complete deliverance) lest they boast against the Lord saying that their own works saved them. They carried lights covered with earthen vessels in their left hands and trumpets in their right hands, leaving no chance for the men to win the battle with their own hands. When the perfect moment came (the fullness of times), they trumpeted the pure word (sword) of the Lord which broke open the earthen vessels—and out came the victorious light!

In the book of James we are told to receive with meekness, the engrafted word. The engrafted word is not that word which is written on pieces of parchment. It is not the Bible that you hold on your lap, although the Bible is given by inspiration of God. It is divinely breathed (2 Timothy 3:16). Only the Holy Spirit can cause the word to become reality to us. The engrafted word is that which is written by the Holy Spirit upon our hearts and upon our minds. God said, "I will put my laws into their mind, and write them in their hearts: and I will be to them a God, and they shall be to me a people." We are the book within because we are living epistles not written with ink, but with the Spirit of the living God; not in tables of stone, but in fleshy tables of the heart.

The <u>third</u> reason we are the book within, is that throughout the book of Revelation, we see pictures that the body of Christ is the expression of Christ, who is the word made flesh. For example, in Revelation 1:20, the seven candlesticks are symbolic of the seven Churches. In John 1:4 we see that light and life is the same person. In Psalm 36:9 we read, "In thy light shall we see light." The Candlesticks are the body of Christ. He is the central shaft and it is *one piece* of gold.

<u>Fourth,</u> in Revelation 5:1, this book is in the *right hand* of the Lord. The right hand speaks of anointing, valiancy, and power. The power of God is the preaching of the cross. Also, in looking at the lives of Joseph and Benjamin, we find that Joseph had ten brothers before him. Ten speaks of the law. Joseph represents a perfect type of Christ. Benjamin (son of the right hand) is his only full brother. In Benjamin's sack of corn was something that none of the other brothers had—a silver cup. Silver speaks of redemption. Joseph's silver cup was empty when it was placed in Benjamin's sack. Why? It typifies that Jesus drank the bitter contents of the cup. We are in the right hand of the one that is seated on the throne. We are Jesus' full brother. He is the first born of *many* brethren, making us joint heirs with him. We share in his inheritance. There are many good things said about us in the word of God. There are many good things said about the anointing of God, the power of God, the valiancy of God, and we are that book that is in his right hand.

When we study the four horses in chapter 6, the understanding of those horses is going to unseal the book within. The book of Revelation is the highest revelation in the entire Bible about the death, burial, and resurrection of Christ. The more we come to understand the signs and symbols in the book of Revelation, what they represent, and how we are identified with them, the more the life of the Lamb is going to flow forth out of us. We will no longer be a garden inclosed, a spring shut up, or a fountain sealed, because Jesus was shut up *as us* over 2000 years ago at Calvary's cross.

Fifth, the little Shulamite represents the Church, the bride, who has been inclosed, shut up, and sealed up, as we find in Song Of Solomon 4:12. The Shulamite had received in type, the baptism of the Holy Spirit when she was courting the king. He wined her and dined her and she passed out in his arms. She woke up in his arms—gripped by him. We are being gripped by him as we enter into rest. As we wake up to the truth about the finished work and enter into rest, we will find ourselves fully gripped by the cross of Jesus Christ. Faith is our grip on God. Redemption is God's grip on us.

When Paul was ready to go to Jerusalem to preach the gospel, the prophet Agabus took Paul's girdle and bound his hands and feet, telling Paul that if he went to Jerusalem he would be bound and delivered into the hands of the Gentiles. But Paul was so fully gripped by the cross of Jesus Christ that he said, "I am ready not to be bound only, but also to die at Jerusalem for the name of the Lord Jesus."

So, the little Shulamite represents the Church. Before she received the baptism of the Holy Spirit in type, the king told the Shulamite, "Our bed is green," symbolizing life. He was saying, "I am Life. When we marry and become one, we are going to produce life because I am going to reproduce myself through you. I don't want you to be a garden inclosed, a spring shut up, or a fountain sealed any longer, but I want that seed that I planted in your spirit to impregnate your soul with myself, so that there can be a birthing of my nature through your life."

The sixth and last reason that we are the book within is found in Ephesians 1:10-14. Paul tells us that we are sealed with the Holy Spirit of promise, which is the earnest or the down payment of the inheritance, until the redemption of the purchased possession. Remember the story in Jeremiah chapter 32? In Jewish history, when someone defaulted on their purchased property, they had to sell it to a near-kinsman redeemer. Then they would take the scroll to the redeemer and he would break the seals as evidence that he owned that purchased possession. Jeremiah *engraved* or subscribed the evidence (the deed, the scroll, the book), took *witnesses,* and *weighed in the balances seventeen pieces of silver* while he was *shut up* in the court of the *prison,* which was in the religious king of

Judah's house. With those seventeen shekels of silver, he purchased *the field* of Hanameel in Anathoth. We are the scroll—the world is the field. Every generation has signed this scroll saying, "No man can redeem this property." Each generation has defaulted because in Adam, no man can redeem us. No man possesses the seventeen shekels of silver that are required to redeem us. We needed a new creation redeemer—a man without sin—a man with redemption's silver. E. W. Bullinger wrote:

> Seventeen is the combination or sum of two perfect numbers—seven and ten—seven being the number of spiritual perfection, and ten of ordinal perfection. We see a beautiful illustration in Romans 8:35-39, which concludes the first great division of that all-important Epistle, and sums up the blessings of *those who are dead and risen in Christ.* First we have a series of seven, then a series of ten. The seven are marked off by being put in the form of a question, while the ten are given as the answer to it. Who shall separate us from the love of Christ? Shall (1) tribulation, (2) or distress, (3) or persecution, (4) or famine, (5) or nakedness, (6) or peril, (7) or sword? As it is written, For Thy sake are we killed all the day long; we are accounted as sheep for the slaughter. Nay, in all these things we are more than conquerors through Him that loved us. For I am persuaded, that, (1) neither death, (2) nor life, (3) nor angels, (4) nor principalities, (5) nor things present, (6) nor things to come, (7) nor powers, (8) nor height, (9) nor depth, (10) nor any other creature, shall be able to separate us from the love of God which is in Christ Jesus our Lord (emphasis added).[29]

And there we have the seventeen reasons that Jeremiah prophetically weighed out the seventeen shekels of silver to purchase the field of Hanameel with. Isn't it interesting that the name "Hanameel" means "the grace that comes from God"? Jesus Christ paid the price. He is our near-kinsman redeemer. He is the grace that came from

God to purchase the field of the world which is in Anathoth, or poverty, or hell. He has engraved *himself* on the tablets of our hearts. He took us as witnesses when he put us *in him* and weighed *himself* in the balances. Because of sin, we were found wanting. But Jesus was *not* found wanting. He was *not* found wanting. He had what it took to redeem us—seventeen pieces of silver—the righteousness of God. So he took us to the cross within himself, where we were crucified with him, we died with him, and we were buried with him. The religious had Jesus crucified and shut up in the prison of hell and that is where he left the sin that he had become for us, as us. Because of Jesus' finished work of the cross, sin was deposited in hell where it belongs. Now remember, we are in him. So, when the Holy Spirit quickened Jesus, we were quickened too! When the Holy Spirit raised Jesus up from the grave, we were raised too! When Jesus was seated at the right hand of God, we were seated too!

In Spirit, the seals of the book within have been broken. Now the fullness is beginning to walk itself out in us. When the seals are broken within us in experience and the rivers of living water flow out of us, then the residue of the people are going to see the proof that we are God's purchased possession! All people will flow to the mountain of the Lord (Micah 4). That's when *Jesus* will get *his* inheritance!

The Seven Horns And The Seven Eyes Of The Slain Lamb

Revelation 5:1-5:

> And I saw in the right hand of him that sat on the throne a book written within and on the backside, sealed with seven seals. And I saw a strong angel proclaiming with a loud voice, Who is worthy to open the book, and to loose the seals thereof? And no man in heaven, nor in earth, neither under the earth, was able to open the book, neither to look thereon. And I wept much, because no man was found worthy to open and to read the book, neither to look thereon. And one of the elders saith unto me, Weep not: behold, the Lion of the tribe of Judah, the

> Root of David, hath prevailed to open the book, and to loose the seven seals thereof.

Remember, John was weeping and one translation actually says, "One of the elders said unto me, 'Shut up.'" The elder told John that the Lion of the tribe of Judah, the Root of David, hath prevailed to open the book, and to loose the seals thereof. Then, in verse 6, when John looked to see the Lion, he saw a Lamb instead.

> And I beheld, and, lo, in the midst of the throne and of the four beasts, and in the midst of the elders, stood a Lamb as it had been slain, having seven horns and seven eyes, which are the seven Spirits of God sent forth into all the earth.

The Lion of the tribe of Judah speaks of Jesus' overcoming earth walk. We will discuss this in more detail in following issues of this series. But the Lamb speaks of that which took place over 2000 years ago when the spotless Lamb went to the cross. John saw that the Lamb had seven horns representing fullness of power. The horns are not something literal, they are symbolic of power. Seven is symbolic of fullness. Just as the seven seals in verse 1 are not literal, but symbolic, meaning that we are fully sealed. Then he saw that the Lamb had seven eyes, representing perfection of perception, which are the seven Spirits of God sent forth into all the earth. Continuing in Revelation 5:7-11;

> And he came and took the book out of the right hand of him that sat upon the throne. And when he had taken the book, the four beasts and four and twenty elders fell down before the Lamb, having every one of them harps, and golden vials full of odours, which are the prayers of saints. And they sung a new song, saying, Thou art worthy to take the book, and to open the seals thereof: for thou wast slain, and hast redeemed us to God by thy blood out of every kindred, and tongue, and people, and nation; And hast made us unto our God kings and priests: and we shall

> reign on the earth. And I beheld, and I heard the voice of many angels round about the throne and the beasts and the elders: and the number of them was ten thousand times ten thousand, and thousands of thousands;

Notice the phrase in verse 11b, "and the number of them was ten thousand times ten thousand, and thousands of thousands." I like to say, "And the number of them was the whole earth." When Jesus went to the cross, he said in John 12:32, "And I, if I be lifted up from the earth, will *drag all men unto me*," the Greek says. This is the day in which the Church is expressing the very nature (name) of Jesus and every knee is bowing, of things in heaven, and things in earth, and things under the earth, and every tongue is confessing that Jesus Christ is Lord, to the glory of God the Father! Every knee bowed spiritually at the cross over 2000 years ago, but in this Day it is being manifested with increasing intensity until the sound of many waters is heard throughout time and eternity.

We sing the song, "Behold the Lamb," and what we are saying is that we need to just view the Lamb. We need to view the death. When we view the death, out of that will spontaneously come the life. We need to keep viewing the Lamb, eating the Lamb, partaking of bread and wine, until *all men* say with a loud voice:

> Worthy is the Lamb that was slain to receive power, and riches, and wisdom, and strength, and honor, and glory, and blessing. And every creature which is in heaven, and on the earth, and under the earth, and such as are in the sea, and all that are in them, heard I saying, Blessing, and honor, and glory, and power, be unto him that sitteth upon the throne, and unto the Lamb for ever and ever. And the four beasts said, Amen. And the four and twenty elders fell down and worshipped him that liveth for ever and ever. (Revelation 5:12-14).

To some people, the book of Revelation is a sealed book. This is because in order to understand the book of Revelation, one must be in the same spirit that John was in. It was written in sign and symbol. It is a symbolic book. We have discussed some of the reasons people think that the Bible or the book of Revelation is the book that is sealed. The first reason is that one must be *in the spirit* to understand it. Secondly, it is a symbolic book and the symbols must be understood. Thirdly, we must understand that John looked *behind* him. He was not interpreting what he saw as future events. John looked behind him and saw that which was—the crucifixion, the death, the burial—and he saw that which is—what is true *now* because of the death, burial, and resurrection. What is true of us today? We are the righteousness of God in Christ Jesus. We are not just forgiven sinners, but we are brand new creatures in Christ! That is what *is* because of what *was*. Then John saw that which *is to come*—the *product* of a people who understand *what is true of them* because they understand *what was,* over 2000 years ago. John looked behind him. He was not interpreting the revelation as "future events." As we look behind us and see what happened at the cross, the life of the Lamb is going to flow out of us more and more as time goes on. We are not interpreting it as future events. That interpretation only ministers a lot of confusion because future events and current events are always changing. No wonder the Church is full of uncertainty and confusion. *This is the revelation of Jesus Christ!* The time is at hand for us to fill our mind with this truth so we can become *the product* of the book of Revelation.

You Shall Hear A Word Behind You

Let's look into Isaiah 30:20-21:

> And though the Lord give you the bread of adversity, and the water of affliction, yet shall not thy teachers be removed into a corner any more, but thine eyes shall see thy teachers: and thine ears shall hear a word *behind thee,* saying, "This is the way, walk ye in it," when ye turn to the right hand, and when ye turn to the left (emphasis added).

The word "though" in verse 20 is in italics or parenthesis and it was added in the translation, so it was not there originally. The footnote in the Companion Bible says, "Omit 'though' and read it as a direct promise." And the Lord give you the bread of adversity. Who is the bread? Jesus is the bread. When did Jesus, the bread, have adversity? Jesus had adversity at the same time we did—at the cross of Calvary. The Lord also gave us the water of affliction. When was he afflicted? Isaiah 53 tells us that his soul was afflicted at the cross.

Then in verse 21 he says, "Thine ears shall hear a word *behind thee*, saying, 'This is the way, walk ye in it,' when ye turn to the right hand, and when ye turn to the left." John heard this voice *behind him* on the isle of Patmos telling him, "I am the way, walk in me." The isle of Patmos is the isle of "my death." John was bearing record of the word of God and of the martyrdom of Jesus Christ. He was bearing in his body the marks of the Lord Jesus. This is the way we are to walk—by hearing the voice behind us—not by making Revelation a book of some eschatological event that is going to happen tomorrow, or a year from now, or 100 years from now—but interpreting it by looking behind us. This is the way, walk ye in it.

Jesus is the bread of adversity. Leviticus chapter 2 describes the meal offering. Jesus became the meal offering at the cross of Calvary over 2000 years ago. Also, Jesus was the water of affliction. The children of Israel got their water by smiting the rock when they were in the wilderness. Paul told us the rock was Christ. He was the smitten rock. The water of affliction flowed from the cross of Calvary over 2000 years ago. Again, Isaiah foretold this in chapter 53.

There are some that teach suffering so strongly that they have the doctrine of suffering ingrained in them, and they believe that God brings suffering for the purpose of purifying us. It is amazing that when someone comes down with some dreaded disease and they think that God is purifying them through trials, it keeps the works and the lusts of the flesh down for a while, but as soon as the "processing" is over, all of those lusts come back. Why? Because that is not what was happening. Suffering may put a lid on things and it may *look* like something is happening, but God is not saving Adam. No man can open the book. No amount of suffering except Jesus' suffering at the cross of Calvary can open the book.

I know God can use those things. For example, if a man has been eating junk food and not exercising and has a heart attack, in the natural, he can learn to eat right. We can learn natural lessons.

We can even learn some spiritual lessons of stewardship and discipline. But what I'm saying is, just as God does not bring sin into our lives to purify us, neither does God bring sickness to purify us. Believing that God *does* act like that is what gives people the stress that causes their illnesses! That is what idolatry will get you. That is smiting the rock twice and we will *never* experience the Promised Land with that mentality. Jesus was not smitten to take away all our diseases to turn around and put diseases back upon us. That belief is idolatry, and it is ludicrous. It is worshipping some created idol, not the one true God. We must let his smiting be our smiting.

So, the Lord gave you the bread of adversity and the water of affliction at the cross. How did they get water in the wilderness? By smiting the rock. Jesus was the smitten rock. The water of affliction was given when the rock was afflicted. So, let's continue in Isaiah 30:20-21: "And though the Lord give you the bread of adversity, and the water of affliction, yet shall not thy teachers be removed into a corner any more, but thine eyes shall see thy teachers:" (In the King James Version, the sentence does not stop there because there is a colon. It goes on to say:) "And thine ears shall hear a word *behind thee,* saying, 'This is the way, walk ye in it,' when ye turn to the right hand, and when ye turn to the left" (emphasis added). Where are we going to eat the bread of adversity and drink the water of affliction? At the same place John did in Revelation chapter 1—behind us.

When we eat of the bread of adversity and drink of the water of affliction, we are not talking about what "poor old me has to suffer while I trudge along on this earth" or "the more I suffer, the more I'm going to be conformed into his image." His suffering was our suffering and through that suffering at the cross, he sat us on the throne. If we suffer with him, we will reign with him. If we eat of the bread of adversity and drink of the water of affliction, then in Revelation 7:15-17, we see what will happen.

> Therefore are they before the throne of God, and serve him day and night in his temple: and he that sitteth on the throne shall dwell among them. They shall hunger no more, neither thirst any more; neither shall the sun light on them, nor any heat. For the Lamb which is in the midst of the throne shall

feed them, and shall lead them unto living fountains of waters: and God shall wipe away all tears from their eyes.

Ruth was fully satisfied when Boaz fed her bread and wine. It brought her into a rest. Revelation 7:17 tells us that we are to be fed by the Lamb which is in the midst of the throne. What does that mean to us? If you are really hearing a word from the throne, if you are really hearing a word by the Spirit of God in this present day, it is going to be about the death of Jesus Christ. Every piece of furniture in the tabernacle and everything in the Most Holy Place testifies of him!

John says in verses 16-17, "They shall hunger no more, neither thirst any more; neither shall the sun light on them, nor any heat. For the Lamb which is in the midst of the throne shall feed them." What brings the marriage? The *marriage supper* of the Lamb. They shall not thirst any more, because the Lamb shall lead them unto living fountains of waters. We are eating of the bread of adversity and we are drinking of the water of affliction which took place at the cross of Calvary. Why? Because we are looking behind us. This is the way, and we're walking in it. John turned to see the voice behind him and he saw Christ speaking out of the midst of his Church. For the Lamb which is in the midst of the throne shall feed them, and shall lead them unto living fountains of waters, and God shall wipe away all tears from their eyes. Remember Isaiah chapter 6. When Isaiah saw that the old man was dead and that the Lord was high and lifted up, God wiped away the tears from his eyes and changed his cry from that of "Woe" to that of "Holy, Holy, Holy is the Lord of Hosts! The whole earth is full of his glory!"

Only The Lamb Slain Opens The Book

Who then, opens the book? No man opens the book. No amount of suffering opens the book. One school of thought on the death of Christ is this: Jesus is our pattern and what he suffered on the cross, we must also suffer. That thinking is erroneous. Jesus suffered *as* us. We have already suffered being crucified, dead, and buried with Jesus over 2000 years ago and when we came to the cross and accepted him as our savior, we released that truth to work for us in our own lives. Our understanding of that is going to break the seals and bring us out of a suffering, "Woe is me" mentality to a "Holy, holy, holy" mentality that Isaiah experienced after the coals touched his mouth.

We find an interesting character in the Old Testament named Rizpah. "Rizpah" means "burning coals of fire." It is the feminine form of the same word that is used in Isaiah 6 when his mouth was touched with the coal from off the altar. Rizpah stood and watched seven sons being crucified. She stood there to chase away the birds and the beasts that would come and try to eat the dead carcasses. She stood there and watched their bodies from the beginning of harvest time until it began to rain. History tells us that she stood there until the Feast of Tabernacles. We, the Church, are staying at the cross of Christ and viewing his death until water drops upon us from heaven—until the book is opened and the living fountains of water flow freely!

It is not "how much we suffer" that opens the book. We need to have the mindset that his suffering was our suffering and because of that, we're seated right now on the throne in heavenly places. When we have that mindset, then no matter what we go through, we will stay in balance. Sadly, there are people today who glory in what they suffer! "Look at me, I'm going through so much and somehow it is going to cause a greater anointing to come or a higher place of honor for me." That is exactly what Moses did when he smote the rock twice and he missed the Promised Land. The anointing is on the word of God. The anointing abides within us and it is on the word that is engrafted upon the tablets of our hearts and our minds.

Chapter Four

Come And See

*I*n Revelation chapter 6, we see four beasts. These are not wild beasts as in Revelation chapter 13. The beasts in chapter 6 are living creatures expressing life. John looked behind him and saw Christ, the living Word, portrayed as these four beasts in each of the four gospels. The word of God is a divine masterpiece! Four times, at the opening of each seal, and the riding forth of each horse—the white horse, the red horse, the black horse, and the pale horse—these living creatures say three little words that are so important. "Come and see," or "Behold the Lamb!" Look at Revelation 6:1:

> And I saw when the Lamb opened one of the seals, and I heard, as it were the noise of thunder, one of the four beasts saying, "Come and see."

Come and see. Come and view—not come and do! He is not saying, "Come and pay your tithes and then the book is going to be opened." And I believe in paying tithes and giving gifts and showing up when the Church doors are open. We do that out of obedience and because we *want* to—it's our new creation nature to do those things. But we do not do them to become more righteous or to open the book. Come and see. It is like Israel in the wilderness. When they were murmuring against Moses, he went to God because they were snake bitten, and asked God what to do. God told him to take a fiery serpent and put it upon a pole and when they looked, they lived. But they were to do more than just see the fiery serpent on the pole. The word says that when they *beheld* the serpent of bronze, they lived. That word means more than just a glance. It means to look intently at, to have respect for. This denotes understanding. God did not want them to just see it and then forget about it.

Come and see. Come and understand what happened. Come and understand the twelve redemptive aspects of the finished work of Calvary. Come and understand that the Lamb must be roasted with fire, not soddened down with water. Come and hear a message from the throne so that you can see with the eyes of your understanding and the Spirit of wisdom and revelation in the knowledge of him can be opened up unto you.

Look at Revelation 6:3:

> And when he had opened the second seal, I heard the second beast say, "Come and see."

And verse 5:

> And when he had opened the third seal, I heard the third beast say, "Come and see." And I beheld and lo, a black horse; and he that sat on him had a pair of balances in his hand.

And verse 7:

> And when he had opened the fourth seal, I heard the voice of the fourth beast say, "Come and see."

As we view what happened at the finished work of Calvary, it is going to take away the veil that is on our mind. There is only one thing that we have to do to get these seals broken. Behold the Lamb.

What is the thing that is going to keep the book sealed up? Nothing but the residue yet in our mind (2 Corinthians 3:14-15). The veil that was done away in Christ but is not yet *taken* away from our mind is the only thing that is going to keep the book from being opened. If there were a veil between you and I, you might hear my voice, but you would not see me. The world wants to see Christ, so we must remove the veil from our mind that was done away at the cross of Calvary. When Jesus died, the veil in the temple was rent from the top to the bottom. It was done away with. But now the veil that is over our mind must be taken away, and the only way it can be taken away is as we eat the Lamb that is roasted with fire. As we partake of the bread and wine that he feeds us, the veil is taken away. And that is the only way the veil is going to be taken away.

Ashes To Ashes—Dust To Dust
Beauty For Ashes—Shake Off The Dust

God said he would give us beauty for ashes. When they put the bullock on the brazen altar, the bullock became ashes. The ashes were filtered through a filter and fell down. Those ashes represent Jesus as he took into himself all that we were. He said "I am going to give you beauty for ashes." He didn't say he was going to change the ashes into beauty, he said I'm going to *ex*change—I am going to give you beauty *for* your ashes. He became ashes so that we could be arrayed in his beauty. Seeing the finished work of the Lamb roasted with fire will birth within you an awesome humility and a depth of appreciation and love for our Savior that you have never known before. Nothing but the full understanding of the Lamb slain brings about *true* worship.

Then in Isaiah 52 God speaks to the Church and says, "Shake thyself from the dust, arise and sit down, O Jerusalem." God is not saving Adam, the man made from dust. He crucified Adam because he was weighed in the balance and found wanting. Again, the *metamorphoo* from the caterpillar to the butterfly is not an allegory of initial salvation, but of our maturing process. We cannot use that as an allegory of initial salvation, because God is not saving the caterpillar. God is not saving Adam. His days were numbered—and there were only six of them[30]. But we can use metamorphosis for an allegory of a maturing process because we are being changed from realm to realm and from glory to glory as more of the salvation that is in our spirit comes to our soul and a conception of the word takes place. When that happens, we are changed more and more and we manifest him more and more.

The only thing that is keeping the book sealed, the garden inclosed, the spring shut up and the fountain sealed, is the veil that remains in our mind. We are not talking about "mind over matter." We are talking about our spirit man being given dominion over the earth. We are talking about Spirit flowing through soul. Romans 12:2 says that if we *renew our mind* we'll be transformed. Renewing our mind is not merely positive thinking. Renewing our mind is a conception of the word by the spirit, taking place in the womb of the mind and birthing the Christ nature. It is a whole new world compared to the old world mentality of saving Adam.

What is the thing that will redeem Ishamael, the "wild ass" nature that Exodus 13 speaks of? And "redeem" does not mean "modify the old man," it doesn't mean "save the old man," it does not mean "rehabilitate the old man." Look at Exodus 13:13:

> And every firstling of an ass thou shalt redeem with a lamb; and if thou wilt not redeem it, then thou shalt break his neck: and all the firstborn of man among thy children shalt thou redeem.

The Lamb is the answer to the old nature. The Lamb is also the answer to the residue of Adam's thinking yet in our mind. Eat, partake, more and more of the Lamb until the marriage is experienced. Only then are we able to say, "Not my will but thine, be done."

MEGIDDO

The horses in Revelation chapter 6 are war horses. Where is the war? The war is in the mind. How do we win that war? By seeing that it was won at the cross of Calvary. For years we have been taught about a literal battle of Armageddon that will be fought in a place called Megiddo. But when the Holy Spirit imparts to us his meaning of the scriptures, we begin to see things with dove's eyes. Spiritually speaking then, what is in the valley of Megiddo? "I" is. When you realize "I" is crucified, dead, and buried, the war is over!

Then we can cast down *imaginations,* and every high thing that exalts itself against the *knowledge* of God, and bring into captivity every *thought* to the obedience of Christ. Those things—imaginations, knowledge, and thoughts—are in the mind. Every meaningful thought we have leaves a residue in our brain. But these are war horses—and the war is in the mind. As we understand what these horses depict, they will run through our mind and leave hoof prints. The more hoof prints we have of the white horse, the red horse, the black horse, and the pale horse, the more we are going to manifest the mind of Christ. The more of his hoof prints we have, the more residue synthesis of Christ we will have, not just within the brain, but within our mind. Proverbs 21:31 says, "The horse is prepared against the day of battle: but safety is of the Lord."

Now look at Revelation 19:11:

> And I saw heaven opened, and behold, a white horse; and he that sat upon him was called Faithful and True, and in righteousness he doth judge and make war.

Most people teach the white horse in Revelation 6 as the antichrist because the rider has a bow. But when we find out what that bow represents, we will see that it is not the antichrist. Then, they teach this white horse in Revelation 19 as the literal coming of the Lord as if he is raising horses in heaven and one day he's going to jump on a white one and come back. I don't mean to be crude, but sometimes dramatic illustrations must be used just to show how carnal some of that teaching is. Let's continue with verses 12-13:

> His eyes were as a flame of fire, and on his head were many crowns; and he had a name written, that no man knew, but he himself. And he was clothed with a vesture dipped in blood: and his name is called The Word of God.

We are the book within. We are the word made flesh because he is the head and we are his body. And yes, this is the coming of the Lord. Yes, it is his coming in a white horse, but the white horse speaks of strength and power, and in particular, white speaks of the righteousness of the saints. So, because he has *many crowns*, his coming is in a many-membered company.

In verse 13 Jesus is clothed with a vesture dipped in blood. John was looking behind him and he saw what Isaiah looked forward to in Isaiah chapter 63. Both men saw the cross of Christ. Look at Isaiah 63:1-6:

> Who is this that cometh from Edom, with dyed garments from Bozrah? this that is glorious in his apparel, traveling in the greatness of his strength? I that speak in righteousness, mighty to save. Wherefore art thou red in thine apparel, and thy garments like him that treadeth in the winefat? I have trodden the winepress alone; and of the people there was none with me: for I will tread them in mine anger, and trample them in my fury; and their blood shall be sprinkled upon my garments, and I will stain all my raiment. For the day of vengeance is in mine heart, and the year of my redeemed is come. And I looked, and there was none to help; and I wondered that there was none to uphold: therefore mine own arm brought salvation unto me; and my fury, it upheld me. And I will tread down the people in mine anger, and make them drunk in my fury, and I will bring down their strength to the earth.

Jesus' body, his vesture, was dipped in his own blood when he was pressed in the winepress without the city on Calvary's cross. Notice verse 6 of this passage, "And I will tread down the people in mine anger, and make them drunk in my fury, and I will bring down their strength to the earth." We were crucified with Christ.

As The Morning Spread Upon The Mountains

Joel saw the same army of horses. Look at Joel 2:1-11:

> Blow ye the trumpet in Zion, and sound an alarm in

my holy mountain: let all the inhabitants of the land tremble: for the day of the LORD cometh, for it is nigh at hand; A day of darkness and of gloominess, a day of clouds and of thick darkness, as the morning spread upon the mountains: a great people and a strong; there hath not been ever the like, neither shall be any more after it, even to the years of many generations. A fire devoureth before them; and behind them a flame burneth: the land is as the garden of Eden before them, and behind them a desolate wilderness; yea, and nothing shall escape them. The appearance of them is as the appearance of horses; and as horsemen, so shall they run. Like the noise of chariots on the tops of mountains shall they leap, like the noise of a flame of fire that devoureth the stubble, as a strong people set in battle array. Before their face the people shall be much pained: all faces shall gather blackness. They shall run like mighty men; they shall climb the wall like men of war; and they shall march every one on his ways, and they shall not break their ranks: Neither shall one thrust another; they shall walk every one in his path: and when they fall upon the sword, they shall not be wounded. They shall run to and fro in the city; they shall run upon the wall, they shall climb up upon the houses; they shall enter in at the windows like a thief. The earth shall quake before them; the heavens shall tremble: the sun and the moon shall be dark, and the stars shall withdraw their shining: And the LORD shall utter his voice before his army: for his camp is very great: for he is strong that executeth his word: for the day of the LORD is great and very terrible; and who can abide it?

This is the coming of the Lord that Revelation 19 speaks about. It is a many-membered coming. It is his coming in clouds. It is his coming through a firstfruit company of people. For those who do not have understanding, it is going to be a day of darkness and of gloominess until the new day dawns *in them*. Why? Because they are scared to death of the judgment of God—which was fully meted at Calvary's cross! It is not a future event—it is a finished work! People are scared to death because of the deception they've been taught by the god of this world—the religious system—concerning the book of Revelation. It *is* a day of darkness because they are very uncertain about what is going to happen. Ask people who have heard Revelation as futuristic teaching—they are scared to death! So it is a day of darkness to them, a day of clouds and of thick darkness. But notice the phrase in Joel 2:2, "as the morning spread upon the mountains." It is a New Day to those who are a great and a strong people.

When my daughter worked third shift, she would come home in the morning and say "Good night," but I would say "Good morning." It was night-time to her, but morning to me. That is the way it is today. People are preaching, "The end of the world is coming and it is going to be blown to smithereens." It is night-time to them. But to those who are bondservants, to a people great and strong, it is the dawning of a New Day, because they have understanding. This is The Day that the Lord has made. The New Day is Christ our Lord. We will rejoice and be glad *in him!*

In verse 3, "a fire devoureth before them; and *behind* them a flame burneth." There is that word again—behind. When did the flame burn behind us? At the cross of Calvary. That was the judgment. Notice, "the land is as the garden of Eden *before* them." That is what we have to look forward to. Jesus made the graveyard a garden. As we realize this, our lives will bloom like a garden, complete with fountain stream—not shut up, but flowing out. Again, he says, "and *behind* them a desolate wilderness; yea, and nothing shall escape them." Behind us is the desolate wilderness where all in Adam died at Calvary's cross and none escaped! In Adam, all died. In Christ shall all be made alive. If you want life, that is where it comes from—in Christ. Then in verses 4-11 it speaks of the army in Revelation chapter 19, and the coming of the Lord through that army.

These are war horses in Revelation 6. Where is the battle? We wrestle not against flesh and blood, but against principalities and powers. And the principalities and powers are not just something on the outside of the city. The principalities and powers are things that are warring within our mind, the residue of Adam that is still there.

What are the principalities and powers? Ephesians 6:12 says, "For we wrestle not against flesh and blood, but against principalities, against powers, against the rulers of the darkness of this world, against spiritual wickedness in high places. Where are they? In high places. What is to be done with them? 2 Corinthians 10:5-7 tells us: "Casting down *imaginations*, and every high and lofty thing that exalteth itself against the *knowledge* of God, and bringing into captivity every *thought* to the obedience of Christ." Principalities and powers are the thoughts and the thought processes that go on in our minds that are not of God. We are to cast them down, throw them down, and bring them into captivity by putting on the mind of Christ concerning the death, burial, and resurrection.

Metamorphosis

Romans 12:1-2 says, "I beseech you therefore, brethren, by the mercies of God, that ye present your bodies a living sacrifice, holy, acceptable unto God, which is your reasonable service. And be not conformed to this world: but be ye transformed by the renewing of your mind, that ye may prove what is that good, and acceptable, and perfect, will of God." Be not conformed to this outer world. Don't be conformed to Adam, thinking you have two natures. But be *transformed* by the renewing of the mind. The word "transformed" there is the same word that is used in Matthew chapter 17, when Jesus was transfigured before them—*metamorphoo*. On the mountain of transfiguration, his spirit swallowed up the realm of soul and body and he dissolved into the realm of spirit, which is a picture of the body of Christ who will experience total transformation. This is happening as our minds are fully renewed. We are *experiencing* the transfiguration power, or realm, or dimension that we're already seated in. And as time goes on it will only intensify and flow out to a greater degree.

This is what Nahum 1:9 says about Jesus and the cross of Calvary:

> What do ye imagine against the Lord? He will make an utter end: affliction shall not rise up the second time.

In other words, he did it once and for all. We're not going to smite the rock twice. Jesus does not have to go back and do it all over again. His suffering was our suffering. Jesus is our pattern, but that does not mean that we have to suffer with anything that he nailed to the cross. *He* did it once and *for all.* Jesus is our pattern in humility, in comforting, in meekness, in righteousness, in mercy, in purity, in peace, and in persecution for *righteousness'* sake. Many people who *think* they are being persecuted are *not* being persecuted for righteousness' sake. They may be being persecuted for the sake of their religion. But religion is not righteousness. The theme of the Bible is redemption. Jesus, the bread, partook of the affliction. Jesus, the living water, partook of the adversity. And if we eat the bread of affliction and drink the water of adversity, we will never hunger or thirst again.

Romans 8:6 says, "For to be carnally minded is death, but to be spiritually minded is life and peace." To have the residue of Adam in our mind, and to think out of that, is death. But to have the mind of Christ is life and peace. 1 Corinthians 15:26 says that the last enemy to be destroyed is death. In the past we have heard that this death is only physical death. The mortal can be changed to immortal when this corruption puts on incorruption. But another way to look at the last enemy, death, which is being destroyed, is the death of the residue of Adam that is in our mind. When that is destroyed, we don't have to worry about our physical bodies being changed. When corruption puts on incorruption, the mortal *must* put on immortality. So, the last enemy that *was* destroyed and *should be* destroyed *experientially* in our lives is that residue, that veil, the carnal mind. The carnal mind is death! In Romans 8:7, the carnal mind is *an enemy* against God. *That* is God's enemy. *That* is *the* principality and power. The *true enemy* of God is the carnal mind.

Divine Equine

The horses of Revelation 6 are divine equine. When the first seal was opened, it sounded like thunder. Paul said the preaching of the cross is the *power* of God. Thunder, power, emanated from the throne when the first seal was opened. This is the beginning of the preaching of the horses, or the thundering of the preaching of the cross. James and John were "the sons of thunder." These horses represent the life, death, and burial of Jesus. The white horse represents the righteous earth walk. He knew no sin in his earth walk. But then he became sin as us, died spiritually, and went into hell. When you see lightning and hear thunder, there is some power involved with that! The preaching of the cross is the power of God! Look at Job 39:19-25:

> Hast thou given the horse strength? Hast thou clothed his neck with thunder? Canst thou make him afraid as a grasshopper? The glory of his nostrils is terrible. He paweth in the valley, and rejoiceth in his strength: he goeth on to meet the armed men. He mocketh at fear, and is not affrighted; neither turneth he back from the sword. The quiver rattleth against him, the glittering spear and the shield. He swalloweth the ground with fierceness and rage: neither believeth he that it is the sound of the trumpet. He saith among the trumpets, 'Ha, ha; and he smelleth the battle afar off, the thunder of the captains, and the shouting.

Here, power or strength in the horse's neck is likened to thunder. Look at the next question, "Canst thou make him afraid as a grasshopper?" The thing that kept the children of Israel from entering the Promised Land was a grasshopper mentality of fear. Grasshoppers eat the foliage of the garden. Fear is the Palmerworm and the Cankerworm. Fear will devour your garden. Fear is the thief of dreams. And God would not let any fear enter into the Promised Land! Isn't it interesting that in Revelation 21:8 we read that the fearful and unbelieving will not enter into the Holy City. It is terribly sad because there are multitudes chained by fear to their religion, their doctrines, and their traditions and they will not enter the Holy City until they loose themselves from those chains (Isaiah 52:2). But we, the holy remnant, are not going to let any grasshoppers keep us from having Jesus, our Promised Land Man manifested. Nor will we allow fear to keep the seals unbroken. The life of the Lamb is going to flow out because there will not be a grasshopper mentality in the body of Christ! There can't be with the understanding of the death of Christ.

This horse is not afraid! In verse 24, he swalloweth the ground with fierceness and rage. He will swallow up all of the residue of the flesh that is in our mind! The understanding of these horses will do that! In verse 25, he is not afraid, because the battle is over and he is more than a conqueror.

These horses of Revelation chapter 6 have the goods! They have the power, the thunder. They are not afraid, like grasshoppers. They swallow up the fleshly mentality, the residue of Adam. These horses are swifter than eagles, meaning God is doing a quick work as he reveals these horses to us. Jeremiah 4:13 says, "Behold, he shall come up as clouds, and his chariots shall be as a whirlwind: his horses are swifter than eagles. Woe unto us! For we are spoiled." The book of Revelation is the height of understanding the Lord Jesus because it brings to us the product. After 65 books, we should be ready for Revelation. And we should be able to interpret it symbolically, as it was written, and not literally. We should be able to look behind us and see what it typifies. It is the ultimate and it gives the product.

In Revelation chapter 1, we discussed the fact that Jesus was the firstbegotten of the dead. That does not mean that he was the first one physically raised because there were other people physically raised from the dead. It means that he was the first one raised from spiritual death unto life. Being quickened and raised are two separate operations. Some do not understand that Jesus died spiritually. But you can't loose a bird that is already loose. You can't cause something to be alive that is already alive. Why would he have to be quickened if he were already spiritually alive? Jesus was quickened when he was in the depths of hell. He was made alive. That quickening was first spiritual.

The resurrection was his *physical* raising. Jesus was made alive from death unto life. He was the first one born from spiritual death to life. He was quickened and made alive from more than just physical death. He was quickened and made alive from spiritual death. The book of Acts says that *when he was raised,* he was loosed from the pains of death. One would think that when he died physically, he was loosed from the pains of death. But in his raising, he was loosed from the pains of death, which means that he died spiritually. Paul wrote it like this:

> [For I always pray to] the God of our Lord Jesus Christ, the Father of glory, that He may grant you a spirit of wisdom and revelation [of insight into mysteries and secrets] in the [deep and intimate] knowledge of Him, by having the eyes of your heart flooded with light, so that you can know and understand the hope to which He has called you, and how rich is His glorious inheritance in the saints (His set-apart ones), and [so that you can know and understand] what is the immeasurable and unlimited and surpassing greatness of His power in and for us who believe, as demonstrated in the working of His mighty strength, which He exerted in Christ when He raised Him from the dead and seated Him at His [own] right hand in the heavenly [places], far above all rule and authority and power and dominion and every name that is named [above every title that can be conferred], not only in this age and in this world, but also in the age and the world which are to come. And he has put all things under His feet and has appointed Him the universal and supreme *Head of the church* [a headship exercised throughout *the church*], *which is his body,* the fullness of Him Who fills all in all *[for in that body lives the full measure of Him Who makes everything complete, and Who fills everything everywhere with Himself]*. And *you* [He made *alive*], when you were *dead (slain)* by [your] *trespasses and sins* ... (Ephesians 1:17-2:1, Amplified Bible. Emphasis added).

This passage is packed with power! Take care to read the emphases. But I want you to notice the last sentence, Ephesians 2:1: "And you [He made alive], when you were dead (slain) by [your] trespasses and sins." This is clearly referring to spiritual death. We follow the Lamb wherever he goes. We were crucified with him. He died for us and as us. Father God raised the Lord Jesus Christ and seated him at his own right hand in heavenly places, over all rule and authority and power and dominion and every name that is named, not only in that age, but in this age. Christ is the Head and we are his body. If we are his body, that means we are spiritually alive in him. We are raised to new life in him. We are seated with him, and we reign with him *today*. And in his body, the Church, lives the full measure of him who makes everything complete, and who fills everything everywhere with himself! Are you getting the message?

"Name" Means "Nature"

Look what Revelation 6:8a says about this:

> And I looked, and behold, a pale horse: and his name that sat on him was Death, and Hell followed with him.

His name that sat on him was Death. What does "name" mean? Name means character, or nature. Jesus' nature became death at Calvary. He drank the bitter cup. If you drink something, you take it into the inside of you. The priests had to eat the sin offering in the Old Testament. If you eat something, it becomes you. When your nature is of a certain type, it means you *are* that. When you drink something into yourself, it becomes a part of you. So, Jesus drank the bitter cup. He became sin. The only way we are going to get rid of the residue of Adam and see the expression of Christ is when we see the death and see *what happened to* the old man, Adam. The only way we will see the book of life opened, and the life of the Lamb flow out, is to see the death—the doing away with the old nature.

Then when you're tempted to think otherwise, you can say, "No, I know how it happened." Jesus, the holy, righteous Son of God was tempted in every way that we were tempted and yet he never sinned. That is what qualified him to become sin, to die spiritually and to go into hell. It is vitally important that we understand that, because religion has taught that he was just a "sin offering," so "God just sees us as righteous." He does not just *see* us as righteous; we were *made* the righteousness of God in Christ. We *are* righteous! We were bad to the bone, but now we are righteous to the core with the righteousness of Jesus. That is who we are through and through. He laid the ax to the root. He dealt with the sin nature. Now we have the very nature of Christ. God does not just see us as righteous—we are righteous. We are not trying to heal the deadly wound. We are loving not our lives unto the death. We are not trying to raise an old man or tell you that you have two natures. You do not have two natures, *and you are not in the flesh!* Is the word the word? Romans 8:9 says, "But ye are not in the flesh, but in the Spirit, if so be that the Spirit of God dwell in you." 1 John 5:12a says, "He that hath the Son hath life." So, if you have the Son, you have life and you are not in the flesh, but in the Spirit. We must know no man after the flesh, including ourselves. We do not judge by the appearance realm. This conduct will bring us to the understanding that we are not in the flesh, we are in the Spirit.

This engrafted understanding written on the tablets of our hearts will empower us to live above sin. Paul said, "Awake to righteousness and sin not." He did not say that we are to fight this sin and fight that sin. He said, "Awake to righteousness and sin not." Adam fell asleep in death when he sinned. How do we awake to righteousness? By seeing what happened at the cross and seeing that we are the righteousness of God in Christ Jesus. Paul said, "Walk in the Spirit and you shall not fulfill the lust of the flesh." Well, we *are* in the Spirit. But we have to *know* we are in the Spirit. The Bible says "And ye shall *know* the truth, and the truth shall make you free." When you know you are in the Spirit, you are empowered. Jesus said, "Whatever ye shall ask in my name, that will I do, that the Father may be glorified in the Son. If ye shall ask anything in my name, I will do it." Remember, "name" means "nature." Jesus was saying, "Whatever you ask *in my nature*—meaning, if your nature is my nature—I will do it, that the Father may be glorified in the Son. You will have whatever you want because you'll want what I want." If we want to give outward expression to what is true of us inwardly, then we are going to have to focus on what is true of us inwardly—what was and what is. And then the "shall be" shall be.

A Finished Work Of Love

Some people take only a futuristic view of the book of Revelation and interpret it literally, with a seven year tribulation, a beast in some temple in the Middle East, and an antichrist that they are waiting to see unveiled. The antichrist is not the one who is unveiled in the book of Revelation! It's the unveiling of the Lord Jesus Christ, the Lord of glory! And then some take the preterist view in which they interpret the book of Revelation only historically, yet look at nothing concerning the fact that John looked behind him and saw a finished work.

We have to understand that John saw the revelation of Jesus Christ. If we are going to minister the book of Revelation as the unveiling of Jesus Christ, then it will come forth as what John saw in Revelation chapter 1. He saw he who *was*—the finished work of Calvary. He saw he who *is*—what is true of us because of the finished work of Calvary. And he saw he who *is to come*—the product of a people who understand what is true of them because of he who was and what happened in he who was—the crucifixion, death, and burial of Jesus Christ—a finished work of love.

1 John 3:2 says:

> Beloved, now are we the sons of God, and it doth not yet appear what we shall be: but we know that, when he shall appear, we shall be like him; for we shall see him as he is.

The New King James version says it this way:

> Beloved, now we are children of God; and it has not yet been revealed what we shall be, but we know that when He is *revealed,* we shall be like Him, for we shall see Him as He is (emphasis added).

This same John saw the Lord revealed! He saw him as he is and that is what he recorded for us in the book of Revelation. Now we too may see him revealed! The marriage supper of the Lamb is not far away somewhere out there beyond the universe. It is right here, right now, in the great day of the feast. The food on the table is Lamb. When he shall appear, we shall be like him. *Then* we are going to see him as he is.

But no man can ascend unless he first descends (John 3:13, Ephesians 4:9). We can't ascend by just looking at the glorified, ascended Christ. We must see our descent *with him* by looking into all that he accomplished during those three days of his death, burial, and resurrection—seeing how it happened and how we were involved. Remember, the Greek word "soul" is written in the feminine gender and refers to the mind, the will, and the emotions. We can't get an old woman out of our mind by showing ourselves another man. The old woman is the veil, the residue of Adam in our soul, our thinking. We are going to get rid of an old woman by showing ourselves what happened to Adam and how we were identified with that.

The book of Revelation is a book about a de-creation. Adam created certain things in our lives through the fall. As we see that the book of Revelation is primarily the death of Christ, and as we look at how low he went, then we can see how high he went. When we see that it is about the death of Christ then we will understand that the plagues and all the things that seem negative in the book of Revelation speak to us about that which was destroyed at Calvary. As we continue in the book of Revelation, we will see the curse of the law being de-created through the death of Christ.

We see a lot of things from the book of Genesis in the book of Revelation. One of those things is the question God asked Adam: "Adam, where art thou?" We find the answer to that in the book of Revelation and we will locate where Adam is. That is going to cause the veil to be taken away from our mind because the veil is the residue of Adam, the old nature that we had at one time. That is why the woman in Revelation, the Babylonian system says, "I sit as a queen, and am no widow, and shall see no sorrow." We must show our old woman that we were widowed from our first husband and that we are now married to the glorified Christ.

We have formerly been taught that we must crucify the flesh and die daily. The spirit of Judas will take the redemptive truths of God and throw them down in the temple and try to work itself. Judas did something that represents people today who think they must die to self and crucify their flesh *by works of the flesh.* What we need to do is realize daily that the flesh is already crucified. His death was our death. We will then be empowered to live righteously. Grace is a divine enablement. Salvation is not by works, it is by grace, through faith, that we are saved.

You May Kiss The Bride

As it is in the natural, so it is in the spiritual. What happens when a man and woman are united in marriage? Before the marriage, the two are virgins. During the wedding ceremony, the bride has a veil covering her face. After the wedding ceremony, the groom lifts the veil from her face and kisses her. After that takes place, the two produce seed through intimacy. When the veil is taken away from a woman who is married, she never puts that veil back on again. When the veil has been taken away from our mind by seeing the death of Christ, we are going to manifest *him*. Then the world is going to see the glorified Christ being birthed out of us. Another thing that occurs when a man and a woman are united in marriage is a name change. "Name" means "nature." When we are married to Christ, we receive a nature change—from Adam to Christ. The true Church is Mr. and Mrs. Jesus Christ the Lord!

The veil is being removed today as we renew our mind by viewing the crucifixion, the death, and the burial of Jesus Christ. The veil that was done away in Christ, is now being taken away—not as we behold the glorified Christ—but as we see that everything Adam brought to us, including the residue, was done away at the cross of Calvary. The only way we will see the glorified Christ is as we look *through* the crucified Christ. That is why Paul said, "I determined not to know anything among you, save Jesus Christ, and him crucified."

Get The Message!

By the time we get from the book of Genesis to the book of Revelation, we should have enough understanding to know that this is the Revelation of Jesus Christ—not of some literal battle of Armageddon. The transliteration of the Greek "Armageddon" really refers to a mountain range. This speaks of a Mt. Zion people. Jesus tells us to "flee to the mountains." Even though it is a mountain range, mountains have valleys. The valley of Megiddo is in a mountain range. The battle of Armageddon is fought in a valley—the battlefield of the mind. The mountain is our mind and the valley is our low, carnal thinking, our old woman thinking. The book of Proverbs says that an adulterous woman is an open ditch. So the valley is between the mountain range of our mind. This is even true anatomically—the right and left hemispheres of our brain are the mountains. The "limbic system" is located in a valley between both hemispheres. The limbic system houses the emotions, or "affective brain," which is a part of the soul. It is interesting to note that *limbus* means "ring." Remember—the only veil in the New Testament is the one over the mind.

The battle of Armageddon has nothing to do with a literal battle over in the Middle East. We've been so duped with religious junk food that we have missed the whole point. We haven't even preached Jesus out of this book. We've only preached the doctrines of the evil imaginations of man. At the beginning of the Lord's address to each Church in Revelation chapters 2 and 3, he says, "To the angel of the Church." An angel is a messenger with a message—*and we need to get the message!* Thank God that we are beginning to minister the revelation of Jesus Christ. Thank God that a people are beginning to see that the only thing that will cause the appearing of the Lord is the taking away of the veil as the mind is renewed. When we go to his word *just to see him,* we will see *from* Genesis *to* Revelation that it is *the* revelation of Jesus Christ!

Adam made the garden a grave yard. Jesus came along and made the grave yard a garden. He is the gardener. For example, the hill of Golgotha is where David buried the skull of Goliath, who was a Philistine. The word "Philistine" means "dust roller." He was Goliath of Gath, and that is where we get the word "Golgotha." David, who represents a type of Christ, killed Goliath and buried his head, his skull, on the hill of Golgotha, the place of the skull. Then the seed of David, Jesus, destroyed Adam, the man of dust, on the hill of the skull. And Jesus destroyed the enemy that lives within *our* skull, our un-renewed, carnal mind, on the hill of the skull. Every picture in the Old Testament is a piece of the mosaic of the finished work of the cross.

Before We Had The Written Word, The Word Was Written In The Stars

Another picture is found in Job 38:31. God asks, "Canst thou bind the sweet influences of the Pleiades, or loose the bands of Orion?" Pleiades consists of a cluster of seven stars (fullness of light) found in the constellation Taurus. "Pleiades" means "Congregation of the ruler." The Syriac name for the Pleiades is "Succoth," which means "booths." "Orion" means "The glorious one." The ancient Hebrew meaning of the names of the stars that make up the constellation Orion is: "This is he who triumphs coming forth as light." Orion is the most brilliant of all the constellations. God is describing the heavens as the tabernacle or the tent or the chamber for the sun (Psalm 19:4). He is describing Succoth, the Feast of Booths, the Feast of Tabernacles. He is asking Job, "Can you loose the light and the understanding that will bring the people into the experience of the Feast of Tabernacles?" The birth, the life, the death, the burial, and the resurrection of our Lord Jesus Christ is uttered day after day and night after night as the cumulative testimony of the stars show forth this knowledge. And all flesh shall see it together (Isaiah 40:5) as all see now the beauty of Orion's glory—he who triumphs coming forth as light[31] is the bridegroom coming out of his chamber (Psalm 19:5). Jesus is the bridegroom and we are his chamber! We are his tabernacle! We are his dwelling place! The tabernacle of God is among men!

Then in Job 38:32, he says, "Canst thou bring forth Mazzaroth in his season? Or canst thou guide Arcturus with his sons?" Mazzaroth is the twelve signs of the Zodiac. Twelve is the number of governmental perfection or rule. The heavens declare the twelve redemptive aspects of the cross and our identification with it—crucified, died, buried, quickened, raised, seated; crucified with, died with, buried with, quickened with, raised with, seated with. Arcturus means "the greater sheepfold." Today Arcturus is known as Ursa Major or "the great bear." In Arcturus, we see the innumerable seed gathered by him who scattered (Jeremiah 31:10, Ezekiel 34:12-16). The truth was enshrined and written in the heavens where no human hand could touch it. Before we had the written word, the word was written in the stars. The heavens declare the glory of God, *speaking of this very day* as the whole earth is filled with his glory, as the glory of the Lord is being revealed. How shall all flesh see it together? As *our* heaven, *our* tent, *our* tabernacle, *our* dwelling place for the Son is opened up and out of our lives flow the rivers of refreshing—the presence of the Lord—which God hath spoken by the mouth of all his holy prophets since the world began (Acts 3:19-21)[32].

The Bible says that Job was a perfect man. The only one I can think of that is perfect, is the Lord Jesus. He was sinless and was qualified to go to the cross. Isn't it amazing that Job had ten children, representing the Ten Commandments, the law? Jesus came not to destroy the law, but to fulfill (abolish or end) the law. "Fulfill" means "to imbue, diffuse, finish a period, end, expire" (see Romans 10:4, 2 Corinthians 3:7-11, Ephesians 2:15, Colossians 2:13-17, Hebrews 7:18). The hand of God afflicted Job and brought boils. In the Old Testament God *did* bring negative things to people. Since Calvary he uses his *word* to chastise and cleanse and correct. Job is a picture of Jesus at Calvary.

We see the boils in the book of Revelation, a part of the curse. Jesus became the curse. The hand of God touched Job. It was the hand of God that brought about the plan of salvation and brought it to the finish at the cross.

We have been taught that since the hand of God touched Job, then it must be God who brings all kinds of cancer and tuberculosis and diabetes and disease into our lives to "process us." God created the waster to destroy. We thought that meant that he created that dirty rat to come and buffet us into the realm of glory to mature us and cause us to grow up. But this is really what he did: he created the waster to destroy *him* and he did that at the cross of Calvary. When we say that God is going to bring suffering (meaning the things that he nailed to the cross) into our lives to perfect us, then we are smiting the rock twice. With that kind of mentality, we are also saying that *we* can open the book. No man can open the book. The only one who can open the book is the Lamb. The only thing that can take the veil away from our mind is seeing that the old man is dead and that we are a new creation in Jesus Christ.

Behold The Lamb

We're not going to ascend by ascending. Ephesians 4:9 says, "Now that he ascended, what is it but that he also *descended first* into the lower parts of the earth?" We can't get rid of the veil by beholding the glorified Christ. We're not going to ascend by viewing an ascending Christ. We're going to ascend when we first see how low he went. *Then* we will see how high he went. *Then* we will see the glorified Christ, and not until then. The other truth in this is, when we see how low he went, we see how low *we* went when we were crucified with him. *Then* we will be able to see how high we ascended and were seated *with him*. This is the very thing that is going to remove the veil so that we can realize like the Shulamite, "I'm not black, I don't have any spot in me." The thing that allows us to sin and do things out of character with the nature of God is this: we think that our black spots were not taken away. The only thing that released the Shulamite into a love relationship with the king was her understanding that her black spots were done away with at the cross of Calvary. Then and only then could the king reproduce himself through her. It was not the other way around. It was not by beholding the king. It was by beholding the Lamb. *Then* she could behold the King.

The king wants to appear. That is what Revelation is about—*apokalupsis*—the appearing, the unveiling, the uncovering of something that has been hidden. How is the unveiling going to take place? By beholding the Lamb. Four times, the four beasts or living creatures in Revelation chapter 6 say, "Come and see." Not come and do, but come and view. The word "see" denotes understanding. Then John says, "And I saw." In Revelation 22 the last thing John saw was a river of water of life, clear as crystal, flowing out of a people and everything they came in contact with, lived.

In Revelation 22:10, the angel told John, "Don't seal up the sayings of the prophecy of this book." In the book of Daniel, he is told to seal the book until the time of the end. The vision and the prophecy and the book are sealed up in Daniel only until the full manifestation comes forth. This refers to the fact that we have been sealed up, but now Jesus is being made visible. He is galloping out of us as we come to the understanding of the death. The vision is no longer sealed. What was sealed up in the book of Daniel is unsealed in the book of Revelation. When we received the Holy Spirit, we were sealed until the day of redemption. Now we are being unsealed in Revelation chapters 5 and 6—as we behold the Lamb. Then, in Revelation chapter 7 we are sealed again with a different kind of sealing. We will look at Daniel's seventy weeks in the last chapter of this book.

In Revelation 5:5-6 when John looked to see the Lion of Judah, he saw the Lamb. The Lion of Judah represents his overcoming, victorious earth walk—the holy, righteous earth walk of Jesus that caused him to be the spotless Lamb. So, John looks and does not just see that Jesus was tempted in all points, but that he overcame every temptation. When John looks, the text says more than that. It says he *beheld*. The Vine's expository dictionary defines "behold" as "calling attention to what may be seen or heard or *mentally apprehended in any way* (emphasis added.)" John studied the vision. He gave it all of his heart, all of his soul, and all of his might. When he beheld, he saw more than the Lion of the tribe of Judah—Jesus overcoming in his earth walk—but he saw the Lamb. He was trying to find out who is going to break the seals and open the book so that the life of the Lamb can flow out and he does not see just a Lion, but he sees the Lamb. He saw the nature of Christ who, although he was the God of creation, the Majestic of majesties, wholly right and radiantly righteous, the luminescence of light in whom there is no variance, wisdom itself, the essence of the quintessence of love—he humbled himself—he laid it all aside to be rejected by his very own people, loved only for what he could do for others, betrayed by his best friends, ridiculed, shamed, spat upon, plucked, pierced, whipped beyond recognition and tortured upon a cruel cross. And then—after all that—he was lowered even further—he became sin—he became all that Adam was and all that Adam ever brought into the world—and descended into hell. Behold the Lamb.

What is going to be on the table at the marriage supper? Lamb. We can not identify the glorified Christ with the term "Lamb." If we put a title or a name on The One that was quickened, raised, ascended and seated, we must call him Christ and Lord. The term "Lamb" always refers to the Lamb slain at Calvary. If there is Lamb on the table, it is not yet the glorified Christ, but the Lamb slain—

we must begin with that. We must eat the bread and drink the wine.

Most Holy Place Mentality

In Revelation 5:8, they were praying from the Most Holy Place. They were worshipping from the Most Holy Place. When you pray from the Most Holy Place, your prayer is not "God, heal me." It is "God, I thank you for healing me." Prayer from the Most Holy Place is no longer petition, it is realizing reality. When you have a need in your life, whether it is spiritual, emotional, physical, or financial, the prayer is not "God please, will you ...." It is "God, thank you for supplying all of my needs more than 2000 years ago at the cross of Calvary." *That* is praying from the throne.

There are some in the church today proclaiming: "Jesus said, 'My house shall be called the house of prayer!' He did not say it shall be called the house of praise or the house of worship." So, they go out of balance saying, "We've got to pray more than we sing and worship. We have to have more prayer meetings." The majority of the Church has been out of balance with this narrow mindset. Quite frankly, some have even made prayer "all about me." Some people have the mentality that "prayer" means asking for what they need. That is one type of prayer and it is valid. We call it "petition." But let me ask you, what is prayer? Prayer is communication with God. The prayer of petition is communicating our needs to our Father. The prayer of intercession communicates to our Father the needs of others. The prayer of thanksgiving is communicating our thankfulness to Father God and it springs from the understanding the finished work of the cross. The prayer of praise—with or without music—communicates our recognition of him whom we esteem and love above all others. With praise we communicate our validation of all his valiant deeds. The prayer of worship communicates our recognition of the highest worth—to him who sits on the throne and unto the Lamb. In the prayer of worship, we communicate our love for him, our love for who he is. Our every thought is communication with God and when we realize this, we pray without ceasing. Even silence is prayer. This is when we communicate our awe of his Awesomeness. Sometimes in silence we're just hanging out with our best friend. So when we come to the place of Love, which is the Most Holy Place, most of our communication (prayer) with Father God is worship!

When you worship from the throne, it is not just mouthing words or going through the motions and it is certainly not mouthing words when your heart is not in it. When you worship from the throne, that worship is awakened because you have an understanding of the death, burial, and resurrection—and specifically the death. The golden altar of incense represents praise and worship, and the coals that burned the incense came from the brazen altar where the death took place. The first mention of worship in the Bible takes place at the death of the sacrifice that Jehovah-jireh provided (Genesis 22). There is power in the principle of first mention.

When you worship from the throne, your mouth is touched, like Isaiah, with a burning coal. You are like Rizpah who stood and watched the seven sons being crucified. We are going to stay at the death of Christ until it rains! We are going to eat Lamb until it rains! "Drop down, ye heavens, from above, and let the skies pour down righteousness; let the earth open, and let them bring forth salvation, and let righteousness spring up together; I, the Lord, have created it" (Isaiah 45:8). We are going to eat the bread and drink of the cup showing forth his death until he comes forth and fully appears!

Some will say he has already come. Yes, he has, in one form, but he is always coming. It is not a coming of the Lord as in a future event. It is an ongoing experience! It is "comings" of the Lord. He came to you when you were born again. He came to you when you were baptized in the Holy Spirit. He came to you when he healed you. He came to you when he brought you form one level of glory to another level of glory. He came to you between those realms and he is coming to us in the Feast of Tabernacles. We are to eat of the death until he comes so that our mouth is touched with the coals. Then the ministry that comes out of our mouths comes out of the Most Holy. When the ministry comes out from the throne, instead of "Woe, woe, woe," it is going to be "Holy, holy, holy."

Like Isaiah and Rizpah, our mouth is being touched with a live coal so that when we speak, when we pray, when we worship, it is from the throne, the dimension of the place in which we are already seated. This is the "It is finished" dimension where we realize that Jesus has gone before us and prepared a place for us. He has come again to us to bring us into the Most Holy and now we're just growing into that Place. There is no more petition when you see that. When you come into this dimension in God, the only thing you're able to do is rest. Then the banks of your river will overflow with thanksgiving, praise, and worship forever. In Revelation 5:9 we find out who is worthy—the Lamb slain. Then in verses 11-13 we see all humanity worshipping the Lamb forever!

The Church—The Book Within

I want to recapitulate "the book within" at this point. To some, the book in Revelation chapter 5, speaks of the Bible. There are three reasons for that. First, they are not in the spirit that John was in. John was in the Spirit on the *Lord's Day*. Jesus *is* the Lord's Day. Jesus *is* the Jubilee. Jesus is referred to as "The Day" in scripture. Psalm 118:24 foretells this, declaring; "This is *the day* which the Lord has made; we will rejoice and be glad in it." John was in the Spirit in the Lord's Day and he saw and began to experience Jubilee.

Second, those who do not understand the book of Revelation are not looking *behind* them, but are interpreting Revelation literally and futuristically. One of the keys to interpreting Revelation is in looking behind us. In the garden, God asked, "Adam, where art thou?" He is crucified. We have to visit the grave site and see where Adam is. That is how we get rid of the veil that remains in our mind. We need to see that Adam was crucified, he died, and was buried, and that will take the veil away.

The third reason for this misunderstanding is that some have not fully grasped that the book of Revelation was written in sign and symbol. There is nothing literal in this book. For example, we read about men who are tormented for *five months* and they are trying to die. They *want* to die. The worst thing that can happen to us is that we do *not* get the revelation that we already died. And because we do not get that revelation, we continue trying to kill ourselves, we continue trying to hang ourselves like Judas, or crucify our flesh. There are five months from the last day of Passover to the first day of Tabernacles, which begins with the blowing of the trumpets. It was also five months that Noah's Ark was afloat. The Ark represents Jesus. Noah, whose name means rest, got in the Ark and the judgment beat upon that Ark. His judgment was our judgment. After five months, the Ark landed on Mt. Ararat, which means the curse is reversed.

Our Old Man Was Crucified With Christ

Revelation chapter 9 says that those who are tormented five months seek death and do not find it. It is possible for people to be tormented right now, even though they are positionally seated in the Most Holy Place. If they are trying to open the book and have the life of the Lamb flow out of them by what they suffer or by what they do or don't do, they are in torment. We are *seated* in a position that people are literally dying to go to! And people are *miserable* in the Church! I know of two people who were in mental institutions because they think they have committed the unpardonable sin, simply because they do not understand what took place at the cross of Calvary. That is torment! Those people, above all people, wish they could die! Anguish in that realm can be so intense that people wish death! But let's look at it in the spiritual realm. People are trying to crucify themselves, and die to the flesh. For five months, they are tormented. When we study that part of Revelation, there are some glorious truths that we will see concerning the bottomless pit.

In chapter 1 of Revelation, John was on the isle of Patmos, which means "my killing." This tells us that our killing is not future. John looked behind him and he came to bear record of the word of God and the martyrdom of Jesus Christ, meaning that he got a revelation that his killing was not in the future. His killing happened at the cross when he was crucified with Christ.

John turned to see a voice and he saw seven golden candlesticks, meaning he heard and saw a voice coming out of the Church. That voice is declaring bread and wine—the bread of adversity and the water of affliction—and we get it by looking behind us. Then we will hear his voice saying, "This is the way, walk ye in it." When we turn to the right hand and when we turn to the left, we are to always keep in mind what happened at the cross of Calvary.

When the people in Paul's day heard this message of grace, they thought it was a license to sin so that more grace could abound. That has not changed in over 2000 years for some in the Church.

Some people in this day think the same thing. There are at least two reasons for their misunderstanding. First, they do not understand that grace is not a license to sin. Titus 2:11-12 says that grace teaches us to deny ungodliness and worldly lusts, that we should live soberly, righteously, and godly, *in this present world!* As Joyce Meyer said, "Grace is not a license to sin—it is the power not to!" Besides, if you're in Adam you don't need a license—you sin perfectly well without one! Secondly, they do not have an understanding of the new creation. They thought they had two natures. Paul said in Romans 6:1-7:

> God forbid! How can you who are dead to sin live any longer therein? Know ye not, that so many of us as were baptized into Jesus Christ were baptized into his death? Therefore we are buried with him by baptism into death: that like as Christ was raised up from the dead by the glory of the Father, even so we also should walk in newness of life. For if we have been planted together in the likeness of his death, we shall be also in the likeness of his resurrection: knowing this, that *our old man is crucified with him,* that the body of sin might be destroyed, that henceforth we should not serve sin. For he that is dead is freed from sin (emphasis added).

As we minister Grace and Truth we are empowered to live above sin. The preaching of the cross is the power of God. When we understand what happened at the cross, and our identification with it, we can utilize the power of the cross in our lives. When we eat the bread of affliction and drink of the water of adversity, it releases a power within us to overcome and to live above sin that to date, few have experienced!

An Invitation To All Creation—Come And See!

Four times, the beasts in Revelation chapter 6 say, "Come and see," just like Moses said to snake bitten Israel. God told Moses to take a fiery serpent and set it upon a pole and they would live for a look, but not just a look—they were to behold it. It was a snake on a pole. It was not a lion or a lamb or an ox or a man. It was a snake. What is the message? Jesus became sin. We must come and see. Come and behold. When the beast says "Come and see," the first four seals are broken and this releases the four horses. The white, the red, the black and the pale horses are released when we come and see.

What are we to come and see? What is going to break the seals and open the book so the life of the Lamb can flow out of us? Viewing the opening of the seals and the release of these horses and *seeing* what they represent and how we were identified with each of them is going to do it. Four times, one of the four beasts tells John to "Come and see," and each time John wrote about what he saw. On the third "Come and see," John said that he *beheld*—and it just happened to be the black horse—Jesus' spiritual death. Behold the Lamb!

In Revelation John saw the product of a people who understand "what is" because they understand "what was." John saw he who is, who was, and who is to come. When John said "And I saw," he saw that which *we* are saying "is to come." He saw the fulfillment. He saw the product. He saw the manifestation of a people that have the appearing of the Lord coming out of them on a consistent basis. When the Church becomes gripped with the cross, there will be such a release of the flow of the river of life that it will no longer be something "which is to come." It will be a river that overtakes the nations!

Spiritual Indicators

Let's look at some biblical concepts regarding the horses in Revelation chapter 6. These horses are war horses. John did not receive anything that had not already been given, but he was seeing for the first time, the whole picture, the finished product. All of his imagery came from the Old Testament and from what he was just beginning to understand by the Spirit of the life of his beloved Jesus. For example, the horses were seen by Ezekiel as well as other places in the Old Testament, like Job and Proverbs. We also see some imagery from the book of Joel in the book of Revelation. Paul had the same revelation that John had, but Paul wrote in more contemporary, practical terms and John wrote in more visionary, sign and symbol terms. That is just like Haggai and Zechariah who both said the same thing to the same people at nearly the same time, but used different literary styles to convey the message. Haggai was more practical, Zechariah more mystical. John and Paul both wrote to seven Churches about similar problems. And they both wrote to the Church at *Ephesus* about that Church's problems. Selah.

These horses are war horses. Where is the battle? Where is the war? We wrestle not against flesh and blood, but against principalities and powers. Principalities and powers are *not* principalities and powers "out there." The principalities and powers are in "high places," as Ephesians 6 tells us. Those high places are in our thinking, as 2 Corinthians 10:5 explains; "Casting down imaginations, and every high thing that exalteth itself against the knowledge of God and bringing into captivity every thought to the obedience of Christ." It's just like the *children* of Israel who blamed all their trials in the wilderness on the "ites" out there instead of their own attitudes and issues. Those "ites" in the wilderness became principalities and powers in the New Testament and the Church is still blaming it on the "out there." The Church is projecting instead of discerning.

What is the Church projecting? We've all had the experience of having our temperature, pulse, respiration rate, and blood pressure taken. These are indicators of what is going on inside our body. We call them "vital signs." They show the presence or absence of vitality or life. Likewise, we can find the vital signs of the Church world. What we see happening in the Church and in the world is a natural picture of a spiritual condition— spiritual indicators. For example, Romans 4:17 says that God calls those things which are not, as though they were. The Church is the mouth of God in the earth. The majority of the Church world—the religious system— has called into existence those things that are going on in the world today by trumpeting religion and a sin-conscious message of law that only ministers death. The spiritual indicators of the Church today call for more than just a revival. The time for revival is over (Hosea 6:2). We do not need to revive something only to let it die again. This is the time for revolution!

For example, there are preachers who stand in the pulpit every week magnifying the sin of abortion by preaching damnation and condemnation to those who abort their children. And, yes, abortion is a sin, just like gluttony or jealousy. There is no question about it.

We are not condoning sin. An overwhelming majority of those who abort their own children grew up in Church. And the religious system has given them the strength to sin! The law is the strength of sin. They have called those things into existence by their very own "messages." How many of those same preachers abort their own spiritual children every single week in Church by stoning them with the law or with their man-made doctrines? Instead of carrying the little children with grace (those who come to the Church to find God and to be born again) they stone them to death with the law. Or they push them out of the womb with the attitude of, "If you don't believe the way I believe, you're an unwanted child." You may be thinking that we are lenient toward sin. We are not lenient toward sin. We are lethal on religion! Jesus hated religion and we can hate it too.

The religious Church ministers judgment and condemnation to those in bondage to homosexuality, which truly is an abomination to the Lord. And yet if those who "minister" this message of condemnation believe themselves to have two natures, then they too go to bed every night with two men—Adam and Christ. Jesus said, "In that night there shall be two men in one bed; the one shall be taken, and the other shall be left." A few verses later he said, "Wherever the carcass is, there will the eagles be gathered together." He was talking about his death, burial, and resurrection and our identification with him in it. Adam is the one who is crucified, dead, and buried. And we are leaving him there! The one who was taken out of the grave bed is Jesus Christ. So there is only one man in the earth, Christ the Lord—and we are in him!

Church, it is time to wake up, rise up, and minister the bread and the wine to deliver a confused religious system. Abortion and homosexuality are just two of the many natural pictures or indicators of the spiritual condition of the Babylonian system. The world we know has not yet had a chance to reject Jesus because the religious system has never presented the real Jesus to the world—and they never will. The best the religious system can produce is Ishmael.

The true Church, God's holy remnant, must go forth with *great grace* to the multitudes (Acts 4:33). The word "Church" means "the called out ones." We were called out of the darkness of the religious system and into the marvelous light of a brand New Day who is Jesus Christ, the Lord! It is an issue of dominion. We're not here to take sides in a war of good versus evil. We are here to take dominion! We are here to turn this thing around by being the mouth of God in the earth which trumpets a pure word from the throne, changing the very face of creation—from Adam to Christ!

So where are the high places? Right there in our minds! "For though we walk in the flesh, we do not war after the flesh (for the weapons of our warfare and not carnal, but mighty through God to the pulling down of strongholds;) Casting down imaginations, and every high thing that exalteth itself against the knowledge of God, and bringing into captivity every thought to the obedience of Christ" (2 Corinthians 10:3-4). Imaginations, knowledge, and thoughts reside in no other place than in our mind.

These horses are war horses and as they gallop through our mind, they will leave hoof prints in our mind. They are trampling out the vintage where the grapes of wrath are stored! When the four horses leave hoof prints as to what they represent—the crucifixion, death, and burial and how we were identified with it—they are going to *imprint* from their hoof prints, the Lamb slain.

Everything that Adam brought into our lives, Jesus did something significant to get rid of. When he wore the crown of thorns representing cursed thinking, he identified with our cursed thinking so that we could identify with and have the mind of Christ. He knew exactly why he came. He said, "To this end was I born and for this cause came I into the world, that I should bear witness unto the truth. Everyone that is of the truth heareth my voice" (John 18:37). But when he got to the cross, he said "My God, my God, why hast thou forsaken me?" In this, he identified with our confusion so that we could identify with and have his peace and soundness of mind. Jesus became all that we were in Adam.

It Is Our Destiny To Manifest

In Psalm 88:8, a Psalm concerning the cross, we see that Jesus was sealed up. Jesus identified with us in being sealed up. Even though we are born again and Spirit-filled, we have been a garden inclosed, a spring shut up, and a fountain sealed, like the little Shulamite. When we get the understanding of the Lamb slain and we are opened up, the life of the Lamb is going to come out of us—

and it is already happening! It is happening at an accelerated level!

There are those who say, "We've come a long way, but we still have a long way to go." We do not have that far to go! God is doing a quick work and cutting it short in righteousness! Because of the word that is going forth, we do not have that far to go! We are right on the verge of the full manifestation (Romans 9:28)! The word that is coming from the Most Holy Place is of the finished work! When you are in the Most Holy Place, you are *behind* the veil. If you are behind the veil, what are you seeing? You're seeing a "done deal," a finished work. The veil was rent.

Beside the fact that the Ark of the Covenant and the contents in the Ark represent the death, burial, and resurrection, when we are speaking from the throne, when we are praying and worshipping from the throne, it is because we see that it is a finished work. We are behind the veil, we are already there! Paul knew he had attained in spirit, but the full manifestation was not realized (Philippians 3:3-16). Christ the Lord is manifesting in this day as the veil is taken away from our mind. It is our destiny to manifest the nature of Christ!

The book of Revelation is the zenith of the Bible. By the time we get from Genesis to the book of Revelation, we should be able to see that the entire Bible is the revelation of Jesus Christ! The book of Revelation is the highest sounding trumpet, it is the seventh trumpet, it is the archangel, it is the highest message, *and it is about the death of Christ*. It is about de-creating something that Adam created.

So, these are war horses that are galloping through our mind. Proverbs 21:31 says, "The horse is prepared against the day of battle: but safety is of the Lord." We have discussed the white horse in Revelation chapter 6. In Revelation chapter 19, we see another magnificent white horse. Those who teach the book of Revelation literally say that the rider on the white horse in Revelation 6 is the antichrist because he has a bow and a crown and he went forth conquering and to conquer. Then they teach the white horse in Revelation 19 as only the future coming of the Lord, splitting the sky, coming back on this white horse. But look at that passage in Revelation 19:11-14:

> And I saw heaven opened, and behold, a white horse; and he that sat upon him was called Faithful

> and True, and in righteousness he doth judge and make war. His eyes were as a flame of fire, and on his head were many crowns; and he had a name written, that no man knew, but he himself. And he was clothed with a vesture dipped in blood: and his name is called The Word of God. And the armies which were in heaven followed him upon white horses, clothed in fine linen, white and clean.

We will discuss this passage in detail when we study Revelation chapter 19, but for now, notice the phrase in verse 12 which says, "and on his head were many crowns." This speaks of the many-membered coming of the Lord through a people. Then the phrase, "and he had a name written, that no man knew, but he himself" speaks to us of the fact that no one but those who are part of this many-membered body know the true nature of God. Verse 14 describes us. We have established the fact that we are seated in the heavenlies. We are a heavenly company. We follow the Lamb wherever he goes in our righteous earth walk, our very own white horse. Now that we know who we are in Christ—totally new creations—we are clothed in fine linen, white and clean because of the blood of the Lamb.

When Jesus was born, he came in the flesh, he came bodily or literally. Jesus *has* come in the flesh and now he is in your flesh (earthen vessel) and he is in my flesh. *We are the body of Christ.* So, what does the word of God say about those who are still depending on an external coming of the Lord to suddenly make them what they are supposed to be? Look at 1 John 4:1-6 in the Amplified Bible:

> Beloved, do not put faith in every spirit, but prove (test) the spirits to discover whether they proceed from God; for many false prophets have gone forth into the world. By this you may know (perceive and recognize) the Spirit of God: every spirit which acknowledges and confesses [the fact] that Jesus Christ (the Messiah) [actually] *has* become man and *has* come in the flesh is of God [has God as its

source]; And every spirit which does not acknowledge and confess that Jesus Christ *has* come in the flesh [but would annul, destroy, sever, disunite Him] is not of God [does not proceed from Him]. This [nonconfession] is the [spirit] of the antichrist, [of] which you heard that it was coming, and *now it is already in the world.* Little children, you are of God [you belong to Him] and have [already] defeated and overcome them [the agents of the antichrist], because He Who lives in you is greater (mightier) than he who is in the world. They proceed from the world and are of the world; therefore it is out of the world [its whole economy morally considered] that they speak, and the world listens (pays attention) to them. We are [children] of God. Whoever is learning to know God [progressively to perceive, recognize, and understand God by observation and experience, and to get an ever-clearer knowledge of Him] listens to us; and he who is not of God does not listen or pay attention to us. By this we know (recognize) the Spirit of Truth and the spirit of error (emphasis added).

The religious system continues to mar the visage of our Lord. Teaching that Jesus' coming is merely a literal coming *hides the truth from the people that we are his body.* And because they do not see the truth, they annul, destroy, sever, and disunite him from his body. If people are looking only for a literal, external coming of the Lord they are not realizing all the potential that has been placed within them to mature. That mindset is no different than the religious Jews who are still waiting for the Messiah—they do not believe the Messiah *has* come.

There is something else that the religious system is waiting for and that is the "future coming of the antichrist"—but notice—John wrote that the antichrist is *already* in the world. This was written sometime between A. D. 85-95! The coming of the antichrist is not a future event either! We have been blinded! But he who lives in us is greater and mightier than he who is in the world! Our focus, as far as the coming of the Lord, is his coming within and through us rather than outside of us. 2 Peter 1:3-4 says this:

> According as his divine power hath given unto us all things that pertain unto life and godliness, through the knowledge of him that hath called us to glory and virtue; whereby are given unto us exceeding great and precious promises; that by these ye might be partakers of the divine nature, having escaped the corruption that is in the world through lust.

The Lord has already placed in us all that we need to live natural, spiritual lives in maturity. We are partakers of the divine nature. We have escaped the corruption that is in the world. Our old man is dead and our life is hidden with Christ in God. When Christ, our life, shall appear, then shall we also appear with him in glory (Colossians 3:3-4). The word "appear" comes from a word that means "shining." The book of Proverbs tells us that the path of the just is like the shining light, that shineth more and more unto the perfect day. We know that "the perfect day" is Jesus Christ the Lord. Jesus appeared to us when we were born again, when we were baptized into his death. He appeared to us again when he baptized us with the Holy Spirit. And he is appearing to us as we partake of the feast of maturity, the great day of the feast, the Feast of Tabernacles, where out of our bellies is flowing rivers of living water with which to baptize the nations.

John wrote of him who is, and who was, and who is to come. Paul said that he had been delivered, is being delivered, and shall yet be delivered. The word declares that we are made in the image of God—we are a spirit, we have a soul, and we live in a body. So yes, the Lord is coming, but not as the Church has taught. Rather, it is comings of the Lord. His coming is an excellent (three-fold) progression (Proverbs 22:20). He shines brighter and brighter to us, in us, and through us—until the whole earth is full of his glory.

It is time to come out of the dusty dead letter literal mindset and plunge into the *spirit* of the word—into the life-giving power of the word. We will only live by the *proceeding* word, the present word.

"Man shall not live by bread alone, but by every word that *proceedeth* out of the mouth of God" (Deuteronomy 8:3, Matthew 4:4). God speaks a present word to every generation. It is time to come out of confusion. It is time to come out of how we have been programmed to believe and actually begin to think with the mind of Christ. Instead of believing what the carnal mind of the religious system has said about spiritual things, we need to believe what the Spirit of Jesus Christ *is saying* about spiritual things. We need to get rid of the veil. We have become more skilled at defending beliefs that we have conceived through the carnal mind than we are at simply believing the spiritual truths of God's word.

Heavenly Horsemen

In Revelation 19:12, we read:

> His eyes were as a flame of fire, and on his head were many crowns; and he had a name written, that no man knew, but he himself.

His eyes were as a flame of fire. Jesus does not judge by the sight of his eyes, neither reproves after the hearing of his ears, but with righteousness does he judge the poor, and reproves with equity for the meek. On his head were many crowns—referring to a many-membered coming of the Lord. Joel chapter 2 foretells the picture of the white horse of Revelation 19 and he says, "The appearance of them is as the appearance of horses; and as horsemen, so shall they run." Joel talks about an army who, behind them is a desolate wilderness, but the land before them is as the Garden of Eden! He is talking about a horseman company. He is talking about none other than a people who have had the seals broken and out of them is flowing the life of the Lamb. There is an appearing coming out of these people. Christ *within and among* us, the hope of *realizing* the glory, as the Amplified Bible says, is now beginning to be realized (Colossians 1:27)! Proverbs 13:12 tells us that hope deferred makes the heart sick, but when the desire cometh, it is a tree of life. Christ in us is the hope of glory—and he is fulfilling that hope. He is bringing us to the place of the manifestation of his glory. He is the tree of life (Revelation 22:2)!

The weapons of our warfare are not carnal, but they are mighty. As these horses run through our mind leaving hoof prints, then the imaginations and the thoughts will be brought into the obedience of Christ and the war will cease because the only place there is a war is in our mind! When we get peace in our mind, we will see peace on earth. What we see in the world is what we project out of ourselves. Out of the heart flows the issues of life (Proverbs 4:23). What we project is what we see. And what we see is what we get (Genesis 13:14-15). What is in your projector? What is in your heart?

There are many people in the Church today who are battling a lot of things. The reason for that is because they are told that the devil is so mighty and powerful. And I'll say it again—all I want to teach is a great big God, a defeated devil, a dead old man, and an old woman (residue of Adam's thinking) who's on her way out! That reminds me of a children's riddle: What is bigger than God, more defeated than the devil, and if you eat it you'll die? The answer: Nothing! And if the children of Israel would get the message they would be no longer children tossed to and fro and carried about with every wind of doctrine. We would be grown up in all things into him who is the head—Christ the Messiah!

The new woman now, is the mind of Christ—the salvation of the spirit that comes to the soul. It is no longer an old woman, but we're a brand-new woman walking! Just like the Greek word "soul," the Greek word "city" in Revelation chapters 20-22 is written in the feminine gender. All of us have a woman—including men! We are the bride of Christ. We are becoming a brand new woman as these horses gallop through our mind.

Paul writes to us in Romans 12, "Be not conformed to this world," or "Don't be conformed to the Adamic thinking, don't let the residue of Adam rule you—but be *transformed!*" Have the seals broken and the book that you are, opened so that the life of the Lamb can flow out, for you are no longer a garden inclosed or a spring shut up, or a fountain sealed. Renew your mind and you will be transformed. The book within will be opened.

Jesus is not going to be afflicted twice. Every time we say that the book is going to be opened by works or by what we suffer, we are crucifying the Son of God afresh, we are smiting the rock twice

(Hebrews 6:6). Those who teach the Feast of Tabernacles but smite the rock twice and crucify the Son of God afresh, are wondering why they keep wandering around the mountain, and around the mountain, and don't seem to be any closer to experiencing the Feast of Tabernacles than they were when they started preaching it many years ago. We must partake of the bread and the wine. We have to quit smiting the rock twice. We must let his suffering be our suffering. We must let his death be our death. Nahum 1:9 says:

> What do ye imagine *against* the Lord? He will make an utter end: affliction shall not rise up the second time (emphasis added).

What do you imagine *against* the Lord? It is an evil imagination against the Lord to think that affliction will come upon someone and be from God. That thinking is against or anti-the Lord. It is the spirit of error, the spirit of antichrist. It is an "instead of." God is not going to put on you again what he put on you at the cross of Calvary. He is not going to put it on you a second time because Jesus suffered it *once and for all*. It does not have to be done over again. Affliction is not going to rise up a second time, and be from God. It might be from other sources, like not taking care of ourselves, or having un-renewed minds, or genetic predispositions. But when we understand that our genes were cut off and the curse was reversed, we will see that our roots are not in man, our roots are in Christ! As we renew our minds those things have to go.

The Last Enemy

The last enemy to be destroyed was destroyed at the cross and in *experience* it is *being* destroyed. We have taught that the last enemy was physical death. But we do not have to worry about the body changing from mortal to immortality when the last enemy—our carnal mind—is destroyed. When the veil is taken away from our mind, we do not have to worry about the body. This mortal *must* put on immortality when this corruptible (our mind) puts on incorruption. The body will automatically follow suit. Medical science has shown that when something goes wrong with the brain, it can affect the organs of the body. But I'm talking about something more than just the brain. I'm talking about the mind. When we put on the mind of Christ, and put in our mind the right things, corruption is going to be swallowed up and the mortal *must* put on immortality. The mortal body will have no choice in the matter.

The last enemy is not *physical* death. Romans 8:6-7 says:

> For to be *carnally minded is death;* but to be spiritually minded is life and peace. Because the carnal mind is enmity against God: for it is not subject to the law of God, neither indeed can be (emphasis added).

The carnal mind is the enemy of God. So the last enemy to be destroyed is the residue of Adam in our mind. There is already a people who have bypassed the grave and walked right into the kingdom, which is righteousness, peace, and joy in the Holy Spirit. They have allowed the Holy Spirit to do his work of renewing their mind. That is happening right now because "as it is appointed unto men once to die, but after this the judgment, so Christ was once offered to bear the sins of many; and unto them that look for him shall he appear the second time without sin, unto salvation." But the real issue is Christ. What happens in our outer life is a result of our identification with him.

How can we crucify again the Son of God afresh? By thinking that we are going to enter in by works or by how much we suffer, or in any other way than by the Way Maker, the Lord Jesus Christ, who did away with the veil and is now taking away the veil that remains in our mind. We are going to enter into the Kingdom *in experience*, as the veil is taken away from our mind and the last enemy is destroyed.

In The Throne Zone

Scientists say that every time we have a meaningful thought a residue synthesis is formed in the brain. It is like the oil that drips from your car onto the cement in the garage floor. Even after you try to wash it off with the hose there is a residue left. So, when we have the full manifestation of the mind of Christ, something is going to happen within our lives. These horses in Revelation have the goods! Look at Job 39:19-25:

> Hast thou given the horse strength? Hast thou clothed his neck with thunder? Canst thou make him afraid as a grasshopper? The glory of his nostrils is terrible. He paweth in the valley, and rejoiceth in his strength: he goeth on to meet the armed men. He mocketh at fear, and is not affrighted; neither turneth he back from the sword. The quiver rattleth against him, the glittering spear and the shield. He swalloweth the ground with fierceness and rage: neither believeth he that it is the sound of the trumpet. He saith among the trumpets, 'Ha, ha; and he smelleth the battle afar off, the thunder of the captains, and the shouting.

Of course God has given the horse strength, or John would not have received the vision and written about it in the book of Revelation. His neck is clothed with thunder. When the first seal was opened in Revelation 6, there was thunder—something that is powerful and loud! Canst thou make him afraid as a grasshopper? What was the thing that kept the children of Israel from going into the Promised Land? A fearful, grasshopper mentality.

Then, in Job 39:24, we read, "He swalloweth the ground with fierceness and rage." These horses are going to swallow up the ground as they gallop through our mind. All the earthly, carnal thinking, which is death, is going to be swallowed up in the death of Christ! That is the victory. Any residue of the flesh that is yet in our mind is being taken away by the understanding of these horses, and we are going to experience the throne room dominion, the throne room dimension, the "throne zone"—the place where we are already seated.

These horses are swifter than eagles because God is doing a swift work, cutting it short in righteousness. Jeremiah 4:13 shows us the picture:

> Behold, he shall come up as clouds, and his chariots shall be as a whirlwind: his horses are swifter than eagles. Woe unto us! For we are spoiled.

Adam was spoiled at Calvary. And his residue is being spoiled by the heavenly horsemen. Why is God doing a quick work? Because a people are eating Lamb. We've preached so many messages that were not about Jesus, thinking that they were what God was saying. They were just messages. But now we are preaching the King, which brings the manifestation of the kingdom!

The horses in Revelation chapter 6 represent the career of Christ from his birth to his quickening while he was yet in hell. Let's read Revelation 6:1-2:

> And I saw when the Lamb opened one of the seals, and I heard, as it were the noise of thunder, one of the four beasts saying, 'Come and see.' And I saw, and behold a white horse: and he that sat on him had a bow; and a crown was given unto him: and he went forth conquering, and to conquer.

This white horse represents the righteous, holy earth walk of Jesus. Hebrews 4:15 tells us that Jesus was tempted in all points like as we are, yet without sin. He never sinned one time. Then in 2 Corinthians 5:21 it says, "For he hath made him to be sin for us, *who knew no sin*; that we might be made the righteousness of God in him." That is what qualified him to become the one who went to the cross. He died for us and as us because he knew no sin.

Jesus was sinless. He was the spotless Lamb of God. He shed precious blood. And when he said, "Father, into thy hands, I commend my spirit," at that point, he became sin. He became the red horse. And we will study that in further detail later[33]. Until that point, he was the spotless Lamb of God that shed precious blood.

John 8:46 says, "Which of you convinceth me of sin? And if I say the truth, why do ye not believe me?" And John 7:18: "He that speaketh of himself seeketh his own glory: but he that seeketh his glory that sent him, the same is true, and no unrighteousness is in him." The white horse represents the righteous, holy earth walk of

Jesus. He had to be sinless to qualify to be the one that went to the cross. It was always a perfect lamb they were to offer in the Old Testament—otherwise, it wouldn't qualify.

The Career Of Christ

Revelation 4:7 lists the four beasts of Revelation chapter 6:

> And the first beast was like a lion, and the second beast like a calf, and the third beast had a face as a man, and the fourth beast was like a flying eagle.

Notice the order; lion, calf, man, flying eagle. Now look at Ezekiel 1:5:

> Also out of the midst thereof came the likeness of four living creatures. And this was their appearance; they had the likeness of a man.

They had the likeness of a man. These beasts all speak concerning the career of Christ. Now, look at Ezekiel 1:10:

> And as for the likeness of their faces, they four had the face of a man, and the face of a lion, on the right side: and they four had the face of an ox on the left side; they four also had the face of an eagle.

Notice the order; man, lion, ox, eagle.
Why are these beasts in that order in Ezekiel, but in a different order in the book of Revelation, the lion, the calf (ox), the man, and the flying eagle? Because Ezekiel *fore*told the story of Jesus' birth, life, death, and resurrection. Jesus came as a man, lived as a lion, died as an ox, and was quickened and raised as an eagle. Then in the book of Revelation, John *forth*told what he saw when he looked behind to the cross. Both foretelling and forthtelling, prophesying and explaining, are the ministry of prophecy. And remember, the spirit of prophecy is the testimony of Jesus. We're looking behind us and we see the lion—Jesus' righteous earth walk which qualified

him to be the suffering servant—that is the calf or ox. On the cross where he suffered and died, he died as man, the first Adam. Then while in hell, he was quickened, and raised becoming the flying eagle—the ruler of heaven and earth. Each one of these four beasts opens a different one of the first four seals.

In Revelation 4:7, the lion is listed first. The lion is the king of beasts. He speaks of power, authority, and overcoming, which correlates with the white horse. So with the first seal that the Lamb opens, the beast who says "Come and see," is a lion. And when John comes to see, he sees a white horse. This is the righteous, holy, earth walk of Jesus, who is the Lion of the tribe of Judah. Remember, in the gospel of Matthew, the lion nature of Jesus is portrayed as Jesus the King.

The next beast in Revelation 4:7 was like a calf or an ox. The Lamb opens the second seal and the second beast who says "Come and see," is a calf or an ox. Out rides the red horse—Jesus, the suffering servant, becoming sin. In the gospel of Mark, the ox nature of Jesus is portrayed as Jesus the Servant.

The third beast who says "Come and see," had the face of a man and out rides the black horse—Jesus identifying completely with man in that he became sin and received sin's penalty for all men—death. Paul tells us in the book of Philippians that Jesus emptied himself, came in the form of a servant, did not care about his reputation and in fact *made himself of no reputation*. This third beast, the man, opens the third seal, the black horse, which is Jesus dying spiritually. In the gospel of Luke, the man nature of Jesus is portrayed as the Branch (Zechariah 6:12). The human genealogy, the family tree upward to Adam, is given in the book of Luke.

The fourth beast who says "Come and see," is a flying eagle and out rides the pale horse—a two-fold reciprocal action—Jesus going into hell (the pale horse) and Jesus being quickened unto life (the flying eagle)^{34}. Jesus was quickened to life when he was in hell, then he preached to the captives, and then he was resurrected. Quickening and resurrection are two different actions. Another way of showing that Jesus was not just our sin offering, but he literally became sin and died spiritually, is that he had to be quickened. You cannot give life to someone that is already alive. You can't loose a bird that is already loosed. Jesus became sin and he died spiritually.

So when he was quickened, he was spiritually made alive. Then from the time that Jesus was quickened in hell until he was resurrected, he preached to the captives and later those captives were seen walking the streets of Jerusalem—which is typical that those who have died physically, are going to experience a resurrection and those who are physically alive are experiencing a spiritual resurrection. In his quickening and raising, Jesus became the flying eagle—the ruler of heaven and earth. This is the portrayal of Jesus in the gospel of John.

The Rider

So the lion, the overcomer, is the first beast or living creature that opens the first seal, the white horse. Now let's look at the rider on the white horse. White speaks of righteousness and purity. If there is a one-man antichrist, he is certainly not going to ride in on righteousness and purity. If this is the revelation of Jesus Christ, this white horse represents the righteous, holy, earth walk of Jesus.

The rider has a bow—he is the covenant of God. This word "bow" in the Septuagint is the word "rainbow." In Genesis 9:13 God set the bow in the cloud, and it was a token of the covenant between God and Noah. God covenanted with himself and it was worked out at the cross of Calvary over 2000 years ago—and I was there. We have a covenant—an everlasting covenant with our God!

There are two places in the book of Revelation where we see a rainbow. In Revelation 4, we see a rainbow around the throne as an emerald. In Revelation 10, we see another mighty messenger from heaven clothed with a cloud with a rainbow over his head, representing the understanding of the covenant. Where did the New Covenant begin? It began at the cross of Calvary because there was one man who was righteous and holy and even though he was tempted in all points, he remained unscathed by sin. Then he went to the cross and became sin and died spiritually. So the bow that the rider has represents a covenant. In chapter 4 the rainbow is green, which speaks of life. Jesus overcame by the life of God flowing through him. His covenant with God caused him to overcome.

The White Horse

Let's continue in Revelation 6:2:

> And I saw, and behold a white horse: and he that sat on him had a bow; and a crown was given unto him: and he went forth conquering, and to conquer.

The white horse represents the righteous, holy, earth walk of Jesus, who was tempted in all points like as we are, yet without sin. He, who knew no sin, became sin, that we might be made the righteousness of God in him. In John 8:46, Jesus said, "Who convinceth me of sin?" He was stating himself, that he had absolutely no sin in his life.

Revelation 6:2 continues, "And I saw, and behold a white horse: and he that sat on him had a bow; *and a crown was given unto him.*" The same Greek word for this "crown" in Revelation 6:2 is used in Matthew 27:29:

> And when they platted a crown of thorns, they put it upon his head, and a reed in his right hand: and they bowed the knee before him, and mocked him, saying, 'Hail, King of the Jews!'

This is the same crown that is on the rider of the white horse in Revelation 6:2. Many teach that the rider on the white horse in Revelation chapter 6 is the antichrist because he has a bow, and they say, "Well, obviously, if he has a bow, he must have an arrow." But this bow is a covenant, not a weapon. The white horse really represents the holy, righteous earth walk of Jesus. The antichrist will never ride in on righteousness and purity because God is not saving Adam! We were weighed in the balances and found wanting. Jesus knew that if he is going to appear through a people, he must crucify Adam, cause Adam's death, and cause him to be buried. Our antichrist spirit was done away with at the cross of Calvary even though there is a residue of that which tries to manifest. Christ cannot appear through Adam!

The rider on this white horse is not symbolic of the antichrist. If this is the antichrist who goes forth conquering and to conquering, a crown of thorns does not sound like too much conquering to me. But, it certainly was conquering for the true Christ and for those that are his. Because in the crown of thorns, Christ identified with our cursed thinking so we can have the mind of Christ! *That* is conquering! We are conquering as we put on the mind of Christ. There is no conquering; there is no overcoming in Adam or in the residue of Adam in our mind. But there is conquering in the mind of Christ. As we put on the mind of Christ, not just concerning any word, but concerning the cross of Calvary, we are more than conquerors!

The white horse represents the perfect, holy earth walk of Jesus. He has a bow—a covenant with God. Through the life of God he overcomes. The crown on the rider of the white horse is the crown of thorns. Because of Jesus' righteous earth walk, there comes a time when the religious people plat a crown of thorns and place it upon his head. And before Jesus even gets to the cross, he begins to identify with our cursed thinking so that we can have and manifest the mind of Christ. He has a crown upon his head—he is the King of kings, the Lion of the tribe of Judah. He went forth conquering to make us *more* than conquerors. Now *we* have a righteous earth walk. We're riding a white horse with him!

Then we read in the end of Revelation 6:2, "And he went forth conquering and to conquer." Jesus was in union with the Father and that is why he overcame. He went forth conquering—he lived a victorious life of righteousness—and to conquer—he conquered death, hell, and the grave. In 1 John 5:4-5 we find that "Whatsoever is born of God overcometh the world: and this is the victory that overcometh the world, even our faith. Who is he that overcometh the world, but he that believeth that Jesus is the Son of God?" So now, he has made us more than conquerors! Now, it sure did not seem like he was the conqueror to those standing at the cross that day. But things are not as they appear. That is why we must not judge according to the appearance realm.

There were five major offerings in the Old Testament. Five is the number of grace. Each of these offerings represents exactly what the horses represent in Revelation 6. The meal offering represents the holy, righteous, earth walk of Jesus. The burnt offering represents Jesus being the burnt offering. The peace offering represents Jesus who became our peace by identifying with our lack of peace. He *became* the sin offering. He *became* the trespass offering. He literally became that—not just a sin *offering,* but he literally became trespasses and sin.

In Leviticus chapter 1, we first see the burnt offering, each of which represents Jesus as the burnt offering. In chapter 2 of Leviticus, we see a meat offering or a meal offering. It was a recipe for making bread. Jesus is the bread of life. The meal offering or the meat offering represents the white horse, the holy, righteous earth walk of Jesus. Let's read Leviticus 2:1:

> And when any will offer a meat offering unto the Lord, his offering shall be of fine flour; and he shall pour oil upon it, and put frankincense thereon:

The fine flour represents the word. In his righteous earth walk, Jesus was the word made flesh. John 1:14 says, "And the Word was made flesh, and dwelt among us, (and we beheld his glory, the glory as of the only begotten of the Father), full of grace and truth." This is the fine flour. Jesus is the bread. Another ingredient in the meal offering was oil, which represents the Holy Spirit. Jesus, in his earth walk, was led and guided by the Holy Spirit. The next ingredient was frankincense, which is typical of prayer. Jesus overcame by being directed and governed by the Holy Spirit. Jesus was a man of prayer. He was continually in communion with the Father, and every time he had an opportunity, he would get away from the multitudes and the disciples to be alone with God in prayer.

The apostle Paul was a millstone in that he broke the word down to fine flour. He did not just declare the gospel. He *explained it.* In Luke 17:35 Jesus said, "Two women shall be grinding together; the one shall be taken, and the other left." They are grinding together or studying the word of God. One woman is the mind of Christ. The other woman is the carnal mind of the flesh—the old woman. Then in Revelation chapter 18, a great millstone is cast into the sea of humanity and it destroys Babylon, or confusion. When we become a millstone and explain the word, Babylon is destroyed and its captives are *released!* The Church is groaning for this release.

Jesus was the word made flesh. He was led by the Spirit. He was a man of prayer. And then, in Leviticus 2:13, we see the prophetic picture that he was full of grace and truth:

> And every oblation of thy meat offering shalt thou season with salt; neither shalt thou suffer the salt of the covenant of thy God to be lacking from thy meat offering: with all thine offerings thou shalt offer salt.

In Colossians 4:6, salt speaks of grace; "Let your speech be alway with grace, seasoned with salt, that ye may know how ye ought to answer every man." Jesus was full of grace and truth. When they brought to him the woman that was caught in the very act of adultery, he ministered grace to her. He did not condemn her. His life was one of truth and grace.

Now, look back to Leviticus 2:11:

> No meat offering, which ye shall bring unto the Lord, shall be made with leaven: for ye shall burn no leaven, nor any honey, in any offering of the Lord made by fire.

Leaven represents sin. In the white horse earth walk of Jesus, he was without sin even though he was tempted in all points. Jesus had no leaven, no sin. And notice what else this scripture says; there was to be no honey in the meal offering. Honey is a natural sweetener. That which emanated from the Lord Jesus was not just a natural sweetness, but supernatural. He said, "He that hath seen me, hath seen the Father" and "The Son can do nothing of himself, but what he seeth the Father do." There was not just a natural sweetness in his earth walk. He was one with the Father and out of him came the nature of the Father.

The meal offering correlates with the white horse, which is the holy, righteous earth walk of Jesus. He had to be holy, he had to be sinless, in order to be the one that was qualified to go to the cross and become sin for us and as us.

The Red Horse

Now, let's look at the red horse in Revelation 6:3-4:

> And when he had opened the second seal, I heard the second beast say, 'Come and see.' And there went out another horse that was red: and power was given to him that sat thereon to take peace from the earth, and that they should kill one another: and there was given unto him a great sword.

This beast who says "Come and see," is the calf or ox. An ox is one who has a servant nature. Oxen are beasts of burden. They are bred to be servants and to bear burdens. When he opened the second seal, a red horse rode out. The word "red" is the Greek *purrhos*, which speaks of fire. It connects us with the first offering in Leviticus 1, the burnt offering, which was burnt with fire. That represents the red horse, or Jesus becoming sin. Jesus was not just a sin offering, otherwise we have not been *made* the righteousness of God in him.

If we think that sin was just *laid* upon Jesus somehow, as in the Old Testament when the sin was laid upon the head of the bulls and goats, then our sin was only covered, and just for a year. In the Old Testament they had to be reminded of that sin again each year, so they developed a sin-consciousness. In order for us to have a God-consciousness, we must see that Jesus became sin. He not only died physically, but he died spiritually. We are not just sinners saved by grace—though we are saved by grace. We are not just forgiven sinners—though we are forgiven. We have a brand new nature! We have been *made* the righteousness of God in Christ Jesus.

And we must not only come to know that, but according to Romans 6, we must reckon it. This happens when we go to the word of God and do more than just read it and "know" it, or memorize it, but when we reckon, we account, "How did that happen?" If you do not understand *how* you became the righteousness of God in Christ Jesus, the enemy of your soul can come to you and try to tell you that you are not the righteousness of God in Christ Jesus, and he can steal that away if you just "know" it. But when you reckon it or when you know *how* it happened, then the enemy of our soul cannot steal that away. Even if you have forty foot tidal waves coming against you in all directions, when you know who you are in Christ Jesus, and you know *how* you got there, it just does not matter! When you know who you are in Christ, you know that even though you may be temporarily experiencing poverty or sickness or sin or whatever it is, it was done away with at the cross. That will remove any residue that might still be in your mind that tries to say, "No, I'm not the righteousness of God in Christ Jesus because of what I'm experiencing in my life." No matter what we are experiencing in our lives, we do not judge by the appearance realm.

When the seals are broken, and the life of the Lamb flows out of us, it will change our circumstances and we will give outward expression to that which is true of us inwardly. Then the glory of the Lord is going to fill the temple to the extent that when people look upon us, they are not even going to see the temple, they are only going to see God.

This is comparable to Enoch, who was taken and not found. He was translated, because he walked with God—left foot, right foot—death, resurrection. Enoch walked with God in this manner for 300 years, which speaks of complete deliverance. The old man that we were was left at the cross of Calvary and as the residue is removed from our mind, we are going to experience the self-fulfilling power of the word (Isaiah 61:11, Amplified Bible). The new man is being taken out of the grave of our mind and he is appearing in resurrection power! The word of God will fulfill itself in our lives! *It is not something that we do!* It is not even something that we have to "walk out." If it is truly a reckoning, the word of God will fulfill itself and we'll do nothing other than manifest the word made flesh! The time is at hand!

The red horse represents Jesus becoming sin. In Psalm 22 we see a Messianic Psalm foretelling the suffering Savior. He said, "I am a worm and no man." He became a maggot. He drank the bitter cup. He became our bitterness or our wormwood. Then he took our wormwood (bitterness) and nailed it to the wood. He became the worm that was nailed to the wood—and we were there. So our wormwood or our bitterness, which comes out of the old man, has been done away with at the cross of Calvary. That is GOOD NEWS! That is what the gospel is all about! That is why the Bible says the gospel must be preached *and then* the consummation of salvation will come. And the gospel is the death, the burial, and the resurrection and our identification with it. Then the end of our salvation will come. Who is the end? Jesus is the Alpha and the Omega. He is the last Adam. He is the end. And when his gospel is preached, then he will appear! There will no longer be a veil that will prevent him from appearing. It won't just be a hidden spiritual thing within us, but it will be a *manifestation,* an appearing of the Lord of glory.

Jesus drank the bitter cup. When we drink something, we take it into the inside of ourselves. In the Old Testament, the priests were to *eat* the sin offering. When we eat something, it's digested, and it eventually goes into the cells of our body. Jesus was not just a sin offering, he drank the bitter cup. He laid the ax to the root by becoming sin, not just a sin offering. He did not just die a *physical* death on an old rugged cross. He also took it in, he drank the bitter cup—he became sin. He literally became sin. This is what the red horse speaks of in Revelation 6:4:

> And there went out another horse that was red: and power was given to him that sat thereon to take peace from the earth, and that they should kill one another: and there was given unto him a great sword.

Again, the word "red" here is *purrhos,* and it means "fiery" or "fire-like." Fire speaks of judgment. This represents Jesus becoming sin—not just a sin offering. If Jesus was just our sin offering, then our sins were just covered. But because he became this red horse, he became sin. He, who knew no sin, became sin. Our sins are not just covered. We are not just forgiven sinners. We are not just sinners saved by grace—even though we *are* forgiven and we *are* saved by grace—*but we are new creations in Christ Jesus!*

Again, our sins are not just covered as in the Old Testament. When they offered the blood of bulls and goats their sin was covered and only covered for one year. They had to go back and be reminded of their sins every year, which produced a sin consciousness. But because Jesus became sin, our sins were forgiven. As Paul said, if any man be in Christ, he is a new creature; old things are passed away; behold, all things are become new. Once again, John saw the same thing as Paul and writes to us in Revelation 21:4b- 5a, "For the former things are passed away. And he that sat upon the throne said, Behold, I make all things new."

God not only forgave us, he took away all of the old. The old man is crucified, dead, and buried. "But ye are not in the flesh but in the Spirit, if so be that the Spirit of God dwell in you. Now if any man have not the Spirit of Christ, he is none of his" (Romans 8:9). If you have the Spirit of God in you, you are not in the flesh, but in the Spirit. It does not matter how it looks. I don't care what you did today before you opened this book, you are in the Spirit. It may *look* as if you're in the flesh if you are not mature yet, but we do not judge by appearance (1 Samuel 16:7, 1 Thessalonians 5:22). It may not *look* like you're healed, but you are healed. If you are speaking from the throne, by his stripes you are healed even before you became sick.

When we speak from the throne, we are speaking Spirit. That empowers us to live above sin, to awake to righteousness and sin not. We awake to righteousness by seeing that there were two men—Adam and Christ. Adam was done away with. That only leaves Christ. He cannot sin and he cannot be sick—it is not in his nature. When we really get the revelation, he is going to appear. When he appears, there will not be any sin or sickness or carnality or death. It was done away at the cross because Jesus became sin. He was not just a sin offering. He became who we were in every sense of every definition—in all that it could possibly mean. I believe that he partook of more than Adam could have ever thought about bringing into our lives. Jesus took it all to the cross and from that, he brought exceedingly, abundantly more into our lives than we could ever ask or think, according to the power that worketh in us. What is the power? The preaching of the cross. Unto him be glory in the Church by Christ Jesus throughout all ages, world without end! Amen.

Isaiah 1:18 says "Come now, and let us reason together, saith the Lord: though your sins be as scarlet, they shall be as white as snow; though they be red like crimson, they shall be as wool." How can they be as wool? Because the Lamb takes them away. But it is more than just a taking away. It is an exchange. We exchange our sin for the Lamb nature. He became our sin; we became new creations with his nature. So we become as wool, or receive the nature of the Lamb. That did not happen by Jesus just covering our sins, but by him becoming sin and doing away with them—removing them as far as the east is from the west. God does not look at us "unrighteous people" and then just choose to see us as righteous, as some teach. That is not the way it is. We were *made* the righteousness of God in Christ Jesus. If Jesus just became a sin offering, then we were not really *made* the righteousness of God. God does not see us as something that we are not. "Justified" does not mean "just as if I'd never sinned." It means you have never sinned as far as God is concerned[35]. When you see that you indeed are dead unto sin, you are not going to want to live in sin because light has no communion with darkness. Instead of raking them over the coals, you can say to your children, "You're too good to do that." As the cliché goes, "accentuate the positive and you eliminate the negative."

To see more of the meaning of the red horse, let's look at Isaiah 53:9:

> And he made his *grave* with the wicked, and with the rich *in his death;* because he had done no violence, neither was any deceit in his mouth (emphasis added).

The word "grave" in the Hebrew, is "hell," and the word "death" is "deaths" (plural).[36] He did not just die a physical death. That would mean he was just a sin offering and our sins were just *covered*. He died two deaths. He died physically and he died spiritually.

Why would Acts 2:24 say that Jesus was loosed from the pains of death when he was *raised,* if he did not die spiritually? If he just died physically it would say that he was loosed from the pains of death when he died. When a person is in pain, if they die, they are out of pain. But the scripture does not say that Jesus was loosed from the pains of death when he died *physically*. He was loosed from the pains of death when he was *raised*. He was loosed from *that* death grip. He was loosed from that sin that he had become, from that *spiritual* death that he died.

Another example in scripture of Jesus' spiritual death is found in Ephesians 2:1 and 2:5, respectively:

> You hath he made alive, who were dead in trespasses and sins; Even when we were dead in sins, hath made us alive together with Christ.

Paul is making a distinction between physical death and spiritual death, because these people were physically alive. So, the death he was talking about was spiritual death. And then he says, "... hath made us alive together *with Christ*." When was Christ spiritually dead for us to be made alive together *with* him? When he became sin. That was when he died spiritually, as scripture reveals[37].

It is so important for us to understand that we were not just forgiven when we accepted Jesus as our Savior, but we became a new creation, because he, who knew no sin, became sin, that we might be made the righteousness of God in Christ Jesus. We must locate Adam. "Adam, where art thou?" When we see where he is, it takes away the residue because the residue is part of that old Adamic thinking. So, I want to show you the old man. I want to show what happened to Adam and where he is, because that is where *your* old man is—crucified, dead, and buried. And the residue, that veil untaken away that was done away, will be taken away. Then the life of Jesus will be reproduced through his body, which we are. When the veil is lifted from a bride after a woman is married, that veil is never put back over her face again.

We can find the red horse in the book of Joshua. The harlot Rahab represents the Church who has said "Amen" to everything that has come down the pike, and has not really learned how to discern and rightly divide the word of truth. She realizes that all she needs to do is take a scarlet thread (the red horse) and put it in the window. That is what we are doing. We are putting a scarlet thread in the window of our soul. We are seeing that it is a finished work. Rahab and her whole family received more in one day than all of Israel received in forty years! And some of them still didn't get it!

In the Song Of Solomon, we see a little more about the red horse. Remember, the little Shulamite thought that the king was never going to love her because she saw herself as black as the tents of Kedar, or the second son of Ishmael. In other words, "I'm just in the flesh. The king is never going to love me." Then he took her to the mountain of Bether or the mountain of suffering and there he showed her that all of her flesh—all of her black spots were done away with. *Then and only then,* was she released to come into a love relationship with the king. Because of this relationship, he reproduced himself through her and she gave birth to his child. The king knew the little Shulamite could not come into this relationship until he took her to the mountain of suffering and showed her, in type, what took place at the cross of Calvary. He did not show her the resurrection. He did not show her the resurrected Christ. He showed her the Lamb slain and her identification with it. Showing her what happened to her old nature and what he did to bring about its death is what released her to come into a love relationship with the king, where he could reproduce his life through her. That is GOOD NEWS!

We've had it completely wrong in the Church with the mindset of "We've got to fight this sin and we've got to fight that sin," and "The way to get rid of the residue of Adam is beholding the glorified Christ." Neither of those will do for us what God wants done in us. Taking us to Mt. Bether is the only thing that will show us that our black spots were done away with at Calvary. That will release us to come into a love relationship with the King, where he can appear. But we've ministered it in such a legalistic way. We've ministered it in such a message of works. This is not a "processing" per se, but it is waking up to a provision! There is a processing in renewing our mind daily, but we have taught so much processing via suffering as in "The more we suffer, the more we are going to rule and reign." Well, yes it is via suffering—his suffering was our suffering. We are already seated in the place of ruling and reigning. So the mindset of "The more we suffer, the more we are going to rule and reign," must be brought into captivity to the obedience of Christ. The truth is, the more we wake up to what happened at Mt. Bether because of Christ's obedience, the more we are going to rule and reign. When we wake up to the fact that his suffering was our suffering and we are already seated in the throne, we will release the King to rule and reign through us (Matthew 16:19). That is GOOD NEWS!

Look at Song Of Solomon 4:1-4:

> Behold, thou art fair, my love; behold, thou art fair; thou hast doves' eyes within thy locks: thy hair is as a flock of goats, that appear from mount Gilead. Thy teeth are like a flock of sheep that are even shorn, which came up from the washing; whereof every one

bear twins, and none is barren among them. Thy lips are like a thread of scarlet, and thy speech is comely: thy temples are like a piece of a pomegranate within thy locks. Thy neck is like the tower of David builded for an armory, whereon there hang a thousand bucklers, all shields of mighty men.

He said, "You have doves' eyes. You went to the mountain of Bether with me and I did not point out all your black spots. I took you to the mountain of suffering, and in type, showed you that my suffering was your suffering and now you have doves' eyes—you can see by the Spirit." Then he says, "Your hair is like a flock of goats." Can you imagine? This is a man courting a woman! The last thing he wants to tell her is that her hair is like a flock of goats—unless it means something beautiful and something spiritual. Goats' hair was used to cover the Most Holy Place in Moses' tabernacle. He was telling her that she was a tabernacle for him to dwell in!

Then he talks about her teeth. We use teeth to chew with. He compares her teeth with sheep. Sheep are those that follow Jesus and reproduce. They bear the fruit of the womb. He told her that her teeth were like a flock of sheep that are even shorn, which came up from the washing and every one bore twins and there was none barren among them. When you see with doves' eyes, when you've chewed up this word—the good news that you were already taken to Mt. Bether, the mountain of suffering—and when you come up from the washing of the water by the word, you are going to bear twins. You're going to reproduce the King! And none is barren among them! The Church in confusion or the Church in Babylon has been barren, unable to produce the life of the Lord. The "twins" speak of the fact that what is true of Christ is true of us.

Now, verse 3 is the focus in reference to the red horse: "Thy lips are like a thread of scarlet, and thy speech is comely." When you see that Jesus became sin not only *for* you, but *as* you, at the cross of Calvary the word on your lips becomes a scarlet thread that all may hear the Good News. When the word on your lips is the death of Christ, proclaiming that he, who knew no sin, was made to be sin for us, that we might be made the righteousness of God in him; your speech is comely to all who will hear. In fact, your speech will be so comely that they will want to hear more and more about Jesus—their ear will become nailed to the door.

Then he tells her, "Thy temples are like a piece of a pomegranate within thy locks." In other words, you're going to manifest fruit as your mind is renewed. "Thy neck is like the tower of David builded for an armory, whereon there hang a thousand bucklers, all shields of mighty men." The neck speaks of the will. In other words, "You're not studying war any more. You've beaten your swords into plowshares and your spears into pruning hooks. You've hung up your buckler and your shields of the mighty men of war because you realize that it is a finished work."

The word of God is releasing the Christ within us. I don't think we realize how much his word is releasing and bringing an appearing of the Lord Jesus Christ—beyond our quintessential hopes and dreams. As he comes, everything about us will change through the self fulfilling power of his word!

Now, let's read Revelation 6:4 again:

> And there went out another horse that was red: and power was given to him that sat thereon to take peace from the earth, and that they should kill one another: and there was given unto him a great sword.

Notice the phrase "to take peace from the earth." When you come to understand that it is not by the works that you're so used to doing, doing, doing—the length of your hair, the clothes that you wear, what you do, what you don't do, to make you more fair—it is going to take a little peace away from you. When Jesus came to town, only the simpletons, paupers, outcasts, whores, and thieves believed him. So why were the Pharisees so worried? Because this man of no reputation could calm the storm, move mountains, heal the sick, raise the dead, write a new nature in the ground of an adulterous woman's heart, and teach with an authority that caused the "fools" to be able to believe him but caused the Doctors of the law to hate him! He disturbed their peace! They were confused, but not by the things Jesus taught. His teaching only exposed their own Babylonian confusion and they felt all that confusion rise to the surface when he spoke. That is what they hated. His truth brought revolution—it set the captives free! Yes, I'd say that Jesus took "peace" from the earthly Pharisees.

Here is one way to know whether or not you or someone you know is a Pharisee: If your doctrine, your traditions, or your rules are more important than *loving people,* you can be sure that you are a Pharisee. When you see that you can't do your own thing anymore, it takes away your peace, especially if you're used to "doing for" God rather than *being with* God. This takes away your false sense of peace. You can get so involved in doing and thinking you are meriting brownie points with God and becoming more righteous, that when the word of God takes that away from you, you feel naked because you are so used to doing all those works. That false sense of peace is stripped away so that you can receive the real peace of God. Isn't it a rest to realize that the work was completed at the cross of Calvary and we're not trying to impress God—we couldn't impress him with our works anyway. We're not trying to impress anyone. We just be—because we see. We see what happened at the cross of Calvary and that we were there. What rest! We cease from our own labors and that false sense of peace is stripped away. Now our works are no longer dead works. Our works spring out of our understanding of the finished work. Now our works are the works of God.

Jesus has been taking away from us our false sense of peace to the point that we finally trust in the fact that his suffering was our suffering. Now he has brought about a true peace to us because of what took place at the cross. He experienced our confusion, he experienced our lack of peace, and that brought *true peace.* When we come to understand the Lamb slain, we receive true peace. Jesus said, "Peace I leave with you, my peace I give unto you; not as the world giveth, give I unto you. Let not your heart be troubled, neither let it be afraid."

I thank God that when we come to this understanding, the false sense of peace that we've had, thinking that we are going to mature through works, has been taken away, stripped away from us. And now, we are coming into a true peace, realizing by grace we are saved through faith, not by works, lest any man should boast. That will release the peace of God in our midst! And I don't care what comes against you, you can rule and reign in the peace of God. Did you know that peace rules (Colossians 3:15)? Peace rules! That is what we have lacked. We have lacked that peace because we have not fully understood the finished work and because we have not understood that there is nothing that we can add to it. It is a "done deal."

Now look at the next phrase in Revelation 6:4, "... and that they should kill one another." The very ones that killed him, were killed themselves at the cross of Calvary. In Adam, those who hung Jesus on the cross were crucified *with him* on that cross over 2000 years ago. Jesus' becoming sin accomplished that.

The last phrase in Revelation 6:4 is: "... and there was given unto him a great sword." The great sword is the word about his finished work. It gives us great discernment. In the Old Testament they were to cut the offerings right down the middle and slay them and flay them and lay them open. Every organ and all the entrails were exposed. So the priests took a sword, a knife, and they cut the offering in half and lay it open. Then they would cut it in pieces and lay it upon the altar. We've all seen nice little pictures of Jesus where he is portrayed with a little trickle of blood here and there. But one translation says that his visage was so marred that he looked like hamburger meat. He was unrecognizable. His visage was marred more than any man. That does not sound like a little trickle of blood here and there. It sounds like he was beaten so badly that in looking upon him, you could not even be certain that he was a man!

That great sword in Revelation 6:4 is the word of God. As we understand the four horses we receive a great sword of discernment. In the Old Testament, when people came to offer an offering, the priest had to have enough discernment to know whether they needed to offer a burnt offering, a meal offering, a sin offering, a trespass offering, or a peace offering. That great sword is the word that we receive, to know exactly what people need wherever they are in their lives. For example, if someone needs physical healing to be manifested in their lives, you do not show them the crown of thorns. You show them that by the stripes of Jesus, they were healed. The priests had to know which offering was to be applied to every situation. The great sword is the word that Jesus was all of these offerings himself.

The Church is coming to realize that what they have heard and what they have had has not been enough. It is going to take more to bring them to maturity. They are coming to understand that it is not in works of the flesh. They've heard these great swelling messages, they have seen miracles, as well and good as that is—and signs will follow the preaching of the truth—but they have depended on signs with very little truth, and that has not matured them. Like Jesus said, miracles and signs won't make you believe! What is the wisdom of God and the power of God? The preaching of the cross. That is going to release the faith of God out of our midst in progressive degrees!

So, as we come to understand the twelve redemptive aspects of the finished work of Calvary, our identification with it, and how that took place, we know exactly what part of that needs to be applied to our lives and what needs to be applied to others, as we minister unto them from the throne. This great sword is the sword of discernment. We have a great sword—the word of God!

This red horse is represented in Leviticus chapter 1 by the burnt offering. Look at Leviticus 1:3-7:

> If his offering be a burnt sacrifice of the herd, let him offer a male without blemish: he shall offer it of his own voluntary will at the door of the tabernacle of the congregation before the Lord. And he shall put his hand upon the head of the burnt offering; and it shall be accepted for him to make atonement for him. And he shall kill the bullock before the Lord: and the priests, Aaron's sons, shall bring the blood, and sprinkle the blood round about the altar that is by the door of the tabernacle of the congregation. And he shall flay the burnt offering, and cut it into his pieces. And the sons of Aaron the priest shall put fire upon the altar, and lay the wood in order upon the fire: and the priests, Aaron's sons, shall lay the parts, the head, and the fat, in order upon the wood that is on the fire which is upon the altar: but his inwards and his legs shall he wash in water: and the priest shall burn all on the altar, to be a burnt sacrifice, an offering made by fire, of a sweet savour unto the Lord.

In verse 3, we see Jesus—the male without blemish. He was the spotless Lamb without blemish, because he did not sin. Jesus offered his life of his own voluntary will. Jesus was also the bullock—the calf or ox. He is the door of the tabernacle of the congregation before the Lord. He is our burnt offering. He is our atonement. He is the great high priest who sprinkled his own blood. Are you coming to the realization that Jesus is everything? He is Lord of all, above all, through all, in all, over all—our all in all!

If the lamb that the priests brought to offer put up any kind of a fight, they had to go and get another lamb. Jesus prayed in the garden that the Father's will be done, not his will. It had to be a willing sacrifice. The person offering the lamb had to be willing to offer it, as verse 3 says, "He shall offer it of his own voluntary will." Jesus was both the offerer and the offering.

Then the sons of Aaron the priest put fire upon the altar. What color is fire? It is red. Remember, the red horse is fiery or fire-like. The burnt offering represents Jesus and that is why the second beast in Revelation 6 that opened up the seal that loosed the red horse, was a calf (Revelation 4:7). Jesus became the suffering servant, he became the bullock, he became sin—not just a sin offering, but in the full sense of the word, he became sin.

Then, in Leviticus 1:7, they were to *lay the wood in order* upon the fire. They did not just throw the wood on the fire in any old way. In Romans 6:17 we find that Paul had a *system* of truth, or a form of doctrine. In other words, the reason these horses are presented in the order of white, red, black, and pale, is because there is a systematic way of presenting the work of Jesus, his death, his burial, and his resurrection that people will come to grasp and to be grasped by the cross.

In Leviticus 1:8, the priests laid the parts, the sacrifice that had been cut up in pieces, in order upon the wood. The head was first—the mind of Christ—then the fat, which was the most prosperous, superabundant part of the animal. The fat also refers to oil. The fat was the priest's portion (Jeremiah 31:14). In Isaiah 10:27, the Amplified Bible says, "The yoke shall be destroyed because of fatness [which prevents it from going around your neck]." *This* is the anointing that destroys the yoke—the anointing that flows from Christ, the head—the most prosperous and superabundant part of the body!

Verse 9 of Leviticus chapter 1 says, "But its inwards and his legs shall he wash in water." The sacrifice was washed from the residue. In our identification with Christ, the inwards speak of our inward parts; the legs speak of our walk. Our soul and our walk are being washed today—not with any old word—but with the word of the crucifixion, the death, and the burial. That is what gets rid of the residue.

Then verse 9 continues, "And the priests shall burn all on the altar to be a burnt sacrifice, an offering made by fire, of a sweet savour unto the Lord." The red horse, which represents Jesus' becoming sin, correlates with the burnt offering in that it was a male, it was spotless, it was laid apart, and it was burnt with fire. You won't find a more detailed description of what Jesus suffered on the cross than that of the Old Testament offerings. His visage was marred more than any man. As we understand the white horse and the red horse, we are beginning to get this great sword of discernment, as Hebrews 4:12 says, the word of God is quick and it is alive! Not just any word that man may preach, but the word concerning the death, the burial, and the resurrection is giving us a great sword of discernment. We know what we need according to the finished work of Calvary, and we know what others need when they come to us.

The first beast in Revelation 6 said, "Come and see," and he showed John the white horse, the righteous, holy, earth walk of Jesus. The second beast said, "Come and see." Not come and do, just come and view. This is the consecration of the priests. In the consecration of the priests, several criteria had to be met and I'll mention just a few: The priests had to be a son of Aaron, and they had to be at least thirty years of age. They were to have no physical flaws like a mole, a speck in the eye, or a broken bone (Leviticus 21:18-24). If they were not consecrated, they could not actively execute the ministry of the priest. Yet, a priest-to-be could meet all these criteria and still not be consecrated. Part of the consecration was just standing *to watch* the offering of a bullock and two rams (Leviticus 8:13-36). Just watch. Just view. Just see. Then the offering was laid in the priests' hands, completing the consecration.

Consecration is not something you do—as much as we want to do it sometimes, to become more consecrated and more dedicated to the Lord. Consecration is to have our hands full of the sacrifice. Melchisedec has his hands full of bread and wine and he is offering that unto the Church and unto the nations.

Our mouths are being touched with the coals of fire. The word of the brazen altar is on our lips. And as the book of Revelation says, the coals of fire are being thrown out into the earth and we are ministering this word unto the nations. We are not going to minister judgment and condemnation, telling people they need to quit this and quit that. Through the word of his death, Jesus will turn them away from their iniquities. It will not happen by telling people to stop sinning. In the understanding of these horses, we who have had judgment given to us will minister judgment by showing the nations the white horse, the red horse, the black horse, and the pale horse. We will feed them Lamb and invite them to the super supper, the greatest meal of the day, at the end of the day. The only thing on the menu is Lamb served as bread and wine. As we partake, the book is opened and out flows the life of the Lamb.

It's All About Jesus

When we view the book of Revelation as a book of redemption and as the revelation of Jesus Christ, we cannot help but experience and express the life of the Lamb. Where is the life of the Lamb being revealed in this hour? We used to say (and the majority of the Church world still says) that the Lord will be revealed when he comes literally. People have taken the book of Revelation and taught the white horse as the antichrist, the red horse as war, the black horse as famine, and the pale horse as disease and poverty, but that does not line up with the revelation of Jesus Christ. If the revelation of the book of Revelation is to make us blessed if we read it and understand it and keep it, it cannot be about war and famine and pestilence and disease and poverty. That does not make us happy and that does not bless us.

But when we see that it is the revelation of Jesus Christ, it changes the whole picture. He wants to be revealed. He is being revealed in one place—out of the midst of a people. As we have previously said, we can be born again, Spirit-filled, operating in the gifts of the Spirit and speak in tongues all the live long day—and still be a garden inclosed, a spring shut up, and a fountain sealed. Jesus identified with us being sealed up when he went to the cross, as we read in Psalm 88:8. He was sealed up in death *until the time* of his quickening. But there is a place where he is still sealed up. He is sealed up in us and he wants out! Not "out" in the sense that he is going to leave us, but "out" in the sense that when the world looks at the Church, the only person they will see is Jesus! The Amplified version of Ecclesiastes 3:11 says that God has planted eternity in men's hearts and minds! Then, in Acts 3:21, we see that the heaven (including the eternity that he has planted in us) must receive Jesus Christ *until the times of restitution of all things.* Christ in us (Colossians 1:27) wants out! He wants to be unsealed, unveiled. He wants us to know him and the power of his resurrection that lifts us out from among the dead even while in the body (Philippians 3:10-11, Amplified Bible)! In this is the appearing of the Lord! He wants to appear to the world!

We are coming to understand that as we look behind us as did John, we are hearing a voice behind us saying, "This is the way, walk ye in it." The One who is behind us is the Lamb slain—the crucifixion, the death, and the burial.

The book that is sealed on the backside represents crucifixion, death, and burial. That which comes out of us, the life of the Lamb, is the quickening, the raising, and the seating. The horses in Revelation chapter 6 represent the career of Christ, from his holy, righteous earth walk until the time that he was in hell. Then he was quickened, raised, and seated in heavenly places. Not only did Jesus experience this, but the word of God tells us that we were there also. We experienced it over 2000 years ago.

In Revelation chapter 5, we found out who was the only one that could open the book. John was weeping and the angel said "Hush up," or "Weep not, for the Lion of the tribe of Judah has prevailed to open the book, and to loose the seven seals thereof." But then, when John looked to see the Lion of the tribe of Judah, *he beheld the Lamb slain.* The one who opens up the book is the Lamb slain. Our understanding of the crucifixion, the death, and the burial is what is going to open the book that has been sealed on the backside.

When I speak of the residue of Adam, I am speaking of the veiled mind of 2 Corinthians 3:14. As we know, the word "soul," refers to the mind, the will, the intellect, and the emotions, and in the Greek, it is written in the feminine tense. So I refer to the veiled mind as "The old woman." There is no way we are going to get rid of the old woman by showing ourselves another man. The way we are going to get rid of the old woman is by showing ourselves that Adam was crucified, he died, and was buried, because that residue is a part of Adam's memory. Paul said in Romans chapter 7, if you are married to another and your first husband is not dead, you are living in adultery. As in the natural; so in the spiritual. When we show the old woman that Adam was crucified, he died, and he was buried, that will remove the veil from our minds. When we remove the veil from our mind, it will be removed in our experience, or in our day to day lives. When the veil is removed in experience, we will move into a place of intimacy, a place of rest, a place of fruitfulness. We will become consistently aware that we actually do live, and move, and have our being in him. We will come to realize that the change we so desperately want in the world must first take place in us. We will come to realize that the rapture we have been waiting for has actually been waiting for us. *Jesus has been waiting for us* to come up hither. His desire is a rapture that takes place *within us*. And it is only going to happen by showing the old woman that Adam is crucified, dead and buried and now the only life being lived is lived in the last Adam, the quickening or the life-giving spirit, Jesus Christ the Lord (1 Corinthians 15:42-50, Galatians 2:20). Now we are beginning to experience our marriage to Christ and bear fruit unto God. There is a people who are experiencing this today, in this Great Day of the Feast of Tabernacles, and it only intensifies as we continue to partake of the bread and the wine.

    I used to teach that when you come into a dark room and turn on the light, the darkness has to flee. The darkness is swallowed up by the light, which is true. But what is the source of that light? It is a negative charge and a positive charge. You must have the negative together with the positive to produce light. We must begin with the Lamb slain if we are ever going to see the glorified Christ. Again, how do we get rid of the old woman? Not by first showing her the glorified Christ, but by first showing the Lamb slain. We get rid of the old woman by showing her that the old man was crucified, is dead, and buried.

People say Jesus came to give us life, which is true. But how did he give us life? By giving us a death. Then he was *quickened* to give us life. That *resurrection life* swallows up the death that is in our mortal bodies (2 Corinthians 5:4). Jesus came to give us a death. Death comes first. Death killed death. Death was swallowed up in the victory that was won by the death on the cross. And now mortality is swallowed up in resurrection life. Again, Jesus did not die to gives us life. He died to bring death to our old nature. He then *lived* to give us life. 2 Corinthians 15:54 says that death is swallowed up *in victory*. That victory came through *the death* of Jesus Christ.

When Jesus died, Adam, the man of sin died. We have victory over the sin nature! We have victory over the man of sin and we overcame him by the blood of the Lamb and by the word of *our* death (testimony). We must start with the death and then we will have the life and the light. Showing the glorified Christ is not going to get rid of the old woman. She is going to be taken away when she sees the crucifixion, the death, and the burial. Only then can we see the glorified Christ. When was Christ glorified? After his death. It is death that consumes death, not life that consumes death in this sense. Once we come to understand that, the book is going to be unsealed.

Jesus' death destroyed death. Many are big on preaching life. They say, "Give us resurrection life!" No, it is death we need—but not the death that comes from ministering legalism and the letter and the law. We need to see the death of Christ and our identification with it. The ministry of this third day is the death of Christ, the bread and the wine, the broken body and the shed blood. Paul said it. Eat the bread and drink of the cup and show forth his ... *death*— until he comes! It is the marriage supper of the Lamb. Of course we are already in union in the Most Holy. But the thing that is going to cause that to be *expressed* in our lives is not in showing our woman (soul) another man, but showing her the old man that she was widowed from at Calvary. Now we are free to be married to the last Adam, the life-giving spirit, the Lord Jesus Christ. In fact, we are married to the Lord; we just haven't known it and we haven't really reckoned it.

The Books Are Being Opened

> And I saw in the right hand of him that sat on the throne a book written within and on the backside, sealed with seven seals (Revelation 5:1).

We who have been sealed up, the born-again and Spirit-filled Christians, are being unsealed. The seven seals of Revelation 5:1 are not seven literal seals. Seven speaks of fullness. We have been fully sealed up even though we have been born again and Spirit-filled. The reason we have been sealed up is because we have been immature. But thank God, the understanding of the Lamb slain is breaking the seals on the backside of the book so that out of us can flow quickened, raised, and seated—the glorified, risen Christ, the resurrected life.

The understanding of each of these horses in Revelation chapter 6 is going to cause our book that has been sealed up, to be unsealed so that out of us can gallop the life of the white horse, the red horse, the black horse, and the pale horse. Then our soul will be completely under the brazen altar and we will experience the earthquake in Revelation chapter 6—the resurrection will flow out of us. There will be earthquakes in diverse places—as a people come to experience the resurrection life of Jesus Christ! Then the sun will become black as sackcloth of hair and the moon will become blood. Later, we will experience a sealing which brings silence in heaven for about half an hour.

You may be thinking, "Wait a minute. You talk about being unsealed, and then you talk about being sealed." We have to first be unsealed on the backside so the life of the Lamb can flow out. Then we are going to be sealed in that dimension, as a people who go in and come out no more (Revelation 3:12). So we have to be unsealed to let the life of the Lamb flow out, and then we will be sealed in that realm of tabernacling. That does not mean that we won't come out and minister to people in the Outer Court and the Holy Place. We will. But we will never experientially leave the dimension of the Holy of Holies that we are sealed in. We will never leave; we will be sealed in that dimension of spirit, never again to manifest the old residue of Adam that was in our minds. We are in that time. How do

I know that? Because bread and wine is being served on the table. The marriage supper, the super supper is being served and there is Lamb on the table—and the Lamb is not the glorified Christ. The Lamb is the Lamb slain.

Those who do not interpret this as the revelation of Jesus Christ say that the white horse in Revelation 6 is the antichrist, the red horse is war, the black horse is famine, and the pale horse is pestilence and poverty and death. But that cannot be if this book is to make us blessed, if this book is to make us happy, if this is the revelation of Jesus Christ. There is no way it can be interpreted according to current events or what is happening out there in the world, because what is happening out there is always changing and Jesus Christ is the same yesterday, today, and forever!

World events are always changing and the interpretation of a literal antichrist is always changing. The "antichrist" is not the same person they said he was when I first heard Revelation taught literally. The beast has changed, the false prophet has changed and somebody (though they're not sure who) is going to be literally cast into some lake of fire. The mark of the beast is not the same as it was when they first taught it. The ten horns are not the same as they were first interpreted some years ago—if it is to be interpreted according to external, outside events. That will keep you busy! Talk about the wearing down of the saints!

Revelation 6:1 mentions thunder:

> And I saw when the Lamb opened one of the seals,
> and I heard, as it were the noise of thunder, one of
> the four beasts saying, 'Come and see.'

These horses are galloping out in thunderous, tumultuous noise. What is Jubilee? It is a long, loud, thunderous blast of a ram's horn until Jesus appears. And where do we get a ram's horn? From the death of a male lamb. We are sounding the ram's horn! And we are going to continue to eat Lamb and sound the ram's horn until he fully and completely appears. Then we are going to continue to eat Lamb to be sealed and to stay in that dimension. We are continually realizing that *it is not us*. It is him that must be glorified and magnified out of our lives and through our lives!

Notice the last part of Revelation 6:1: "And I heard, as it were the noise of thunder, one of the four beasts saying, "Come and see." Come and view. Not come and do, but come and view. Why? Because our salvation is not based upon works. It's by grace that we are saved through faith, not by works, lest any man should boast. Consecration of the priesthood was not anything they did—it was something they saw. It was viewing three sacrifices that were offered and then the last one was laid in their hands along with the bread, constituting our having bread and wine laid in our hands.

The Spirit Of Truth Will Guide You Into All Truth

> But when He, the Spirit of Truth (the Truth-giving Spirit) comes, He will guide you into all the Truth (the whole, full Truth). For He will not speak His own message [on his own authority]; but He will tell whatever He hears [from the Father; He will give the message that has been given to Him], and He will announce and declare to you the things that are to come [that will happen in the future] (John 16:13, Amplified Bible).

There are many different levels of "knowing." The Lord began to explain something to me that I have been saying since I began teaching the book of Revelation. At the time, I was ill and was experiencing more physical pain than I had for a while. I was at the point of physical exhaustion, probably from a lack of sleep. But when my feet hit the floor that morning, the Lord caused me to experience him on a deeper level. As the word says, "When the enemy comes in, like a flood the Spirit of the Lord shall lift up a standard against him." Something went off on the inside of me. Seeing the joining together of the body of Christ unlocked something in me. It was just what I needed. It was not a new revelation; it was just a deeper understanding of revelation. The Lord explained something to me in a greater sense.

Unless you have been daily searching the scriptures as were the Bereans, then you may not understand the remainder of this book. The first thing that I want to say is what the Lord explained to me that morning in a deeper sense. I knew it, but now I know it, and maybe tomorrow I'll know it even more. The book of Revelation is a de-creation of everything that Adam created. And the Lord began to expound on that in a greater sense that morning. He came in with a *whoosh!* I love it when he speaks to me when I am not even studying the word, and then I go to the scriptures and the word confirms the word. Even when our thoughts may be on something else, the Lord can just come in and explain the scriptures to us.

The religious system teaches a literal seven year tribulation, a literal battle of Armageddon with blood up to the horses bridle, literal trumpets—they teach almost everything in this symbolic book as something literal. But the Lord began to show me how it *is* fullness of tribulation. Yes, the book of Revelation *is* a battle of Armageddon. Yes, it *is* the beast and the false prophet thrown into the lake of fire. It is all of that! The book of Revelation and the understanding of it is a de-creation of everything Adam created. But it has been thrown into the future and applied literally to the earth "out there," rather than applying it inwardly and showing us that it has already happened! There was a symbolic "seven year" tribulation. The fullness of what it took to destroy Adam took place at the cross of Calvary. There was a symbolic seven year tribulation over 2000 years ago at the cross of Calvary, and man—the first Adam, the beast, and the false prophet—was thrown into the lake of fire! Fire speaks of judgment, and Jesus' fire was our fire. To a certain extent, there is still some of the veil, Adam's old woman, hanging around in our minds, but as we come to the understanding of the revelation of Jesus Christ, even that is being destroyed.

I often teach by comparison and when I compare what the Babylonian system or denominationalism is teaching, I am not saying those things to run them down or criticize them. If people do not know you by the spirit, they may think that comparison is criticism. But Jesus taught by comparison. Paul taught by comparison. For example, Jesus said, "The *law* says 'an eye for an eye and a tooth for a tooth' *but I say* that ye resist not evil, but whosoever shall smite thee on thy right cheek, turn to him the other also" (emphasis added). Paul talked about what the traditions of man have taught and then he taught the opposite of that, or what God teaches by the spirit.

I saw a "preacher" on television preaching current events and "what's going to happen," and he was offering a video that dramatizes the things he was preaching. I would like to see the video. Not because I want to criticize, but because there may be some things that the religious system is teaching that I may not have heard yet and if I see the video, I can teach the comparison of that with the truth. How can I come before you and tell you that the religious system teaches that there is going to be a literal rapture of the Church and that the world is going to be thrown into a seven year tribulation if I don't know they teach that? And of course they use scripture from 2 Thessalonians to say that when the Church is removed, the Holy Spirit is removed, but yet they say that during the seven year tribulation, people are going to be saved. Talk about Babylonian confusion!

But how could I bring that before you for comparison unless I heard it declared in the religious system. I am teaching some things by comparison. Jesus did it, Paul did it, and we have a biblical example to follow in doing the same. It is not a spirit of criticism that we are ministering. To whom much is given, much is required. And I trust that the message of grace has not caused the pendulum to swing to the extreme left and cause us to be lackadaisical and say, "Well, it's all by grace. I don't have to pray, I don't have to study, I don't have to do any of this stuff." That is not what we are declaring. It is not just grace that we are teaching—it is grace *and* truth. That is balance. Remember, grace is not a license to sin—it is the power not to sin. When we come to understand what happened at the cross of Calvary, that causes the Christ to rise up within us to a greater degree and we will do those things—not out of legalism, and not because we have to, but because it's our nature—it will just be a spontaneous outflow. Jesus got away to pray every time he had an opportunity. He got away from the disciples, and he got away from the crowds, because he could not wait to be alone with the Father. And that is our nature also.

The Black Horse

Now let's look at the black horse in Revelation 6:5-6:

> And when he had opened the third seal, I heard the third beast say, 'Come and see.' And I beheld, and lo, a black horse; and he that sat on him had a pair of balances in his hand. And I heard a voice in the midst of the four beasts say, 'A measure of wheat for a penny, and three measures of barley for a penny; and see thou hurt not the oil and the wine.'

The black horse represents Jesus dying spiritually. And he has a pair of balances in his hand. We were weighed in the balance and found wanting. Remember the handwriting on the wall in Daniel chapter 5? That is a picture of the finished work of Calvary. We were weighed in the balances and God knew that he could not express his life through the seven candlesticks of Revelation; he could not express his life through a many-membered body unless Adam was done away with. The wages of sin is death—we got exactly what we deserved at Calvary because of Adam's sin. At the cross of Calvary, Jesus' death was our death. We were weighed in the balances and found wanting. God knew he could not modify Adam, he could not save Adam. He had to do away with him completely and totally.

The beam of the pair of balances is found in Matthew 11:29-30, where we find the word "yoke." This is the Greek word *zugos* which means, "The beam of the balance" or "a pair of balances." It comes from a word that means "a coupling." In this scripture Jesus said, "Take my yoke upon you, and learn of me; for I am meek and lowly in heart: and ye shall find rest unto your souls. For my yoke is easy, and my burden is light." God is bringing a balance in the midst of the Church today with the message of the cross and our yoking, our coupling, our identification with it.

Now, back to Revelation 6:6:

> And I heard a voice in the midst of the four beasts say, "A measure of wheat for a penny, and three measures of barley for a penny; and see thou hurt not the oil and the wine."

Again, wheat speaks of death, barley speaks of life. When the children of Israel came into the Promised Land, the bread they ate was made of wheat and barley—death and resurrection. In this scripture, a voice in the midst of the four beasts said, "A measure of wheat for a penny, and three measures of barley for a penny." Three measures of barley is the same price as one measure of wheat. One price did it all! Jesus died once, for all! Complete resurrection for all (three measures of barley) for the price of one innocent Lamb who became all that we ever were before we came to the cross and accepted his priceless sacrifice. Jesus, I love you.

Verse 6 continues, "hurt not the oil and the wine." The oil is the precious ointment poured on the head, that ran down on the beard, even the beard of Aaron [the first high priest], that come down upon the collar and skirts of his garments [consecrating the whole body]" (Psalm 133:2, Amplified Bible). The oil is something that is put on the outside of us. It represents something that is made visible. (This is an important point and we will discuss it further in the next chapter.) Jesus was crucified on Mt. Calvary, near Gethsemane where the olive oil press was. That is where the olives were crushed to produce the oil—and that is where Jesus prayed that crushing prayer, "O my Father, if it be possible, let this cup pass from me: nevertheless, not as I will, but as thou wilt." His crushing was our crushing. When we see his death, it is going to bring about his appearing!

The wine, of course, is something that we take within us. They made wine by "dancing" on the grapes to crush them. His beating was our beating, his crushing was our crushing. That produced the wine. "See thou hurt not the oil and the wine." The oil and the wine were not hurt—they were produced through *his* hurt.

The beasts in Revelation 6 are not "beasts" as we think of wild beasts or a furry creature out there in the barn yard. These beasts are living creatures expressing life. The book of Ezekiel talks about these living creatures, and later we will discover more of what Ezekiel chapter 1 says about the living creatures in relation to the "terrible crystal." These living beasts or living creatures are Cherubim. In the Most Holy Place were the Cherubim. The Cherubim represent people that have been apprehended, or gripped by the cross. *You* are a Cherubic company today! Cherubim are not angels with wings. An angel is a messenger with a message. We are going to find out what the wings are. John saw more wings on these angels than Ezekiel saw. There has to be something to this, and we are going to find out. But these Cherubim represent apprehended people—people who are gripped by the cross of Calvary.

We are being gripped, just like Paul. The prophet Agabus took Paul's girdle and bound up his own hands and feet and told Paul that if he went to minister this gospel over in Jerusalem, they would persecute him and may even kill him. And Paul said "I'm ready not only to be bound, but also to die for the name of the Lord Jesus!" That's what he meant when he said "I die daily." He was saying, "I'm so full of this gospel, this death, burial, and resurrection, that I am not afraid of those who can kill my body. I am ready and willing to lay down my physical life if that is what it takes to get this word to them!"

What we are seeing is that these Cherubim represent a people like Paul the apostle, who are apprehended—gripped by the cross. Paul said "I have not yet apprehended that for which Christ apprehended me." Paul was saying that something had a hold of him that he did not yet have a hold of fully. We were apprehended at the cross of Calvary. Now we are apprehending that which apprehended us (Philippians 3:12).

Remember, the first beast that said, "Come and see" was a lion. The second beast that said, "Come and see" was a calf or an ox, the servant nature, which represents Jesus becoming sin. The third beast that released the rider of the black horse had the face of a man. The black horse represents Jesus fully identifying with man in the sense that he died spiritually. He was not just a sin offering, he died spiritually. His death was not just one death, a physical death; his death was also a spiritual death. He died two deaths as we saw in Isaiah 53.

There is an Amish community near my home town. When I drive by there in the springtime I see them working their fields with horses and plows. Sometimes there is more than one horse and those horses are linked together or yoked together. These horses in Revelation 6 are linked together and they represent a transaction. Paul talked about his "form of doctrine," which was Paul's system of truth. Meaning, if we teach the death, burial, and resurrection and our identification with it in a systematic way, people will be able to grasp it and they will be able to come to understanding. And notice these horses—it is not the black horse first, or the red horse, because Jesus had to be righteous and holy and sinless in order to qualify to be the one that went to the cross. If he had sinned, then he would have died for himself because the wages of sin is death. But he died for us and he died as us. The white horse is first and it leads into the red horse. The red horse leads into the black horse. The black horse leads into the pale horse.

So let's look at Revelation 6:5-6 again:

> And when he had opened the third seal, I heard the third beast say, 'Come and see.' And I beheld, and lo, a black horse; and he that sat on him had a pair of balances in his hand. And I heard a voice in the midst of the four beasts say, 'A measure of wheat for a penny, and three measures of barley for a penny; and see thou hurt not the oil and the wine.'

Again, John heard the third beast, which is the man, say, "Come and see." Don't come and do, come and view. Come and see that Jesus, who became sin for us and as us, died spiritually as well as physically.

Now, with this scripture in mind look at 2 Corinthians 4:10-11:

> Always bearing about in the body the dying of the Lord Jesus, that the life also of Jesus might be made manifest in our body. For we which live are alway delivered unto death for Jesus' sake, that the life also of Jesus might be made manifest in our mortal flesh.

My paraphrase is this: "We are always meditating about the death of Christ—not just the resurrection life—but the death of Christ. Why? That the life also of Jesus might be made manifest in our body!" This is not saying that we should always meditate on the resurrection life. However, we are not God's army of dead men because we died in Christ over 2000 years ago. We are very much alive. But how are we going to see that life resurrected and released in our experience? By always bearing about in the body the dying of the Lord Jesus Christ. This black horse speaks to us of Jesus dying spiritually, and we must meditate on all aspects of his death.

We must constantly renew our minds to the fact that the body of sin, the man of sin was crucified, is dead, and was buried, in order for us to live victoriously and to overcome. When Paul was preaching grace they said, "Does that mean that we can just sin and the more we sin, the more grace will abound?" Paul said to them, "Who in the world would come to understand that you are dead indeed unto sin and want to continue therein? You're dead to sin, why would you want to continue in sin?"

Always bearing about *in the body* the *dying* of the Lord Jesus—we must constantly minister the death. We must constantly renew our mind to what happened at the cross of Calvary. What is the preaching of the cross? It is the power of God and the wisdom of God. If we are going to get rid of any residue, it is going to be by seeing the death. "Beloved, now are we the sons of God, and it doth not yet appear what we shall be: but we know that, when he shall appear, we shall be like him; for we shall see him as he is" (1 John 3:2). That does not mean that you see him as he is and then you will be like him. It means as you view what happened at the cross of Calvary, he is going to appear. And then, as he is, you will see him and you will see that you are like him. We will see him as he is. How is he in this Day? He is quickened, raised, and seated as the result of the death. He is a finished work and so are you! Only as we view the death will we see the resurrection. It is not the other way around.

We have ministered it the other way around for years saying, "If you behold the glorified Christ that is going to make you be like him." But as we behold the death of Christ, now are we the sons of God. It does not appear what we shall be, but we know that as we view his death, he shall appear, and then all men are going to see him as he is because it will be him appearing in them and through them. The Cherubim were positioned on the Ark of the Covenant so that they were *always beholding the blood* upon the *mercy* seat—that is where the glory of God appeared and abided. In type, those two angels were always beholding the death of Christ.

If you remember, when Mary Magdalene went to the garden tomb and found that the stone had been rolled away. She stood outside the tomb weeping, and as she wept, she stopped down and looked into the tomb. It is no accident that she saw two angels in white sitting, one at the head, and the other at the feet where the body of Jesus had lain. In bearing the judgment of God on the cross, Jesus came up from the judgment seat and *became himself* the mercy seat. The two angels spoke with her and after their conversation, what did she do? She *turned to look behind her* and when she did that, she saw what she thought was the gardener. These words were not just written randomly to fill up space in John's gospel. Jesus *is* the gardener, the husbandman, who, at Calvary's cross, planted a garden inside of a woman who had previously been a graveyard, inhabited by seven devils.

It is well and good to see the woman, Mary Magdalene in this picture. But don't miss the bigger picture of the woman, the Church, who has been an inhabitant of and inhabited by Babylon, confusion. The Church has been in the wilderness—an unkempt garden. The same thing is happening within her. She is about to bud with righteousness, with fruit and spices that spring forth from the understanding of the death of Jesus Christ that she has been planted in. I'm speaking of a garden, the likes of which this earth has *never* experienced! The Sun-clothed woman is coming forth to manifest the crown royal (Esther 1:11)—and her name is not Vashti—her name is Esther, which is the feminine form of "hidden secret," the bride of Christ.

When a bride gets married, once the veil is removed, she never puts that veil over her face again. When the veil is removed, we are sealed in the dimension of the Most Holy. The veil represents the veil that was done away in Christ, but now is being taken away from our minds as we *behold the death of Christ.*

Paul said, "Always bearing about in the body *the dying* of the Lord Jesus." Why didn't he say, "Always bearing about in the body the glorified Christ?" Why didn't he say "Always viewing the glorified Christ?" There is a super supper in the Feast of Tabernacles and there is Lamb on the table. The Lamb always denotes the Lamb slain, and not the glorified Christ. So it is in 2 Corinthians 4:10; "Always bearing about in the body the dying of the Lord Jesus, *that the life* also of Jesus might be made manifest in our body." The life of Jesus will be made manifest in our body (the Church) as we bear about the dying of the Lord Jesus—in our minds, in our ministering, in our worship, in our daily experience. View the death, experience the life!

We used to teach this scripture as, "The more I suffer in this life, the more his life is going to emanate from me." That is not consistent with the word of God. If we always bear about in the body of Christ the dying of the Lord Jesus, if we continue to partake of bread and wine, feast on the death—if the eagles are continually gathered around the carcass, what is going to happen? The seals on the backside—crucified, died, buried—are going to be broken so the life of the Lamb can come forth. Then we are going to be sealed in the dimension of being quickened, raised, and seated in the throne.

"For we which live are alway delivered unto death for Jesus' sake, that the life also of Jesus might be made manifest in our mortal flesh." It is not life that swallows up death; it is death that swallows up death. Understanding *the* death brings light that will swallow up any residue of Adam yet in our minds.

When we bear about in the body the dying of the Lord Jesus, then as we minister the word, as we are praying, as we are worshipping, it is all done from the throne. If we suffer with him, we reign with him. But I'm not talking about the kind of suffering that you may be thinking about. I understand that we go through fiery trials. It is much easier to go through those things when we understand that God did not bring those things to buffet us into a realm of glory. When we quit smiting the rock twice, it will cause us to overcome quickly and easily.

We also used to teach, "The more we suffer, the more we are going to rule and reign with him." Our Father is not an "Indian-giver." He did not build a hedge around us at the cross of Calvary to turn around and let it down to "buffet us into the realm of glory." It is not God that is letting down the hedge one iota. We do not have to go through a "Job experience." As we have previously discussed, Jesus had our Job experience. The hand of God touched Job to bring him forth as pure gold. The hand of God is what caused Jesus Christ to go to the cross. That was the plan and the purpose of God that he might come forth in a people as pure gold, when we come to understand that his suffering was our suffering at the cross of Calvary. As this happens, the Ten Commandments become no longer commands, but they become *a promise* that God will not break. Because of our new nature, we are *promised* that the nature of Christ in us will fulfill them, for when you love, you will not break the Ten Commandments.

We which live are always delivered unto death for Jesus' sake. Why? "That the life also of Jesus might be *made manifest* in our mortal flesh." This is the appearing of the Lord! That is what we want to see. His death took any death in us away, that his life might be manifested out of our mortal flesh. It is already happening! It is not just something that is going to happen. The measure to which our minds are renewed to the finished work of Calvary, is the measure in which we are experiencing the birthing of the nature of Jesus Christ. What we see, we become. And when we see him as he is, we will be like him. When we view the finished work of Calvary, we will manifest that completely and totally. And it has already begun.

Now let's go on to Revelation 7:1-3:

> And after these things I saw four angels standing on the four corners of the earth, holding the four winds of the earth, that the wind should not blow on the earth, nor on the sea, nor on any tree. And I saw another angel ascending from the east, having the seal of the living God: and he cried with a loud voice to the four angels, to whom it was given to hurt the earth and the sea, Saying, 'Hurt not the earth, neither the sea, nor the trees, till we have sealed the servants of our God in their foreheads.'

In verse 1 John writes, "After these things." After what things? After the loosing of the seals that took place in chapter 6. We will study these verses in more detail in the succeeding book in this series. But now we will look at the sealing that takes place once the seals have been broken. Look at the phrase in verse 3, "Hurt not the earth, neither the sea, nor the trees, till we have sealed the servants of our God in their foreheads." Once the seals that have sealed the book on the backside have been broken, there will be a people who are sealed in the dimension of the Most Holy, the realm of life, the realm of Spirit, and they will go out no more. When they go out, it is a going out to minister to people in the Holy Place and the Outer Court and on out into the world, but they do not leave that dimension of Spirit that they have been sealed in. They are sealed in that realm. They are sealed in that dimension.

There is a people right now that are being *unsealed* and the life of the Lamb is flowing out of them, but they are also being *sealed* in that dimension as they continue to partake of bread and wine. In verse 3 he says, "Hurt not the earth, the sea, or the trees." We are not going to go forth and show humanity that they received a deadly blow until we are sealed in this realm. We must first have the revelation before we can give it to humanity. Having the revelation *is* the sealing.

Remember, in Ezekiel 9:1-4, they were to go forth into the City and they were to mark certain people. That word "mark" in the Hebrew is "tav," which is written in the form of a cross, and we'll look at that again later on. Today we are being sealed in our foreheads as our minds are being renewed with the finished work of Calvary and our identification with it. This is the system of truth that God gave the apostle Paul.

We are being sealed in that realm of life as on the Day of Atonement. On the Day of Atonement, there was a fit man that laid hands upon two goats. One goat was killed and blood was sprinkled seven times before the Ark. But the other goat was sent out into the wilderness never to return again. History tells us that the first time they sent that goat out that was never to return, it returned! So, they took it and shoved it off a cliff so that it would never return again! That is what Jesus did on the Day of Atonement. He took our old man and got rid of him so he would never return again.

This is exactly what we have done in saying we have two natures—the goat nature versus the sheep nature. The goat that was sent out returned the first time, but now we are taking a *second look* and it will never return again! We will never again think that we have two natures. Jesus said he shall separate the sheep from the goats—and the sheep inherit the kingdom! Let's make sure the goat does not return this time! And *this is the Day* of Atonement! When we get to Revelation chapter 16 and see the seven vials that are poured out upon a people, that represents the Day of Atonement to us. That is what is happening right now! I *want* seven vials—the fullness of the death of Christ—to be poured out between my ears, so there can come an *apokalupsis,* an unveiling of the Christ—the revelation of Jesus Christ. This is exactly why the book of

Revelation was given to John for us.

I have shared with you that Joseph of Arimathaea begged the body of Jesus after his death. He spent his whole life carving a tomb out of the rock. That is what we are doing—carving a tomb out of the rock. Seeing the tomb that we were placed in and buried in over 2000 years ago—and the Rock is Christ. Joseph spent his lifetime carving that tomb and he thought that he was going to be buried in it. But he begged the body of Jesus after his death and he buried Jesus there instead, typifying that Jesus' death was Joseph of Arimathaea's death. That is what is happening to us. We are seeing that Jesus' death was our death.

In the past, when our minds were only renewed in part, we just had our old man laid away in some parlor. We saw him crucified and dead, but not buried. If he is not buried we think he is able to resurrect at any time. We must see him buried. That will bring closure. Then we will know that he cannot return or be resurrected. The first Adam was not resurrected. If we are going to overcome on a consistent basis, then we need to understand not only that our old man was crucified, dead, and buried, but we need to understand *how* that happened. When we understand how that happened, then when the enemy of our soul comes or situations come, we can say, "There is no way I am going to receive that because over 2000 years ago at the cross of Calvary, that was done away with. My old man and the effects of Adam were crucified, done away with, and buried." When we see how that happened—and that is what we are gaining when we understand these horses—we have overcoming power that begins to be released within our lives. When the enemy of our soul comes and begins to tempt us with, "You aren't this and you aren't that"—as the little Shulamite thought, "I am black as the tents of Kedar"—if we understand *how* the old man was done away with, we have overcoming power. Applying the cross to our lives removes who we used to be until only Jesus remains.

The world is crying out, "We would see Jesus." The Church world is crying out—they may not fully know it—they've seen miracles and heard great, swelling messages, but their heart's cry is, "We would see Jesus!" That is why they are saying so strongly, "He could physically come any minute." Why? Because they want to get out of the wilderness they are in. In other words, they want to experience freedom and release and they think that if the Lord comes and literally raptures them away, they are going to have a cabin in the corner of glory land and *then* they'll be happy. And that is what they are looking for. It is true that they need to be looking for the coming of the Lord because he is going to come to them that look for him, but they are looking in the wrong place. Jesus spoke of those who look for him in many places except *the one place* where he will appear. Look at Matthew 24:26-28:

> Wherefore if they shall say unto you, 'Behold, he is in the desert;' go not forth: 'behold, he is in the secret chambers;' believe it not. For as the *lightning* cometh out of the *east,* and shineth even unto the west; so shall also *the coming of the Son of man be. For wheresoever the carcase is, there will the eagles be gathered together* (emphasis added).

This is my paraphrase: "If they say to you, 'He is in the desert, the Church in the wilderness,' or 'He is in some literal temple in natural Israel,' or 'He is in the literal eastern sky on a literal white horse,' go not forth. Believe it not. But to those of you who can hear what the Spirit is saying, to those of you who are mine, I'll tell you where I appear." Then Jesus spoke of lightning that comes out of the east. Lightning can come from any direction. So he was talking about a certain kind of lightning. This lightning comes out of the east and shines even unto the west. It lit up the whole sky! The east is the place where the sun rises only after it has gone down in the west. Jesus, the Son arose only after the death. This special lightning that Jesus spoke of is the enlightening that we receive because we have, as the eagles, gathered around the carcass, the death of Christ. Remember, Jesus was resurrected as the flying eagle. When we view the death, when we focus on the death, when we partake of the death, we express his eagle nature and we share in his resurrection life. Only when we follow him in the baptism of his death will we come forth manifesting his resurrection life.

To view the death from the viewpoint of the followers of Jesus who stood around the cross that day—from the viewpoint of the ground up—is to walk away thinking that your hopes and dreams died that day. But to view the death from the viewpoint of the eagle is to see that your hope and your dream is within you waiting to be manifested and expressed. To view the death from the viewpoint of the eagle is to see the finished work of Christ in you and in others. Jesus is appearing to the eagles (plural) who are gathered around the carcass, those who are focusing and feasting on the death. Do you want to see his appearing? Gather round the carcass.

In John chapter 12, Philip and Andrew came to Jesus and said, "Jesus, the Greeks want to see you." But instead of going out to meet the Greeks, Jesus gave Philip and Andrew an agricultural lesson. In verse 24, Jesus said, "Except a corn of wheat fall into the ground and die, it abideth alone: but if it die, it bringeth forth much fruit." Many people take "the ground" here as Jesus' burial. But Jesus was not buried under the ground. Jesus was laid in a tomb that Joseph of Arimathaea spent his whole life carving out. We are going to spend the rest of our lives carving out a tomb—coming to realize that his death was our death—so we can be sealed in the forehead and manifest the life of the Lamb.

Let's look at the story in John 12:20-21:

> And there were certain Greeks among them that came up to worship at the feast: The same came therefore to Philip, which was of Bethsaida of Galilee, and desired him, saying, 'Sir, we would see Jesus.'

This is what the Church is saying! This is what the world is saying! We want to see Jesus! We want to see an appearing of the Lord in the midst of the body! And even though many are declaring that the appearing is going to be as Jesus splits a literal sky and comes on a literal white horse, they do not even realize it, but they are hungering for his appearing in the midst of a people. Even though they may not understand it, their spirit is hungering for the manifestation of the body of Christ in the earth!

Continuing in John 12:22-23:

> Philip cometh and telleth Andrew: and again Andrew and Philip tell Jesus. And Jesus answered

them, saying, 'The hour is come, that the son of man should be glorified.'

Then in verse 24 Jesus says, "Verily, verily," or "truly, truly," or *"pay attention to this because this is important:"*

> Verily, verily, I say unto you, except a corn of wheat fall into the ground and die, it abideth alone: but if it die, it bringeth forth much fruit.

Wheat speaks of death. Barley speaks of life. People want to see Jesus appearing out of us, his body. The appearing of the Lord does not come forth out of a people who are always meditating only on the resurrection life. The appearing of the Lord comes forth from a people who always bear about in the body, the death of Christ. The eagles are gathered around the carcass. Eat the bread, drink the wine, and show forth his ... *death* ... until he appears. Jesus says, "Except a corn of wheat fall into the ground and die, it abideth alone: but if it die, it bringeth forth much fruit." Not just fruit, not just more fruit, but *much* fruit—a full manifestation of Christ.

John 12:24 has been so misrepresented. The death of Jesus is implied, *and we* are included in this scripture too. The seed falls into the ground. What does the ground represent? It is not talking about Jesus being buried. He was not buried six-feet under. He was buried in Joseph of Arimathaea's tomb. The ground represents the ground of our hearts. We read in Matthew's gospel about the sower sowing seed. Some of the seed fell on good ground and some fell on not such good ground. This is talking about the word concerning his death falling into the ground of our hearts, our understanding. This is about our coming once and for all to understand it is not first the glorified Christ that is going to release the life of the Lamb. But we are first sealed in our forehead concerning the crucifixion, the death, the burial, and our identification with it. The seed concerning his death is falling into the ground of our heart and we are coming to understand what happened at the cross of Calvary.

That word of his death is falling into the ground of our heart and notice, if it dies—in the ground of our heart, our understanding—it is going to bring forth not just fruit, not just more fruit, but much fruit! A complete reproduction of the king! And his life will only be reproduced when we realize that we were crucified with him. He is the firstborn among *many* brethren—*much* fruit! And I believe with all of my heart that right now, I am sowing seed in good soil! The whole truth of his death is falling in the ground, on good soil, and it is going to bring forth much fruit in our midst! There is coming forth a manifestation like we have never experienced before! When we come to Mt. Bether, the mountain of suffering, and we see that his death was our death, his suffering was our suffering, his burial was our burial, the life of the Lamb is going to appear. The residue that is yet in our minds will be moved out of the way completely.

We need to understand this and let the word fall into the ground of our hearts. What word? The word of Jesus' death. Jesus became sin and died spiritually. We have to know that and we have to reckon it. Paul talks about the fact that we were crucified with Christ and that we need to know this in order to overcome. Our old man was crucified and now we are to reckon it.

What does it mean to "reckon?" "Reckon" is an accounting term. It is like balancing your checkbook to the penny so that you know how much money you can draw out of your account. Reckoning goes beyond just knowing that you were crucified at the cross of Calvary. But as you look at every scripture and every detail, you're reckoning it to be so. You're counting on the fact that when you write the check, the money is going to be there. You know that you were crucified with Christ and now you're reckoning it to be so. Now you can count on the fact that you were crucified with Christ and that Jesus was made to be sin so that you could be made the righteousness of God in him. Righteousness was deposited into your account. An exchange took place. That reckoning is going to release the power of God in your midst to live and to walk above sin or whatever it is that seems to be harassing you from the natural realm. You are reckoning that the word of God will fulfill itself in your life.

To reckon also means to know *how* it happened. You are "thinking on these things" and simply believing the word. We must know and we must reckon. We have to know that we can count on the fact that righteousness was deposited in our account. As we have said many times, he was not just a sin offering, otherwise, we are just forgiven sinners, or sinners saved by grace. We are forgiven and we are saved by grace—but we are new creations in Christ Jesus! As we know *and* reckon, as we renew our minds to this, there will come an appearing of the Lord!

I receive news letters from month to month by many that blatantly come out and say that Jesus did not become sin, he was just a sin offering. Well then, if that is true, we must have a new sin offering every year! We've been crucifying the Son of God afresh! No wonder his visage is marred more than any mans! Jesus drank the bitter cup. He took it within himself. He became sin. When you take something into yourself whether eating or drinking, it becomes you. Jesus drank the bitter cup.

So, in Revelation chapter 6 why are the horses in this order? The horses are not just arbitrarily there. They are there for a reason. They are there in a certain, systematic order for a reason—so that we can gain understanding from Paul's system of truth, through John, who heard from the Holy Spirit. If they are taught in the proper order, they will release life.

Let's look again at Romans 6:1-11:

> What shall we say then? Shall we continue in sin, that grace may abound? God forbid. How shall we, that are dead to sin, live any longer therein? Know ye not, that so many of us as were baptized into Jesus Christ were baptized into his death? Therefore we are buried with him by baptism into death: that like as Christ was raised up from the dead by the glory of the Father, even so we also should walk in newness of life. For if we have been planted together in the likeness of his death, we shall be also in the likeness of his resurrection: Knowing this, that our old man is crucified with him, that the body of sin might be destroyed, that henceforth we should not serve sin. For he that is dead is freed from sin. Now if we be dead with Christ, we believe that we shall also live with him: Knowing that Christ being raised from the dead dieth no more; death hath no more dominion over him. For in that he died, he died unto sin once: but in that he liveth, he liveth unto God.

> Likewise reckon ye also yourselves to be dead indeed unto sin, but alive unto God through Jesus Christ our Lord.

In verse 1, Paul says, "What shall we say then? Shall we continue in sin, that grace may abound?" There is the question. In verses 2 and 3, is the argument: "God forbid. How shall we, that are dead to sin, live any longer therein? Know ye not, that so many of us as were baptized into Jesus Christ were baptized into his death?" In other words, the argument is, how can a dead man sin? If you would walk up to a dead man in a casket and slap him on his face, he would not slap you back. He is dead. If we are dead indeed unto sin, we will not live any longer therein. Seeing that the old man is crucified, dead, and buried is going to release the power to live above sin. When we come to know this as verse 6 says, and to reckon this as verse 11 says, it is going to release the ability of God in our midst to overcome whatever it is that came as a result of the curse of Adam and that which was nailed to the cross of Calvary. When we know this *and reckon this* it will break the seals on the backside and it will release the life of the Lamb to flow out of us on a consistent basis.

What Paul is saying in Romans 6:3 is, "Don't you know this—that you were baptized into his death?" Notice what he says next, in verse 4: "Therefore we are buried with him by baptism into death: that like as Christ was raised up from the dead by the glory of the Father, even so we also should walk in newness of life." You are not only crucified and dead in that death, but you are buried with him by baptism into death. Because of our death with him we are also raised with him, so we should walk in newness of life. Now Romans 6:5-7:

> For if we have been planted (notice that—planted) together in the likeness of his death, we shall be also in the likeness of his resurrection: Knowing this, that our old man is crucified with him that the body of sin might be destroyed, that henceforth we should not serve sin. For he that is dead is freed from sin (parenthesis added).

In verse 6, the Greek says, "That our old man *was* crucified with him." A dead man can't sin. "The body of sin" in verse 6 is the man of sin, the first Adam, who was destroyed at Calvary.

You may be thinking, "But I sin every once in a while." Reality says, "That isn't you. That is the residue of that old man that is yet over your mind." People say, "Get real." But do we really want people to get real? Because reality means that we speak what is true of ourselves and of others in the realm of Spirit, the realm of truth, and not from the appearance realm—no matter what that is— whether it is sickness, poverty, despair, or sin. To get real means that I speak of what is true of me in the heavens. When we speak of what is true of us in the heavens we are just releasing something that God already created.

I heard someone say that there is a difference between fact and truth. I agree. The factual realm is the appearance realm. If we speak from the appearance realm, the people will faint. For example; the appearance realm says that people have problems. The appearance realm says that someone may be depressed and taking antidepressants. The appearance realm says they may have received a bad report from their doctor. The appearances say their kids need braces. The appearances say it's time to balance the checkbook. The appearance realm says college tuition is due next week. The appearance realm says that someone was laid off from their job last week. The appearances say that someone may be doing something they should not do. The appearances say that they are acting like sinners. Are you feeling faint yet?

But the truth is that if we speak from the realm of appearance, people will become discouraged. The truth is that they are the head and not the tail, above only and not beneath! The truth is that the blessings of God are chasing them down and overtaking them! The truth is, the fruit of their body is blessed! The truth is, they're blessed when they come in, and blessed when they go out! The truth is, their enemies are smitten before their face! The truth is the Lord has commanded blessing upon their storehouses and in everything that they set their hands to! The truth is that they are rich— exceedingly abundantly above all that they could ever think or hope or ask or dream! The truth is that they are healed! The truth is they are *not* sinners—they are new creations in Christ Jesus! The truth is, the Lord has established them as a holy people unto himself and all the people of the earth see that they are called by the Name of the Lord! The truth is that all of this happened at the cross of Christ Jesus our Lord—and we are in him!

If you are not mature enough to hear me by the Spirit, you will think that I just gave you a license to sin. If you understand the book of Galations, then you will know that the immature cannot experience or enjoy their inheritance because they are in bondage under the elements of the world and under the law. Children will spend their inheritance on riotous living instead of Godly living. This is not a children's book. This is for bondservants only.

Paul ministers grace to the Roman Christians and in so many words, he is saying, "The reason you cannot live above sin, the reason you are having such a hard time in your life is simply because you do not know this: our old man was crucified. He did *not* say, "The reason you cannot live above the natural is because you don't know that Jesus was quickened and resurrected." Let's read it in Romans 6:6:

> Knowing this, that our old man is crucified with him, that the body of sin might be destroyed, that henceforth we should not serve sin.

So, how are we going to live above sin? By knowing this! The majority of the Church has not known this: our old man was crucified. If the Church did know this—in experience—there would be holiness and righteousness and virtue in the Church today. So we must know this, and we must go beyond just knowing, because all of us "know" that our old man was crucified. To understand this, look at Romans 6:11:

> Likewise reckon ye also yourselves to be dead indeed to sin, but alive unto God through Jesus Christ our Lord.

Notice the word "reckon." We know something, but now we have to reckon it. How is this going to happen? Let's look at Romans 6:17:

> But God be thanked, that ye *were* the servants of sin, but ye have obeyed from the heart *that form of doctrine* which was delivered you (emphasis added).

This is Paul's system of truth, his form of doctrine. This is like the wood that is laid *in order* upon the fire in Leviticus chapter 1. And the horses ride out *in order* in Revelation chapter 6—a systematic way of teaching the death, the burial, and the resurrection. As I explained earlier, these horses in Revelation 6 are a transaction. They are connected to one another. The white horse leads us to the red horse which leads us to the black horse which leads us to the pale horse. There is a systematic way of teaching the death, burial, and resurrection. We do not just throw these seeds out, but we teach it in a specific order so the Holy Spirit can quicken it to our hearts. Unless you know that Jesus walked in his earthly life, in total righteousness and holiness and did not sin one time, it would not mean anything to know that he became sin. If he had sinned, then he would have had to go to the cross for himself and die for himself, because the wages of sin is death.

But Jesus did not sin and that leads us to the red horse. He became sin for us and as us. The red horse then, leads us to the black horse. After Jesus became sin, he died spiritually. After he died spiritually, the black horse leads us to the pale horse—he went into hell. Death and hell followed after him, after he became sin and died spiritually (Revelation 6:8).

Notice the past tense in Romans 6:17, "Ye *were* the servants of sin." Then he talks about the "form of doctrine." Now, the Weymouth's translation of Romans 6:17 is:

> But thanks be to God, that though you were once enthralled unto sin, you have now yielded a hearty obedience to that *system of truth* in which you have been instructed (emphasis added).

So, these horses travel, if you will, in a systematic way. These horses reveal the same message that Paul the apostle revealed.

In the book of Revelation we see what must be sealed after we are unsealed. If you are thinking, "You said we have to be unsealed and then we have to be sealed," you are right on. Let's look at what must be sealed after we are unsealed, beginning with Revelation 7:1-3:

> And after these things I saw four angels standing on the four corners of the earth, holding the four winds of the earth, that the wind should not blow on the earth, nor on the sea, nor on any tree. And I saw another angel ascending from the east, having the seal of the living God: and he cried with a loud voice to the four angels, to whom it was given to hurt the earth and the sea, Saying, 'Hurt not the earth, neither the sea, nor the trees, till we have sealed the servants of our God in their foreheads.'

"After these things," he said in verse 1. After what things? After we have beheld the Lamb slain and the seals have been broken—crucified, died, buried, crucified with, died with, buried with—we will be sealed in our foreheads. Not until those seals are broken and out of us comes the understanding—quickened, raised, and seated, quickened with, raised with, and seated with—will the life of the Lamb flow out of us bringing a full manifestation of Christ in the earth. After these things, after the loosing of the first six seals, John saw four angels standing on the four corners of the earth, holding the four winds of the earth, that the wind should not blow on the earth, nor on the sea, nor on any tree.

It is interesting that we are being unsealed from that which has sealed up the book, but at the same time, we are being sealed in a dimension and in a realm of Spirit—the Most Holy Place. As it says in Revelation 3:12; we go *in* the temple of God and out no more. When we have been *unsealed,* we experience a life in God that *seals us in.* That is understanding. That is knowing and reckoning. Once the seals are broken and the life of the Lamb flows out, this sealing, beginning in Revelation chapter 7, brings us into a place where we no longer manifest anything except the nature of God at all times. Do you think that is impossible? God deals in the realm of the impossible! What is impossible with man is possible with God. We are living in a time when a people are being sealed in that dimension right now. As they behold the Lamb slain, the seals are broken and out of them is flowing the life of the Lamb.

Now let's look at Revelation 7:2-3 again:

> And I saw another angel ascending from the east, having the seal of the living God: and he cried with a *loud voice* to the four angels, to whom it was given to hur.t the earth and the sea, saying, 'hurt not the earth, neither the sea, nor the trees, till we have sealed the servants of our God *in* their foreheads' (emphasis added).

Ezekiel wrote about a people that cried and sighed for the abominations that were in the midst of the Church, and they were marked with a mark in the forehead. Look at Ezekiel 9:1-4, to see what it is that we are going to be, *and are being* sealed with, in type:

> He cried also in mine ears with a *loud voice,* saying, Cause them that have charge over the city to draw near, even every man with his destroying weapon in his hand. And, behold, six men came from the way of the higher gate, which lieth toward the north, and every man a slaughter weapon in his hand; and one man among them was clothed with linen, with a writer's inkhorn by his side: and they went in, and stood beside the brasen altar. And the glory of the God of Israel was gone up from the cherub, whereupon he was, to the threshold of the house. And he called to the man clothed with linen, which had the writer's inkhorn by his side; And the LORD said unto him, Go through the midst of the city, through the midst of Jerusalem, and set a mark *upon* the foreheads of the men that sigh and that cry for all the abominations that be done in the midst thereof (emphasis added).

Here we see some people that were sealed upon their forehead. In Revelation 7, we read that we are being sealed *in* our foreheads—not *on* our foreheads! Why was it *upon* the forehead in Ezekiel and *in* the forehead in Revelation? Before Jesus' death on the cross, man had an "outside" relationship with God. It is only because of the death of Christ that we can have an intimate inner relationship with God. This is not some Hebrew or Greek inscription or any other inscription for that matter, written on the outside that can only be seen with a laser beam of light. Those that teach the book of Revelation as anything other than the revelation of Jesus Christ say that if you have the mark of the beast, you're going to get stamped with a number and only a laser or a digital signal can read that mark or that number—or whatever it is that they are teaching now—and it has probably changed since last week. But the word of God says, "Sealed *in* the forehead." It is not some literal inscription or some mark of God on the outside, but we are sealed on the inside with One Thing.

In type, we see this sealing in Ezekiel 9:1. "He cried also in mine ears with a loud voice." This is the same loud voice as in Revelation 7:2. Ezekiel continues, saying, "Cause them that have charge over the city to draw near." Those that have charge over the city are the Church. The ministers need to draw near today. There is a famine for the hearing of the word in the midst of the ministry today. The Lord promised that if we'd draw near unto him, he would draw near unto us.

Let's continue in Ezekiel 9. "Cause them that have charge over the city to draw near, even every man with his destroying weapon in his hand. And, behold, six men (crucified, died, buried, crucified with, died with, buried with), came from the way of the *higher gate,* which lieth toward the north, and every man a slaughter weapon in his hand; and *one man among them was clothed with linen,* with a writer's inkhorn by his side: and they went in, and stood beside (of all places) *the brazen altar,*" (which represents the cross). As we know, the number 6 is the number of man. Again we see the story of the first Adam being done away with at the cross. Notice, it says "One man among them was clothed with linen." Jesus was that one man without sin. He hath made him to be sin for us, who knew no sin; that we might be made the righteousness of God in him.

Ezekiel 9:3-4 continues, "And the glory of the God of Israel was gone up from the cherub, whereupon he was, to the threshold of the house. And he called to the man clothed with linen, which had the writer's inkhorn by his side; And the Lord said unto him, go through the midst of the city, through the midst of Jerusalem (go through the midst of the Church), and set a mark upon the foreheads of the men that sigh and that cry for all the abominations that be done in the midst thereof." Today this is being done spiritually.

When we look at the word "mark" in verse 4, the Hebrew takes us to "tav." The word "tav" is the last letter of the Hebrew alphabet and it was originally written in the form of a cross.[38] Those in the midst of the Church that are sighing and crying because of all the abominations, or because there is not an appearing of the Lord in manifestation, are being marked with the form of a cross. We are being sealed in our forehead (in our mind) with the understanding of the cross. The sealing of the saints in the forehead in Revelation chapter 7 refers to being sealed with the cross. Because of the cross of Jesus Christ we are sealed in the Most Holy Place dimension.

We are being sealed with the death of Christ. Again, the sealing is exactly what happened in type, on the Day of Atonement when the scapegoat was taken by the hand of a *fit man,* out into the wilderness, never again to return (Leviticus 16). There were two goats and they cast lots upon them. One of them was to be killed and the blood was sprinkled seven times before the Ark of the Covenant. The killing of the first goat represented Jesus dying physically. Then, by the hand of a fit man, the second goat was taken and loosed into the wilderness, into an uninhabited place. We are being sealed in our forehead with the cross, the death of Christ. We are "fit." We are the righteousness of God in Christ. This uninhabited place represents the place where Jesus died outside the camp. That goat was never to return again. The man of sin, the first Adam, will never return again because he is crucified, dead, and buried. We are being sealed in a dimension that we are never going to come out of again because of Jesus' death outside the camp. We are being sealed with the cross, sealed with the understanding of the crucifixion, the death, and the burial. That is what seals us in our forehead never again to express anything but his life.

Dr. Kay Fairchild and Lisa Perdue, R.N.

The Pale Horse

Now we will look at the pale horse in Revelation 6:7-8:

> And when he had opened the fourth seal, I heard the voice of the fourth beast say, 'Come and see.' And I looked, and behold a pale horse: and his name that sat on him was Death, and Hell followed with him. And power was given unto them over the fourth part of the earth, to kill with sword, and with hunger, and with death, and with the beasts of the earth.

The beast who said, "Come and see" when the fourth seal was loosed was the flying eagle—and the pale horse came forth. John saw the pale horse and notice what he wrote next: "And his name ...." The word "name" means "nature." John saw a pale horse, and his name that sat on him was Death. John was saying that his *nature* that sat on him was death. Jesus' nature became death and he went into hell. He became sin. He died spiritually. He became all that we were in Adam. We have *already experienced* all of these devastating things—at the cross of Calvary over 2000 years ago. Why is it a pale horse or a "green" horse when "green" speaks of life? It was when Jesus was in hell that he was born from death unto life. He was born from death to life because he had become our sin and he died spiritually.

Jesus preached to the captives while he was in hell *after* he was quickened to life and *before* he was resurrected. Quickening, resurrection, and being seated are three different operations, as are crucified, died, and buried. For example, being buried is not the same as being crucified. So, we see three operations taking place after Jesus was laid in the tomb: he was quickened or made alive, he was raised, and he was seated. Between the time that he was quickened and raised he preached to the captives in hell.

How could a man that became death and hell—that became all that Adam was—preach to captives in hell, loose them from hell, and have them walk the streets of Jerusalem with him after his resurrection? Because from the time he was quickened, or made alive, and before he was resurrected, is when he preached to the captives, spoiled principalities and powers, and made an open show of them triumphing over them in the cross. They were not resurrected until after Jesus was resurrected. That is when he led captivity captive—he led a train of vanquished foes and he bestowed gifts on men (Ephesians 4:8, Amplified Bible). So John wrote, "And I looked, and behold a pale horse: and his name that sat on him was Death, and Hell followed with him." Jesus not only took on the nature of sin and death, but he went even further! He went into hell. And hell followed with him.

Now, Revelation 6:8b reads: "And power was given unto them over the fourth part of the earth, to kill with sword, and with hunger, and with death, and with the beasts of the earth." Four is the number of the universe. Four is the number of creation. It is always used in reference to all that is created—including Adam. Four is the number of the earthly nature, the number of the earth. So, the fourth part of the earth, which represents Adam and fallen creation, was completely done away with at the cross of Calvary. Power was given unto Jesus! Power has been given unto us also, as our mind is renewed to the death of Christ—understanding that he became sin, he died spiritually, and he went into hell. We have power over all that Adam brought into the world! Why? *A dead man has no power!* Now, we may try to resurrect him if we just leave him in the parlor. But if we see that he has been buried, and we get rid of that residue, we have power over him. He is gone! There is nothing to him! There is nothing to a dead man that is buried.

We need to see that no man ascends; no man is going to experience the *apokalupsis,* the appearing of Christ the Lord, unless he first descends! What does this mean to our lives? We need to always bear about in the body, the dying of the Lord Jesus Christ, that the life also of Jesus may be made manifest in our mortal bodies. We need to meditate first and foremost on the death of Christ. His death swallowed up death. That will release life! Ephesians 4:9 says, "Now that he ascended, what is it but that he also descended first into the lower parts of the earth?" He descended *first.* And where did he descend to? To the lower parts of the earth. That speaks of hell. Again, Jesus was not buried six feet under. He was laid in a tomb. The "lower parts of the earth" is hell. Ephesians 4:10: "He that descended is the same also that ascended up far above all heavens, that he might fill all things." And he took us with him! When he was quickened, when he was raised, when he was seated, he took us with him!

Whatever residue is left after the first three horses gallop through our minds, the fourth one will get rid of! Philippians 2:5-8 says:

> Let this mind be in you, which was also in Christ Jesus: Who, being in the form of God, thought it not robbery to be equal with God: But made himself of no reputation, and took upon him the form of a servant, and was made in the likeness of men: And being found in fashion as a man, he humbled himself, and became obedient unto death, even the death of the cross.

Let this mind be in you—this is what you should meditate about. What does the phrase mean, that he "was made in the likeness of men?" He became sin. Jesus emptied himself of everything that would be inconsistent with him being 100% man and he went to the cross, he became sin, and he died spiritually. He fully and completely identified with us in our fallen nature!

Now, let's see the quickening. When Jesus was in hell, in the heart of the earth, was when he was quickened. We looked at the scripture in Acts 2:24, that says he was loosed from the pains from death when he was raised. If he just died physically and not spiritually, he would have been loosed from the pains of death when he physically died. But it was when he was raised that he was loosed from the pains of death, which shows that he died spiritually and he was in hell.

Look at Ephesians 2:4-5. "But God, who is rich in mercy, for his great love wherewith he loved us, even when we were dead in sins, hath quickened us together with Christ ... ." The word "quickened" means "made alive." A person can be physically alive, yet if they are not in Christ they are spiritually dead. This passage clearly refers to spiritual death. If Jesus did not die spiritually how could we have been quickened (made alive) with him? He died a spiritual death because he became all that we were in Adam and when he was quickened or made alive, we were quickened and made alive together with him. Why would he have to be made alive if he did not die spiritually? We had to be made alive and we were made alive together at the same time that he was quickened and made alive. As Revelation chapter 1 says, he was the firstbegotten of the dead. Again, he was not the first one raised from physical death, so how could he be the firstbegotten of the dead? He was the first one that was born from spiritual death into spiritual life.

Jesus was made alive; he was quickened *in the spirit.* If he had to be quickened and justified in the spirit, then he had to have become sin and died spiritually. It is vitally important for us to understand that he became sin and died spiritually. It is also vitally important for us to understand that because of this, we are not just forgiven sinners! We *are* forgiven—our sins have been removed as far as the east is from the west—*and* we are brand new creations in Christ Jesus. I don't care if it doesn't look like it or if it doesn't feel like it, I am declaring reality! We are new creations in Christ Jesus! We are the righteousness of God in Jesus Christ, and that is not dependent on what we do or what we don't do! We are God's righteousness in the realm of Spirit and when we get that message, there will come a manifestation because of the self-fulfilling power of the word! Once we know it and reckon it, it is going to manifest!

1 Peter 3:18 says:

> For Christ also hath once suffered for sins, the just for the unjust, that he might bring us to God, being put to death *in* the flesh, but quickened *by* the Spirit.

Notice the words "in" and "by." They are the same Greek words. If they are the same Greek word, then we must either use the word "in," or "by." So, is it more correct to say, "Being put to death in the flesh, but quickened in the Spirit?" Or is it more correct to say, "Being put to death by the flesh, but quickened by the Spirit?" The second choice does not make sense. Jesus was put to death *in* the flesh, but quickened *in* the spirit. Then, 1 Peter 3:19 says, "By which also he went and preached unto the spirits in prison." When did he preach to them? Between the times that he was quickened and before he was physically raised. This is 1 Peter 3:18-19 in the

Amplified Bible:

> For Christ [the Messiah Himself] died for sins once for all, the Righteous for the unrighteous (the Just for the unjust, the Innocent for the guilty), that He might bring us to God. In His human body He was put to death, but He was made alive in the Spirit, in which He went and preached to the spirits in prison.

Jesus did so much more than we could ever realize with just one look at the cross. How can we truly give him all the praise, all the glory, all the honor due his name, unless we take a second look at the cross in this, the Feast of Tabernacles? It is vitally important that we partake of this bread and wine. How long? Until he comes! Look at 1 Timothy 3:16:

> And without controversy great is the mystery of godliness: God was manifest in the flesh, *justified in the Spirit,* seen of angels, preached unto the Gentiles, believed on in the world, received up into glory (emphasis added).

How would *God* have to be justified in the Spirit? Only when he emptied himself, identified with man through Jesus Christ, became sin, died spiritually, and went into hell—only then would he have to be justified in the Spirit. At the cross of Calvary, it was not that Jews and Gentiles became one. It is not even about Jews or Gentiles. It is about a new creation in Christ Jesus. And all of those things that pertain to whether we are Jew in the natural or whether we are Gentile in the natural have nothing to do with the plan of salvation.

Now look again, Revelation 6:8b:

> And power was given unto them over the fourth part of the earth, to kill with sword, and with hunger, and with death, and with the beasts of the earth.

My paraphrase is this: "And power was given unto them over

the fourth part of the earth, to kill *along with* the sword, and with hunger, and with death, and with the beasts of the earth." All of that is part of the curse that is found in Deuteronomy chapter 28. In Deuteronomy 28:22 we find:

> The Lord shall smite thee with a consumption, and with fever, and with an inflammation, and with an extreme burning, and with sword, and with blasting, and with mildew; and they shall pursue thee until thou perish.

Now compare the sword in Deuteronomy 28:22, with Isaiah 54:17 which says, "No weapon formed against you shall prosper." Why will no weapon formed against you prosper? Because over 2000 years ago, it was destroyed at the cross of Calvary. We see hunger in Deuteronomy 28:48. We see death in Deuteronomy 28:21-22 and 48. And we see the beasts of the earth in Deuteronomy 28:26. All of that was part of the curse. And cursed is everyone that hangeth on a tree!

Do you feel an overwhelming thanksgiving, praise, and worship exploding in your spirit right now? God is AWESOME! His word is a masterful masterpiece! Roasting the Lamb with fire evokes a holy awe and reverence which shakes the posts of the door and fills the temple with glory!

The Fifth Seal—The Souls Under The Altar

The fifth seal that is loosed involves our soul being under the altar. That is happening right now as we understand these horses in a systematic way, according to Paul's system of truth. If you are following with me in your understanding, we are now in Revelation chapter 6, verses 9-11. Our souls are under the altar. Then we are going to see a great earthquake—the resurrection. We will see something begin to happen to the natural light, the sun, which we've had over our minds. Then something will happen to the lesser light, the moon, that has also been in our minds. Then we are going to see a sealing in Revelation chapter 7. And in chapter 8, there is silence in heaven for about a half an hour.

All of this is what is happening right now. It has nothing to do with current events, although it is going to change the events that currently are. It has nothing to do with taking the book of Revelation and teaching a literal war, or a literal battle of Armageddon. It is a people—Mt. Zion—who are victors in the battle of the mind. We wrestle not against flesh and blood, but against principalities and powers in high places. Our minds are the high places. We win this war by casting down imaginations, by seeing the death, by bringing every thought into captivity, and by all of that which happens in our minds. It is not just knowledge. It is not just mind over matter. It is the truth of the death of Christ that is in our spirits flowing through our souls, manifesting outwardly so that every eye will see him.

As we appropriate these horses, the residue of Adam, or our old woman, or the veil that is yet untaken away, is being taken away from our minds. John wrote about the fifth seal (and five is the number of grace) in Revelation 6:9:

> And when he had opened the fifth seal, I saw under the altar the souls of them that were slain for the word of God, and for the testimony which they held:

The key word is "souls." John saw under the altar, the *souls* of them that were slain for the word of God, and for the testimony (or martyrdom), which they had—the death which they held. Notice it does not say that *they* were under the altar, but that their *souls* were under the altar. If it did say "they" were under the altar, it would be talking about literal martyrdom, which has happened and may happen in the future, but that is not what this is talking about. This is the revelation of Jesus Christ. They held this death in their understanding and they carried it in the life they lived unto God.

Notice, he says, "I saw under the altar." What altar? The brazen altar where, in type, Jesus, the perfect sacrifice was laid. Not the people, but their souls, were under the altar. Our old woman is being consumed. Any residue is being taken away because we are seeing that Adam was crucified, he's dead, and he is buried. Any residue of that Adam, as we understand *the* death, is being consumed. Our soul is under the brazen altar. We understand the sacrifice, we understand the death of Christ and notice—we are slain by what[39] and for what? We are slain by and for the word of God *and* for the testimony or martyrdom which we hold. Our testimony is this: "We are dead and our new, *real* life is hidden with Christ in God!" The sword of the word gets rid of the old mentality, the old soul thinking.

The apostle Paul wrote in Colossians chapters 2-3 of his great concern for the believers that they would come to know Christ in this same way—their souls under the altar, slain by and for the word of God and for the testimony which they held. And although he does not use the same words that John used, he spoke the same message to the body of Christ. It is a beautiful passage of scripture and I encourage you to read it.

On to Revelation 6:10:

> And they cried with a loud voice, saying, How long, O Lord, holy and true, dost thou not judge and avenge our blood on them that dwell on the earth?

If this is the revelation of Jesus Christ, they are *not* saying, "Lord, just how long is it going to be until you really zap those people that have persecuted us?" That is *not* the revelation! We're not saying, "O Lord, how long until you just really give them what they deserve?" Remember John looked behind him and saw everything that was accomplished in the work that Jesus finished at the cross. John's salutation was from he which is, and which was, and which is to come (Revelation 1:4). But John *saw* he who was (past), he who is (present), and he who is to come (future), in his second look at the cross (Revelation 1:19). John heard the saints of old saying, "How long now before you will sit in judgment and avenge our blood on them that dwell on the earth?" And he also heard God's answer—"Holy justice was satisfied upon the cross of Calvary where my judgment was fully poured out upon my only begotten Son." John also heard us today saying, "Lord, how long is it going to be until we are sealed in this dimension so that we can go out and give them the same bread and wine and feed them Lamb until the appearing of yourself takes place in them too?"

John completes the description of the fifth seal in Revelation 6:11:

> And white robes were given unto every one of them; and it was said unto them, that they should rest yet a little season, until their fellowservants also and their brethren, that should be killed as they were, should be fulfilled.

White robes speak of us being clothed with Jesus. He is our garment. He is the righteousness of God. Through his willingness to be made sin, we are made the righteousness of God in him. John goes on to speak of rest. We have been seated with him in his throne and our resting place is glorious! Look at Isaiah 11:10-11:

> And in that day there shall be a Root of Jesse, which shall stand for an ensign of the people; to It shall the Gentiles seek: *and His rest shall be glorious*. And it shall come to pass in that day, that the Lord shall set His hand again *the second time* to recover the remnant of His people ... (emphasis added).

His rest shall be glorious! And now his rest is our rest—just like the little Shulamite found—his bed is our bed. Did you catch the rest of that scripture? The Lord shall set his hand again *the second time* to recover the remnant of his people. This speaks of right here, right now, the Great Day of the feast—the Feast of Tabernacles—*the second look* at Passover. *In This Day,* our fellow servants and our brethren are realizing that they too were crucified with Christ. Now they are experiencing being quickened, raised, and seated in his resting place which is indeed, *glorious!*

Behold! He cometh with clouds, and every eye shall see him because there is a people who are beholding the Lamb. We will see the glorified Christ when we get into the quickening, the raising and the seating, but we must first see the dark side of Calvary because the treasures are in the darkness (Isaiah 45). There must first be a death before there can be a resurrection. We are not going to fully experience our marriage to Christ until we first realize that we were widowed from the old man. As we see that, the residue of Adam's thinking will be removed and Christ will appear, shining through our earthen vessels.

The Sixth Seal

To recap; Revelation chapters 2 and 3 are to him that overcomes, and the Lord tells us what is required of us in these chapters. But before he told us what is required of us, he told us something about himself, because we overcome by the blood of the Lamb and by the word of our testimony.

Unleavened bread is also seen in chapters 2 and 3. Leaven represents sin. The Feast of Unleavened Bread represents getting the dirt out of our house. How? Through the blood of the Lamb and by the word of our martyrdom—understanding the death of Christ and our identification with it.

Then, the Feast of Firstfruits is seen in Revelation chapters 4 and 5, where it speaks of a seating. In Revelation chapter 4, John sees the vision of the throne. Then, in chapter 5, he sees the book within, which represents Firstfruits—we were seated in heavenly places with Christ.

Then, in Revelation chapters 6 and 7 we see the Feast of Pentecost—the sealing of the saints. When we received the baptism of the Holy Spirit, that was a sealing—we were sealed with the Holy Spirit of promise which was a down-payment of something greater to come. We were sealed until the day of redemption with the Holy Spirit of Promise.

Let's look at the sixth seal in Revelation 6:12-17:

> And I beheld when he had opened the sixth seal, and, lo, there was a great earthquake; and the sun became black as sackcloth of hair, and the moon became as blood; And the stars of heaven fell unto the earth, even as a fig tree casteth her untimely figs, when she is shaken of a mighty wind. And the heaven departed as a scroll when it is rolled together; and every mountain and island were moved out of their places. And the kings of the earth, and the great men, and the rich men, and the chief captains, and the mighty men, and every bondman, and every free man, hid themselves in the dens and in the rocks of the mountains; And said to the moun-

> tains and rocks, Fall on us, and hide us from the face of him that sitteth on the throne, and from the wrath of the Lamb: For the great day of his wrath is come; and who shall be able to stand?

With the sixth seal, there is an earthquake recorded in verse 12. When did the great earthquake of earthquakes happen? It happened when Jesus was raised! Then the sun became black as sackcloth of hair, and the moon became as blood. Revelation 6:13 says, "And the stars of heaven fell unto the earth, even as a fig tree casteth her untimely figs, when she is shaken of a mighty wind." Now, let me ask you, what does the fig tree throughout the word of God symbolically point to? The fig tree represents natural Israel. It was lights out for natural Israel on the day of Pentecost. That does not mean that natural Israel was excluded, but that God has extended this salvation that Jesus bought and paid for, to all men—to every tongue and tribe and nation! So it was lights out for natural Israel, not in the sense that it is all over for Israel and they can never be saved. But it was lights out for natural Israel as far as being God's chosen, peculiar people. Now *all men* can become God's chosen, peculiar people as they accept the salvation of God. The same thing that happened on the day of Pentecost is recorded here in Revelation 6. Look at Acts 2:1 and 2:16-21:

> And when the day of Pentecost was fully come, they were all with one accord in one place. (Verses 16-21) But this is that which was spoken by the prophet Joel; 'And it shall come to pass in the last days, saith God, I will pour out of my Spirit upon all flesh: and your sons and your daughters shall prophesy, and your young men shall see visions, and your old men shall dream dreams: and on my servants and on my handmaidens I will pour out in those days of my Spirit, and they shall prophesy: and I will show wonders in heaven above, and signs in the earth beneath; blood, and fire, and vapour of smoke: The sun shall be turned into darkness, and the moon into blood, before that great and notable day of the Lord

come: and it shall come to pass, that whosoever shall call on the name of the Lord shall be saved.'

The sixth seal, the great earthquake, reveals Jesus' resurrection. On the day of Pentecost, the sun was turned into darkness and the moon into blood. The resurrected Christ baptizing us with the Holy Spirit correlates with Revelation 6:12, "There was a great earthquake and the sun became black as sackcloth of hair, and the moon became as blood." Isn't that what we just read in Acts chapter 2? So, it was "lights out" for natural Israel as far as their being the only ones that can receive salvation, and it was *lights on for the whole world!* Welcome Holy Spirit! Now, all Israel will be saved and all Russia will be saved, and all the United States will be saved, and all China will be saved, and every knee is going to bow out of *every* kindred, and tongue, and people, and nation! That is what we are going to see! There are some glorious truths concerning the sun, moon, and stars to be revealed in succeeding volumes that you won't want to miss.

Then, in Revelation 6:13, the stars, like the figs, fell from heaven, which again, refers to former rulers. In verse 14 the old heaven—the old way of thinking—departed as a scroll and every other kingdom of man was moved out of the way. Then Revelation 6:15-17 mentions seven levels of men. This represents the fullness of man. Man's system has tried with all of his strength to protect his kingdom from being destroyed, but it did not and cannot stand.

The River Of God

In Revelation chapter 7, we will see the seventh seal opened. We will look at that in the succeeding volume. But for now, let's jump into the river of God. In the latter part of the book of Revelation, John describes a City who has come to understand the death of Christ. Out of them flows a river of life as clear as crystal. Ezekiel was shown this same river in chapter 47. The river flows from a people who look eastward or toward the rising of the sun. This is a people who are always beholding the face of the Lord. Then the Lord, with a measuring line *in* his hand, measured a thousand cubits and there the waters were ankle deep. He measured another thousand cubits to waters that were knee deep. Then he measured another thousand cubits to waters that were waist deep. The fourth time, the Lord measures another thousand cubits and the waters were so deep that they were waters to swim in. It was a river that could not be passed over. Four times (the number of all creation), the Lord measures this river of life which reaches out to all creation and *everything* that comes in contact with this river lives! This precious river then flows to the Dead Sea (those who are spiritually dead) and all of lost humanity is healed and made fresh, or made alive by the river of life! The water that flows from the east side of the temple is pristine and deep—calling unto deep—as we come to understand the finished work of Calvary where the water first began to flow at the piercing of Jesus' side.

The book of Revelation is a carbon copy of the book of Ezekiel. At the end of Revelation, we see a City out of which flows a river, which is God. And in the end of the book of Ezekiel, there is a City and the name of the City is "The Lord is there!"

The Firmament Stretched Forth

With that in mind, let's read Ezekiel 1:22:

> And the likeness of the firmament upon the heads of the living creature was as the colour of the terrible crystal, stretched forth over their heads above.

Living creatures or Cherubim are those who are apprehended—gripped by the cross of Calvary. The word "firmament," in the Hebrew refers to "seed" and also refers to having our mind renewed to the word of God because the firmament is stretched forth upon our mind. A seed speaks of reproduction. So as our minds are renewed to God's word, a reproduction of his nature takes place.

An example of this is found in 2 Corinthians 5:1-8:

> For we know that if our earthly house of this tabernacle were dissolved, we have a building of God, an house not made with hands, eternal in the heavens. For in this we groan, earnestly desiring to be

clothed upon with our house which is from heaven: If so be that being clothed we shall not be found naked. For we that are in this tabernacle do groan, being burdened: not for that we would be unclothed, but clothed upon, that mortality might be swallowed up of life. Now he that hath wrought us for the selfsame thing is God, who also hath given unto us the earnest of the Spirit. Therefore we are always confident, knowing that, whilst we are at home in the body, we are absent from the Lord: (For we walk by faith, not by sight:) We are confident, I say, and willing rather to be absent from the body, and to be present with the Lord.

There is a firmament that is stretched forth. The word "firmament" also means "expanse," which comes from the root word meaning "burdened" or "to expand by hammering." It is like taking a piece of gold and hammering it until it is a thin sheet that can be overlaid onto something else, as was the Ark of the Covenant. And that is what God is doing. He is hammering on our minds with the finished work. Our minds are experiencing a labor as they are being changed.

2 Corinthians chapter 5 is usually preached at funerals, but I believe it is applicable to right now. And I believe this is what is happening as our minds are being burdened or renewed as we are laboring to enter into rest by seeing the death of Christ and our identification with that. Verse 1 says, "For we know that if our earthly house of this tabernacle were dissolved, we have a building of God, an house not made with hands, eternal in the heavens." That word "dissolved" is "thoroughly loosened." In other words, as we hear the word, the salvation that is in our spirit is coming into our mind and changing this outward house.

Notice 2 Corinthians 5:2; "For in this we groan, earnestly desiring to be clothed upon with our house which is from heaven." What does it mean to be clothed upon with our house which is from heaven? The death of Christ got rid of the old man which was nothing but death. Then the life we receive as a result of seeing that death swallows up any residue in our soul and bodies. Right now, this house which is from heaven, our spirit, is clothing our soul. Our mind is being renewed. The spirit is clothing, flowing to the soul and we are getting the same God, the same salvation that is in our spirit, into our soul—our mind, our will, and our emotions. We are the Sun-clothed woman!

Continuing with 2 Corinthians 5:3, "If so be that being clothed we shall not be found naked." When our house, our spirit, clothes our soul, we are not going to be naked but we are going to realize that we are the righteousness of God in Christ Jesus and it is going change everything that needs changing.

2 Corinthians 5:4 says, "For we that are in this tabernacle do groan." Do you ever find yourself groaning that there can be that change within your life? Not only do we groan to manifest the nature of Christ and no longer live in guilt and condemnation, but we even groan for the changing of our bodies. "For we that are in this tabernacle do groan, being burdened: not for that we would be unclothed, but clothed upon, that mortality might be swallowed up of life." When this tabernacle of spirit clothes our soul, it is going to change the physical body! In the Old Testament, the priests garment was made of three layers. Paul prayed that our spirit and soul and body would be preserved blameless unto the coming of our Lord Jesus Christ. Paul also wrote of the redemption of our body in the book of Romans. Salvation is three-fold—spirit, soul, and body.

Then he wrote in 2 Corinthians 5:8, "We are confident, I say, and willing rather to be absent from the body, and to be present with the Lord." He is speaking of a place in God where we are no longer body-conscious—no longer led by the senses—no longer led by the appearance realm. This is a dimension of the Most Holy Place. When we see that we who are crucified with Christ in his death are now resurrected with him in his life (Colossians 3), we see that we are *now* a sun-clothed woman—and in Revelation 12, the sun-clothed woman births a manchild.

The word "burdened" in 2 Corinthians 5:4 comes from a word that means "a weighty or a grave matter." Something that is a weighty matter or a grave matter is something that has great significance. To see that his burden at Calvary was our burden is very important. What are our minds being burdened with, hammered on, and filled with? The fact that the old man is not only crucified, but he is dead and he has been buried.

So in Ezekiel 1:22, we read: "And the likeness of the firmament upon the heads of the living creature was as the colour of the terrible crystal, stretched forth over their heads above." Again, this phrase, "stretched forth," speaks of reproduction and mind renewal. Romans 12:2 says we are to be "transformed"—the same word that is used in the gospels when Jesus was on the mountain and was "transfigured" before them. We are transformed or transfigured by the renewing of our mind.

We also get the word "seed" from the phrase "stretched forth." We've already looked at John 12 where a seed falls into the ground of our heart renewing our mind to the death of Christ. As this takes place we will bring forth *much* fruit. There will be a *great* appearing of the Lord. That is what the phrase "stretched forth over our heads above" refers to.

Notice, it says, "stretched forth *over* their heads." It does not say "upon." If interpreted literally, one would say that it is referring to the atmospheric clouds or the firmament above. But it says, "stretched forth over" the Cherubim, or over the living creatures heads. The living creatures refer to people—meaning their minds are renewed or burdened about something that has to do with a weighty matter. This passage portrays the spirit being stretched forth, clothing our soul—and notice, it says it is as the colour of the "terrible crystal."

The Terrible Crystal

The word "terrible" means "awesome" and "reverence." The event that is going to ignite an awe and a reverence in us individually and corporately both in the Church world and in humanity, is when a Cherubim company, who are gripped by the cross, the death of Christ, have partaken of bread and wine long enough to enter into rest. This is something that is not happening out in the future so much as it is happening right now. And it is going to promote and ignite reverence in us and in others. It is going to ignite awe—the awe of the Lord.

The Star Of David

Some people are afraid to think in these terms, because when they hear the word "crystal," they immediately think about some "new age movement." However, if it's in the word, God wants us to understand it. Everything in the word of God is for the Church. But the Church has let religion steal the truth from them and pervert it. This word, "crystal," in the book of Ezekiel and in the book of Revelation is just one example.

The word "crystal" is the rock crystal or the quartz crystal. In Revelation, John shows us a river that flows out of the City that is as clear as crystal. There are two primary things about a crystal. First, it is hexagonal in shape, meaning there are six sides—crucified, died, buried, quickened, raised, seated. It is also bi-pyramidal, which means that it consists of two identical pyramids base to base. This is portraying the fact that because we have eaten Lamb, because we have partaken of bread and wine, we have the firmament that is as the color of the terrible crystal, stretched forth over our mind, causing spirit and soul to becoming one. The two pyramids—spirit and soul—have become one. It is the marriage supper of the Lamb. These two pyramids are base to base and as they become one they move into each other, forming the Star of David. We are the star of David—the Church—the bride of Christ who has become one with Jesus Christ the Lord, the Day Star, the Bright and Morning Star. ("And I will show wonders in the heaven above.")

The Pivot Of God

The crystal or the quartz has two primary uses. First, it was used for optical instruments. Today we are seeing as we've never seen before. Who needs a "crystal ball" when we have the Holy Spirit, the crystal of God who guides us into all truth? The crystal was also used in points of balance in pivots. Today crystals are still used as bearings for pivots in watches or compasses. Through a balanced people, God is pivoting and he is changing things according to his purpose and his will. Through these living creatures that are gripped by the cross, that have the firmament stretched forth, or their minds renewed to the finished work of Calvary, God is revolving and he is transforming things. One of the definitions of "resurrection" is "reversal." Adam made the garden a grave yard. At the cross, Jesus made the grave yard a garden! That was the great pivot of God. In the New Testament period, huge stone pivots were used in olive presses and wine presses. Jesus' pressing reversed the curse. God has a people today who are living in the beginning of the full manifestation of the pivot of God.

The Father's Vision, The Father's Dream

Also, Ezekiel 1:22 mentions the "color" of the terrible crystal. First of all, rock quartz crystal has no color. This word "colour" is the Hebrew "'ayin," which means "an eye." Jesus said, "If the eye be single, the whole body will be filled with light." He was referring to vision. We are a people who are no longer asking Father God to fulfill our vision, but we want to fulfill the *Father's* vision! We are a people who want to make *God's* dreams come true!

The word from which crystal is translated is found three times as "frost," three times as "ice," and one time as "crystal" in the Old Testament. I want you to see what the awesome crystal, the single-mindedness, the expanse, the firmament stretched-forth, the seed falling into the ground of our hearts, will do in the midst of a people.

Look at Job 37:10; "By the breath of God frost is given: and the breadth of the waters is straitened." What will this crystal do that is stretched forth over our heads? What will this spirit and soul do—this spirit and soul that become one through the repetitious hammering of the bread, the wine, and the Lamb—in the midst of our lives and in the midst of those that we come in contact with? When our mind is renewed, the rivers of living water clear as crystal flows out. Remember—everything that this crystal river comes in contact with is going to live. It is a river so deep it has to be swum in.

Now look at Job 38:29. "Out of whose womb came the ice? And the hoary frost of heaven, who hath gendered it?" The word "ice" here is the same word "crystal." Peter referred to the mind as the womb when he said "gird up the *loins* of your mind." Out of whose womb came the ice or the crystal? Out of the womb of our mind is coming this river that is clear as crystal. There is a people who are having this firmament stretched forth over their heads as the color or the eye of the terrible crystal. Their womb is being renewed with the finished work of Calvary. They have one mind. One vision. One purpose. One body. One spirit. One hope. One Lord. One faith. One baptism. One God and Father of all, who is above all and through all and in all!

God's Great Adventure

In Psalm 147:17, we find the word "crystal" again:

> He casteth forth his ice like morsels: Who can stand
> before his cold?

The word "ice" is "crystal." The phrase, "casteth forth" is "to hurl or to throw," and "adventure." The word "morsels" comes from a word that means "an opening" or "to open." When we understand that the book of Revelation is about Jesus, we come to see that his precious sacrifice, his death, brings one opening after another. This crystal, this gem, these hidden treasures of darkness (Isaiah 45:3, Colossians 2:3), become an adventure! As we cast forth this seed of the finished work of Calvary, talk about adventure! There is a huge amount of progress being made today in outer space adventure. This is just another natural picture of a spiritual happening—the adventure of inner space! And the morsel is opening! There is one opening after another. The Bible will become a brand new book when there comes a focusing.

What is the result of this crystal that is stretched forth over our head, renewing our minds to this finished work of Calvary? We'll find the answer in Genesis 31:40:

> Thus I was; in the day the drought consumed me,
> and the frost by night; and my sleep departed from
> mine eyes.

This frost will consume every bit of the residue of Adam.

In Job chapter 6, Job talks about people in verse 15—the deceitful brethren. Then he talks about discernment in verse 16:

> My brethren have dealt deceitfully as a brook, and as the stream of brooks they pass away; Which are blackish by reason of the ice, and wherein the snow is hid.

This crystal will bring forth discernment. Remember the red horse—a great sword of discernment is given to us. We can see those things that are "blackish." We can discern when this crystal is stretched forth over our heads and our minds are renewed to the finished work. We can see the deceitful brethren. We can see that residue of Adam that is manifesting. As we see that residue and confusion, we simply see an issue that needs to be ministered to by the cross of Christ. We don't condemn but neither do we condone. *We minister!*

Another example of words translated from the word crystal is found in the incident where Jeremiah the prophet brought a prophetic roll to king Jehoiakim and the king destroyed the roll. Look what he says in Jeremiah 36:30, using the word "frost" which is also translated "crystal:"

> Therefore thus saith the Lord of Jehoiakim king of Judah; He shall have none to sit upon the throne of David; and his dead body shall be cast out in the day to the heat, and in the night to the frost.

In other words, the gospel will bring the conviction of the Holy Spirit into people's lives destroying all residue of Adam.

The Revelation Of Jesus Christ

Can you see now, that the visions Ezekiel saw were the same visions that John received? We must completely identify with the finished work. In Revelation chapters 21-22, we see the Feast of Tabernacles. We see a people that is completed and manifesting the fullness because they understand the Lamb slain, they understand the horses, and they understand that the book of Revelation is a de-creation of what Adam created. It is *not* a seven year tribulation *in our future*. It is *not* blood up to the horses bridle *in our future*. It is *not* a literal battle of Armageddon *in our future.* It is something that took place over 2000 years ago at the cross of Calvary and the book of Revelation bears that out because it is the revelation of Jesus Christ. It is *continuing* to destroy the residue that is in our minds as we come to understand it.

So, lets read Ezekiel 1:22-25 again (parenthesis added): "And the likeness of the firmament upon the heads of the living creatures (the Cherubim, those gripped by the cross) was as the (eye or the) color of the terrible crystal, stretched forth over their heads above. And under the firmament were their wings straight, the one toward the other: every one had two, which covered on this side, and every one had two, which covered on that side, their bodies. And when they went, I heard the noise of their wings, like the noise of great waters, (we see this in Revelation!) as the voice of the Almighty, the voice of speech (because they are all speaking with the tongue of the learned), as the noise of an host: when they stood, they let down their wings. And there was a voice from the firmament that was over their heads, when they stood, and had let down their wings." Then Ezekiel goes on to write about opened heavens and the glory of the Lord that again, is seen in the book of Revelation.

So, what do we see in Ezekiel? We see a carbon copy of the book of Revelation. He sees a City out of which flows a river with water as clear as crystal because the firmament has been stretched forth over our heads (the seed of Christ) as the eye of the terrible crystal (we are single-minded). We can apply every use for the word crystal into the realm of spirit and what is happening to us right now—as in the natural; so in the spiritual. We are becoming one in our experience as we come to understanding. As I've mentioned before, the reason for the order of the books in the Bible, with Revelation being the sixty-sixth, is because God designed a progression of growth. After sixty-five books, we ought to know what this is all about! By now, we ought to understand that the whole Bible is about the Revelation of Jesus Christ—not the revelation of Newsweek Magazine! We ought to understand that we do not read the Bible like we read our newspaper, seeing horses as literal horses, seeing battles as literal battles, seeing wars as literal wars where there is devastation and famine and death. It already happened! It happened at Calvary. Now we are really beginning to understand it. The things John saw and wrote to us in the book of Revelation are a picture of what happened at the cross of Calvary and what is taking place as the residue of Adam's thinking is being taken away!

What a privileged people we are to live in such a time as this. This Day is unlike any day that humanity has ever known—the Day of The Revelation of Jesus Christ!

Chapter Five

The Origin Of The Religious World Order's Dispensational Theology

Most of us were taught that the book of Revelation is the revelation of future catastrophic events. We were also taught that Revelation chapter 4 describes a literal rapture of the Church. One reason we have not understood that the book of Revelation is the revelation of Jesus Christ and that Revelation chapter 4 speaks of the spiritual dimension of the Most Holy Place is because we have not been aware of the error that has been taught by the religious system. Some Christians have never even questioned the origin of those doctrines of man. The majority of the Church's dispensational theology was taught to *stop* the reformation! M. L. Moser, Jr. wrote[40]:

> Not only did the Reformers proclaim the mighty truth of justification by faith for the liberation of men's souls, but they nerved thousands to break from the tyranny of the dark ages of the papacy by clearly identifying the antichrist of Bible prophecy. The symbols of Daniel, Paul and John were applied with tremendous effect. The realization that the incriminating finger of prophecy rested squarely on Rome aroused the consciousness of Europe. In

alarm Rome saw that she must successfully counteract this identification of antichrist with the papacy or lose the battle. She must present plausible arguments which would cause men to look outside the medieval period for the development of antichrist. Jesuit scholarship rallied to the Roman cause by providing two plausible alternatives to the historical interpretation of the Protestants. 1.) Luis de Alcazar (1554-1630) of Seville, Spain, devised what became known as the 'preterist' system of prophetic interpretation. This theory proposed that the Revelation deals with events in the Pagan Roman Empire, that antichrist refers to Nero and that the prophecies were therefore fulfilled long before the time of the medieval church. Alcazar's preterist system has never made any impact on the conservative, or evangelical wing of the Protestant rationalists and liberals. 2.) A far more successful attack was taken by Fransisco Ribera (1537-1591) of Salamanca, Spain. He was the founder of the 'futurist' system of prophetic interpretation. Instead of placing antichrist way in the past as did Alcazar, Ribera argues that antichrist would appear way in the future. About 1590 Ribera published a five hundred page commentary on the Apocalypse, denying Protestant application of antichrist to the church of Rome.

While we do not agree with Moser's identification of antichrist, we are seekers of the truth and we want to show you where these doctrines originated. Moser gives historical information of religion's attempt to save their Babylonian kingdom. But religion is not confined to the Catholic Church. Religion is deeply ingrained in all who have a veil that remains untaken away, whether in the Church *or* in the world. Now, on the subject of futurism, this is what H. Grattan Guinness wrote[41]:

> Futurism is literalism, and literalism in the interpretation of symbols is a denial of their symbolic

character. It is an abuse and degradation of the prophetic word, and a destruction of its influence, It substitutes the imaginary for the real, the grotesque and monstrous for the sober and reasonable. It quenches the precious light which has guided the saints for ages, and kindles a wild, delusive marshfire in its place, It obscures the wisdom of Divine prophecy (and) it denies the true character of the days in which we live ...

Alcazar ran to the left, Ribera to the right, engendering the Babylonian confusion that exists in much of the Church world today. Hosea 10:1-8 says:

Israel is an *empty* vine, he bringeth forth *fruit unto himself:* according to the multitude of his fruit he hath *increased the altars;* according to the goodness of his land they have *made goodly images. Their heart is divided;* now shall they be found faulty: he shall break down their altars, he shall spoil their images. For now they shall say, 'We have no king, because we feared not the Lord; what then should a king do to us?' They have spoken words, swearing falsely in making a covenant: thus judgment springeth up as hemlock in the furrows of the field. The inhabitants of Samaria shall fear because of the calves of Beth-aven: for the people thereof that rejoiced on it, for the *glory* thereof, because *it is departed* from it. It shall be also carried unto Assyria for a present to king Jareb: Ephraim shall receive shame, and Israel shall be ashamed of his own counsel. As for Samaria, her king is cut off as the foam upon the water. The high places also of Aven, the sin of Israel, shall be destroyed: the thorn and the thistle shall come up on their altars; *and they shall say to the mountains, 'Cover us;' and to the hills, 'Fall on us.'* (Emphasis added).

Any ministry which brings forth fruit unto itself is an empty vine. Bringing forth fruit unto oneself causes the altars and places of worship to be built unto oneself. This causes the Church to make images according to their own pattern of goodness. But the basic problem in the Church today is that of a divided heart. Israel's heart was divided, therefore, they were found with fault before God. As a result, the glory has departed from the Church, just as it departed from Israel. Notice the last phrase in verse 8, "And they shall say to the mountains, 'Cover us;' and to the hills, 'Fall on us.'" Does that sound familiar? We read the same thing in Revelation 6:15-17:

> And the kings of the earth, and the great men, and the rich men, and the chief captains, and the mighty men, and every bondman, and every free man, hid themselves in the dens and in the rocks of the mountains; And said to the mountains and rocks, Fall on us, and hide us from the face of him that sitteth on the throne, and from the wrath of the Lamb: For the great day of his wrath is come; and who shall be able to stand?

This all took place spiritually at the cross of our Lord. In This Day, all of this is taking place *in manifestation* as a people come into unity, realizing everything that took place in the finished work of the cross. We are not saving Adam's kingdom. We are bringing forth fruit unto God as we become married to Christ in experience, by partaking of the marriage supper of the Lamb (Romans 7:4). We are enjoying the Kingdom of God and everything is done unto his glory.

If you study the word "dispensation" in the Greek and take it back to its source, you will find that it comes from a word that means, "a dwelling, a family, a home, a household, a temple," and from a word that means, "to feed the sheep." Religion has taken the simple truth of God and made it diabolically distorted drama, a nightmare of gloom, despair, and agony on thee. The nightmare is over Church. It is time to wake up.

That in the dispensation of the fullness of times he

might gather together in one all things in Christ, both which are in heaven, and which are on earth; even in him: in whom also we have obtained an inheritance, being predestinated according to the purpose of him who worketh all things after the counsel of his own will: *that we should be to the praise of his glory,* who first trusted in Christ. (Ephesians 1:10-12, emphasis added).

From the beginning, God has had a temple to feed his sheep. God's glory filled each temple from tent to tent. The first temple God created was Adam. The second was Moses' Tabernacle. The third was David's Tabernacle. The fourth was Solomon's Temple. The fifth was Zerubbabel's Temple. The sixth was Herod's Temple (when Jesus went into it). The seventh was Jesus himself. The eighth temple or tabernacle is the body of Christ (2 Corinthians 6:16, Ephesians 2:19-22, Revelation 21:3, 11).

Daniel Chapter 9:24-27

The prophecy of Daniel 9:24-27 is the basic eschatology of the religious world order. They say that part of this prophecy was fulfilled and then there was a gap of 2000 years. Then they say that the final week is going to be fulfilled at some future time. But the truth is that this entire prophecy was fulfilled over 2000 years ago when Jesus hung on the cross and died. Let's read this portion of the book of Daniel:

> Seventy weeks are determined upon thy people and upon thy holy city, to finish the transgression, and to make an end of sins, and to make reconciliation for iniquity, and to bring in everlasting righteousness, and to seal up the vision and prophecy, and to anoint the most Holy. Know therefore and understand, that from the going forth of the commandment to restore and to build Jerusalem unto the Messiah the Prince shall be seven weeks, and threescore and two weeks: the street shall be built again,

and the wall, even in troublous times. And after threescore and two weeks shall Messiah be cut off, but not for Himself: and the people of the prince that shall come shall destroy the city and the sanctuary; and the end thereof shall be with a flood, and unto the end of the war desolations are determined. And he shall confirm the covenant with many for one week: and in the midst of the week he shall cause the sacrifice and the oblation to cease, and for the overspreading of abominations he shall make it desolate, even until the consummation, and that determined shall be poured upon the desolate.

What is this spiritually foretelling? What is the present truth of this scripture? It is something that has happened and is continuing to happen in the lives of a people who are focusing on Christ, taking a second look at the finished work. Verse 1 speaks of the Holy City, who is a people. Over 2000 years ago the holy city was a place in the Middle East. But because of the cross of Jesus Christ our Lord, today the Holy City is a people.

This prophecy was given to Daniel as he was seeking God for an answer to the utter confusion that the people lived in and among. Israel had been in Babylonian captivity for 490 years. Daniel was asking the Lord to give him instruction as to how his people could be brought out of captivity and bondage. The angel Gabriel appeared to Daniel, bringing the message of the cross. Gabriel is the same angel that appeared to Mary and said, "Thou shalt conceive in thy womb, and bring forth a Son, and shalt call his name Jesus. He shall be great, and shall be called the Son of the Highest; and the Lord God shall give unto him the throne of his father, David. And he shall reign over the house of Jacob for ever; and of his kingdom there shall be no end." The name "Gabriel" means "hero" or "man of God." There is a man in the midst of the Holy City today. That man is not a man or a woman as we know one another. That man, that Gabriel, that angel, that message that is standing up, is Christ himself. If our focus is Christ, if our purpose in going to the Bible is to see Christ in every book and in every chapter, then we are going to see him. Where the kingdom of God has gone wrong in the past is in seeking revelation and knowledge. But if we will go to the book to see Christ in that revelation and that knowledge, we will get the Truth. The Truth is a person! We will have more than just revelation and knowledge, we will have Christ!

We must protect the seed. The people of God, like the Virgin Mary, are virgin soil and they have a virgin seed within them. We must be very careful that the word we bring forth is a balanced word, backed up with scripture as the Bible interprets itself. We must be sure that the word brought forth will protect the seed and will not pollute or corrupt the seed like a spiritual teratogen. We must be a virgin people as it were, and not "kingdom harlots," who have received the seed of every man. We must be a people that have a pure seed within us. So, Daniel was seeking God for instruction to bring Israel out of captivity. Today we are seeking God for instruction as to how we may walk out of Babylon, having absolutely nothing that would bind us, nothing that would deter or stop the flowing of the Christ out of us. For us to have Babylon consumed and removed out of our lives, the instruction is to realize that over 2000 years ago, it was destroyed, it was consumed, and it was done away with.

The prophecy of Daniel chapter 9 speaks of nothing more or less than the finished work of Christ. The seventy weeks ran concurrently. The end of the sixty-ninth week was fulfilled when Jesus entered Jerusalem in his triumphal entry, recorded in John chapter 12. The seventieth week was fulfilled completely when Jesus hung on the cross and he cried, "It is finished." The thing that brought natural Israel out of bondage and captivity is the same thing that brings us out of bondage and captivity! So first, he says in Daniel 9:24, "Seventy weeks are *determined* upon thy people and upon thy holy city." That word "determined" is "chopped off." But we have been taught a "parenthesis theory" by the religious system that says something like, "God is going to stop time here for 2000 years and save the last seven years for the future." Seventy weeks are determined—chopped off—set aside in time. So this seven year period that we have been taught as "future" was fulfilled when Messiah was cut off at the cross!

The next phrase in verse 24 is, "To finish the transgression." How did he finish the transgression? He was crucified. That is the answer! Again, we see this all the way through the word of God.

Those who lived in the time of the Old Testament had to look forward to Messiah's crucifixion. But we are looking behind us. If we can hear the voice behind us, we can hear him saying, "It is finished. Rest in my finished work." When we enter into that rest, the temple of God will be completed—and when the temple is completed, God fills it with his glory! As we enter into the rest that remaineth, God is finishing us (Hebrews 4).

What was Israel to do on the Day of Atonement, before the Feast of Tabernacles? They were to afflict their soul. Your Day of Atonement is this: afflicting your soul. What is the affliction of our soul? It is our asking God the question, "Isn't there anything I can do?" And God's answer is, "Rest!" He has made it so simple that most of us have missed it through the programming of the religious concepts and the mentality of Adam, and we think that if we can't *do* something, we are not going to have salvation. Entering into rest is *affliction* to most of us because of what we've been taught by the religious system of works! The Day of Atonement comes to each of us individually as we afflict our soul in our struggle to realize that we cannot add one cubit to our stature. Jesus took care of the sins of the world. He is not concerned about the sins of the world. The only thing he is concerned about is unbelief! He has already taken care of the sin issue—it is no longer an issue! Now he wants a people who believe! And the only way a people are going to believe—the only way a people will be able to eat of the Most Holy things—is when there is a priesthood in the earth with the Urim (light) and the Thummim (perfection and completion), which is the understanding of maturity. This priesthood understands that maturity comes by viewing, not by doing. Viewing the death of Christ will bring maturity and out of that maturity will come the "doing," or the works of righteousness. But the Church and the world will not eat of the Most Holy things until a priest arises with the Urim and the Thummim. The Most High Priest is Jesus Christ flowing through a people, flowing through his priesthood. He is Melchisedec, the Priest.

So the phrase, "To finish the transgression," has to do with being crucified. Look at Isaiah 43:25:

> I, even I, am he that blotteth out thy transgressions
> for mine own sake, and will not remember thy sins.

He finished the transgression and blotted them out when he was blotted out as the first Adam at the cross of Calvary—and we were in him. Look at Colossians 2:10-14:

> And ye are complete in him, which is the head of all principality and power: In whom also ye are circumcised with the circumcision made without hands, in putting off the body of the sins of the flesh, by the circumcision of Christ: Buried with him in baptism, wherein also ye are risen with him through the faith of the operation of God who hath raised him from the dead. And you, being dead in your sins and the uncircumcision of your flesh, hath he quickened together with him, having forgiven you all trespasses; *Blotting out the handwriting of ordinances that was against us, which was contrary to us, and took it out of the way, nailing it to his cross* (emphasis added).

This took place over 2000 years ago and we are looking behind us, taking a second look at the cross, to see *everything* that was finished in Jesus' death, burial, and resurrection. It was not one man that died there "in our place," or "instead of us." He became sin. He became who we were in Adam. In the Psalms, when David prophetically spoke of Christ on the cross of Calvary, he said, "I am a worm, and no man." That word "worm" actually means something that is even *lower* than a worm. It means "a crimson maggot." Jesus became who we were! He became sin—not just a sin *offering*. He became who we were. We were crucified with Christ. And when he was quickened, he was born again—not because he sinned, but because he *became* sin. Jesus is the firstborn from the dead. He is the firstborn *among many* brethren because we were quickened in him, with him. This is *not* elementary—especially if you think you are still living with two natures. You may think that you know that Jesus was crucified and you may say, "Yes, everyone knows that Paul said, 'I am crucified with Christ.'" But if you think you are still living with two natures, if you are still just a forgiven sinner, then you have *missed* what you have said is "basic and elementary."

Jesus finished the transgression through his crucifixion. Look at

Isaiah 53:4-5:

> Surely he that borne our griefs, and carried our sorrows: yet we did esteem him stricken, smitten of God, and afflicted. But he was wounded for our transgressions, he was bruised for our iniquities: the chastisement of our peace was upon him; and with his stripes we are healed.

The wounding for our transgressions was the physical wounding that Jesus suffered. He was bruised for our iniquities. A bruise is something that takes place on the inside. Jesus was bruised for our inner hurts, our emotional scars. Jesus finished the transgression. He was physically wounded for our transgressions. Now look at Hebrews 9:11-15:

> But Christ being come an High Priest of good things to come, by a greater and more perfect tabernacle, not made with hands, that is to say, not of this building; Neither by the blood of goats and calves, but by his own blood he entered in once into the holy place, having obtained eternal redemption for us. For if the blood of bulls and of goats, and the ashes of an heifer sprinkling the unclean, sanctifieth to the purifying of the flesh: How much more shall the blood of Christ, who through the eternal Spirit offered himself without spot to God, purge your conscience from dead works to serve the living God? And for this cause he is the mediator of the new testament, that by means of death, *for the redemption of the transgressions* that were under the first testament, they which are called might receive the promise of eternal inheritance (emphasis added).

If the shedding of the blood of bulls and goats under the Law would have brought maturity, then there would not have been the need for another priesthood. There would not have been any need for Christ to come and become the once and for all sacrifice. All that the sacrifices under the Law could do was cleanse their fleshly sins. But the "once and for all" sacrifice of Christ did more than just forgive us—he gave us a new nature! God is not saving Adam. The old man was crucified. We do not have two natures. The book of Revelation talks about a people who try to "heal the deadly wound." This refers to ministries and ministers who have tried for nearly 2000 years to reform Adam and to make Adam act right and live right and clean up his act—but Adam is dead! He's crucified, dead, and buried. These ministries actually preach and teach that we have two natures. It may *appear* like we have two natures if we are not mature in Christ and our mind is not renewed, but we do not have two natures! We only have one nature and it is the nature of Christ. Our conscience has been purged from dead works. We have received a new consciousness, a new awareness. We have received a new nature.

Notice the phrase in Hebrews 9:15, "For the redemption of the transgressions." According to Daniel 9, Jesus finished the transgression. Israel's *flesh* was cleansed with the Old Testament sacrifices, but in Hebrews 9 we find that through the blood of Christ, our *consciousness* was cleansed, or our *nature* was changed. Death brought the redemption of transgressions.

Remember, in Daniel chapter 9, Daniel was receiving instruction from the angel of the Lord, or from a messenger with a message, as to how Israel could be set free from their captivity and bondage. How was Israel set free when they were snake-bitten? By viewing the snake on the pole. How are we going to be set free? By viewing. How was the priesthood consecrated in Leviticus? By viewing. Not by trying to live right, but by viewing right. They were looking forward to the cross of Christ and we are looking behind us to the cross of Christ where we are all brought together into One. Out of this view, automatically, right living will come. We will awake to righteousness and we will not sin.

Let's look at the next phrase in Daniel 9:24:

> Seventy weeks are determined upon thy people and upon thy holy city, to finish the transgression, and *to make an end of sins,* and to make reconciliation for iniquity, and to bring in everlasting righteousness, and to seal up the vision and prophecy, and to anoint

the most Holy (emphasis added).

Notice the second reason the seventy weeks are set aside, chopped off, or determined for the people in Babylonian captivity and for God's Holy City—to make an end of sins. How did Jesus make an end of sins? Look at John 1:29:

> The next day John seeth Jesus coming unto him, and saith, 'Behold the Lamb of God, which taketh away the sin of the world.'

Jesus finished the transgression in his crucifixion. But he made an end of sins in his death. Are you beginning to see that the seventy weeks that the Church has taught as "future" is not future at all? How can it happen in the future when it happened at the cross of Calvary over 2000 years ago? To say that this is something that is yet to happen is to crucify to themselves the Son of God afresh and put him to an open shame (Hebrews 6:6). Jesus *meant* what he said—it is finished! The religious system says that the last week in Daniel 9:27, is yet to happen in the future. But it has already happened, as we will see momentarily.

As we see in John 1:29, sin is no longer the issue. Does that mean that we are condoning sin? God forbid! It means that Jesus has taken care of the sin of the world. It is unbelief that must be dealt with and that is removed as we renew our minds to the finished work of the cross. We do not have a "sin problem" in the world. We have a sin*ner* problem because of unbelief. Jesus already took away the sins of the world, and removed them as far as the east is from the west, but do we *believe* that? Look at Matthew 1:21:

> And she shall bring forth a Son, and thou shalt call his name Jesus: for he shall save his people from their sins.

He shall save his people from their sins. Did he do that? Yes, he was crucified. He died for the whole world. It's like Joseph marrying the Egyptian. It's like Hosea marrying a harlot. Jesus married the whole world at the cross. He forgave them of their sins (plural)

and all he is asking is for them to believe that.
Look at Hebrews 9:26:

> For then must he often have suffered since the foundation of the world; but now once in the end of the world hath he appeared to put away sin by the sacrifice of himself.

Jesus put away the sin of the world at Calvary's cross. And notice the earlier phrase, "but now once *in the end of the world.*" The world came to an end at the cross of Christ. For over 2000 years the Church *has not known* that the cross of Christ was the end of the world, or the end of the age. Jesus said it this way: "For as Jonas was three days and three nights in the whale's belly; so shall the Son of man be three days and three nights in the heart of the earth." Why has the Church been in the dark? Because one day with the Lord is as a thousand years, and a thousand years as one day. The Church has been asleep in death, dreaming the dream of hell—but on the third day, he arose! Church, we are the body of Christ in the earth, and it's resurrection morning! This is the third day! Awake unto righteousness Church! Awake O sleeper, and arise from the dead, and Christ shall give thee light (Jonah 1:6, Ephesians 5:14).

So the world came to an end at the cross. How is it that Jesus, Paul and John said that we are not of the world? Because the world came to an end for us at the cross. Paul said we are dead with Christ from the rudiments *of* the world. Paul also said that we shine as lights *in* the world. So, we are *in* the world, but we are not *of* the world. If we are not of the world, then what are we of? 1 John 4:6 tells us:

> We are of God: he that knoweth God heareth us; he that is not of God heareth not us. Hereby know we the spirit of truth, and the spirit of error.

Now let's look at Hebrews 8:12:

> For I will be merciful to their unrighteousness, and their sins and their iniquities will I remember no more.

Jesus has wiped the slate clean! Unrighteousness and sins have been done away. Iniquity is a little different than sin. "Iniquity" is wanting to "do your own thing." Iniquity is self-will. It is the mindset that says, "I'm going to do it my way, when I want, how I want. I'm not going to submit to anything or anyone, not even God." Iniquities are the thoughts that go on *inside* of us that, if we listen to them and act on them, produce sin. But remember, Jesus was bruised for our iniquities and his bruises were his inward bleeding that cleansed us from our strong self will. In many cases, it is the inward hurts that cause people to act in self will. He cleansed our soul. Jesus took care of our whole being at the cross where we were made whole. We have victory over all these things—unrighteousness, sins and iniquities. The only thing that separates us from experiencing God today is unbelief. The gospel holds a beautiful story for the solution of unbelief. Look at Mark 9:23-24:

> Jesus said unto him, 'If thou canst believe, all things are possible to him that believeth.' And straightway the father of the child cried out, and said with tears, 'Lord, I believe, *help thou mine unbelief*' (emphasis added).

Jesus is the answer for unbelief. This man said that he believed, then he said, "Jesus, please help my unbelief." In other words, "I believe in part, now help me believe perfectly, fully, completely—help me to mature in believing." We have churches full of unbelieving believers—but Jesus is the answer! He is the only one who can create belief—His belief. All we need to do is ask.

Forty-two times, Israel stopped in their wilderness wanderings and each one of these forty-two stops were illustrated sermons—prophetic pictures of the gospel of the *finished* work of Jesus Christ. There were forty-two groups of people that built the wall in the book of Nehemiah. All of those different gates that they built, the prison gate, the dung gate, the sheep gate and so on, represent the twelve redemptive aspects of the finished work of the cross of Jesus Christ, namely: crucified, died, buried, quickened, raised, and seated; crucified with, died with, buried with, quickened with, raised with, and seated with. The wall that Nehemiah and his people built speaks of the salvation of our soul. Then in Matthew chapter 1 we see the forty-second generation mentioned.

The first stop in the wilderness was when the children of Israel came to the waters of Marah. The water was bitter and they could not drink it. The Lord showed Moses a tree that was *already there*—a finished work—and when Moses cast it into the bitter waters, the waters then became sweet. This is a prophetic picture of Jesus, the tree of Life, being cut down and cut off at the cross, cast out for us and as us. And because of his sacrifice, we, the bitter waters, became sweet. Jesus Christ, on the tree, took away the man of bitterness, Adam. Now look at 1 Peter 2:24:

> Who his own self bare *our sins in his own body on the tree,* that we, being *dead to sins,* should live unto righteousness: by whose stripes ye were healed (emphasis added).

When we *see* that Jesus bore our sins in his own body on the cross or on the tree, and now we are dead to sin and sins, we're going to live unto righteousness! Jesus was crucified to finish the transgression. He died to make an end of sins (plural). And sin is the *acts* of sin—meaning, we do not condone sin but it is even more than that—sin is not the issue! The issue before us now is unbelief—what are we going to do with it? When the Holy Spirit brings understanding, even unbelief is no longer an issue! As we realize that God is all-powerful, and as the priesthood sees every man hanging on that cross, we can remit their sin by seeing them and their sin hanging on the cross. That will release the faith of God, and that will release the presence of the Holy Spirit and he will make them an offer they can't refuse! Every knee will bow and every tongue will confess that Jesus is Lord to the glory of God, the Father, when there is a priesthood going forth with bread and wine. It may be easy for us to see us hanging there—but our enemies? We need the Holy Spirit! We need our minds renewed. We need the faith of Christ in operation. When the priesthood can see every man hanging on the cross with Christ, we will see an unlimited ability of God flow out of the corporate priesthood in the earth!

We can look at the religious order and see that something has been missing. And this is not criticism—it is the truth. Do you see the Church as a whole, the religious order, living above sin, being righteousness personified, being holiness personified? The world is *tired* of people preaching one thing and living another! The reason people have not been able to live what they've preached is because they've had everything backwards. They've had the cart before the horse. They've tried to fight this sin and that sin and put this stronghold down and cast that imagination down—and they will never accomplish it that way because where you put something down in one area, it will jump up in another! There is something missing! There is something that the Church has not known—and it is this:

> Knowing this, that our old man is crucified with him, that the body of sin might be destroyed, that henceforth we should not serve sin (Romans 6:6).

Our old man is crucified with him! Remember the curious girdle that was tied to the *back* of the ephod? You can't understand who you are in Christ as a new creation until you have an understanding that the old man is crucified, dead, and buried. Remember Eli, the fleshly priest? The Ark had been captured by the Philistines. "Philistine" means "dust roller." The Ark had been captured by the religious people who were rolling in the dust. There are still some "holy rollers" today. This represents Jesus being captured by the religious people of the man of dust, the first Adam, and being hung on the cross and crucified. When they came and told Eli what had happened, the Bible says that Eli fell *backwards* and broke his neck and died—*for he was an old man.*

Back, and backwards—these stories in the Old Testament are typical for us today, Paul says. We're supposed to *get the message* from them. We are to look back, backwards, behind us to the cross of Christ where the old man was crucified, has died, and is buried. Jesus was captured over 2000 years ago and hung on a cross. Had the prince of this world known, they never would have crucified the Lord of glory. The Romans 6:6 key that will free us, is *realizing* that we are already free—realizing the old man is dead. As a priesthood holds before the people a view of the death, and as the people *view,* they are going to walk in righteousness and holiness in Christ experientially.

So, in Romans 6:6 we see that the body of sin was destroyed. Jesus was crucified to finish the transgression. He died to make an end of sins. It is finished. It has been accomplished. "Comfort ye, comfort ye my people, saith your God. Speak ye comfortably to Jerusalem, and cry unto her, that *her warfare has been accomplished,* that her *iniquity* has been pardoned: for she hath received of the Lord's hand *double* for all her sins." There were two deaths. It is completely finished and we are complete in him. We want to take our sword and beat it into a plowshare and study war no more. We do not want to take our sword and cut off the servant's ear. We want to nail his ear to the door, and Jesus is the door. But many people in the Church today use their sword to cut people up with. They say, "Bless God, if you don't do it our way, you're a heretic!" That kind of teaching is way off base. Let's look at the next reason for the seventy weeks in Daniel 9:24:

> Seventy weeks are determined upon thy people and upon thy holy city, to finish the transgression, and to make an end of sins, and *to make reconciliation for iniquity,* and to bring in everlasting righteousness, and to seal up the vision and prophecy, and to anoint the most Holy (emphasis added).

Seventy weeks are determined upon thy people and upon thy holy city, to finish the transgression (crucified), and to make an end of sins (died), and to make reconciliation for iniquity. Look at 2 Corinthians 5:16-21:

> Wherefore henceforth know we no man after the flesh: yea, though we have known Christ after the flesh, yet now henceforth know we him no more. Therefore if any man be in Christ, he is a new creature: old things are passed away; behold, all things are become new. And all things are of God, who hath reconciled us to himself by Jesus Christ, and hath given to us the ministry of reconciliation; To wit, that God was in Christ, reconciling the world unto himself, not imputing their trespasses unto

them, and hath committed unto us the word of reconciliation. Now then we are ambassadors for Christ, as though God did beseech you by us: we pray you in Christ's stead, be ye reconciled to God. For he hath made him to be sin for us, who knew no sin; that we might be made the righteousness of God in him.

We know no man after the flesh. That does not mean that we condone sin when we meet a person who has sin in their life. I counsel people on a regular basis and I can minister to their issues yet all the while see them crucified in Christ and a new creation. I'm not focusing on what is coming out of their life. I'm not condoning either. I'm seeing them complete. That is what Paul meant when he said we know no man after the flesh. We do not harshly, critically judge people.

Then Paul said that we have known Christ after the flesh, yet now henceforth know we him no more. We saw Jesus hanging on the cross, suffering. But we must realize that Jesus experienced much more than just physical suffering. We must see the suffering that went on *beyond* the suffering in the flesh. We must see that three days and three nights he went into hell. He became a crimson maggot. He became who we were in Adam.

To know Jesus Christ after the flesh is to think that he just died a physical death and not a spiritual death. Paul gave us another nugget of truth when he said, "Yet now henceforth know we him no more after the flesh." Now we know him spiritually. The Spirit of Christ is in us. When that reality dawns on our consciousness, we *know* him in spirit, or we are one with him spiritually. Therefore if any man be in Christ, he is a new creature—brand new. The phrase "new creature" means "one completely higher in a totally new dimension and completely different than the old man." We're not even the same species. We're not even a butterfly from a worm because the worm is dead. The butterfly has worm blood in it. We cannot use that message any longer to illustrate the born-again experience. We do not have Adam's blood in us! We have a brand new bloodstream! We're a brand new creation. God destroyed the vessel on the potters' wheel, started all over again and made *another* vessel. God is not patching up Adam! God loved us to death! Adam was marred in the potters hand so he crucified him, killed him, got him out of the way and made The Way for us to become a brand new creation. Old things are passed away; behold all things are become new, and all things are of God! In the book of Revelation Jesus said, "I make all things new." He did not say "I make all new things." He said, "I make all things new!" To make something new, you take away the old first.

Then Paul said that God has given *to us* the ministry of reconciliation. Do you want to be a part of this priesthood that has the bread and wine? Here it is: "To wit that God was in Christ, reconciling *the world* unto himself, *not imputing* their trespasses unto them, and hath committed unto us the word of reconciliation." The phrase "not imputing" means "not holding against, not keeping a record." God has nothing against us. He is not keeping a record of our trespasses. "Trespasses" means "deviations, sideslips, willful transgressions, and unintentional error." O the love of God! He destroyed the man of sin! We no longer serve sin! No matter how vile a person is, we do not condone what they're doing, but we must see them crucified on that cross. That will release the faith of God which cannot fail. That will release the Spirit of God because you have remitted their sin and God will begin to draw them. The book of Revelation says that there is a people being tormented in the presence of the Lamb, which is "Lambkin" in the Greek, which, when carried through, means "a Lambkin company." They're going to be brought under the conviction of the Holy Spirit as we can see them hanging there on the cross. The only way we can do that is as our minds are renewed. The more descriptive we can be of the prophetic picture of the finished work of the cross, the more we explain the death, burial, and resurrection, the more Christ will stand up in us and minister through us through the power of the Holy Spirit!

Paul had a message! Every other writer in the New Testament was influenced by Paul's message. Remember the ship caught in the storm Euroclydon? Paul ministered to the sailors, breaking bread. Well, if he was breaking bread, what do you think he was preaching to them? He was preaching his message, his gospel, the death, burial, and resurrection. An east wind came; the wind of God, and Paul told them that the ship would be destroyed. But they wanted to save the ship so they starting throwing things overboard. This is what we do when we try to salvage our religious ways. But Paul said the ship would be destroyed, and he was breaking bread with them. Paul was trying to get a message through to them, but they were not getting the message.

In the next chapter, Paul built a bonfire with the pieces of the ship and a beast came up out of the heat. What comes out of *not knowing* that the old man was crucified, dead, and buried and we've been quickened, raised and seated with Christ? The residue of the old beast man comes out every time! A *brood* of vipers! The old beast is not some beast over in the Middle East that is going to rise up in some temple they have built. The beast is Adam. When the beast came up out of the heat and grabbed Paul by the hand, Paul just shook it off. Are you shaking off the residue of the beast by realizing that your old man was crucified, is dead, and buried? After Paul shook off the beast, he laid hands on and healed every sick person on the island!

Our ship is bound for destruction. It was totally destroyed at the cross and now it is being destroyed in manifestation as we shake off the residue that remains. So don't try to throw things overboard to save the ship. Don't try to work it in the energy of the flesh with the mentality of "I must salvage the old religious ship." Just wake up to what happened at the cross. Wake up to righteousness. It is that simple. The carnal mind of the religious system is what has made it all so difficult. They have libraries and bookstores full of books and so very much knowledge! And all that knowledge has done nothing but puff them up into one big cloud without water, without any life-giving substance to give the earth! The religious system is just a vapor! An empty void! An uninhabited waste place! All we have needed is the Spirit of wisdom and revelation in knowledge of *him!* We're beginning to realize what it is going to take to have God habitate us—which is nothing but viewing the finished work of the cross. What a rest to enter into!

So, in 2 Corinthians 5:20-21, Paul said, "Now then we are ambassadors for Christ, as though God did beseech you by us: we pray you in Christ's stead, be ye reconciled to God. For he hath made him to be sin for us, who knew no sin; that we might be made the righteousness of God in him." The transgression was finished in

Christ's crucifixion. Christ made an end of sins in his death. And he made reconciliation for iniquity in his death and all that he suffered *beyond* his physical death.

Now look at Romans 5:10:

> For if, when we were enemies, we were reconciled to God by the death of his Son, much more, being reconciled, we shall be saved by his life.

God reconciled us when we were enemies! We hung on that cross even though we were an enemy of God. Yes, Adam was God's enemy. But we were reconciled by the death of God's own Son. Much more, being reconciled, we shall be saved by his life. Every man woman and child has been reconciled—not saved—reconciled. They were reconciled whether they wanted to be reconciled or not. In John 12:32, Jesus said, "And I, if I be lifted up from the earth, will *draw all men* unto me." The Greek says, "I will *drag all men* unto me." Jesus was lifted up from the earth on Calvary's cross. Whether you wanted to or not, Jesus dragged you to that cross.

But to be saved, Romans 5:10 says we shall be saved by his *life*. To be saved means you have accepted his sacrifice. And not only have you accepted it, but now you *believe it*. When you believe in his life, that *activates* his life in you and you will begin your journey of salvation. We need to clearly understand this because some teach pantheism, which says God is in everything. The *bios* life of God is in everything, the biological life, because God gave *that* life to everything, without choice. But the divine life of God, the *Zoe* life, which means "life as God has it," comes only from accepting the sacrifice of Christ and partaking of the Lamb slain, which is the ultimate gift from God—and we choose it as God draws us. There is no greater gift to choose.

One more scripture among many, that reveals that Daniel's prophecy was fulfilled when Christ made reconciliation for iniquity and *finished the work* at the cross, is Zechariah 3:9-10:

> For behold the stone that I have laid before Joshua; upon one stone shall be seven eyes: behold I will engrave the graving thereof, saith the Lord of hosts,

> and I will remove the iniquity of that land in one day. In that day, saith the Lord of hosts, shall ye call every man his neighbour under the vine and under the fig tree (emphasis added).

That Stone with seven eyes is the Lamb with seven eyes in the book of Revelation. The Amplified Bible says of that stone in Zechariah 3:9, "For behold, upon the stone which I have set before Joshua, upon that one stone are seven eyes or facets [the all-embracing providence of God and the sevenfold radiations of the Spirit of God.]" Next he says, "I will engrave the graving." How did the Lord engrave the graving? He was wounded for our transgressions, he was bruised for our iniquities: the chastisement of our peace was upon him; and with his stripes we are healed. And notice the phrase, "I will remove the iniquity of that land *in one day.*" This speaks of the crucifixion, the death, *and the burial* of Jesus Christ where the iniquity of the land was *removed* in one day. The Lord goes on to say in verse 10, "In that day shall ye *call every man his neighbor* under the vine and under the fig tree." When Jesus was lifted up on the cross, he drew all men unto himself—in that day—in one day—in *The Day.*

Now let's look at the last three aspects of Daniel 9:24:

> Seventy weeks are determined upon thy people and upon thy holy city, to finish the transgression, and to make an end of sins, and to make reconciliation for iniquity, *and to bring in everlasting righteousness,* and to seal up the vision and prophecy, and to anoint the most Holy (emphasis added).

How did Jesus bring in everlasting righteousness? Look back to 2 Corinthians 5:21:

> For he hath made him to be sin for us, who knew no sin; that we might be made the righteousness of God in him.

When Jesus was quickened or made alive, he brought in everlasting righteousness. If we are made the righteousness of God in him, then when Jesus was made to be sin, he also had to be made righteous again, and that happened when he was quickened. This is when Jesus became the firstborn from *spiritual* death. Jesus was the first one to be born again. That may blow your religious theology, but the old ship has to be destroyed along with everything in it to make ready for the new vessel! In our second look at the cross we're seeing everything we missed in the first look, when we ate the Lamb in haste. We are roasting the Lamb with fire. *We are no longer going to sodden the Lamb down with water!* We are seeing the half that has never yet been told, with our second look at the cross. We're not going to close our eyes to this. We are going to view the Lamb! We're going all the way in, past the veil that has been done away, to the very presence of the Ancient of Days—and the Lamb is the light of his glory!

Jesus, who had become sin, had to be made the righteousness of God so *we* could be made the righteousness of God in him. 1 Timothy 3:16 says that God was *justified* in the Spirit. Why would *God* have to be justified in the Spirit? Because he used the flesh of Jesus to enter into death's dark door of sin, as anointed worship leader, Lynn Garner sings. So amazing is the love of God! We have a *loving* God! The only way we are righteous is because we are in him. The only way we are the holiness of God is because we are in the Holy One. So Jesus brought in everlasting righteousness when he was quickened. Look at Revelation 19:8-9:

> And to her was granted that she should be arrayed in fine linen, clean and white: for the fine linen is the righteousness of saints. And he saith unto me, 'Write, 'Blessed are they which are called unto the marriage supper of the Lamb.'

This speaks of a people who become righteousness personified. This is not just a spiritual position of righteousness. The moment you accept Jesus as your savior, as a baby Christian, you are the righteousness of God in Jesus Christ. But the Bible speaks of the *fruit* of righteousness. We bear the fruit of righteousness by drawing out of the soil of the death we have been planted in. What is the marriage supper of the Lamb? It is when spirit, the masculine part, becomes one with the feminine part, the soul—the mind, the will, the intellect, and the emotions. When we are born again, our spirit is wall to wall God. Just as in the natural, it takes male and female to produce children, so it is in the Spirit. The masculine spirit and the feminine soul become one and produce the nature of Jesus Christ. For this to happen, your mind must be renewed, your will must be in harmony with the Spirit of God, your emotions and your intellect must be flowing with what is in the Spirit. That is the marriage supper of the Lamb. How does all this take place? By the marriage supper of the *Lamb*. It takes place as we partake of the Lamb slain and roasted with fire.

Now, the fifth aspect of the seventy weeks:

> Seventy weeks are determined upon thy people and upon thy holy city, to finish the transgression, and to make an end of sins, and to make reconciliation for iniquity, and to bring in everlasting righteousness, *and to seal up the vision and prophecy,* and to anoint the most Holy (emphasis added).

In the Old Testament, one part of the garments of the high priest was the mitre, which represents the renewing of the mind and the sealing of the saints. There is a people who are drawing out of the death that they have been planted in, and life is being produced out of them. We're putting on what all the garments of the high priest spiritually represent. We're being clothed with Christ as we take the second look at the cross and as we get all of his garments on. The mitre is the last garment to be put on as the high priest raises it to seal his head. We are being sealed by this word. In the book of Ephesians, we find that we have been sealed with the Holy Spirit of promise until the day of redemption. Now, as we take a look at the Lamb slain, we are beginning to be *un*sealed as never before. Out of us is galloping the white horse of righteousness, the red horse—the understanding of our judgment that took place over 2000 years ago, the black horse, where Jesus completely identified with us in spiritual death, and the green (pale) horse of quickening life where we were quickened to life with Jesus when he was in the pit of hell.

God is sealing up the vision and the prophecy as we focus on what happened at the cross. Then we begin to be unsealed, and out of us gallops the Lord Jesus Christ in all of those magnifications and levels of anointing that those horses represent. Look at Revelation 5:5-6:

> And one of the elders saith unto me, 'Weep not: behold, the Lion of the tribe of Juda, the Root of David, hath prevailed to open the book, and to loose the seven seals thereof.' And I beheld, and lo, in the midst of the throne and of the four beasts, and in the midst of the elders, stood a Lamb as it had been slain, having seven horns and seven eyes, which are the seven Spirits of God sent forth into all the earth.

The seven horns speak of the fullness of power and unlimited anointing that a people with the bread and the wine are moving in. The seven eyes speak of the perfection of perception, the spiritual maturity of a people who are unsealed—a people that have nothing unclean within them—no debris, no traditions, no dogma or doctrine of man—they are a crystal sea. And when that river of life begins to flow out of them, it is as pure as it started its flow in the Spirit. That is what we want and we are only going to get that by seeing the death, by partaking of bread and wine.

To bring in everlasting righteousness speaks of Christ's quickening. Sealing up the vision and the prophecy speaks of being raised. Now for the last aspect of Daniel's prophecy:

> Seventy weeks are determined upon thy people and upon thy holy city, to finish the transgression, and to make an end of sins, and to make reconciliation for iniquity, and to bring in everlasting righteousness, and to seal up the vision and prophecy, *and to anoint the most Holy* (emphasis added).

We are waking up to the fact that we are seated in heavenly places with him above all heavens—the Most Holy Place. We are already at the finish line. Salvation is realizing that we are at the finish line, and now we are coming out to the cross (the Outer Court) to see how we got to the finish line (the Holy of Holies). When that happens, we become the habitation of God. We *become* the Most Holy Place of God and what flows out of us is nothing but him. Look at Jude 14:

> And Enoch also, the seventh from Adam, prophesied of these, saying, 'Behold, the Lord cometh with ten thousands of his saints,

"Enoch" means "initiated." We're being initiated into the kingdom by the Spirit of God. Enoch was the seventh from Adam. We know that he was not literally "the seventh" from Adam, but "seventh" speaks of something that has to do with fullness. In the Greek this verse says, "Behold, the Lord cometh *with myriads of himself.*" This speaks of anointing the Most Holy. This speaks of quickened, raised, and seated in the Most Holy Place. When Solomon told the Shulamite that she had "goats' hair," he was telling her that she was his dwelling place, the Most Holy Place. When the Lord comes with myriads of himself to anoint the Most Holy, we *become* the Most Holy Place. We are his habitation. The tabernacle of God is among men. We are not God. We are one with God. Because of the cross we are one with him and one in him. Look at James 1:18:

> Of his own will he begat us with the word of truth, that we should be a kind of firstfruits of his creatures.

In the Greek, this verse says, "That we should be creatures of himself." Myriads of himself, creatures of himself—God is so habitated in us that we can't tell where he starts and we end or where we end and he starts! The hills have melted like wax at the presence of the Lord! The heavens declare his righteousness, and all the peoples see his glory! We have partaken of a dimension in God where we *realize* crucified, died, buried, quickened, raised, seated, crucified with, died with, buried with, quickened with, raised with, seated with. We have come to a place where we realize as Daniel chapter 9 says, the only way we can come out of all bondage and all corruption and all slavery and anything that binds us is by realizing that over 2000 years ago, it happened! As we just believe that, as we just *hear* the Ram's horn of Jubilee, we enter into rest. We're free from indebtedness. We have no bondage or slavery within our life. We've received our inheritance, which is the Christ flowing out of us. Now we've become his inheritance.

It is all based on a death. Did you know that every piece of fruit that you eat first went through a death before it could bring you life? Every tree that produces fruit goes through death first before it produces life. That is the cycle of God. First death and then life. Look at Hebrews 2:11:

> For both he that sanctifieth and they who are sanctified are all of One: for which cause he is not ashamed to call them brethren.

Jesus sanctified us over 2000 years ago. We are the ones he sanctified. Both he that sanctifieth and they who are sanctified are all of One and he is not ashamed to call us brethren! Hallelujah! Look at Colossians 3:4:

> When Christ, *who is* our life, shall appear, then shall ye also appear with him in glory.

In the original King James Version, the words "who is" is in italics, meaning that it was not in the Greek. So it really says, "When Christ, our life!" "When Christ, our life, shall appear, then shall ye also appear with him in glory." In other words, when you take the second look and see the death, Christ will appear. He will become expressed. He will become tangible. He will come out of heaven to your earth. He will come from the invisible to the visible. This is the anointing of the Most Holy.

The word "Christ" in the Greek is *Christos,* which means "anointed." The historical man Jesus is the Christ. He is God's perfect idea of *giving visibility* to himself. Christ is the image of God. "Image" speaks of something made visible, a representation of something. Jesus was the visible manifestation of God. He gave

God visibility. One does not see God with the natural eyesight. One does not hear God with the natural hearing. One does not touch God with the natural sense of touch. God is Spirit, and Spirit is invisible. The spiritual dimension is not the physical dimension, but Spirit manifests *as* the physical dimension. Therefore, when the scripture in Daniel 9:24 speaks of anointing the Most Holy Place, it speaks of giving visibility.

God gave visibility to the Outer Court. We have seen multitudes of people converted in a born-again experience, doing the works of the Outer Court. It was made visible. We have seen the Holy Place, or the Pentecostal, Charismatic, Spirit-filled realm made visible with the gifts, signs, and wonders. Now God is anointing, or making visible the Most Holy Place. This anointing is taking place as a people begin to experience in reality, the knowledge and the depth of that which concerns the Most Holy Place. In the Outer Court we met Jesus. We met someone outside of ourselves, as it were. In the Holy Place, we met Christ. That which we came in contact with was the Spirit of God, the realization and awareness that we were empowered. While those realms are glorious, still there is a lot of struggling going on in those realms.

The Holy Place realm was not given to us because we were perfect, nor was it given to us to make us perfect. In fact, even though one is born again and Spirit-filled, he is like a huge contradiction. He is no longer that which he was, but is still not what he is supposed to be in manifestation. For many years we have condemned ourselves because of this, as we felt that we were not living up to that which we know is good and right, according to the knowledge of good and evil.

In the type and shadow of Pentecost, it was a new meal offering which was sown with leaven. Leaven is a type of sin. Typically, God was showing us that in the Holy Place we are not mature yet. There is still sin in our life when we are living in the Holy Place. Actually, we are a monster in the Holy Place because we are in duality in that dimension of our experience in God. Sometimes we feel on top of the world, spiritually. We feel like prophesying, speaking in tongues, dancing, praising God, yet at other times we feel the exact opposite. This is duality. We have a spiritual consciousness which is empowered within us, but at the same time, we are very much aware of an old identity. This is why one can prophesy in a meeting and yet be carnal minded when the meeting is over. He senses God, but still senses the old, because of hanging on to an old identity. This is where the majority of Christendom has been for over 2000 years. Many have believed that God was going to "pop" them into some instantaneous experience, which would completely deliver them from their duality. True and lasting deliverance is progressive. God is progressive. The Holy Place is only the second dimension of our experience.

Webster's dictionary defines the word "duality" as "The quality or state of being dual, made up of two elements or aspects." Duality is a doctrine which states that the universe is under the domination of two opposing principles of good and evil.

Webster's dictionary defines "oneness" as "The quality or state of being one, whole, concord, harmony, and integrity. Being a single unit or entire being or thing, and *no more*. Existing as something actually or virtually the same as something else."

Duality says that there is me and there is God. But oneness and identification in Christ is saying that we are one single unit existing as virtually the same. This is the discovery of our true self. Paul said, "But he that is joined to the Lord is one spirit." This is the mystery of God.

Look at 1 Corinthians 15:45-47:

> And so it is written, 'The first man Adam was made a living soul;' the last Adam was made a quickening spirit. Howbeit that was not first which is spiritual, but that which is natural; and afterward that which is spiritual. The first man is of the earth, earthy: the second man is the Lord from heaven.

All men are born in Adam. Adam is a nature. We have absolutely no trouble believing that we are like him! But the word of God says the second man, or the second nature, or the rebirth experience is— the Lord from heaven. Our first conscious awareness of ourselves was earthy, but our second conscious awareness of ourselves is the Lord! That is the awakening of our true self, and the Lord is that Spirit. When we are joined to the Lord there is only One Spirit. So the anointing of the Most Holy Place is God giving visibility to himself in and through a people. *A people* are becoming the Most Holy Place—a people becoming Spirit in the Day of the Lord!

Now let's proceed in Daniel chapter 9. Those seventy weeks were fulfilled over 2000 years ago. Many teach that sixty-nine weeks were completed, then there was a gap of 2000 years, and then the last week (verse 27) will be fulfilled at a future time. But we are going to know the truth. Let's read verse 27:

> And he shall confirm the covenant with many for one week: and in the midst of the week he shall cause the sacrifice and the oblation to cease.

Jesus confirmed the covenant when he preached for three-and-a-half years to the lost sheep of the house of Israel. He confirmed that with *many*. But he also confirmed it when he was raised from the dead and he preached first to the Jews. Then in the midst of the week he caused the sacrifice and the oblation to cease when he offered his own body as the once and for all sacrifice. The offering of himself caused the sacrifice of bulls and goats and heifers and turtle doves and all that blood to cease! In the midst of the week he went to the cross and at the end of the week he was resurrected. All of Daniel's prophecy foretells the cross of Jesus Christ! The entire Bible is the revelation of Jesus Christ!

Daniel was seeking instruction as to how his people could come out of the Babylonian captivity and bondage they had been under for 490 years. They looked forward to it, we look behind to it. It is a prophetic picture of the death, burial, and resurrection. We are having communion. We are eating the bread and drinking the wine until the Lord comes. And when we do this, we are showing forth his death until he comes—not come out there in the sky—but from spirit to soul—manifest, express—come out of the invisible and give visibility through a people. He has come, he is coming, and he shall come. Thank God that we are involved in the coming of the Lord—the *apokalupsis,* the uncovering of Christ within us, the *epiphaneia,* his manifestation, his outshining, his outraying, and the *parousia,* the presence of the Lord flowing through a people—through viewing the cross a second time.

This next statement has nothing to do with condoning sin. You need to read it very carefully so that you don't go around like those that Paul ministered to in the book of Romans when he ministered grace so purely that they said, "Paul, do you mean that we can sin?" Paul said, "God forbid." And I say, "God forbid." Did you know that you had nothing to do with being a sinner? You were shaped in iniquity and conceived in sin in your Mother's womb. You did not sin to become a sinner. You were born a sinner. Because you were born a sinner, you sinned. There was nothing you could do about the matter. That was your nature and you automatically sinned just like a tree automatically produces fruit. You did not have to work at sinning; you did it because that was your nature.

When you were born *again,* when you were born from above, spiritually, you became the righteousness of God in Jesus Christ. When you were re-born, you received the nature of Jesus Christ. When you were born again, you received everything that he paid for over 2000 years ago. When you were born again, your spirit became wall to wall God. When you're born again, you have within you everything needed for you to mature into the full measure of the stature of the Lord Jesus Christ. There is nothing we can do to earn or merit salvation.

The gospel of Matthew tells us that the lily does not spin or toil. It does not labor. But what it does to grow or to mature, is draw its life out of the death, or out of the soil that it has been planted in. Romans 6:5 says that we were planted in the death of Christ! As we draw out of the death, not working, not laboring, but as we draw out of the death that we have been planted in, Christ resurrects more and more within us, as Romans 6:5 explains. Then out of maturity we will "do." We don't *do* to mature. We *view* to mature and out of viewing will come right doing. We need to get the horse in front of the cart, awake to righteousness, and walk in the spirit. The only "doing" there is to mature is to renew the mind. Romans 12:1-2 tells us to present our bodies a living sacrifice, holy, acceptable unto God, which is your reasonable service. "Reasonable service" means "the least you can do." Just present yourself. "Here I am Lord. I'm saved, but not by my works. I didn't merit salvation. All I can do is look to see what happened over 2000 years ago and accept the sacrifice."

It's not right living we're preaching, it's right viewing. And out of right viewing will come right living. But the Church has had it backwards. That's why Paul said, "Awake to righteousness and sin not." He said, "Walk in the Spirit and you'll not fulfill the lust of the flesh." But what we've been doing in the Church is handing out a list of rules. "Do this. Do not do that. Do. Do." And it has all been according to the knowledge of good and evil. What we want to do is eat from the tree of life. The only way to eat from the tree of life is to recognize that his death was my death, his suffering was my suffering, and his judgment was the judgment to my old man. If you can understand the breastplate of judgment and realize that was the judgment of your old man, you will escape a judgment to come. If you'll judge yourself you will not be judged. Christ cannot be judged.

You may ask, "Isn't there a judgment coming upon the world?" Yes. They are reaping what they are sowing. But there is a further judgment for the world when the sons of God show them that Jesus' judgment *was* their judgment. When we can understand that through Jesus' death we experienced our judgment, then as we view Christ, right living will come. The only way to be a victorious Church who lives above sin, who lives and moves and has our being in him, not faltering and floundering around and experiencing shipwreck after shipwreck, is if we minister as did Paul the apostle, and *explain* the word of God and break it down, becoming a millstone that destroys confusion. Then we will experience walking above sin, walking in maturity, in perfection, and it will be as easy as taking one step after another. We won't even have to think about it. When the brain is functioning normally, we do not have to think about what foot to put out next as we walk—it just naturally, supernaturally happens!

God is bringing his people to the place of their identity. He is bringing his people home. He is bringing us to the realization of who we are. He is bringing us to the realization that the old man is dead, and only Christ remains. We're beginning to focus on the second look at the cross and that is bringing us to the place where we are supernaturally, naturally walking in Christ. He is bringing us to the place where the Church is *his* body for *him* to live and to move and to have *his* being in. We are the tabernacle of God. We are coming to the place where there is no energy of the flesh expended because we live like the lily, planted in his death. This is the lost coin that the woman swept her house for! This is the thing we have been yearning for. We've known that something was not right. Yes, the truth we had was good, but there was something missing and we *knew* that there was something missing. It was a silver redemptive coin. We are a Church so gripped by the cross that when people say, "You had better be careful or you're going to be persecuted," we're going to say, "Persecuted? We'll lay down our lives for the gospel of Christ!"

Years ago the Lord showed me in a vision, a tree with dead, brown leaves on it. In the vision, someone took a rake and tried to knock the remaining dead leaves off the tree but they would not come off. Then in the spring, when the life came through the root system, up through the trunk, and out through the limbs, those dead leaves automatically fell off and were replaced with life. But the tree went through the death of the winter before the life could come forth.

It's not that there is no discipline involved. But once you know who you are, once you know that the old man is crucified, you will not yield your members as instruments of unrighteousness to sin. Because you know who you are you will not go to the same places your old man went to. You won't look at the things your old man looked at. The book of James says we sin when we are drawn away of our own lusts and when lust has conceived, it brings forth sin, and sin brings forth death. Now that you know who you are, the Spirit governs your life and you no longer look at the things your old man looked at. In the past, we have tried to do all of this without the understanding of the finished work of the cross and it just produced a beast. But as we take the second look at the cross in this Feast of Tabernacles, the veil is taken away and Jesus steps out in the clouds to minister bread and wine to the earth.

Appendix A

Christ's Spiritual Death

<u>1 Peter 3:18</u>: "For Christ also hath once suffered for sins, the just for the unjust, that he might bring us to God, being put to death in the flesh, but quickened by the Spirit."
> (Barclay) He underwent physical death, but in his spirit he was brought to life.
> (Beck) ... made alive in His spirit.
> (Godbey) ... quickened in spirit. * (Footnote: His own human spirit)
> (Norlie) ... made alive again in His spirit.
> (Wuest) ... made alive with respect to the spirit (His human spirit) ...
> (Knox) ... endowed with fresh life in his spirit.
> (RSV, ASV, NASV, Alford, Young, Weymouth, Amplified) ... made alive in the spirit.
> (Concordant) ... vivified in spirit.
> (Rotherham) ... made alive in spirit. (Centenary)
> (Douay) ... enlivened in the spirit.
> (Confraternity) ... he was brought to life in the spirit. (NEB)
> (New Life, Laubach) ... His spirit was made alive.
> (Jordan) ... his spirit was made very much alive.
> (Marshall) ... quickened ... in [the] spirit.

If he was made alive in His spirit, He must have been spiritually dead.

<u>Hebrews 2:9</u>: "But we see Jesus, who was made a little lower than the angels for the suffering of death, crowned with glory and honor, that he by the grace of God should taste death for every man."

(Knox) ... he was to taste death, and taste it on behalf of all.
(NEB) ... in tasting death, he should stand for us all.
(Diaglott) ... by God's Favour, he might taste of Death on behalf of every one.

Isaiah 53:9: "And he made his grave with the wicked, and with the rich in his death*: because he had done no violence, neither was any deceit in his mouth."
* (Cambridge) "Death" is plural in the Hebrew: "deaths."

Matthew 27:46: "And about the ninth hour Jesus cried with a loud voice, saying, 'Eli, Eli, lama sabachthani?' that is to say, 'My God, my God, why hast thou forsaken me?'"

27:50: "Jesus, when he had cried again with a loud voice, yielded up the ghost."
Jesus died twice; spiritually, then physically.

Romans 6:23: "For the wages of sin is death; but the gift of God is eternal life through Jesus Christ our Lord."
The wages of sin is first spiritual death (Genesis 2:17). Since Jesus was made to be sin, he of necessity, died spiritually.

2 Corinthians 5:21: "For he hath made him to be sin for us, who knew no sin that we might be made the righteousness of God in him."
(Translator's NT) ... God made him to be sin itself on our behalf ...
(GNB) ... God made him share our sin in order that in union with him we might share the righteousness of God.
(NEB) ... God made him one with the sinfulness of men ...
(Knox) ... God made Him into sin for us ...
He was so literally made sin in spirit that He had to be made righteous in spirit again.

1 Timothy 3:16: "And without controversy great is the mystery of godliness: God was manifest in the flesh, justified in the Spirit, seen

of angels. preached unto the Gentiles, believed on in the world, received up into glory."
> (Beck) ... became righteous in spirit ...
> (Young) ... declared righteous in spirit ...
> (20th Century) ... Pronounced righteous in spirit ...
> (Weekes) ... was made righteous in spirit ...
> (Knox) ... justification won in the realm of the Spirit; a vision seen by angels. "Manifested in the flesh" would include His birth to His actual physical death when He no longer was in the flesh. "Justified (made righteous) in spirit, seen of angels, preached unto the Gentiles" would all have to be in the spirit before He was raised from the dead physically because the Gentiles were not preached to in His earthly ministry - only the lost sheep of the house of Israel. "Believed on in the world" refers to His post-resurrection appearances; "received up into glory" is the Ascension. He was made righteous in spirit after He had first been made sin in spirit and died physically.

<u>1 Corinthians 1:30</u>: "But of him are ye in Christ Jesus, who of God is made unto us wisdom, and righteousness, and sanctification, and redemption."
> He has been *made* (lit.) righteousness unto us, after having been made sin first.

<u>Romans 6:6</u>: "Knowing this, that our old man is crucified with him, that the body of sin might be destroyed, that henceforth we should not serve sin."
> (Weymouth, 20th Century, Amplified, New Berkeley, Laubach, Beck, Moffat, Goodspeed, Wade, Centenary, NASNT, NIV) ... our old self ...
> (Nearly all versions, lit.) ... was crucified ...
> "Our old *self* was crucified ... so that our *bodies* ..." It was the condition of our spirit that was crucified with him. What was the condition of our old self?

<u>Ephesians 2:1</u>: "And you hath he quickened, who were dead in trespasses and sins."

Romans 8:2: "For the law of the Spirit of life in Christ Jesus hath made me free from the law of sin and death."
> We were formerly dead (spiritually) in sin. This former condition of our spirit (old self) was crucified with Him. He became exactly what we were.

Ephesians 2:5: "Even when we were dead in sins, hath quickened us together with Christ, (by grace ye are saved;)"
> (Way) ... thrilled us with the same new life wherewith He quickened our Messiah
> (20th Century) ... gave Life to us in giving Life to the Christ.
> (Amplified) ... He gave us the very life of Christ Himself, the same new life with which He quickened Him.
> (Knox) ... he, in giving life to Christ, gave life to us too ...
> (Jordan) ... God in his overflowing sympathy and great love breathed the same new life into us as into Christ ...
>
> We and He were made alive together. This is not physical resurrection; verse 6 refers to that. If we were made alive *together*, then He was made alive at some time. If He was made alive, then He must have been spiritually dead.

Colossians 2:13: "And you, being dead in your sins and the uncircumcision of your flesh, hath he quickened together with him, having forgiven you all trespasses."
> (20th Century) ... to you God gave life in giving life to Christ!
> (Knox) And in giving life to him, he gave life to you, too ...
> (Marshall Interlinear) ... he co-quickened you with him ...

Revelation 1:5: "And from Jesus Christ, who is the faithful witness, and the firstbegotten of the dead ..."
> (Weymouth) ... the first of the dead to be born to Life ...
> (Wade) ... the First of the dead to be born into renewed Life ...
> (Noli) ... the pioneer of the resurrection ...
> (20th Century, 1st) ... the First of the Dead to be born again ...

Colossians 1:18: "And he is the head of the body, the church: who is the beginning, the firstborn from the dead ..."
> (Knox) ... it begins with him, since his was the first birth out of death ...
>
> (20th Century 1st) Being the first to be born again from the dead, he is the source of its life ...

Acts 2:24: "Whom God hath raised up, having loosed the pains of death: because it was not possible that he should be holden of it."
> (New Berkeley) Him God raised up by setting Him free from the pangs of death; for He could not be held in its grip.
>
> (Cunnington) ... whom God raised, relieving the birth-pangs of death ...
>
> (Williams) ... But God raised Him up by loosing Him from the pangs of death ...
>
> (Plain English) ... having loosed the birth-pangs of death ...
>
> (Marshall Interlinear) ... Whom God raised up loosening the pangs of death ...
>
> (Rotherham) ... whom God raised up, loosing the pangs of death ...
>
> (Weymouth) But God has raised Him to life, having terminated the throes of death ...
>
> (W.E. Vine) "pangs:" Greek *odin* - a birth pang, travail pain, translated "sorrows" in Matthew 24:8 and Mark 13:8. Greek verb *odino*: "travail in birth" in Galatians 4:19; "travail upon a woman with child" in Revelation 12:2 and in 1 Thessalonians 5:3. If God loosed Him from the pangs of death when He raised Him up, the pangs of death would have to be spiritual because He was released from physical death pangs as soon as He left His body, three days before His resurrection. It is interesting to note that Catholic versions, based on other manuscripts, say "hades" instead of "death."
>
> (Jerusalem Bible) God raised him to life, freeing him from the pangs of Hades; for it was impossible for him to be held in its power.
>
> (Douay) Whom God hath raised up having loosed the

sorrows of hell, as it was impossible that he should be holden by it.

(Confraternity) ... having loosed the sorrows of hell, because it was not possible that he should be held fast by it.

Jesus had a two-fold resurrection—from spiritual death and from physical death:

Acts 13: 33-34: "God hath fulfilled the same unto us their children, in that he hath raised up Jesus again; as it is also written in the second psalm, Thou art my Son, this day have I begotten thee. And as concerning that he raised him up from the dead, now no more to return to corruption, he said on this wise, I will give you the sure mercies of David."

(1) Spritual: "... this day have I begotten thee ..."
(2) Physical: "And as concerning that he raised him up from the dead, now no more to return to *corruption* ..."
(New Berkeley) But that He raised Him from the dead, never to return to decay, He has expressed this way ...
(New Life) ... I have given you life today*
*Remember Ephesians 2:5-6.

Acts 2:31: "He, seeing this before, spake of the resurrection of Christ, that his soul was not left in hell, neither his flesh did see corruption."

(1) His soul was not left in hades.
(2) Neither did his flesh see corruption.
(New Berkeley) ... abandoned to the realm of the dead ...
(Weymouth) ... He was not left forsaken in the Unseen World ...
(Rotherham) ... neither was he abandoned unto hades ...
(Translator's NT) ... he was not abandoned to Hades ...

Job 25:4-6: "How then can man be justified with God? Or how can he be clean that is born of a woman? Behold even to the moon, and it shineth not; yea, the stars are not pure in His sight. How much less man, that is a worm; and the son of man, which is a worm?"

A worm is serpent-like. Man is a partaker of the sin

nature due to the fall; Jesus bore that nature.

John 3:14: "And as Moses lifted up the serpent in the wilderness, even so must the Son of man be lifted up."

Numbers 21:6-9: "And the Lord sent fiery serpents among the people, and they bit the people; and much people of Israel died. Therefore the people came to Moses, and said, We have sinned for we have spoken against the Lord, and against thee; pray unto the Lord, that he take away the serpents from us. And Moses prayed for the people. And the Lord said unto Moses, Make thee a fiery serpent, and set it upon a pole: and it shall come to pass, that every one that is bitten, when he looketh upon it, shall live. And Moses made a serpent of brass, and put it upon a pole, and it came to pass, that if a serpent had bitten any man, when he beheld the serpent of brass he lived."

> The serpent was the likeness of the thing destroying the Israelites. Jesus became sin and died spiritually. The worm and the serpent denote union and harmony with the nature of the old man and adversary.

Appendix B

Jesus In Hell Scriptures

Acts 2:27: "Because thou wilt not leave my soul in hell, neither wilt thou suffer thine Holy One to see corruption."
>(New Berkeley) ... Thou wilt not abandon my soul to the realm of the dead.
>(Weymouth) For thou wilt not leave me in the unseen world forsaken ...
>(Amplified) For you will not abandon My soul, leaving it helpless in Hades [the state of departed spirits] ...
>(Rotherham) Thou wilt not abandon my soul unto hades ...
>(Translator's NT) ... you will not abandon my soul to Hades ...
>The key to the significance of this verse in our study is found in the word "leave." W.E. Vine, "leave:" Greek *enkataleipo* - to forsake, abandon, leave in straits, or helpless, said by or of, Christ, as in Matthew 27:46, 2 Timothy 4:10, 16 and Hebrews 13:5 Those in paradise or Abraham's bosom were comforted, not abandoned or forsaken (Luke 16:22-26). Jesus was on the ungodly side.

Matthew 12:40: "For as Jonas was three days and three nights in the whale's belly; so shall the Son of man be three days and three nights in the heart of the earth."
>(Good News) In the same way that Jonah spent three days and three nights in the depths of the earth.
>Since Jesus' stay in the heart of the earth (not the grave) was like Jonah's stay in the belly of the whale, what was Jonah's experience like? This would tell us something of

what Jesus' experience was like.

Jonah 2:1-6: "Then Jonah prayed unto the Lord his God out of the fish's belly. And said, I cried by reason of mine affliction unto the Lord, and he heard; out of the belly of hell cried I, and thou heardest my voice, For thou hadst cast me into the deep, in the midst of the seas; and the floods compassed me about; all thy billows and thy waves passed over me. Then I said, I am cast out of thy sight; yet I will look again toward thy holy temple. The waters compassed me about, even to the soul; the depth closed me round about, the weeds were wrapped about my head. I went down to the bottoms of the mountains; and the earth with her bars was about me for ever: yet hast thou brought up my life from corruption, O Lord my God."

>Notice the terms "affliction," "the deep," "floods," "billows," "waves," "cast out," "the deep," "weeds," "corruption" (margin, "the pit"). Jonah did not have a restful, paradise-type experience to say the least.
>(GNB) From deep in the world of the dead I cried for help and you heard me. I thought I had been banished from your presence and would never see your holy temple again. I went down to the very roots of the mountains into the land whose gates lock shut forever. But you, O Lord my God, brought me back from the depth alive.
>(Basic English) ... out of the deepest underworld I sent up a cry, and you gave ear to my voice ... you have taken up my life from the underworld, O Lord my God.
>(Masoretic OT) Out of the belly of the netherworld cried I ... Yet hast Thou brought up my life from the pit ...
>(Rotherham) ... Then didst thou bring up - out of the pit my life ...
>(New American) ... From the midst of the nether world I cried for help ... the abyss enveloped me ... the bars of the nether world were closing behind me forever, you brought my life up from the pit ...
>(Berkeley) ... From the innermost part* of Sheol I cried for help ...
>>*or "womb"

Psalm 88: 4-8, 11, 12, 16: "I am counted with them that go down into the pit: I am as a man that hath no strength: Free among the dead, like the slain that lie in the grave whom thou rememberest no more: And they are cut off from thy hand. Thou hast laid me in the lowest pit, in darkness, in the deeps. Thy wrath lieth hard upon me, and thou hast afflicted me with all thy waves. Selah. Thou hast put away mine acquaintance far from me; thou hast made me an abomination unto them: I am shut up, and I cannot come forth. Shall thy lovingkindness be declared in the grave? Or thy faithfulness in destruction? Shall thy wonders be known in the dark? And thy righteousness in the land of forgetfulness? Thy fierce wrath goeth over me; thy terrors have cut me off."

>(Knox) ... a man past all help, there among the lordless dead ...I lie in a prison whence there is no escape.
>(Basic English) My soul is among the dead, like those in the underworld, to whom you give no more thought; for they are cut off from your care.
>(Jerusalem) You have plunged me to the bottom of the Pit, to its darkest, deepest place, weighted down by your anger, drowned beneath your waves.
>(Moffat) In the nethermost pit thou hast placed me, in abysses dark and deep; thy wrath lies heavy upon me, thy waves all overwhelm me ... I cannot escape from my prison ... thy faithfulness in the world below.
>(New American) You have plunged me into the bottom of the pit, into the dark abyss.
>(New English) Thy burning fury has swept over me, thy onslaughts have put me to silence.

Romans 10:6,7: "But the righteousness which is of faith speaketh on this wise, 'Say not in thine heart, Who shall ascend into heaven?' (that is, to bring Christ down from above): Or, 'Who shall descend into the deep?' (that is to bring up Christ again from the dead)."

>The Greek word for "the deep" is *abussos*. W.E. Vine's definition for *abussos* is found under "bottom, bottomless," and reads: "bottomless ...is used as a noun denoting the abyss (A.V., "bottomless pit.") It describes an immeasurable

depth, the underworld, the lower regions, the abyss of Sheol ... the reference is to the lower regions as the abode of demons, out of which they can be let loose, Revelation 11:7; 17:8. It is found seven times in the Apocalypse, 9:1, 2, 11; 11:7; 17:8; 20:1, 3; ... See also Luke 8:31

<u>Colossians 2:15</u>: "And having spoiled principalities and powers, he made a show of them openly, triumphing over them in it."

This is what happened in the abyss, the abode of demons. "In it" is the Greek *en auto,* meaning "in Him," not "in it." Thus, the 14th verse is parenthetical, and the 15th verse here is connected with the 13th verse which says we were made alive together. In other words, the 15th verse took place after He was quickened, not at the cross.

(Knox) ... the dominions and powers he (God) robbed of their prey, put them to an open shame, led them away in triumph, through him.

(Alford) ... stripping off from himself the principalities and the powers, he (God) made a show of them openly, triumphing over them in him.

(Conybeare) And he (God) disarmed the Principalities and the Powers [which fought against Him,] and put them to open shame, leading them captive in the triumph of Christ.

(Phillips) And then, having drawn the sting of all the powers ranged against us, he exposed them, shattered, empty and defeated, in his final glorious triumphant act!

(Weymouth) And the hostile princes and rulers He shook off from Himself, and boldly displayed them as his conquests ...

(Barclay) ... he stripped the demonic powers and authorities of their power, and made a public spectacle of them, as if they had been captives in a victor's triumphal act!

(Wand) ... he stripped away like a cast-off garment every demonic Rule and Authority and made a public exhibition of them ...

(Noli) He despoiled the infernal dominions and realms. He dragged their rulers as captives in procession ...

The word for "spoiled" is *enekduo*, from *ekduo*. Under "strip," W.E. Vine's definition for *ekduo* is "to take off, strip off, is used especially of clothes."

Romans 5:6: "For when we were yet without strength, in due time Christ died for the ungodly."

Romans 5:8: "But God commendeth his love toward us, in that, while we were yet sinners, Christ died for us."
If He died *for*, that is, on the behalf of or in the stead of the ungodly (not just the righteous dead in Abraham's bosom), then He suffered the consequences of the ungodly's death. He went where they would have gone.

The most common objection to all of this is taken from Luke 23:43: "And Jesus said unto him, Verily I say unto thee, To day shalt thou be with me in paradise." The Greek word for "today" is *semeron*. Bullinger's Critical Lexicon and Concordance to the English and Greek New Testament says: "*Semeron* when it comes after a verb, belongs to that verb, unless it is separated from it and thrown into the next clause by the presence of *oti* (that). For example:
Luke 19:9: "*oti* this is salvation come."
Luke 4:21: "*oti* this day is the Scripture fulfilled."
Mark 14:30: "*oti* this day before the cock crow you will deny me."
Without *oti*::
Matthew 21:28: "go today."
Luke 22:34: "this day"
Luke 23:43: "Verily to thee I say To day, with Me shalt thou be in Paradise." (The words to day being made solemn and emphatic).
This is in harmony with numerous Old Testament passages: Deuteronomy 6:6; 7:11; 8:1; 10:13; 11:8, 13, 28; 13:18; 19:9; 27:4; 31:2; etc. where the Septuagint corresponds to Luke 23:43."

Other references: Matthew 6:30; 16:3; 21:28; Luke

5:26; 12:28; 13:32, 33; 19:5; 23:43; 24:21; Hebrews 3:7, 13, 15; 4:7; 5:5; 8:8; James 4:13

(Tomanek) Indeed today I say to you, you shall be with Me in paradise.

(Lamsa) Truly I say to you today, You will be with me in Paradise.

Notice what the thief's request was, "Lord remember me when thou comest into thy kingdom." Jesus seemed to be saying, "I'll do more than remember you at some future time; I give you my word this very day that you will be with me in my kingdom."

It seems strange that many stack everything concerning the intermediate state of Jesus on Luke 23:43 in the King James and ignore all the evidence on the other side.

Appendix C

Three Feasts of the Lord

Passover

Revelation chapters 2 and 3 (Revelation 12:11)	To him that overcomes We overcome by the blood of the Lamb and the word of our testimony (death)
Revelation chapters 2 and 3	Things the Lord required of them
(Unleavened Bread)	Get leaven out by seeing finished work
	He did not tell them what was required of them until he *first* said something about himself and his finished work
Revelation chapters 4 and 5	We are raised and seated in the throne
(Firstfruits)	His raising was our raising
	We are seated in the heavenlies

Pentecost

Revelation chapters 6 and 7   Sealing of the Saints

Sealed with the Holy Spirit of Promise

Tabernacles

Revelation chapters 8, 9 and 11:15 (Trumpets)	We see seven trumpets
Revelation chapter 16 (Atonements)	We see seven vials of blood poured out
Revelation chapters 21 and 22 (Tabernacles)	God tabernacles with men

Appendix D

The 7 Churches of Revelation and Present Truth

	EPHESUS (INVENTOR OF WORKS)	SMYRNA (EMBITTER, MINGLE WITH MYRRH)	PERGAMOS (FORTIFIED, TOWER, CASTLE)	THYATIRA (FEMALE WOMAN)	SARDIS (A GEM)	PHILADELPHIA (BROTHERLY LOVE)	LAODICEA (A PEOPLE)
	"REMOVE LIGHT"	"HEAVENLY PEOPLE VS NATURAL PEOPLE"	"HIDDEN MANNA" "WHITE STONE"	"MORNING STAR" "RULE"	"SPIRITUAL, CARNAL, DEAD ONES"	"PILLAR" "GOD TAB. WITH MEN"	"REST" "SIT ON THRONE"
	DAY 1 LIGHT	DAY 2 SEPARATION	DAY 3 FOOD	DAY 4 SUN, MOON, STARS	DAY 5 BIRDS IN HEAVEN, ANIMALS ON LAND, FISH IN SEA	DAY 6 MAN	DAY 7 REST
	EAT OF TREE OF LIFE	GARDEN IN EDEN	AGE OF PATRIARCHS	CROWN OF LIFE	HIDDEN MANNA	WILDERNESS WANDERING	KINGDOM AGE, BABYLONIAN CAPTIVITY	RULE & REIGN	WHITE LINEN	PILLAR IN HOUSE OF GOD	BABYLONIAN RELEASE	JEW OF JESUS' DAY	SIT IN THRONE WITH HIM

THE OVERCOMERS GET MOST HOLY PLACE BLESSINGS

7 KINGDOM PARABLES - 7 CHURCHES

| MATT. 13:18-23 SEED SOWN - MINISTERS ARE SEED SOWERS REV. 2:2 | MATT. 13:24-30 TARES & WHEAT-SOME DOCTRINE OF SYNAGOGUE OF SATAN REV. 2:9 | MATT. 13:31-32 BIRDS IN BRANCHES - BALAAM REV. 2:14 | MATT. 13:33 3 MEASURES LEAVEN IN MEAL - JEZEBEL TEACHES TO EAT THINGS SACRIFICED TO IDOLS REV. 2:20 | MATT. 13:44 TREASURE HID IN FIELD. MAN SELLS ALL - IN MIDST OF DEATH IS TREASURE JESUS BOUGHT REV. 3:24 | MATT. 13:45-46 JESUS BUYS WHOLE FIELD TO GET PEARL IN FIELD - JESUS GETS TEMPLE REV. 3:12 | MATT. 13:47-48 BAD FISH THROWN BACK - SOME SPUED OUT REV. 3:16 |

Appendix E

The 7 Days of Creation and the 7 Churches

	DAY 1	DAY 2	DAY 3	DAY 4	DAY 5	DAY 6	DAY 7
	LIGHT	SEPARATION	FOOD	SUN, MOON, STARS	BIRDS IN HEAVEN, ANIMALS ON LAND, FISH IN SEA	MAN	REST
	EPHESUS	SMYRNA	PERGAMOS	THYATIRA	SARDIS	PHILADELPHIA	LAODICEA
	REMOVE LIGHT	HEAVENLY PEOPLE & NATURAL PEOPLE	HIDDEN MANNA, WHITE STONE (PURE WHITE)	MORNING STAR, RULE	SPIRITUAL, CARNAL, DEAD PEOPLE	PILLAR, GOD TAB. WITH MAN	REST SIT ON THRONE
	GARDEN IN EDEN	AGE OF PATRIARCHS	WILDERNESS WANDERING	KINGDOM AGE OF THE KINGS	BABYLONIAN CAPTIVITY	BABYLONIAN RELEASE	JEWS OF JESUS' DAY
			THE OVERCOMERS GIVEN MOST HOLY BLESSINGS				
	EAT OF TREE OF LIFE	CROWN OF LIFE	HIDDEN MANNA	RULE & REIGN	WHITE LINEN	PILLAR IN HOUSE OF GOD	SIT IN THRONE WITH HIM

Appendix F

The Feasts of the Lord

Farming Season	Hebrew Month	Feast (Historical)	Jesus (Prophetic)	Believer (Personal)	Seasonal (Seasonal)
Barley Harvest	Nisan 14 / 15-21 / 17	Passover / Unleavened Bread / Firstfruits	Crucified / Died / Buried / Resurrected	New Birth / Put Off Old / Put On New	Initial Salvation Luther-1517 Wesley-1738
	Iyyar	50 Days From Resurrection to Pentecost			
Wheat Harvest	Sivan 6	Pentecost	Exalted	Baptism in Holy Spirit	Acts 2 Kansas-1901 Los An.-1906
Fruit Harvest	Tammuz / Ab / Elul	No Feast — The Church Period			
Final Ingathering	Tishri 1 / 10 / 15-21	Tabernacles / Trumpets / Day of Atonement / Tabernacles	Total Victory / Ascension / Union	Revelation / Renewed Mind / Glory-Fullness	Present Present Present

Nisan —Mar-Apr Tammuz —Jun-Jul Tishri —Sep-Oct
Iyyar —Apr-May Ab —Jul-Aug
Sivan —May-Jun Elul —Aug-Sep

Appendix G

Literary Structure of Revelation

Passover

(Passover)

Chapter 1

"We overcome by the blood of the Lamb, and by the word of our testimony (martyrdom)." (Revelation 12:11)

(Unleavened Bread)

Chapters 2 and 3

(Firstfruits)

Chapters 4 and 5

Pentecost

Chapters 6 and 7

Tabernacles

(Trumpets)

Chapters 8 - 10

(Atonements)

Chapter 16

(Tabernacles)

Chapters 8 - 22

Appendix H

Revelation 1:19   Revelation 1:4

Hast Seen (Seals)   Which Was

What happened to Jesus at the cross

Which Are (Trumpets)   Which Is

What is true because of what happened at the cross

Which Shall Be (Vials)   Which Is To Come

<u>Product</u> of what is true because of what happened at the cross

Appendix I

Five Schools Of Thought On The Death Of Christ

1. Moral View: This view states that Jesus died as a martyr. It states that he died for a good cause. This concept is that he thought enough of the message to be killed for it. In the moral view one would say, "If Jesus thought enough of the message to die for it, shouldn't I? Shouldn't you?" This view is incorrect because there were others who died as martyrs, but their death could not make us righteous.

2. Pattern View: This view focuses on the fact that Jesus learned obedience through that which he suffered. That is a true statement. However, in saying that Jesus is our pattern, this view states that he was our pattern all the way from his earthly life, up to and including the cross. So what he suffered on the cross, we also have to suffer. Jesus was our pattern in his earth walk. He was tempted in all points, yet without sin. But to say that we have to suffer what he suffered on the cross would make his death *as* us for naught. One cannot really grow with this view. The world suffers a lot of things because as the word declares, that the way of a transgressor is hard; yet we do not see the world growing up in Christ. Those of this persuasion believe that we must crucify the flesh and die to self daily, rather than seeing that we were already crucified and we have already died with Christ. This view also believes that God brings sickness upon us to buffet us into the realm of glory. In this view, there is duality. This concept is that Jesus died *instead of* us rather than *as* us.

3. Ransom View: There are two sides to this view. This view states that there was a payment being made. One view is that this payment was made to the devil. It states that it was a barter for our soul. In essence, it conveys the idea that Jesus said, "Here is the price Mr. Devil, now let those people go." First of all, can you imagine God bartering with the devil? So the devil answers back and says, "If you send your own Son and let him die, and become sin, and go to hell, that will be sufficient for me. I'll let the people go free." The reason "ransom people" believe this is because what Jesus did certainly did free us from the power of darkness. But even though Jesus did destroy the works of the devil, it was not to barter with the enemy. Jesus did not come to barter with the devil, he came to *destroy* him.

4. Ransom View #2: This view says that a ransom was paid to God. This position states that God said, "In order to set man free, I'm going to have to have some kind of a suffering to pay for the wages of sin that has come upon mankind." So God sent his Son to die in order to pay the wage of sin to God. That view still leaves us unchanged on the inside. For example; let's say we have a man that is on death row, and he is ready to be electrocuted. But someone steps us and offers to be electrocuted in his place. The problem with that is, we still have a criminal on our hands. The man is still what he was before. This view still has Jesus in one place and us in another. There can be no nature change if Jesus died *instead of* us. He did something *with* us.

5. Substitution View: Substitution means "one who takes the place of another." We must be careful with the way in which we look at substitution. Romans 5:8 says, "But God commendeth his love toward us, in that, while we were yet sinners, Christ died *for* us." That sounds like Jesus died instead of us. But Galations 2:20 says that we were crucified *with* Christ. Romans 6:5 says that we died *with* him and were buried *with* him. Colossians 2:13 says that we were made alive *with* him. Ephesians 2:6 says that we were raised *with* him and we were seated *with* him. In dying for us as Romans 5:8 says, it means that he died according to the *law of identification.* The Amplified Bible says in Philemon 6, "[And I pray] that the participation in and sharing of your faith may produce and promote full recognition and appreciation and understanding and precise knowledge of every good [thing] that is ours in [our identification with] Christ Jesus [and unto His glory]." Identification means "to consider or treat as the same." Therefore, when Jesus hung on the cross and became sin, there was a substitution that took place. He became who we were in Adam. It is a paradoxical truth, because it was Jesus dying, yet when he became sin, there was a substitution—he became us. He was crucified *as* us, died as us, was buried *as* us. Then Jesus was quickened, raised, and seated as the glorified Christ, the last Adam, the life-giving Spirit—and we are in him.

Endnotes

[1] Deuteronomy 15:16-18, Exodus 21:1-6

[2] Proverbs 31:22

[3] Exodus 30:25, 35 Exodus 37:29, 2 Chronicles 16:14

[4] John 3:5

[5] 2 Corinthians 3:6, Romans 7:6

[6] 2 Corinthians 5:14, Galations 2:20, Ephesians 2:5,6, Colossians 2:13

[7] Lucas, Jerry and Washburn, Del Theomatics Stein and Day. 1977

[8] Bullinger, E. W. Number in Scripture Kregel Publications. 1967

[9] This will be discussed in detail in the study of Revelation chapter 13.

[10] See Isaiah 60:8

[11] Lucas, Jerry and Washburn, Del Theomatics Stein and Day. 1977.

[12] Lucas, Jerry and Washburn, Del Theomatics Stein and Day. 1977.

[13] John 7:23

[14] See appendix G

[15] Exodus 12:1-11

[16] Lucas, Jerry and Washburn, Del Theomatics Stein and Day. 1977.

[17] See appendix B Luke 23:43

[18] Strong, James, Strong's Concordance Nelson. 1990.

[19] See appendix H.

[20] See appendix F

[21] See appendix E

[22] W. E. Vine's Expository Dictionary of New Testament Words - "Earnest"

[23] Romans 9:6, Galatians 3:7, Romans 9:8, Romans 2:28-29, Galatians 4:25-26

[24] Lucas, Jerry, and Washburn, Del Theomatics Stein and Day. 1977.

[25] E. W. Bullinger. Number in Scripture. Kregel Publications. 1967.

[26] E. W. Bullinger. Number in Scripture. Kregel Publications. 1967.

[27] There are twenty different lists given of the 12 tribes. These vary according to

the different objects with which they are given, and the different connections in which they stand, according to birth: mothers, encampment, numeration, blessing, geographical relation. All are worthy of attention and study. In Genesis, the 12 tribes are: Reuben, Simeon, Levi, Judah, Dan, Naphtali, Gad, Asher, Issachar, Zebulun, Joseph, Benjamin. In Revelation, the 12 tribes are: Judah, Reuben, Gad, Asher, Napthali, Manasseh, Simeon, Levi, Issachar, Zebulun, Joseph, Benjamin. From E. W. Bullinger. Companion Bible Zondervan Bible Publishers.

[28] Job 40:9, Psalm 77:18, 81:7, 104:7, Revelation 6:1, 14:2.

[29] Bullinger, E. W. Number in Scripture Kregel Publications. 1967.

[30] See Exodus 20:9-11 and Luke 13:14-17.

[31] Bullinger, E. W. The Witness of the Stars Kregel Publications. Reprint of the 1893 ed.

[32] Bullinger, E. W. The Companion Bible Zondervan Bible Publishers.

[33] See appendix I

[34] Exodus 19:4, Deuteronomy 32:10-11, Psalm 103, Isaiah 40:31

[35] Acts 13:39, Romans 3:24, Romans 4:25, Romans 5:9, and 5:16-18, 2 Corinthians 5:19-21

[36] The Cambridge Bible

[37] See appendix A

[38] Wycliffe Bible Commentary

[39] See Hebrews 4:12

[40] Moser, M. L. Jr. An Apologetic of Premellenialism Challenge Press. Little Rock, AR

[41] Guinness, H. Grattan Romanism and the Reformation From the Standpoint of Prophecy A. C. Armstrong Publishing. 1887.

Printed in the United States
1346400005B/31-255